Proceedings of th to explore the nort Africa, from Tripoly eastward

in MDCCCXXI. and MDCCCXXII., comprehending an account of the Greater Syrtis and Cyrenaica; and of the ancient cities composing the pentapolis

Frederick William Beechey

Alpha Editions

This edition published in 2024

ISBN 9789362512574

Design and Setting By
Alpha Editions
www.alphaedis.com
Email - info@alphaedis.com

As per information held with us this book is in Public Domain.
This book is a reproduction of an important historical work.
Alpha Editions uses the best technology to reproduce historical work
in the same manner it was first published to preserve its original nature.
Any marks or number seen are left intentionally to preserve.

Contents

INTRODUCTION.	- 1 -
CHAPTER I.	- 9 -
CHAPTER II.	- 16 -
CHAPTER III.	- 31 -
CHAPTER IV.	- 42 -
CHAPTER V.	- 62 -
CHAPTER VI.	- 88 -
CHAPTER VII.	- 111 -
CHAPTER VIII.	- 128 -
CHAPTER IX.	- 146 -
CHAPTER X.	- 176 -
CHAPTER XI.	- 196 -
CHAPTER XII.	- 244 -
CHAPTER XIII.	- 262 -
CHAPTER XIV.	- 274 -
CHAPTER XV.	- 290 -
CHAPTER XVI.	- 327 -
CHAPTER XVII.	- 359 -
CHAPTER XVIII.	- 384 -
CHAPTER XIX.	- 418 -

INTRODUCTION.

IN offering to the Public an account of the mission, the proceedings of which will form the subject of the present Narrative, it may be proper to state briefly the circumstances which gave rise to it, and the objects to which its inquiries were chiefly directed.

When Captain Smyth visited the Northern Coast of Africa, in the year 1817, he had many opportunities (during the course of his Survey) of obtaining information connected with the state of the country and the points most deserving of notice which it presented. The exertions of this active and intelligent officer procured at Lebida the matter for the only plan which we have of that city and its antiquities, while his journey to Ghirza made us acquainted with the actual nature of those remains, so important in Arab estimation, the account of which is given at the latter part of our narrative.

Captain Smyth had proposed to extend his journey eastward; for the friendly disposition of the Bashaw of Tripoly had been diligently cultivated by himself and Colonel Warrington, His Majesty's Consul-general at the Regency, and the whole tract of country between Tripoly and Derna was open to the researches of the English. Circumstances, however, prevented him from doing so, and on returning to England he submitted the information which he had been able to collect to the Admiralty, and suggested that a party might be advantageously employed in exploring the Greater Syrtis and Cyrenaica, as well as the country to the eastward of Derna as far as Alexandria and the Oasis of Ammon.

Many spots of more than ordinary interest were comprehended within the limits of the Syrtis and Cyrenaica: some of these had been the favourite themes of mythology, haunts in which the poets of Greece and Rome had loved to linger; and others had been celebrated in the more sober language of historians whose fame is less perishable than the objects which they describe. But whatever might once have been the state of a country placed before us so conspicuously in pages which are dear to us, there had not in our own times been any opportunity of ascertaining its actual condition. The name of Cyrene was familiar to classic ears, but no one had visited its remains; the "secret springs" of Lethe and the Gardens of the Hesperides had almost been confounded with the fables of antiquity; and the deep and burning sands, overspread with venomous serpents, which were supposed to form the barrier between Leptis Magna and Berenice, had rarely been trodden since the army of Cato had nearly found a grave beneath their weight.

The outline of this extensive Gulf (the Greater Syrtis), the coast of which was as formidable to the vessels of the ancients as its sands were supposed to have been to their armies, had never been accurately laid down in modern charts, and the contradictory statements of its form and peculiarities appeared to call for minute investigation. There were many geographical points to be determined in the space between Tripoly and Bengazi, and remains of several ancient towns (besides Cyrene) were known to exist in the Pentapolis, of which no plans had hitherto been made. Under all these circumstances it appeared to Captain Smyth that, as he was himself about to sail in the Adventure to finish his survey of the northern coast of Africa, it might so be arranged that a party on shore should proceed simultaneously along the tract of country mentioned, communicating from time to time with his vessel as occasions might offer in the course of their route. The views of His Majesty's Government were at this period favorable to the cause of research; and the labours of many skilful and enterprising men had been, since the peace, advantageously directed to various points of interest, from the sultry plains of Fezzan to the borders of the Frozen Ocean. It was therefore not long after the plan in question had been submitted to the Admiralty and the Colonial Department, that it was acceded to by Earl Bathurst and Lord Melville; and the means of carrying it into effect were referred to the consideration of one of the heads of the Admiralty, whose well-directed ability had often been manifested in the promotion and arrangement of similar undertakings, and whose exertions in the cause of science and discovery are well known and highly appreciated.

Accordingly, when the necessary dispositions had been made, Lieutenant Beechey was appointed on the part of the Admiralty to undertake the coast line from Tripoly to Derna,—if practicable, as far as Alexandria; and Mr. Tyndall, a young gentleman on board the Adventure, was directed to assist him in the survey. Earl Bathurst appointed Mr. Beechey to examine and report on the antiquities of the country, and Mr. Campbell of the Navy was soon after nominated to accompany the expedition as surgeon. The party was embarked on board His Majesty's Ship Adventure, and sailed from England early in July with Captain Smyth, proceeding directly to Malta: there they were joined by Lieutenant Coffin of the Navy, who had come out in the Adventure, and who handsomely volunteered his services on shore, which were accepted without hesitation. A short time was sufficient to complete the few remaining preparations, and the expedition left Malta for Tripoly.

We have already said that it had been in contemplation to extend our journey farther to the eastward, and to examine the country between that place and Alexandria, in which it seemed probable that interesting remains might be found. We had in that event proposed to return by Siwah, and along the track of Horneman to Augila; from which place we should have re-entered the Greater Syrtis, and explored some of the more inland parts of it in the course of our journey back to Tripoly. Circumstances, however, which it will not here be necessary to explain, prevented our going farther eastward than Derna, and limited the period of our stay in the Pentapolis to a much shorter period than we had originally calculated upon. Our work has in consequence assumed the form of a Journal, and has become more contracted on points of unquestionable interest, and more diffuse in matters which would otherwise have been omitted, than it would have been in the character which we wished it to have taken. We do not, however, mean to apologize for having done less than we might have done under the circumstances in which we were placed; or to underrate the value of the matter which we have been able to lay before the Public: the materials which we had to work upon are in themselves sufficiently interesting to call for the attention of those who read for information, and the labour which has been employed in collecting them (during the whole course of a long and fatiguing journey) has not been thrown away upon trifles.

We have given to the world (we may say with the greatest accuracy) an extensive tract of coast which has been hitherto unsurveyed, and of which our best charts afforded a very imperfect outline, as will appear by a reference to the maps at the head of the work.

We have obtained the plans of towns and places, (rendered interesting by antiquity, and by the rank which they hold in the pages of history,) of which we have hitherto had no details; and have described, or made drawings of every object of note which has presented itself on the field of our operations. In fact, whatever may be the merit of our work in other respects, or the value attached to our exertions, we are satisfied ourselves with the matter acquired and with the labour and diligence which has been employed in collecting it; and it is because our materials are worthy of more attention than we had time and opportunities to bestow upon them, that we regret we are not able to offer them to the Public in a more complete form than we have been able to give them. Had it been in our power to employ excavation, on a more extensive scale than we did, and to bestow as much time upon every object worth attention as its importance appeared to demand, our work could have been a more perfect one; that is to say, it would have treated of art, and its details more exclusively (we mean the details of sculpture, architecture, and painting,) than it does in the shape which it at present assumes. We might also have given additional interest to our narrative by introducing more plates than we have been able to insert; but our number has been (we believe necessarily) limited, and we may add that the selection of those which appear might have been better if we had known, before the drawings went to the engraver, that we should have been obliged to leave out so many of them.

Something should be said to account for the delay which has taken place in publication since the work was first announced. We may state that, so far as we are ourselves concerned, more than three parts of the MS. was finished at least two years ago; and that the remainder was only kept back because it could not be completed till the first portion was printed.

FOOTNOTES:

The plan here alluded to of the City of Lebida was obligingly placed at our disposal by the author, and we wished to have had it engraved for the work; but, in consequence of being obliged to limit our number of plates to much fewer than we had originally anticipated, this plan, with some others of our own, have been omitted.

The poetical account of this tract of country by Lucan is well known to the readers of ancient literature, and we shall have occasion hereafter to advert to it in speaking of the actual appearance of the Syrtis.

A little before this period, an expedition undertaken by the Bashaw of Tripoly against his eldest son Mahommed, now Bey of Derna, afforded to Signor Della Cella, an Italian gentleman residing in Tripoly, the opportunity of visiting the Syrtis and Cyrenaica in the capacity of physician to the Bashaw's second son, who at that time commanded the expedition against his brother.

The account of this journey was published at Genoa soon after the return of Dr. Della Cella; and the interest which uncertainty had given to the country through which he passed was increased by his animated description of its remains. But the opportunities which were afforded to the Doctor were not sufficient for the accomplishment of his object; and although his pen described the extensive ruins which he witnessed, the reader had to regret that the shortness of his stay prevented him from examining them with attention.

We subjoin the errata which we have been able to detect in a hasty perusal of the Narrative after the whole was printed off. There may possibly, however, be others which have escaped us. The few errors which occur in some of the passages quoted from foreign languages, we have not thought it necessary to include in this list, since the proper readings will be obvious to all who understand them, and it will be unnecessary to point them out to those who do not.

Page

52, *for* who has obligingly, *read and* who has, &c. (Note.)

65, *for* this range, *read* the range.

292, *for* ti stan bono, *read* ti sta bono.

293, *for* a te. *read* été.

397, *for* its site should be *fixed, read* looked for.

397, *for of* the accounts of the city of Barca, *read* if the accounts, &c.

471, *for* at the roadstead, *read in* the roadstead.

Coast line of the Gulf OF THE Greater Sertis, BY *Capt.* F. W. *Beechey*, R.N.

J. & C. Walker Sculp^t.   *Published as the act directs, April 1827, by J. Murray, Albemarle S^t. London.*

NARRATIVE

CHAPTER I.

Arrival of the Expedition at Tripoly; pleasing appearance of the Town from the Sea — Friendly Reception of the Party by the Consul — Interview with the Bashaw, who promises his protection and assistance — Appointment of the Escort — Visits to some of the Mahometan Residents in Tripoly — Sidi Mahommed d'Ghies — Preparations for the journey — Adoption of the Costume of the Country — This precaution recommended on the experience of the party — Visit from the Arab Escort — Description of their principal, Shekh Mahommed el Dúbbah — Sketch of the Shekh's former Life — Friendly attentions of the European Residents of Tripoly — Arrival of Dr. Oudney and Lieutenant Clapperton.

IN the beginning of September the Adventure sailed from Malta, and in a few days we made the African shore, at about the situation assigned to Tripoli Vecchio. Running down to the eastward, we soon discovered the place of our destination, and on the morning of the 11th, cast anchor in the harbour of Tripoly. The town makes a respectable appearance from the sea; it is surrounded by a high wall, strengthened with bastions, above which are distinguished the mosques and the baths, whose white minarets and cupolas form no unpleasing contrast with the dark tints presented by thick groves of palm-trees, rising in varied groups, from the gardens at the back of the town. The different coloured flags which were hoisted to salute us on the castle of the Bashaw, and the houses of the several consuls, floated gaily in the clear atmosphere and bright sunshine of a Mediterranean climate; and the whole together, viewed under favourable impressions, gave to Tripoly an appearance of much more interest and importance than it was afterwards found to have deserved.

The reception which we experienced from Mr. Warrington, the British Consul-General at Tripoly, was friendly and attentive in the extreme; and, on our landing, the consulate was assigned to us as a residence, which he obligingly left at our disposal. The arrival of our party was now signified officially to the Bashaw, who appointed a day to receive us; being at the time indisposed, on account of the operation of *burning*, which he had undergone as a cure for the rheumatism. His Highness was provided with a skilful European physician, who had been for some time attached to his person and to the court; but the prejudices of his country were too strong to be overcome by reason, and the remedies of Dr. Dicheson gave way to the popular superstition.

On the day appointed for the interview, we proceeded to the palace of His Highness, accompanied by the Consul and Captain Smyth. The streets through which we had to pass, on our way to the Castle, were by no means fit approaches to a regal abode; they were encumbered with the rubbish of houses fallen into ruin, and with the superfluous produce of those which were yet standing; while swarms of little naked and dirty children, and numerous groups of hungry, half-starved dogs, almost blocked up the little space which was left for our passage. The dust which was unavoidably raised in our progress, together with the heat of the sun, and the myriads of gnats and flies which assailed us in every direction, were no grateful additions to these inconveniences; and we were heartily glad to find ourselves before the gates of the Castle, where a part of the Bashaw's guard was drawn out in due form to receive us. After paying our respects to the Kechia, (who was seated at the end of the skeefa, or entrance hall,) we were ushered along a dark and narrow passage, so irregular and uneven under foot, that we were in danger of falling at almost every step, and having passed at intervals several Tchaouses and soldiers, who were barely discernible through the gloom, we found ourselves at length in a spacious apartment, where a motley crowd of Christians, Turks, Arabs, and Jews, were assembled to wait His Highness's leisure.

We had not been long here before it was announced to us that the Bashaw was prepared to receive us; and, on approaching the presence, we found His Highness seated, with all due solemnity, at the farther end of the apartment, attended by his third son, Sidy Ali, by Reis Moràt, who acted as interpreter, and by other principal officers of the Court. A formidable line of well-armed black soldiers were ranged along the walls of the room, who stood exactly like so many statues, each with a loaded blunderbuss, held with the muzzle pointed downwards; and close to the Bashaw's person was a trusty black slave, who held in readiness His Highness's pistols. The introduction of armed soldiers into the presence-chamber of a Sovereign was rather a novel sight to Europeans, and may be taken as an example of the extremely barbarous state in which the Regency of Tripoly, with all its recent improvements, must still be admitted to remain.

The High Admiral, Reis Moràt, in the name of our party, made known to the Bashaw the friendly disposition of the King of England towards His Highness; in testimony of which he was requested to accept the present of four brass field-pieces, with their accoutrements, which we had brought with us on board the Adventure; and he was then requested to extend his protection to our party in their passage through his extensive dominions. Every assistance was freely offered on the part of the Bashaw, who expressed himself, in return, highly satisfied with the friendly assurances of His Majesty; and the necessary preliminaries being satisfactorily arranged, tea and lemonade were served with all due decorum, and our party took leave of His Highness. The guns were brought up the same afternoon, close under the balcony of the palace, and the Bashaw appeared at the window to inspect them, with some of the officers of his court; various manœuvres were gone through to the admiration and astonishment of the spectators, under the direction of the gunner of the Adventure, and the cannoniers acquitted themselves so highly to the satisfaction of His Highness, that he sent a sword to the gunner, in token of his approbation, and a bag of dollars to be divided among the crew.

In our interview with the Bashaw it had been finally arranged that our party should be escorted as far as Bengazi, by an Arab Shekh who presided over the district of Syrt, and was called Shekh Mahommed el Dúbbah; at Bengazi we were to be consigned to Hadood, Shekh of Barka, who was to conduct us as far as Bomba, beyond which his authority ceased. As Bomba, or its immediate vicinity, may be considered as the eastern limit of the Regency, we were informed that, in our progress from that place to Alexandria, we must depend upon the protection of the Bashaw of Egypt. We had foreseen this circumstance before our arrival in Tripoly, and a letter had been written from Malta to Mr. Salt, His Majesty's Consul-General in Egypt, requesting him, in the name of the British Government, to make the necessary arrangements with His Highness the Viceroy for our passing from Derna to Alexandria; and we afterwards received a firman from Mahommed Ali, which he considered would be sufficient to ensure our advance.

These preliminaries settled we began to make preparations for our journey, and consulted with the most intelligent natives in Tripoly on the best means of forwarding the objects of the Expedition.

We found them on all occasions particularly obliging, and always ready to afford us every information in their power. From Sidi Mahommed D'Ghies, in particular, the same well-informed native who had been of great service to Mr. Ritchie and Captain Lyon, as well as from his son, a most excellent young man, we received at various times much useful advice, and always the most friendly and cordial reception.

At the house of Sidi Mahommed, we were one day introduced to one of the most respectable Mahometan traders to Timbuctoo; who offered to ensure our arrival at that place, and our return in perfect safety to Tripoly, provided we would place ourselves entirely under his directions; allowing, of course, for ill health, as well as for such accidents as could not be foreseen, and may happen to any one in travelling across the desert. As Timbuctoo, however, formed no part of the object of our mission, this offer was naturally declined; and we merely mention it here as one which may be worth consideration, should any future traveller decide upon attempting this journey by way of Tripoly.

Our next care was to provide ourselves with the dress of the country, which was strongly recommended to us by our Mahometan friends, and which, indeed, on the former experience of one of our party, we had before proposed to adopt. The opinion of Colonel Warrington was in favour of the European costume; but as we supposed it to have been founded on the experience of journeys in the neighbourhood of Tripoly only, within the immediate range of the Bashaw's authority, and in places where the natives are more accustomed to the dress; we thought it most advisable to adopt the advice of our Turkish friends, which we knew to be formed on an extensive acquaintance with the prejudices, manners, and customs of the Arabs: this opinion, besides, had the additional recommendation of being quite in unison with our own; and it is probably not unknown to some of our readers that a similar coincidence has usually its weight in decisions of much more importance. The experience of our journey through the Syrtis and Cyrenaica confirmed us still more decidedly in our former opinion; and as the propriety of adopting the Turkish costume has occasionally been questioned and denied, we will venture to add our testimony in its favour to that of all the most experienced travellers in Mahometan countries with whom we have ever been acquainted; so far, at least, as the adoption of it is in question, in places where the principal persons in power, and the bulk of the population are Mussulmen. If it were only on the score of convenience, we should in most cases recommend it; and it is certainly the best calculated to prevent interruption, and all the numerous annoyances arising from idle curiosity and the prejudices of an ignorant people.

On our return, one morning, from a visit to the Bazar, where we had been making some purchases necessary for our journey, we found our apartment occupied by the Bedouin Arabs who had been appointed by the Bashaw to attend us to Bengazi. They had been ranged by our servant on chairs round the room, on which they did not appear to sit much at their ease; and some of them had relinquished their exalted situation for the more convenient level which the chairs themselves occupied, that safe and comfortable position, the ground: here they squatted themselves down with true Arab dignity, and soon found themselves much more at home. There was little in the dress of these swarthy personages by which one might be distinguished from the rest. An ample baracàn, fastened in the usual Arab manner, partially displayed the large, loose sleeves of a cotton shirt, more remarkable than usual for its whiteness; a piece of distinction which is, by Arabs, considered necessary only in towns, and on visits of more than ordinary ceremony: from a leathern belt was suspended a case of the same material, containing a brace of long pistols, near which hung a leathern pouch for powder and ball, and a smaller one which served as a pocket or purse. A red, or white cap, (for some had one, some the other,) and sandals of camel's hide, fastened with thongs of leather, completed the whole costume. One only wore a turban; and, on closer investigation, the pistol-cases and pistols of the person so distinguished appeared to be in better order than those of his companions. But no difference of attire was necessary to mark out Shekh Mahommed el Dúbbah from those who accompanied him. A venerable length of beard, in which white was partially blended with gray, gave an air of patriarchal respectability to his appearance; and a singular mixture of energy and complacency displayed the wild and daring spirit which animated him half subdued by the composure of age, and the decorum which it was necessary to observe on the occasion: a well-acted smile was playing on his lips, with which his voice and his manner, when he addressed us, corresponded; but his large full eye, though its lustre was dimmed by age, was never for a moment at rest; and wandered unceasingly from object to object, with a wildness and rapidity very different from the vacant stare of curiosity so conspicuous in the faces of most of his party.

Shekh Mahommed was at this time nearly sixty years of age, and had early been very formidable as a robber in the district of Syrt. The circumstance of his being the head of a Maràbut tribe, joined to the natural intrepidity of his character, had given him great influence over the Arabs of his neighbourhood; and the daring character of his exploits soon obtained for him the appellation of El Dúbbah, or the Hyæna.

At a more advanced period, when the rigorous measures of the Bashaw seemed likely to reduce the Arab tribes to subjection, Mahommed, finding it probably more to his interest, went over to His Highness's party; and from his knowledge of the country, and the interest which he possessed, was enabled to render him very essential service: he was in consequence established as Shekh of Syrt, a district of more than two hundred miles in extent. We were glad to find that Shekh Mahommed was as eager as ourselves for an early departure from Tripoly; he soon began to enumerate all the various disadvantages which were to be expected from travelling in the rainy season over the low and swampy regions of the Syrtis; and drew such pictures of them as would have determined us to set out immediately had our movements depended upon ourselves. But the delays of the tradesmen, who furnished our supplies, and many others, which could neither be foreseen nor prevented, retarded the movements of the Expedition; and it was not till the morning of the 5th of November that we were able to set out on our journey. It may well be imagined that the attractions of Tripoly are neither very great nor very numerous; and our stay there had been attended with a good deal of trouble and vexation in making the necessary arrangements for our departure: but the friendly attentions which we had invariably received from many of its principal European inhabitants, as well as from several of its Mahometan residents, greatly contributed to enliven the monotony of a Moorish town; and it was not without feelings of sincere regret that we took leave of our little circle of acquaintance. This had latterly been increased by the arrival of Dr. Oudney and Lieutenant Clapperton, of the navy, who were commissioned by Government to make researches in the interior of Africa; and who were to proceed to Bornou, by way of Morzouk, as soon as the preparations could be completed which were necessary for so tedious a journey.

FOOTNOTES:

The practice of cautery is well known to be generally adopted, and confidently depended upon, by the Arabs and Moors, as an effectual remedy for almost every disorder. The custom may be traced to a very remote period, and is alluded to by Herodotus, (Melpomene, 187,) as peculiar to the Libyan Nomades, the early inhabitants of a considerable part of the coast of Northern Africa. The remedy is indeed too indiscriminately applied, but is not, however, unfrequently productive of good effects. We were assured by a man at Bengazi, that he had been cured three times of the plague by the mere application of a hot iron to the tumours which attend the disease; and if we might judge from the dreadful scars which remained, his attacks were by no means slight ones.

This officer holds the second place in the Regency, and is invested with the supreme power whenever His Highness is absent.

Tully observes, "We entered these gloomy passages, which always seem as if they led to some dreadful abode for the purpose of entombing the living."

Reis Moràt, we believe, is a Scotchman, and was formerly mate of a merchant vessel; but having embraced the Mahometan faith, and entered the service of the Bashaw, has now, through his naval skill and abilities, arrived at the head of his profession, and is much considered by His Highness.

Tea is very generally used by the higher classes throughout the Regency of Tripoly, and coffee but rarely.

This young man, who is the second son of Sidi Mahommed d'Ghies, and is also named Mahommed, is an admirable example of true devotion to the religion of his country, united with the more extended and liberal feelings of Europeans. He daily visits the public school where young boys are taught to read the Koran; and superintends the charitable distribution of food which the bounty of Sidi Mahommed provides for the poor who daily present themselves at his gate. Besides his acquaintance with the English and French languages, he is able to converse with the slaves of the family in several languages of the interior of Africa; and when it is considered that Mahometans in general seldom trouble themselves to speak any language but their own, this proficiency is greatly to his credit; we should rather, perhaps, say, to the credit of his father, under whose eye he has been hitherto brought up, and who is himself well acquainted with the French, and we believe with several other languages. The elder son of Sidi Mohammed was in England while we were at Tripoly, and must be remembered by many of the first circles in London.

CHAPTER II.

General description of Tripoly; its Castle and Port — The Buildings of Tripoly commended by Leo Africanus — Present condition of the City — Its existing ancient remains — Burial-ground of the ancient City — Sepulchral urns of glass discovered there by Mr. Consul Warrington — Remarks of Leo Africanus on the soil and level of Tripoly, in the fifteenth and sixteenth centuries — Accumulation of soil since that period — Advance of the sea, mentioned by Leo Africanus, still observable on the coast of Northern Africa — These appearances adduced in confirmation of Major Rennell's remarks on the Lake Tritonis and the Lesser Syrtis — Historical sketch of Tripoly — Its actual state and improved condition under the present Bashaw — Abolition of Piracy, and partial discontinuance of the Slave Trade.

THE town of Tripoly has been built on a foundation of rock, and is washed, to the northward, on two sides, by the sea; while the remaining parts, those to the southward and westward, are bounded by a large sandy plain, which is notwithstanding partially cultivated.

The form of the town is very irregular, but it is completely surrounded by high and thick walls, which appear to have been once very strong. They are now falling fast into ruin; yet wherever any part of the old work is seen, through the mud and irregular fragments of stone, with which the ravages of time have been partially concealed, it appears to be solid and good. The walls are besides provided with ramparts, on which are planted a number of guns quite sufficient to make themselves tolerably respected, were it not that the impertinent interference of rust, and the occasional want of carriages for the guns, might contribute to prevent their effect. The castle is built at the south-eastern angle of the city, close to the water's edge; and may be said to connect the line of ramparts along the beach with that which encloses the town to the southward. The walls of the castle are unusually high, and have been fortunately made to incline a good deal inwards: we say fortunately, for so bad is the state of repair, in which the exterior is kept, that without this convenient inclination to the centre, they would not probably be standing at all. Yet they are certainly of considerable thickness; and it is owing to the very unworkmanlike manner in which the building has been from time to time augmented, for we ought not to call it repaired, that its strength has been materially diminished.

Appearances, however, are by no means disregarded; and the surface of His Highness's castle and residence (for the building is both one and the other) displays a bright coating of plaster and whitewash over the unseemly patchwork beneath it.

The city walls and ramparts are for the most part disguised under a cloak of the same gay material; and the whole together, viewed under an African sun, and contrasted with the deep blue of an African sky, assumes a decent, we may even say, a brilliant appearance. It must, however, be confessed that this is much improved by distance; for a too close inspection will occasionally discover through their veil the defects which we have alluded to above; and large flakes of treacherous plaster will occasionally be found by near observers to have dropt off and left them quite exposed.

Leo Africanus has informed us that the houses and bazars of Tripoly were *handsome* compared with those of Tunis. How far this epithet might have been applicable at the period here alluded to, we are not ourselves able to judge; but we must confess that the beauty of the existing houses and bazars of Tripoly did not appear to us particularly striking: and if the comparison drawn by Leo may be still supposed to hold, we do not envy the architects of Tunis whatever fame they may have acquired by the erection of the most admired buildings of that city. The mosques and colleges, as well as hospitals, enumerated by our author, must have been very different from those now existing to entitle them to any commendation; and the rude and dilapidated masses of mud and stone, or more frequently, perhaps, of mud only, here dignified by the appellation of houses, do not certainly present very brilliant examples either of taste, execution, or convenience. Indeed, if we consider the actual state of Tripoly, we might be authorized, perhaps, in disputing its claims to be ranked as a city at all; and they who are unaccustomed to Mahometan negligence might imagine that they had wandered to some deserted and ruinous part of the town, when in reality they were traversing the most admired streets of a populous and fashionable quarter. This want of discernment, however, is chiefly confined to Europeans; for the greater part of the Mahometan inhabitants of Tripoly are strongly convinced of its beauty and importance; while the wandering Arab who enters its gates, and looks up to the high and whitewashed walls of the Bashaw's castle, expresses strongly in his countenance the astonishment which he feels how human hands and ingenuity could have accomplished such a structure.

Of the ancient remains now existing in Tripoly, the Roman arch we have already alluded to, with a few scattered fragments of tesselated pavement, and some partial ruins of columns and entablatures, here and there built into the walls of modern structures, are all that we were able to discover.

The harbour is formed by a long reef of rocks running out into the sea in a north-easterly direction, and by other reefs at some distance to the eastward of these, all of which make together a very good shelter. In the deepest part, however, there is very little more than five and six fathoms water.

At the extremity of a rocky projection to the northward, forming part of the first-mentioned reef, are two batteries, called the New, and Spanish, forts; and to the westward of these, on an insulated rock, is a circular one called the French fort. Besides these, there are two others on the beach to the eastward, which, with the New and Spanish forts, would prove of considerable annoyance to hostile vessels entering the harbour. The forts are in better condition than the walls and ramparts, which we have already stated to be very much dilapidated, and the guns very little attended to.

The mosques and baths of Tripoly, with its coffee-houses, bazars, &c., as well as the manners and customs, dresses, prejudices, and other peculiarities, of the people who are in the habit of frequenting them, have been so amply, and so well described in other publications, that we need not here attempt any account of them.

We may, however, be allowed a few words on the peculiarities of soil, at present observable in the neighbourhood of Tripoly, as contrasted with those which appear to have existed in the fifteenth and sixteenth centuries.

It has been observed by Leo Africanus, (who flourished during the pontificate and under the protection of Leo the Tenth,) that there was at all times a scarcity of grain in Tripoly, and that the country about it was incapable of cultivation; but it will appear from the passages which we have quoted below, as well as from the actual state of the place, that it is merely the want of rain (which is occasionally experienced) that now prevents the soil in question from producing good crops very regularly.

When we inquire into the cause of this difference, a more interesting result will be afforded by the inquiry than any which relates to the quantity of corn produced at Tripoly. We find, for instance, that the lands to the southward of Tripoly (we mean those in the immediate neighbourhood of the town) were subject, in the time of the African Geographer, to be overflowed for some extent by the sea; while the same parts are now above the level of the water, which never reaches high enough to cover them. "All the country about Tripoly" (says Leo Africanus) "is sandy like that of Numidia; and the reason of this is, that the sea enters freely towards the southward, (entra assai verso mezzogiorno,) so that the lands which ought to be cultivated are all covered with water. The opinion of the inhabitants," he continues, "with respect to this *riviera*, is, that there was formerly a considerable tract of land extending to the northward; but that for many thousand years the sea has been advancing and covering it; which is observable," he adds, "and known to be the case, on the coast of Monasteer, as well as at Mahdia, Sfax, Gabes, and the island of Girbe; with other cities to the eastward, whose shores have but little depth of water; so that one may walk a mile or two into the sea without being up to the waist. Wherever this occurs," (continues Leo) "such places are said to be considered as parts of the *soil* overflowed by the sea;" (that is, not within the original bounds of the latter,) "and the inhabitants of Tripoly," he tells us, "are of opinion, that their city stood formerly more to the northward; but that owing to the continual advance of the sea it has been gradually extended in a southerly direction; they also declare," says our Author, "that remains of houses and other buildings may still be observed under water."

From this account, contrasted with the actual appearance of the place in question, we must either suppose that the level of the lands here alluded to, which are those in the *immediate* neighbourhood of Tripoly, is higher, at the present time, than it was in the age of Leo, or that the sea has retired since that period. For although the soil of Tripoly still continues to be sandy, there is now no part of it, as we have stated above, overflowed to the southward of the town. As we cannot suppose that the sea has retired since the time of the author in question—(for we shall hereafter point out several instances on the coast, between this part of Northern Africa and Alexandria, in which it rather appears to have gained)—we must conclude that, since the age of Leo Africanus, the land alluded to has been rising in a greater proportion than the sea.

This elevation of soil is, at the same time, by no means inconsistent with the rise of the waters already mentioned; for, as the coast is here sandy, we may venture to conclude, that the sea, notwithstanding it continued to rise, threw up, from time to time, a sufficient quantity of sand to raise the level of the country above it; and we shall thus have an additional confirmation of what appears to be actually the case on the coasts of the Greater Syrtis, and Cyrenaica, as well as of the ingenious conjectures of Major Rennell with regard to the Lake Tritonis and the Lesser Syrtis.

It is well known that Tripoly, after the destruction of Carthage, became a Roman province; and that on the conquest of a great part of Northern Africa by the Vandals, it passed into the hands of those barbarians, from which it was rescued, in the reign of Justinian, by the valour and abilities of Belisarius. The rapid and extraordinary progress of Mahometanism, soon after the death of its founder, involved Tripoly, together with the whole of Northern Africa, in the general wreck of civilization and Christianity: since that period it has remained, with few exceptions, in the hands of its Moslem conquerors, passing successively from the government of the Caliphs to the tyranny of Morocco, Fez, Tunis, and the Porte. After the erection of the walls of the town, already mentioned as the work of Dragut, Tripoly became the secure resort of most of the Corsairs who roved under

Turkish colours; and from that port they continually make attacks and descents on the opposite shores of the Mediterranean.

After the death of Dragut, the Porte continued to send Governors to Tripoly under the titles of Sangiac and Bashaw; and the castle was garrisoned by Turkish troops while the Moors inhabited the city. At length, in the year 1714, it was finally rescued from the oppression of the Turks by the great-grandfather of the reigning Bashaw; who, having contrived to assassinate the whole of the garrison, took the reins of government into his own hands, and obtained the title of Hamet the Great. From that time to the present it has remained under the government of the Moors, although the supremacy of the Grand Signor is still acknowledged, and tribute is paid to the Porte.

We may say, in allusion to the actual state of Tripoly, that it appears to be making some advances towards civilization, and is beginning to feel the good effects which result from a state of security and tranquillity. Indeed, when we reflect upon its deplorable condition at the time of the accession of Sidi Yusuf, and look back upon the horrors of civil discord and contention to which it had been for more than eight years exposed—impoverished at the same time by indiscriminate extortion and plunder, and subjected during the period of these heavy calamities to the dreadful effects of famine and plague—we may venture to assert that the present state of Tripoly is far better than might have been expected. It is now secure under the protection of an established government, property is respected, and commerce is improving; its markets are well supplied, its manufactures are encouraged, and its population appears to be increasing.

A considerable portion of the revenue of Tripoly was formerly drawn from the plunder obtained by her corsairs; and a very lucrative branch of her commerce consisted in the traffic of slaves. The humane interference, and the decisive measures, of England, have contributed to check, if not quite to abolish, these execrable sources of profit. Piracy, so far at least as we were able to learn, has been wholly superseded by commerce; and when the Tripolines find that it is more to their interest to give up their traffic in human kind than to continue it, we may hope to see this also relinquished.

It may, however, be added (we fear) that *till then* such a consummation must not be expected, however devoutly it may be wished. Indeed, we cannot reasonably expect that it should; for the feelings which result from a high state of civilization will never be found to precede civilization itself: and humanity, however strongly we may believe, or may wish to believe, it is implanted in the breasts of all mankind, has not often been found to weigh very heavy against the scale in which interest, or inclination, has been opposed to it.

Geographical Remarks on the Towns and District of Tripoly.

The town of Tripoly has been usually considered to occupy the site of the ancient Oea; one of the cities which, with Sabrata and Leptis Magna, the Tripoli Vecchia and Lebida of modern times, composed the three principal towns of a district which took from them the appellation of Tripolis.

At what precise period this tract of country assumed the title of Tripolis does not appear to be clearly ascertained; but we may probably conclude that it acquired it in the reign, either of Titus, or of his successor Domitian; soon after the building of Sabrata and Oea, which may be supposed to have taken place before the middle of the first century.

It seems to be still more uncertain when the name of the *district* was bestowed upon the *cities* of Tripoly; for although Tripoli Vecchia (which we have already called Sabrata) has been said to be the first which assumed it, there does not appear to be any other proof in favour of this supposition, (at least we are not ourselves acquainted with it,) than that which may be inferred from the epithet *vecchia*, by which this town has been for centuries distinguished. Both cities appear to have flourished together under the Romans; and were in all probability destroyed at the same time, in the Saracen invasion of the country. As Sabrata, however, continued to remain in ruins, while a new town sprung up on the site of the ancient Oea, the name of Tripoly may have, perhaps, been first assumed by the latter; while Sabrata, from the circumstance of its being in ruins, was distinguished by the epithet which it retains.

We are not aware of any proof that either Sabrata or Oea had changed their names before their destruction by the Saracens; and as no town appears to have been erected on the ruins of the former, there was no necessity for distinguishing it by another. When a new town arose on the ruins of Oea, it is probable that the appellation by which it is at present known to the Moors, and which is merely a corruption of the Roman term for the district, was the first name which either town assumed after the loss of those which formerly distinguished them. Tráblis would have been known to the nations of Europe as the same name with that of Tripolis; and they would naturally have written the term like that of the district, whenever there might have been occasion to mention it. Supposing this to be the case, we may fairly assume, that the name of Tripolis was never given by the ancients at all to either of the cities in question; and that it is only, in fact, since the Mahometan conquest that the name of the district has been applied to them.

This appears to be more probable when we consider that the title of—*The district of the three cities*—as Tripolis must be translated, would be a very unappropriate term for a single town, although it might be well applied to a department. Such an objection, however, would by no means appear to the Mahometan invaders of the country, who may certainly be imagined to have been ignorant of the language from which the word in question is compounded; and they would discover no reason why the former name of the district might not be a proper one for their new town.

We have not been at the pains to search minutely into this question, which would probably receive light from the writers of the Lower Empire; and we offer the conjectures which we have hazarded above, in the absence of more decided information. At the same time, however, it may here be remarked, that the propriety of adopting the word Tripolis, which appears in the printed copies of Ptolemy, is questioned on very good authority. In support of this assertion we need only refer our readers to the Fourth Book of Cellarius, (chap. 3,) where the question is amply discussed; and as the adoption of this reading, instead of that of Leptis Magna, which appears to be decidedly the proper one, would create an endless and unnecessary confusion in the geography of that part of the country which lies between Tripoli Vecchia and Lebida, we have thought it not irrelevant to allude to it.

It is perhaps the more necessary that we should do so, as Signor Della Cella has availed himself of the reading above mentioned, and of a passage which he has quoted from Pliny, to identify the modern town of Tripoly with Neapolis; which is too evidently the same town with Leptis Magna (or Lebida), to admit of any similar arrangement.

We have by no means any wish to detract from the merits of this gentleman, who deserves every credit for the spirit of inquiry which has led him to encounter the fatigues and privations of a journey like that which he has accomplished. He is the first European who has crossed the Greater Syrtis since the occupation of Northern Africa by the Romans; at least he is the only one that we know of, since that period, who has published any account of such a journey; and he is therefore entitled to the merit of having afforded us the only information which has been given for many centuries of an interesting and extensive tract of country. But as we shall frequently have occasion to refer to his work in the course of the present narrative, we trust that we shall not be suspected of undervaluing its merits, because we may sometimes find it necessary to point out what we conceive to be its errors.

In considering the modern town of Tripoly as Oea, one difficulty will however present itself: Oea is no where mentioned as a port, that we have been able to discover; whereas Tripoly must always have been one. But as many cities are mentioned as ports by one writer, while they are merely styled cities by another, this objection may readily be waived. Garapha is by

Ptolemy styled λιμην, by Scylax πολις, by Pliny, Oppidum; Abrotonum is by Strabo called πολις, by Scylax πολις και λιμην, by Pliny, Oppidum: Leptis Magna is rarely mentioned as a port, although it is well known to have been one; and many more examples might be adduced by those who would take the trouble to collect them.

What is now called modern Tripoly has been said by some writers to have been built by the early inhabitants of Northern Africa, under the name of Tarabilis or Trebiles; and the same authors have stated that the Roman term of Tripolis is derived from the name which they bestowed upon it. We have already noticed the improbability of this latter supposition; and we may now venture to add, that there appears to be no proof of any town having been built upon the site of modern Tripoly before the erection of the city of Oea. Leptis Magna is known to have been built by the Phœnicians, on the authority of several writers of antiquity; but the other two cities composing the Tripolis have always been considered of Roman origin, and no mention is made of any other having ever been assigned to them in works not comparatively modern.

Leo Africanus, who may be supposed to have compiled his account of Africa from the authority chiefly of Mahometan historians, has given his testimony in favour of the native origin of Tripoly, while he states that Tripoli Vecchia was built by the Romans. "Questa," (Tripoli Vecchia) says the African geographer, "è una città antica edificata pur da' Romani;" but of the other town he states, "Tripoli fu edificata da gli Africani, dopo la rovina della Vecchia Tripoli"—without any allusion whatever to the circumstance of its having been originally a Roman city.

Whatever may be the earliest authority for this supposition, it appears to be evidently founded on an imperfect knowledge of the place; for if there were even no reason for supposing Tripoly to be Oea, we must still have allowed it Roman origin; or at least we must have admitted it to have been in existence at the time when the Romans held the country. The Roman arch, which has been given in the work of Captain Lyon, is sufficient to establish this circumstance; and the inscription which it bears, also given in the same publication, and mentioned in the Memoirs of Consul Tully, refers this edifice to the time of Marcus Aurelius. In stating that Tripoly was built by the Africans, *after the ruin of Tripoli Vecchia*, we might have imagined that Leo only meant to allude to its re-construction under the Mahometans; but from the circumstance of his having just before mentioned Tripoli Vecchia, as a city which was built by the Romans, it seems to be probable that, had he been aware of them, he would equally have noticed the pretensions of modern Tripoly to a higher antiquity than he has assigned to it.

Tripoli Vecchia was destroyed, under the caliphate of Omar, by the Saracen invaders of the country. The city was pillaged, after a siege of six months, and its inhabitants either slain or carried prisoners to Egypt and Arabia. This is stated by Leo; and here we have a date for the destruction of the city of Sabrata, which appears to have never been rebuilt: but *how long* after the occurrence of this event Modern Tripoly first appeared on the ruins of Oea we have not been informed by our author. And it seems to be evident that he considered the African town as the first which had been raised upon the spot.

FOOTNOTES:

Three sides of the town of Tripoly are said, in Tully's Memoirs, to be washed by the sea, which is certainly not now the case.

The noted corsair Dragūt is said to have been the author of this defence, and two forts which were situated near the sea are also attributed to this person.

But Leo Africanus, who flourished at the same period with Dragūt, at the beginning of the 16th century, has mentioned the walls of Tripoly as being high and handsome, though not very strong; and as the existing walls of the town, if they be really those of Dragūt, bear all the appearance of having once been very solid, we may perhaps suppose that those mentioned by Leo were standing before the present ones were constructed.

The greatest length of the city, including the walls, may be said to be about 1360 yards, and its extreme breadth about a thousand yards.

The happy confusion of buildings which surmount the walls of the castle, raised at various times for the convenience and accommodation of the royal family, together with the little world which is contained within its limits, have been well, and correctly described in Tully's Memoirs.

To the eastward of the town, however, on a tract of rocky and elevated ground, is the burial-place of the ancient city; where the researches of Mr. Consul Warrington have brought to light some very interesting objects; particularly several large sepulchral urns of glass, the most perfect we have ever seen.

We allude principally to the works of Consul Tully and Captain Lyon, and to Blaquiere's Letters from the Mediterranean.

"In our way home" (says the artless and amiable writer of Tully's Memoirs) "we passed through a street noted for its corn-wells, or rather caverns, dug very deep into the earth. They are situated on each side of the street, at about thirty yards' distance. They were designed for magazines to lay up corn in, where they say it will keep perfectly good for an hundred years.

Happy were it for the inhabitants of this country if these caverns were filled now as they were *formerly* when the country was *so rich in the produce of corn*, that it was from hence exported to many parts of the world, and prized almost above any other. The barley when sown here yields twice as much as it does in Europe. When it grows properly, they reckon thirty and thirty-five ears for one an ordinary produce; while in Europe fourteen or fifteen is considered as a good return." In dry seasons, however, which frequently occur, the case appears to be far otherwise. "The times are so much altered now," (continues the authoress above mentioned,) "that corn is imported at an immense expense. This melancholy change is attributed *to the want of rains*, which have failed for several years past. There have not been more than one or two good harvests for thirty years. If cargoes of wheat do not soon arrive from Tunis, the state of this place will be dreadful beyond description."—*Tully's Narrative*, p. 49.—Again, the same writer says, p. 67, "It has been ascertained by the Bashaw to-day, that there is only barley for sale at two bazars, or market-places, left in the place. *A few years since the barley here grew so favourably, that it produced in return three times as much as in any part of Europe. Such quantities of it were exported, that Tripoly was enriched by its sale;* but the failure of rain has left the country for several years without one good harvest."

This account is consistent with the above, and we have here some idea of what may be meant by the word *formerly*, in the passage first quoted, which is certainly somewhat indefinite.

Part of the sandy plain to the south-eastward is, however, occasionally flooded during the prevalence of strong northerly gales, and there is a tract of marshy ground, to the westward of the town, between the cultivated parts and the sea.

(Leo Africanus in Ramusio, p. 72.)—With respect to the former extension of Tripoly to the northward, here mentioned by the African geographer, the observation is certainly in some degree correct, and consistent with the present appearance of other parts of the coast of Northern Africa; but we must at the same time observe that the town could scarcely have projected any farther to the northward than the sites of the French and Spanish forts; for beyond these we get into five and eight fathoms water.

We must, however, confess, that we cannot altogether understand, why the loss of the ground in the immediate neighbourhood of Tripoly, said by Leo Africanus to have been flooded in his days, should have necessarily occasioned to the inhabitants of the town so great a scarcity of grain as that mentioned by this geographer. For the high grounds immediately beyond the parts which were overflowed, must at all times, we should conceive, from their rocky foundation, have been placed above the level of the sea at its greatest height, and might therefore have been cultivated as we find them to be at present; and the Gharian mountains, as well as the country of Tagiura, both of which are still very productive, are mentioned by Leo as places highly cultivated at the period of the overflow alluded to.

We may remark on this subject—that the coincidence of the former with the present state of the last-mentioned places, appears to be the more worthy of notice, from the circumstance of our finding the actual produce of other districts, both in Tunis and Tripoly, very different from what it appears to have been in earlier periods. Among other examples, in proof of this assertion, we may notice the great difference which has taken place in the produce and soil of Byzacium. This district was formerly much renowned for its fertility; and we are informed by Pliny that one grain of corn from the Byzacium was sent to the Emperor Augustus, which yielded four hundred shoots; and that three hundred and forty stems had been afterwards sent to Nero, produced equally from a single grain of corn. But whatever be the cause of the change which has taken place, we find the soil of the Byzacium to have greatly fallen off from its former extraordinary fertility; in proof of which we need only extract the following observations from Shaw's Travels in Barbary.

"The many parts which I have seen of the ancient Byzacium, or winter circuit, fall vastly short in fertility of the character which has been attributed to them by the ancients. For such as are adjacent to the sea coast are generally of a dry, sandy nature, with no great depth of soil in the very best portion of them. This is called the Sahul, and is planted for the most part with olive-trees, which flourish here in the greatest perfection. Neither is the inland country in a much better condition."

Misit ex eo loco Divo Augusto procurator ejus, ex uno grano, (vix credibile dictu) quadringenta paucis minus germina, extantque de ea re epistolæ. Misit et Neroni similiter CCCXL stipulas ex uno grano.—*Nat. Hist.* l. xviii. c. 10.

Again (lib. v. c. 4.) Ita (Byzacium) appellatur regio CCL. M. P. circuitu, fertilitatis eximiæ, cum centesima fruge agricolis fœnus reddente terra.

Before we take leave of Tripoly it may be proper to recommend, for the information of those who may hereafter visit that country, the useful precaution of not subjecting themselves to the fluctuation which is usual in the exchange of the place. Money, in Tripoly, is in the hands of a few; and its possessors, who are by no means unacquainted with the most profitable methods of laying it out, are not at all times particularly remarkable for a liberal treatment of strangers. We found the exchange get more unfavourable as our demand for money increased; and having been obliged to make some comparatively heavy payments in Spanish dollars, the value of them rose in proportion as it was known we had occasion for them. In order to remedy, or rather to prevent impositions of a similar nature, it would be advisable for travellers to take with them, in Spanish dollars, the amount of the sums they may have occasion for in Tripoly; for even if the exchange should be good on their arrival there, it would most probably lower as they were known to have occasion for money. Should this be inconvenient, bills might be drawn on Malta, and the money in *Spanish dollars* forwarded by the first secure vessel which might be sailing from that port to Tripoly.

It must, however, be observed, in justice to the house of Messrs. Beaussier and Co., that we experienced a more liberal treatment from them than from any other house in Tripoly.

The *Spanish* dollar is the coin in most general request in the northern and inland parts of Africa.

We find both these cities mentioned by Pliny; and one of them (Oea) by Pomponius Mela, while nothing is said by Strabo either of the cities or the district. Pliny died A.D. 79; Mela is supposed to have flourished about the middle of the first century, and Strabo in the reigns of Augustus and Tiberius. We may infer, from the silence of Strabo on the subject, that neither Sabrata nor Oea existed in his time; and as Pliny, though he mentions both cities, appears to have been unacquainted with the name of the district in question, we may also perhaps infer that it was bestowed upon it after his time. What is stated by Cellarius on the subject of Tripolis, appears to confirm this opinion: for he tells us that he knew of no one before the time of Solinus, who made any mention in Africa of the name; and that *he* only applied the term to the district, and not to any particular city.

Solinus is known to have written after Pliny, towards the close of the first century; and we may therefore, perhaps, conclude, that the district called Tripolis, received that appellation between the times of Pliny and Solinus.

Nec qui ante Solinum, non antiquissimum scriptorem, mentionem vocis Tripolis in Africa fecerit succurrit nobis; qui vero, non urbem, sed trium oppidorum regionem intellexit.—(Lib. iv. cap. 3. § 18.)

Tráblis, the Moorish name of the town, is not, however, properly a *corruption* of Tripolis; it is merely the same word articulated through the medium of Arab pronunciation.

Some authors have imagined an early African name *Tarabilis*, or *Trebilis*, from which the Roman name Tripolis was derived; but this is merely imaginary, since the meaning of Tripolis clearly points out its origin to be Greek.

In hoc tractu autem, post Cinyphum fluvium, prima Ptolemæo est Νεαπολις (Neapolis) de qua, in editis, exstat, ἡ καὶ Τριπολις (quæ etiam Tripolis vocatur): in Palatino autem codice nihil de Tripoli legitur, sed ἡ καὶ Λεπτις μεγαλη (quæ, Neapolis, etiam Leptis Magna dicitur.)—Geog. Antiq. lib. iv. cap. 3.

It may be added, in support of the reading in the Palatine manuscript, that Neapolis is mentioned by Ptolemy immediately after the Cinyphus, which lies to the *eastward* of Leptis Magna; so that the geographer, in passing, as he does, from east to west, must be supposed to have omitted Leptis Magna altogether, if Neapolis be not intended to denote it.

This reading of Ptolemy, as will appear from the passage which we have quoted above from Cellarius, is contradicted by the Palatine manuscript; and must be rejected on the authority of Scylax and Strabo, and even of Ptolemy himself.—(See the Fourth Book of Cellarius). The passage of Pliny is not so easily disposed of. After mentioning the city of Sabrata, this author observes, in speaking of the country which lies between the Great and Lesser Syrtis, "Ibi civitas Oensis, Cynips fluvius ac regio, oppida, Neapolis, Taphra, Abrotonum, Leptis altera, quæ cognominatur magna."— (Hist. Nat. lib. v. cap. 5.) Here we find Neapolis mentioned immediately after Oea, and distinguished from Leptis Magna. "Io crederei," says Signor della Cella, "che sia piu conforme al vero, l'ammettere che Tripoli degli antichi geografi debba riconoscersi nelle rovine che trovansi a ponente de' Tripoli tuttora chiamato Tripoli Vecchio. Pare che l'abbandono, qualunque ne fosse la cagione, di questa città, desse luogo alla formazione di quella che attualmente ne porta il nome, e che in quell' epoca fu chiamata *Tripoli il nuovo*, o la nuova città, e da' Greci Νεαπολις. In questa opinione consente la vera lezione di Tolommeo, ove leggesi Νεαπολις ἡ καὶ Τριπολις. (Neapoli che dicesi anche Tripoli.) Ho detto la vera lezione di Tolommeo, perchè io ho per apocrifa quella adottata dal Cellario, dove in vece di Τριπολις, avendo sostituito Λεπτις, tutto rimane alterato e confuso. Con Tolommeo concorda Plinio che ha per due città diverse Neapoli e Leptis Magna, e tra queste due tramette Gaffara e Abrotano; e Plinio, per le cognizione che poteva attinger nella città, e ne' tempi ne' quali scriveva, merita sopra ogni altro credenza intorna alla geografia di questa parte dell' Africa."—(Viaggio da Tripoli, &c. p. 41.)

It will not here be very evident how the modern town of Tripoly can, on the authority of Pliny, be supposed to be the same with Neapolis. For Tripoly is identified by the best authorities with Oea; and Neapolis is mentioned, in the passage alluded to, as situated between Oea and Taphra, (the Graphara and Garapha of Scylax and Ptolemy.) But supposing it to be, as Signor della Cella has stated, that the decay of the "*Tripoli* degli *antichi* geografi" had really given occasion to the building of the present one, under the title he has conferred upon it of Neapolis; it follows that the former city must have borne the name of Tripolis in the time of Pliny, who, so far from knowing any town of that name, does not even recognise the district under the title.

It must, however, be confessed, that the introduction of Neapolis, in the situation which Pliny has assigned to it, is by no means very easily accounted for. At the same time it is certain, that the position in question is directly in opposition to the authority of Strabo, as well as to that of Scylax and of Ptolemy; who, all of them, identify Neapolis with Leptis Magna, as will be seen by a reference to Cellarius. This author, who insists very properly upon the authority of Strabo, &c., that Neapolis is Leptis Magna, supposes, with Hardouin, that Pliny has adopted the passage above quoted from Mela, whom he censures for having brought together places so distant from each other. But Mela is evidently speaking of the country to the westward of the *Lesser* Syrtis; of Leptis Parva, and the Neapolis Colonia of Ptolemy, situated near the extremity of the Mercurii Promontorium, in the vicinity of Clypea; so that, although the towns and cities which he enumerates do not come in the proper succession, they all of them belong to the part of the country which he is describing; and not, as Cellarius imagines, to both sides of the river Triton, which would have made a much more serious confusion. It is therefore less easy to imagine whence Pliny has derived his Neapolis, or what is his authority for the order in which he places the other cities of the district; if indeed he intended them to be in order at all, which from his mention of Oea (the civitas Oeensis) conjointly with the river Cinyphus, we might probably be authorized in denying. We find *Abrotonum* also introduced by Cellarius, instead of *Acholla*, in the passage which he has quoted from Mela: the proper reading is— Hadrumetum, Leptis, Clypea, *Acholla*, Taphrure, Neapolis, hinc ad Syrtim adjacent, ut inter ignobilia celeberrimæ.

The Taphrure of Mela must not be confounded with Pliny's Taphra, which is the same with Graphara or Garapha.

Mela has however done the same (ultra est Oea oppidum, et Cinypus fluvius, per uberrima arva decidens . . .) and the difficulty is increased by what follows—*tum* Leptis altera, &c.; both accounts are very confused, and open to much discussion, but this is not the place for it, and we have already perhaps said too much upon the subject.

Or rather of a female relation of Consul Tully, to whom the work in question is attributed.

It is observed in the same work, "When this arch was built, there were few habitations nearer this place than Lebida, the Leptis Magna of the ancients;" and farther on, "the Romans strayed to the spot where Tripoly now stands, to hunt wild beasts; and under this arch they found a welcome retreat from the burning rays of the sun." But the arch was erected after the middle of the *second* century; and both Sabrata and Oea were extant in the time of Pliny, who flourished in the middle of the *first*,—the conclusion is obvious.

CHAPTER III.

Departure of the Expedition from Tripoly — Passage through Tagiura — Fertile appearance of the latter — Its Mosque, and actual remains — Tagiura considered as the site of Abrotonum — Existence of a salt-water lake at Tagiura, consistent with Strabo's account of Abrotonum — Present tranquil condition of the country in this neighbourhood contrasted with its dangerous state in the time of Consul Tully — Sand-heaps to the eastward of Tagiura — Remarks on their formation, and on the accumulation of sand in other places — Dangers of the sand-storm considered — Passage over the sandy tract to the eastward of Tagiura — Arrive at Wady Ramleh — Stormy weather at that place — Take leave of our European friends who had accompanied us from Tripoly — Continuance of the gale — Arrive at Wady'm'Seyd — Attempt to pass, without success, across the sand-hills to the coast. — Arrive at Guadigmata — Position of Graphara, as laid down by Scylax, considered. — Ancient remains discovered by Captain Smyth in the neighbourhood of Wady'm'Seyd and Abdellata. — Remarks on these, considered as the remains of Graphara — Scuffle with the Arabs at Sidy Abdellati — Remains at that place indicative of an ancient military station — Cross the range of Sélem — Extensive view from its summit over the fertile plains of Lebida and Jumarr — Rains still continue — Distress of the camels — Meet with the English Consul on his return from an excursion to Lebida — Report of a troop of marauding Arabs lying in wait for our party.

ON the 4th of November our arrangements were completed, and we were able to send the greater part of our baggage to the tents which had been pitched in a garden without the town; on the following morning we took a final leave of Tripoly, and set out on our journey to Tagiura.

Our party consisted of three Europeans, who acted equally as interpreters and servants, a Tchaous, or janissary, belonging to the Bashaw, Shekh Mahommed el Dúbbah, with five other Bedouin Arabs, and three Arabs of Tripoly to look after the horses, making altogether (ourselves included) eighteen.

After passing through the Messeah, or cultivated district in the neighbourhood of Tripoly, and along the large Salt Marsh, mentioned in Tully's Memoirs, which was now completely covered with water, we entered the scattered villages of Tagiura. They are surrounded by gardens, yielding abundant crops of corn, fruit and vegetables, and shaded by thickly-planted date and olive-trees, which are equally valuable to the inhabitants. We find Tagiura described by Leo Africanus as a country containing a good many villages, or hamlets, and many gardens of date and other fruit trees; and its present general appearance is probably little different from that which it presented in the time of this geographer.

In consequence of a considerable emigration from Tripoly, this country (he adds) became "assai nobile e civile;" but we must confess that there are at present very little remains of its importance, or extraordinary civilization; unless a large mosque, of some apparent antiquity (highly reverenced by its Mahometan population) and the good-humoured hospitality with which we were received by the natives, may be considered as examples of both.

The people, however, appeared to be contented and happy, and greeted us with many friendly salutations as we passed through their highly-cultivated country. Some Roman columns, which are said to be in the interior of the mosque, would seem to point out its vicinity to an ancient site; and if we must necessarily consider Tagiura to occupy the position of any ancient town, we should suppose it to stand on that of Abrotonum.

But it will be found, upon inquiry, that there are considerable difficulties attendant on such a conclusion. For Abrotonum is stated by Scylax to have been two days' sail from Leptis Magna; and the distance between Tagiura and Lebida (already identified with Leptis Magna) is no more than 59 miles.

The mean rate allowed by Major Rennell, for the sailing of the vessels of the ancients, is 35 miles per day; so that the distance between Leptis Magna and Abrotonum should, at this rate, be 70 miles. It is true that the rate of Nearchus, in the Red Sea and in the Persian Gulf, as estimated by the same author, is no more than 22½ and 30 miles; but this was occasioned by circumstances not attendant on voyages in general, and must be considered (says the Major) as an unusually low rate.

Another difficulty arises from the mention of Abrotonum as a *port*, as well as a city, in the passage we have quoted from Scylax; for Tagiura cannot be said to possess one.

It will here immediately occur to the reader, that Tripoly has a very good port; and that the distance of that town from Lebida will answer remarkably well with the distance of Scylax in question: for Tripoly may be estimated at 67 miles from Lebida, which will be within three of the 70 miles mentioned as the distance between Leptis Magna and Abrotonum. Both these circumstances together will therefore appear very strongly to favour the supposition that Tripoly is Abrotonum; while a third, which we have already mentioned, *viz.*, that Oea is not stated to be a port by ancient writers, (at least, not that we have been able to learn,) will contribute to strengthen the idea.

These facts would undoubtedly make it seem very probable that Modern Tripoly is the Abrotonum of Scylax; but then the authorities of D'Anville and Cellarius, and these are no slender authorities, concur in placing that town on the site of Oea, as which we have accordingly considered it.

We will not pursue the question further; but will leave our readers to judge how far Abrotonum may be placed at Tagiura under the circumstances which we have already stated; merely adding, that the fertile plains of Tagiura are admirably calculated for the position of a town, and that many a pleasant day has been spent among their villages and gardens by the European inhabitants of Tripoly, who often make parties to visit them.

We may at the same time contrast the present quiet state of Tagiura with that in which it was found by Consul Tully a short time before the accession of Sidi Yusuf. It was then considered necessary, in visiting this place, although during what were called tranquil times, that the party of the Consul, amounting to upwards of forty, should be increased by the addition of several of the Bashaw's Chaouses; and it was afterwards reported to His Highness, that he had had, notwithstanding this prudent precaution, a very narrow and fortunate escape.

We found the roads to, and through, Tagiura in most places inundated by the heavy rains which had fallen before the commencement of our journey; a circumstance which, if it did not expedite our travelling, had certainly the good effect of rendering it more pleasant, by cooling the atmosphere and preventing the sand from flying. This was the more fortunate, as the gardens to the eastward of the town are bounded by a dreary tract of sandy desert, which we were obliged to cross. The approach to it was indicated by numerous hillocks of sand accumulated about the date-trees on the outskirts of the villages, leaving their heads exposed, at various heights above the sand, while some of them scarcely appeared above the summit. Judging from the present appearance of Tagiura, we should imagine that many gardens, situated on its eastern limits, have been completely overwhelmed by these heaps.

Any object which is stationary would arrest the progress of sand borne towards it by the violence of the wind; and the low enclosures of Arab gardens in exposed situations might in a few years disappear altogether.

We are not, however, inclined to attribute quite so much to the overwhelming properties of sand, as many other travellers have done; and we do not think that the danger of being actually buried will appear, on consideration, to be altogether so great, to those who are crossing sandy deserts, as writers of high respectability have asserted. The sand which encounters a body in motion, would pass it, we should imagine, without accumulation; and the quantity which might even be heaped upon sleepers could scarcely be more than they might easily shake off in waking. We shudder at the dreadful accounts which have been recorded of whole caravans, and whole armies, destroyed by these formidable waves of the desert; and when our pity is strongly excited by such relations, we are seldom inclined to analyze them very deeply. But a little reflection would probably convince us that many of these are greatly exaggerated: some, because the writers believed what they related; and some, because they wished their readers to believe what they might not be quite convinced of themselves.

In fact, we think it probable that they who have perished in deserts, from the time of the Psylli and Cambyses to the present, have died, as is usual, before they were buried, either from violence, thirst, or exhaustion.

The idea in question has, however, become very general; and we can neither attribute much blame to the reader who believes what is related on respectable authority, or to the writer who simply informs us of what he himself considers to be true. To him whose only view is to excite interest by exaggeration, we may, at least, say it seems to be superfluous: for the hardships and dangers of a journey over the sandy desert may be fully sufficient to satisfy the most adventurous, and to exhaust the most robust, without calling up the airy forms of imaginary horrors, to lengthen out the line of those which really present themselves.

But if the desert have terrors peculiar to itself, it has also its peculiar pleasures. There is something imposing, we may say sublime, in the idea of unbounded space which it occasionally presents; and every trifling object which appears above its untenanted surface, assumes an interest which we should not on other occasions attribute to objects of much greater importance.

The little romance which its stillness and solitude encourage, is at the same time grateful to the feelings; and one may here dream delightfully of undisturbed tranquillity and independence, and of freedom from all the cares, the follies, and the vices of the world. Whenever the wind is cool, without being too strong, the purity of the air is at once refreshing and exhilarating; and, if his stock of water be not very low, the traveller feels disposed to be well pleased with every thing.

Such was precisely the feeling with which our party entered upon the tract of sandy desert before them. We were glad to escape from the continual din and bustle which had attended our preparations at Tripoly; and the very absence of harassing workmen and tradesmen was alone a source of real satisfaction: the coolness of the sea-breeze was unusually refreshing, at least, we persuaded ourselves that it was so; and the anticipation of an interesting journey was acting very strongly upon our minds.

After quitting the cultivated grounds of Tagiura, the traveller is left to pursue his course (in going eastward) as his experience or his compass may direct—there being no indication whatever of any track in the sands of the wide plain before him. As our principal object, in this part of our journey, was to obtain a correct delineation of the coast, we pursued our route along the margin of the sea; which from Tagiura to Cape Sciarra takes the form of a bay, at the head of which lies Wady Ramleh. It was late in the afternoon of the sixth when we reached the Wady, and came up with the party who had preceded us in advance with the camels and heavy baggage.

Wady Ramleh, or Rummel (as it is sometimes pronounced, which signifies, in Arabic, sandy river, or sandy valley), is a small, but constant stream of pure water, which finds its way across the desert from the mountains to the southward. The bed of the stream is much below the surface of the soil; and judging from its width, and the steep banks which confine it, we should conclude that at the periods when the freshes come down from the mountains, Wady Ramleh may be swelled into a considerable body of water. Here our day's journey finished, and we pitched our tents near the stream, making them as comfortable as a stormy night would allow of for the friends who had accompanied us from Tripoly. On the following morning the rain fell in torrents; and as the prospect afforded by the weather was not very inviting, we would not allow our companions to stray farther with us from home; but took our leave of them, as we flattered ourselves, with mutual regret, and they retraced their steps towards Tripoly, while we continued our journey to the eastward.

The wind had by this time increased to a violent gale, and we were very soon wet to the skin: but although such a state may not appear to be at all times an enviable one, it was in fact very much so on this occasion; for the clouds of sand which would have been hurled in our faces by the wind, had the surface of the desert been less wet, would have proved a much greater annoyance. With this reflection we pursued our journey very contentedly, and our Arab friends, composing Shekh Mahommed's escort, appeared to be equally well satisfied; for they soon began to open the several budgets of songs with which an Arab is never unprovided, roaring them out to the full extent of their well-practised and powerful lungs, till they fairly drowned the noise of the gale.

At 10 A.M. we passed through Wady'm'Seyd, a small stream somewhat inferior to Wady Ramleh, and soon entered upon the extensive plain of Jumarr. Wady'm'Seyd may be termed the eastern limit of the long sandy tract which stretches from thence far to the westward, and passing to the southward of Tripoly, is bounded, in that direction, by the Gharian mountains.

The sandy nature of the ground to the westward of Wady'm'Seyd had latterly led us away from that part of the coast, and we now endeavoured to regain the beach; but the sands were so soft that our horses sank up to their saddle-girths, and our utmost efforts to reach it were unavailing: we were in consequence obliged to give up the attempt, and leave this portion of the coast line incomplete. Among the sand-hills we found several patches of rocky ground strewed with fragments of pottery, but no vestiges of building were discernible. The plain of Jumarr, from the excellence of its soil, would no doubt be extremely productive; but notwithstanding this advantage, and its vicinity to the metropolis, a small part of it only is cultivated, and but few Arab tents were to be seen. The Gharian range may here be considered to be about seven miles from the coast; and the heavy rains and torrents from the mountains have made several large ravines in this neighbourhood, which crossed our path in their passage to the sea: the most considerable of these are Wady Terragadt and Wady Booforris. Soon after four o'clock we reached Guadigmata, where we found a small Arab encampment, and pitched our tents for the night.

It is in the neighbourhood of Guadigmata, between that place and Wady'm'Seyd, that we must look for the Graphara of Scylax. For as that city is described by the geographer as being midway between Abrotonum and Leptis Magna, that is, a day's sail from each—Guadigmata being 26 miles from Lebida, and the whole distance from Lebida to Tagiura 58½—it follows that the site of Graphara might be fixed three miles to the westward of Guadigmata; which would place it at 29 miles' distance from each of the cities in question, or half way between Lebida and Tagiura .

There are, however, no remains to the westward of Guadigmata (between that place and Wady'm'Seid) that we could perceive in our route; but two miles beyond Guadigmata there are some remains of building on a rising ground to the eastward of it, which are too much buried under the soil to allow us to give any satisfactory description of them. Two large upright stones, which seem to have been the jambs of a gateway, are all that are now standing; and not even the ground plans of other parts of these remains could be obtained without excavation. We learnt, however, from Captain Smyth that, in the neighbourhood of Wady'm'Seyd, there is a small boat-cove resembling an ancient cothon; and near it the ruins of several baths with tesselated pavements; which must have been situated on that part of the coast which we were not able to visit, for the reasons mentioned above. To the eastward of these, another small port was also discovered by Captain Smyth (formed by a point of land between the Wadies of Ben-z-barra and Abdellata), at which the produce of the country is shipped off in the summer. The mouth of the Abdellata is described by this officer as forming a picturesque cove, and he observed on its left bank (a little way inland) a village consisting of troglodytic caverns, excavated in the sandstone rock; many of which being furnished with doors, are used by the natives instead of the usual matamores, or subterranean storehouses, as granaries.

The former of the ports here described may possibly have been that of Graphara required; but as there are more extensive remains in the neighbourhood of that at Abdellata (or Abdellati), which we shall presently have occasion to mention, we will not venture to fix it as such decidedly.

On the day after our arrival at Guadigmata, the weather proving still very bad, we did not proceed on our route; but spent the day in examining and securing our baskets of provisions many of which we found to have been wet through, and in making those other little arrangements which, notwithstanding all precautions, are usually found to be necessary a day or two after the commencement of a long journey.

We continued our route on the following morning, and found the country beyond become gradually hilly, and the road to be again intersected by Wadys, or ravines, extending themselves from the mountains to the sea. By four we had arrived at Sidy Abdellàti: so called from a celebrated Marábut, whose tomb, surrounded by gardens and date-trees, stands conspicuous on the banks of one of the Wadys. The country about it is everywhere well cultivated, the wells are numerous, and the hills were covered with sheep and goats; but notwithstanding the numerous flocks in our neighbourhood, we found considerable difficulty in procuring a single lamb for our party.

While we were here a disturbance took place which had, at one time, assumed rather an alarming appearance. Our camel-drivers had allowed their beasts to stray over the cultivated grounds of the neighbouring Arabs, who came to demand remuneration, or to revenge themselves, in the event of not obtaining it, upon the owners of the camels: the latter, together with our Arab escort, formed a tolerably strong party, and thinking themselves in a condition to do so, did not hesitate to resist the demand; a scuffle accordingly took place, in which many blows were exchanged, baracans torn, and knives and pistols brought into action. The arrival of Shekh Mahommed put an end to the fray before any serious consequences had ensued, and he satisfied the assailants by reprimanding the camel-drivers, and promising to make them keep their animals within bounds. We were ignorant ourselves of the cause of the disturbance, and seeing our party suddenly attacked, we naturally ran to their assistance, which certainly would not have been the case had we known they had been the aggressors. This made us more cautious afterwards, as we found that our drivers took advantage of the strength of the party to improve the condition of their camels.

The most conspicuous character in this disturbance was a trusty black slave of our conductor the Dúbbah, who appeared to have inherited from his master the art of raising his voice above that of every other person. Having had his pistols wrested from him, he was so hurried away by the violence of his passion as to seem quite unable to give it sufficient vent; and had just raised his knife to plunge it into an Arab, when he was prevented by one of our party, who presented a musket at him and deprived him of his weapon; for although he was fighting on our side, we were not of course desirous that he should proceed to such unjustifiable extremes.

The remains of some strongly-built forts, of quadrangular forms, occupying the heights which command the road, sufficiently point out Sidy Abdellàti as an ancient military station; and indeed, had we found there no vestiges of antiquity, we should have been induced from the nature of the ground to look for some indications of fortification; since the advantages of position, of soil, and of water, which it possesses, are too great to have been overlooked by the ancients.

About the tomb of the Marábut which we have mentioned above, there are frequent traces of building; and the tomb itself is constructed with the fragments of more ancient structures; while the beach and its neighbourhood are strewed with a quantity of pottery and glass. These ruins, although they now, with the exception of the Marábut and the forts, consist only of loose stones and imperfect ground-plans, appear to be more indicative of the site of an ancient town than those which we have mentioned at Guadigmata; and, if Graphara could be placed so near as twenty miles to Leptis Magna, they might probably be considered as its remains. The quadrangular forts which we have just mentioned as occupying the heights of Sidy Abdellàti, might in that case have belonged to a station attached to the town; and the port discovered by Captain Smyth at Abdellata (mentioned above) may then be taken as the one intended by Scylax.

Without carrying the subject further, we may say, in conclusion, that Sidy Abdellàti has undoubtedly been a strong military station, whatever pretensions it may have to be considered as the site of Graphara.

After leaving this place, the road led us, through the valley of Selîn, to a tolerably wide stream called Neggázi, which, winding between the hills, gave an unusual interest to the view. We continued our route for a short time along its banks, and then ascended the range of hills called Sélem, which branches off from the Terhoona range and extends to the sea. From the top of Sélem there is an extensive view westward, over the plain of Jumarr, as far as the sandy desert; and on the eastern side of the ridge there is another view, equally imposing, over the plain of Lebida; so that in spite of the torrents of rain which still continued to deluge us, we could not help stopping occasionally to admire them.

From the summit of this range we noticed several remains of what appeared to be towers, conspicuously situated on the peaks of the hills to the northward; and which, from the strength of their position, might have bid defiance to any attack that could be made upon them: their situations appear to have been chosen with the intention of their being easily distinguished one from another, so as to answer the purpose of communication. The valleys of this range are capable of the highest degree of cultivation, but their fertility has only been partially taken advantage of by the Arabs of the neighbourhood. In some of them we noticed vines and olive-trees flourishing most luxuriantly between patches of ground producing corn and vegetables. Descending on the eastern side of the range, the road lies along the side of the mountain, and several ruins of forts and tombs are conspicuous on either side of it: here also are several remains of ancient wells, and we noticed one, in particular, which had fragments of marble columns lying near it. During the whole of this day the road was so slippery, in consequence of the heavy rains, that our camels could with difficulty proceed: they were continually falling under their burthens, and the alarm which their unsteady footing occasioned them added greatly to the distress of their situation. In the evening we pitched our tents in a valley about a mile from Mergip tower, where we met the English Consul on his return from an excursion to Lebida: he informed us of a report which was in circulation at that place, of a troop of marauding Arabs being in wait for our party two days south of Mesurata. This report was corroborated by Shekh Mahommed el Dúbbah, who seemed inclined to make it of some importance.

We suspected, from the Shekh's manner, that he had himself circulated this story to enhance the value of his protection; and we were determined in consequence not to appear to believe it. As we did not however think it right to omit some precautions, in the event of the report proving after all to be true, we requested the Consul to mention it when he returned to the Bashaw; who might then take whatever measures he should judge to be necessary on the occasion.

FOOTNOTES:

This circumstance is however by no means conclusive, even supposing the columns to be as stated; for Leo Africanus informs us that modern Tripoly was built from the ruins of Leptis Magna, after the final destruction of that city: and the columns in question might as easily have been brought from Lebida, as the materials employed in building the town of Tripoly.

Απο Νεαπολεως, της Καρχηδονιων χωρας, Γραφαρα πολις. Ταυτη παραπλους ἡμερας μιας. απο δε Γραφαρων, Αβροτονον πολις και λιμην. Ταυτη ὁ παραπλους ἡμερας μιας.

Supposing Tripoly to be Oea, we must look for Abrotonum in some place as near to that city as possible; for the distance given by Scylax from Abrotonum to Leptis Magna will become more and more perplexing as we continue to place it farther to the eastward of Oea. Tagiura, under this supposition, is the site we should allow to Abrotonum; but the difficulties which we have stated are against such a conclusion, and we confess that we are unable to reconcile the contending authorities.

Neither Sabrata nor Oea (as we shall hereafter mention) appear to have existed in the time of Strabo: the first town which is mentioned by that geographer to the eastward of the Lesser Syrtis, after the lake Zuchis, and the town of the same name (famous for its purple dye and its salted provisions), is that of Abrotonum in question.

No distance is given by Strabo from Zuchis to Abrotonum; but the mention of a lake much smaller than that of Zuchis, immediately before Abrotonum, (as will be seen in the quotation below,) is consistent with the idea that Tagiura might be the place of the city intended; for we have stated that there is a lake a little to the westward of Tagiura; and although it is of tolerable size, it is nevertheless much smaller than that of Zuchis, which is estimated by Strabo at 400 stadia.

In Ptolemy we find Abrotonum placed to the westward of Oea; and in Pliny to the eastward of Taphra (or Graphara) neither of which positions tend to simplify the matter in question.

Μετα δε την Συρτιν Ζουχις εστι λιμνη . . . και παρ' αυτην πολις ομωνυμος . . . ειτ' αλλη λιμνη πολυ ελαττων· και μετα ταυτην Αβροτονον πολις, και αλλαι τινες. (Lib. 17. κεφ. Γ. § 18.) It must be recollected that Strabo is passing from west to east, and that this is also the course of the Expedition.

The Psylli inhabited the southern parts of the Greater Syrtis, and are said to have been altogether destroyed by clouds of sand which overwhelmed them in their passage to the interior. The Nubian army of Cambyses is thought to have experienced a similar fate.—*Vide* Herodotus, lib. iv.

We would not here be thought to allude to any particular writer; but merely to the general practice, which has obtained in all ages, of exaggerating the effects of the sand-storm in desert travelling; which, without amplification, is sufficiently obnoxious in its genuine native dangers and inconveniences.

These solitary enjoyments are by no means overdrawn; every traveller accustomed to desert journeys must have experienced them: and the late lamented Burckhardt has frequently been heard to declare, that his most pleasant hours in travelling have been passed in the desert.

Lieut. Clapperton, Mr. Carstenson, and some other friends from Tripoly, had rode with us thus far on our journey.

That is, if we suppose Tagiura to be the site of Abrotonum, as we have ourselves already admitted, under the difficulties stated above, and in the absence of more decided information than we have been able to obtain on the subject.

From Guadigmata, two ruins (Selma and Ipsilàta) appear conspicuous on high and pointed hills at the distance of about seven miles; they seem to have been watch-towers commanding the plain; but our guides could only tell us they were *Gussers*, a name which they applied indiscriminately to ruins of every description.

These were the camel-drivers themselves.

The Terhoona range is a branch of the Gharian.

CHAPTER IV.

Arrival at Lebida — Remarks on its position and resources as compared with those of Tripoly — Short account of the city and its remains — Allusion to the African tribe Levatæ (or Levata) by Procopius — The same tribe mentioned by Leo Africanus — Suggestions of Major Rennell on the resemblance between the terms Levata and Lybia — Former position of this tribe near the coast confirmed by Procopius — Remarks on the term Libya — Visit from the Shekh of Lebida — Violent storm at that place retards the advance of the party — Intrusion upon the premises of a celebrated Marábūt — Dangerous consequences of this intrusion predicted by our escort — Departure from Lebida — Remains of the aqueduct, and of the causeway mentioned by Strabo — Arrive at the River Cinyphus, now Wad' el Kháhan — Remarks on the river and the morass in its immediate neighbourhood — Observations on the faulty position of the Cinyphus in the maps of Cellarius — This position probably suggested by some remarks of Pliny, Ptolemy, and Mela — Extreme fertility of the region of the Cinyphus — Remarks on this district, and that of Byzacium — Suggestions of Signor Della Cella with respect to them — Present appearance of the region of the Cinyphus consistent with the description of Herodotus — Neglected condition of the district under the Arabs — Account of Lebida and its remains by Captain Smyth.

ON the following morning we continued our journey to Lebida, the weather being still very bad. The road from Sélem to Lebida leads close along the foot of Mergip-hill, on the summit of which are the ruins of a tower of considerable height, which may be seen from a great distance: at the foot of the hill are the remains of several tombs, but none of those which we saw appeared to be in good style.

On emerging from the valley of Sélem a fertile tract of high ground presents itself, which lies between the valley and Lebida; clusters of olive-trees are scattered over its surface, and contribute with the green turf on which they are planted to give it a very pleasing appearance. From the summit of this appears the whole plain of Lebida, stretching down, in a gentle slope, from the high ground to the sea; and a more beautiful scene can scarcely be witnessed than that which is presented by this fine tract of country. Thick groves of olive and date-trees are seen rising above the villages which are scattered over its surface; and the intermediate spaces are either covered with the most luxuriant turf, or rich with abundant crops of grain.

It must always afford matter for surprise to those who are acquainted with this beautiful and highly-productive country, how Tripoly could ever have been selected, in preference to Lebida, as the metropolis of the regency. Placed in the midst of sand, on the borders of an extensive desert, and situated almost at the extremity of the country in which it stands, Tripoly appears to enjoy scarcely any particular local advantage beyond the possession of its port; while Lebida seems to unite in one beautiful spot all the advantages of plenty, convenience, and security. It is probable that the harbour and strong walls of Tripoly were the principal causes of its adoption as the capital; and the sums of money which would be necessary to rebuild and fortify Lebida, might have been considered as more than equivalent to its local recommendations, by a people who seldom look beyond the present.

But Lebida, once occupied, would be a much stronger post than Tripoly could ever be made; and the good sense of the ancients was conspicuously manifested in its selection as a principal town.

The city of Leptis Magna appears to have been comprehended within little more than a square half mile of ground. It was situated close to the sea, on the banks of a ravine now called Wady Lebda, which might probably in the rainy season have assumed the appearance of a river. When we passed through the place it was, however, nothing more than a small stream, although too deep in some parts to be easily forded; and it is probably dry, or nearly so, in the summer. The inadequacy of this supply to the consumption of the city may be inferred from the remains of an aqueduct communicating with the Cinyphus, still existing, in unconnected portions, in the space between the town and that river. At the back of the town are several large mounds of earth, thrown up in the form of banks; which are supposed to have been raised for the purpose of turning off the water which might occasionally have threatened it from the hills, and which the slope of the ground from the hills to the sea may possibly have rendered very necessary. The quantity of alluvial soil brought down the Wady above mentioned by the winter torrents, have, together with the accumulation of sand from the beach, nearly effaced all traces of the port and cothon of Leptis Magna, which does not indeed appear to have been at any time very capacious. The actual remains of the city are still sufficient to be somewhat imposing; but they are for the most part so deeply buried under the sand which ten centuries of neglect have allowed to accumulate about them, that plans of them could not be obtained without very extensive excavations. The style of the buildings is universally Roman; and they are more remarkable for the regularity and solidity of their construction, than for any great appearance of good taste employed in their embellishment.

A great part of the city has been constructed with brick; and the material which has been used in the instances here alluded to maintains remarkably well the high character which Roman brick has so deservedly acquired. The remains of the stadium are perhaps the most interesting, in speaking of the buildings which have been constructed with stone; they have been partially excavated by Captain Smyth, (to whose account we refer the reader) together with some other buildings; but the task of clearing them entirely would be too Herculean for limited means, and the same may be observed with respect to other parts of Leptis Magna in general.

For our own part, however much we might have been inclined to remain some time at Lebida, the necessity of our immediate advance precluded the possibility of doing so; for the approach of the rainy season made it absolutely necessary that we should cross the low grounds of the Syrtis without delay: and it must be remembered that the coast-line of the Syrtis and Cyrenaica was the principal object of the Expedition.

Leptis Magna was built at an early period by the Phœnicians, and was ranked, after Carthage and Utica, as the first of their maritime cities. After the destruction of Carthage it flourished under the government of the Romans, and was remarkable, as we are informed by Sallust, for its fidelity and obedience.

After the occupation of Northern Africa by the Vandals, the walls and fortifications of Leptis appear to have been dismantled or destroyed: they were probably afterwards restored under Justinian, when the city became the residence of the Prefect Sergius; and we find them, on the authority of Leo Africanus, to have been finally demolished by the Saracens.

From that time the city appears to have been wholly abandoned; and its remains were employed in the construction of Modern Tripoly, as Leo has also informed us.

During the Prefecture of Sergius, who presided over the district of Tripolis, Leptis Magna was attacked by a neighbouring African tribe; and Sergius himself, after some previous successes, was reduced to seek shelter within the walls of the city, to which alone he appears to have been indebted for safety. A party of Moors, of the tribe called *Levatæ*, had encamped under the walls of Leptis, to receive from the governor the reward of past fidelity, and the bribe for their future good conduct. Eighty of their deputies were accordingly introduced into the town, and admitted to a conference with the Prefect. On the statement of certain grievances of which they complained Sergius rose to leave the tribunal; but one of the suppliants detained him by the robe, while the rest of the deputies pressed nearer to his person and urged their demands in louder terms. Provoked at this insolence, an officer of the Prefect drew his sword and plunged it into the

Moor, and the death of this imprudent offender became the signal for a general massacre. One only of the Levatæ escaped from the city to bear the melancholy news of the slaughter of his companions to the rest of the tribe without the walls. They instantly took up arms and invested the city; and though at first repulsed with great loss by a sally of the Romans, they shortly after succeeded in defeating the Prefect; and his general Pudentius, having incautiously exposed himself, was cut off and slain in the field. Sergius retired with the remainder of his army upon the city, and shut himself up within its walls; but as he was incapable of continuing the contest with advantage, he finally withdrew to Carthage, in order to claim the assistance of his uncle, and induce him to march his army against the Moors. The result of the engagement which afterwards took place was fatal to the cause of the Romans; for Solomon, who had so ably filled the place of Belisarius, was slain in the field of Tebeste, and the Prefect was once more compelled to seek safety in flight.

The tribe Levatæ, mentioned in the Narrative of Procopius, of which we have just given the substance, has in later times been noticed by Leo Africanus, and said to have inhabited that part of the desert of Libya which lies between Augela and the Nile. The same author adds that they are of an African race; and we may further remark, with respect to this tribe, that the appellation of Levatæ, by which it was distinguished, has been supposed by Major Rennell (in his illustrations of Herodotus) to have given birth to the Grecian term Libya.

It will be observed that the suggestion of the ingenious author quoted below, with respect to the retreat of the Levatæ into the interior, is confirmed by the account of Procopius; who tells us that "the Moors, called Levatæ, dwelt in the neighbourhood of Leptis Magna;" and we have seen that they were found in the time of Leo Africanus to have inhabited the parts between Augela and the Nile.

With regard to the derivation of the term Libya, suggested by Major Rennell, we may remark that Herodotus has himself derived it from the name of a female native of Africa bearing the same appellation; and it is probable that had there been any other tradition existing in his time on the subject, it would have been mentioned with that which he has recorded. The several tribes which in his æra inhabited the northern coast of Africa have also been enumerated by Herodotus; and no mention is made among these of any race of people called Levatæ. It is evident also that his knowledge of Africa was not confined to recent occurrences or to the actual state of the country in his own time; for he has given us very clear and minute details of events which took place several centuries before that period, among which may be instanced the account which he has transmitted of the first occupation of the country by the Greeks, described in the Fourth Book of his Geography, and alluded to in the passage above quoted from Major Rennell.

We may observe, on the ground of these objections, that, if the derivation suggested be actually correct, it must, in all probability, have taken place long before the period of Herodotus; but there is at the same time no positive proof on their authority that it may not have been possibly the true one.

On the morning after our arrival at Lebida the Shekh of the place came to pay us a visit, and to offer his assistance in procuring us coins and gems, which are constantly found among the ruins by the Jews, who pay a consideration to the Bashaw for the exclusive enjoyment of this privilege. The offer of our new friend was readily accepted, and he himself very cordially entertained by his brother Shekh, Mahommed el Dúbbah; but, his supper being eaten, we never heard more of him or of the antiquities which he professed to procure for us.

The effects of a heavy storm, which had occurred on the preceding night, obliged us to remain at Lebida the whole of this day, in order to dry our provisions and clothes; for we had no sooner pitched the tents, on the evening of our arrival, than we were overtaken by a violent storm of thunder and lightning, accompanied by continued gusts of wind, which kept us employed during the greater part of the night in attending to the tent-pegs.

In the mean time, the rain never ceased to fall in torrents, and soon made its way, impelled by the force of the wind, through every part of a good substantial canvass; one of our tents was completely upset, and the whole of our party, with the better half of the baggage, were wet through long before the dawn of day. Towards morning, however, the storm died away, and the first appearance of the sun, in a tolerably clear sky, was in truth a most comfortable prospect. As it promised to be fine for the rest of the day, we soon spread out our baggage to dry, and gladly availed ourselves of the delay this operation occasioned to walk over the ruins of the town.

Our camel-drivers, however, who had been hired by the journey, were not so well satisfied with this detention, and were urgent in persuading us to advance: but a trifling bakshees soon quieted their remonstrances, and they made up their minds very contentedly to the arrangement. We now began to measure a short base by latitudes, in order to fix a few points with more accuracy; and it was necessary to make use of the summit of a neighbouring hill for one extremity of the base. This spot was the place of residence of a most devout and highly-reverenced Marábūt, the admiration and the terror of the people of Lebida; and as we were proceeding to ascend the hill, our steps were arrested by the voice of the Tchaous whom the Bashaw had commissioned to attend us. As soon as he came up, he began very gravely to assure us, that the holy enthusiast would by no means allow us to encroach upon his domains with impunity; and proceeded to state that he would most certainly kill every person of our party who should dare to ascend, and afterwards sacrifice him (the Tchaous) himself, for having allowed us to intrude upon his retirement. It may be imagined that none of us had any particular wish to offend the holy personage in question; but the hill which he occupied was unluckily the most convenient which could be selected for our purpose; and we did not think it quite necessary to give up our base on the grounds of so ridiculous an objection. The attempt was accordingly made, and the base properly measured, without either of the dreadful results which had been anticipated; and the parties, on descending, received the serious congratulations of the Arabs on having had, what they called, so unexpected and providential an escape.

This formidable personage is the Marábūt mentioned by Della Cella as having threatened to eat him alive; and the Doctor was assured, by a black slave who stood near him, that he was perfectly capable of fulfilling his extraordinary threat.

So much has been written on the subject of these knavish fanatics, that we shall not here attempt any description of them: every book of travels in Mahometan countries contains more or less notice of the wondrous feats which are attributed to them, and of the no less remarkable credulity of those whom they impose upon. We may, however, observe that the country between Lebida and Mesurata, and more especially the neighbourhood of the last-mentioned place, is much infested by these artful and unblushing pretenders to piety and supernatural powers.

On the morning of the 15th we left the ruins of Lebida, and passing between the gardens which are scattered over its plain, proceeded on our road to Zeliten. About nine miles to the eastward of Lebida is the stream called Wad' el Kháhan, which we found to possess more pretensions to the title of river than any which we had hitherto seen. It appears to have its rise in the mountains to the southward; and after spreading itself in shallows over a rocky bed, it falls about twenty feet, and continues its course, though very slowly, to the sea. The banks of Wad' el Kháhan are in some places high, sloping down to the water's edge, and are covered with underwood, among which a few trees may occasionally be observed to rise. The verdure of its banks give it an agreeable appearance, and some remains of building, which are seen here and there through the soil, contribute to increase the interest of the stream.

By the side of the road, at about a mile and a half from where the river empties into the sea, are the remains of the aqueduct mentioned above, which supplied the city of Lebida; and other traces of building are occasionally observable in its neighbourhood. Here also may still be observed the same morasses which formerly characterized this spot, and gave occasion for the construction of the causeway, still existing, which is mentioned by Strabo as having been built by the Carthaginians. All these circumstances contribute to point out Wad' el Kháhan as the Cinyphus, and as such we may reasonably consider it.

The morass is extremely dangerous to cross without a guide, and two of our party, who were unprovided with one, experienced much difficulty in crossing a small quicksand situated between the marsh and the sea. There is another part of this quicksand, more to the eastward, which it was wholly impossible to cross; our horses, in attempting it, sank up to the saddle-girths, and the severity of the Arab spur alone prevented them from sinking much deeper. We may add that the exhalations which rise from the marsh appear to be very unwholesome, for one of our Arab escort, who slept a short time by the side of it, while we were making some observations, was shortly afterwards seized with violent cold shiverings, and every symptom of fever.

At the north-eastern extremity of the morass is the promontory called Tabia Point, on which we found the ruins of what appears to have been a tomb, and at the distance of about a quarter of a mile from the shore may be observed a reef of rocks, which will occasionally afford shelter for boats; the part thus protected is called by the Arabs Marsa Ugrah, from its vicinity to the village of that name. These rocks were above water when visited by Captain Smyth in 1817; but, in consequence, probably, of the prevalence of northerly gales, they were covered when we passed along the coast, and cannot therefore at all times be depended upon for protection.

In considering Wad' el Kháhan as the Cinyphus, which its position with regard to Lebida, and the appearances already pointed out, will very decidedly authorize us to do, one difficulty will be found to arise. It is the impossibility of reconciling the distance from the sea, of the nearest range of hills to the southward, with that assigned by Herodotus to the Hill of the Graces, in which he affirms the Cinyphus to have its source.

The Hill of the Graces is laid down by this geographer at 200 stadia from the sea; whereas the distance of the nearest range of hills, to the southward of Wad' el Kháhan, is little more than four English miles from the coast; and we could perceive in this range no aperture or break through which we might imagine that a stream could have passed in its course from the southward to the sea. We should certainly infer, from the appearance of this chain, that the river must have had its source in it; and one of the hills of which it is composed does certainly present an appearance of three peaks, as we may imagine the Hill of the Graces did; but then we must suppose that some mistake has been made, either by Herodotus himself, or by his editors, in the number of stades above mentioned; and, although it is possible that such an error might have occurred, we have no greater right to dispute the passage in question, than we have to challenge the accuracy of any other statement which is received on the authority of the geographer. We mean, with reference to the text itself, exclusive of local information; for the passage is simply and clearly stated, without the least appearance of ambiguity; and the habit of doubting every statement of an author which does not coincide with our own ideas and observations, is scarcely to be indulged without danger to the cause of truth.

We had determined on our return (among other things which we had no time to examine minutely in advancing) to trace the river Kháhan to its source, and thus decide the point beyond dispute; but unforeseen circumstances prevented our returning by way of Tripoly, and the promised examination never took place. We will not therefore venture decidedly to assert that this stream does not rise to the southward of the chain of hills above mentioned; but we should certainly be surprised (from the view which we had of the range in passing) to learn hereafter that it had been proved, by local observation, to have its source in the mountains farther inland. We may observe, at the same time, that the distance of the Terhoona range from the coast, as it is laid down by Captain Lyon, will answer tolerably well to that of the 200 stadia at which Herodotus has placed his Hill of the Graces from the sea; taking the stade of this geographer at 732 to a degree, or 10¼ to a common English mile, which is the mean allowed by Major Rennell to the stade of Herodotus. There are, however, several other inferior chains of hills (besides the one nearest to the coast) between the Terhoona range and the sea; and we scarcely think it possible that the Cinyphus (or Kháhan) could have found its way through these impediments.

In the chart of Cellarius, as Dr. Della Cella has truly observed, we find the Cinyphus placed to the eastward of the Cephalas Promontorium, in opposition to the testimonies of Strabo and Ptolemy, and of most other writers of respectability. But it is merely with a view to reconcile contending authorities that this position has been assigned to the river; for it will be evident, by a reference to the text of Cellarius, that it is not the one adopted by himself. It may be possible, also, (in addition to the authorities of the Itinerary and the Augustan table which he mentions) that Cellarius has been induced to place his Cinyphus thus far to the eastward, in consequence of a passage in Pliny, and of a remark which he has also quoted from Ptolemy. Pliny fixes the country of the Lotophagi in the most southern recess of the Greater Syrtis, and Ptolemy observes of these people, that they inhabited the neighbourhood of the Cinyphus. It becomes necessary, therefore, in order to reconcile these statements, either to place the Cinyphus nearer to the centre of the Gulf, or to move the Lotophagi nearer to the Cinyphus.

Mela places the Lotophagi still further to the eastward than Pliny, for he tells us that they are said to inhabit the country between the Promontories of Borion and Phycus, which are both of them in the Cyrenaica; and this statement may be considered as an additional reason for moving the Cinyphus to the eastward of its actual position, if the observation of Ptolemy in question be attended to. It is certain, however, that the position of the Cinyphus, on the authorities of Strabo, Ptolemy, and Scylax, is to the westward of the Cephalas Promontorium; Pliny places it in the country between the two Syrtes, and Mela to the westward of Leptis Magna: there is therefore no sufficient authority for moving the river to the eastward of the Cephalas; although it must be confessed that the position of the Lotophagi, in the neighbourhood of the river Cinyphus, is certainly very clear and decided.

We may observe, with regard to these eaters of the lotus, that they have been so very differently placed by different authorities, that it is scarcely possible to say in what part of the map they may, or may not, be laid down; and this circumstance will serve to prove how widely the lotus-tree must have been spread, at various times, over the coast and country of Northern Africa.

The region of the Cinyphus has been celebrated for its extraordinary fertility; Herodotus asserts that it yielded three hundred for one, and other writers have concurred in extolling the richness of its soil. It is remarkable, however, that some authors who have highly commended the soil of the Byzacium, have, at the same time, omitted to notice the fertility of the region of the Cinyphus; while others, on the contrary, who have recorded the extraordinary produce of the district last mentioned, have failed to make any allusion to the productive qualities of the Byzacium. This circumstance has induced Dr. Della Cella to imagine that some of the writers in question intended to include both these districts in one; and in support of this idea he cites passages from Pliny and Strabo, which appear to him decisive in its favour. Pliny says (it is Dr. Della Cella who speaks) that "the people who inhabit the Byzacium are called Libyphœnices;" it is therefore only necessary to ascertain in what country the Libyphœnices dwelt, to determine the position of the Byzacium. And here, continues the Doctor, is a very clear reply of Strabo to this desideratum of ancient geography—"Upon the sea-coast, extending from Carthage to the Cephalas Promontorium, and to the *Masselibii*, is the territory of the Libyphœnices."

But it will scarcely, we imagine, be thought absolutely necessary to conclude, that, because Byzacium may have formed a *part* of the territory of the Libyphœnices, the *whole* of the country inhabited by these people must therefore be called Byzacium; for Strabo himself has informed us that the Byzacians extended only to the *eastern* limits of Carthage (that is, of Carthage Proper, or Zeugitana); whereas the tract which he has assigned to the Libyphœnices generally, comprehended the whole of the Carthagenian territory, from the Cephalas Promontorium to the country of the Massæsyli. The Massæsyli were a people of Numidia, and their district formed the *western* boundary of that country and Mauretania; so that between them and the Byzacians (whom we may, surely, conclude to be the inhabitants of the country from which their name is derived) the whole of Numidia and Carthage Proper intervenes. The Libyphœnices appear to have been the descendants of the Phœnicians (or Carthaginians) and of the several native African, or Libyan, tribes in their neighbourhood; so that Byzacium would naturally be peopled by them to a considerable extent, without its being necessary to infer from that circumstance that all Libyphœnices were Byzacians.

We may add that Strabo does not seem to be aware of any fertility in the soil of the Byzacium; for he continues to state (after the passage above quoted from the Second Book of his Geography) that all the country between Carthage and the *columns of Hercules* is fertile—not including, of course, either the Byzacium, or the region of the Cinyphus.

The extent of the territory which is supposed by Signor Della Cella to have been included in the province of Byzacium, that is, (as we have stated above) from the country of the Massæsyli, on the western side, to the Cephalas Promontorium on the east, would occupy a coast-line of no less than 700 miles, exclusive of its limits in a southerly direction; and it will more readily be seen how much this extent differs, from that of the actual Byzacium, by comparing it with the dimensions which Pliny has given of the country, in the passage which Signor Della Cella has partially quoted above. We shall there find that the district of Byzacium was comprehended within a circuit of no more than 250 Roman miles; so that it is difficult to imagine how Pliny could have intended to extend its limits, either eastward or westward, to the points which the Doctor has claimed for it: since the historian's intentions must have been sadly at variance with his assertions, had he really meant to bestow upon Byzacium so much more than he has stated it to contain.

The region of the Cinyphus has still the same peculiarities which it has been stated to possess by Herodotus; there we still find the rich and dark-coloured soil, and the abundance of water which he mentions: but every thing degenerates in the hand of the Arab, and the produce of the present day bears no proportion to that which the historian has recorded. The average rate of produce of this fine tract of country (so far, at least, as we could learn from the Arabs who inhabit it) is now scarcely more than ten for one; and the lands in the neighbourhood of Zeliten and Mesurata are the only places cultivated to the eastward of the Cinyphus. The produce, in grain, is principally barley, with a moderate proportion only of wheat; but the date-tree and the olive are very generally distributed, and their crops are extremely abundant. We were informed that there was usually a considerable overplus of dates, olive-oil, and barley, both at Mesurata and Zeliten; and that the Arabs of the western parts of the Syrtis draw their principal supplies from the former of these places.

The country to the west of the Cinyphus is, to all appearance, equally productive (we should rather say equally capable of being made so) with that which we have mentioned to the eastward. A small part of this only, however, is cultivated, and we may observe generally, of the region of the Cinyphus, that by far the greater portion of that beautiful tract of country, from the eastern limit of the Syrtis at Mesurata, to the edge of the sandy desert at Wad'm'Seid, is now left in its natural state.

The following short account of the objects most worthy of notice which presented themselves to Captain Smyth in the course of his journey to Lebida in the year 1816, and the succeeding one, have been extracted from his private journal, and obligingly placed at our disposal by the author; and as we think they will not be unacceptable to our readers, we submit them, without further comment, to their notice.

The first principal point to the eastward of Tripoly is Ras al Amra, a projecting low sand, with rocks close in, but possessing a small boat-cove on its east side, resembling an ancient cothon: near it are the ruins of several baths with tesselated pavements.

Beyond Ras al Amra there is another small port, formed by a point of land between the wadies of Ben z barra and Abdellata, whence the produce of the country is shipped off in summer. The mouth of the Abdellata forms a picturesque cove, and on its left bank, a little inland, is a village consisting of troglodytic caverns, excavated in the sandstone rock, and many of which being furnished with doors, are used, instead of the usual matamores, as granaries.

Here begins the tract generally called Zibbi, and the land, rising gradually, exhibits a better, though still neglected, appearance, being thinly planted with olive-trees, and here and there a vineyard.

In the vicinity of the Ganema river frequent vestiges of antiquity announce the approach to a place once more prosperous; and in the valley of Seyd-n-alli are the remains of some Roman fortifications, called by the Moors, the Seven Towers, which from several local indications I think must stand on the site of Quintiliana.

Leptis Magna is situated on a fine level district, of a light and loamy soil, bounded by gentle hills. A great part of this plain is laid out in fields of corn, pulse, carrots, &c., interspersed with groves of olive, pomegranate, and date-trees, among which are a few vineyards; but it is by no means cultivated with the attention due to its susceptibility of improvement; and a great portion of the produce is annually destroyed by the gundy rat, and a species of jerboa, (probably the μυς διπους represented on the Cyrenian coins) which greatly infest all the grounds, yet no means are used to destroy them. The want of enclosures is also greatly felt, the young shoots of the seed being protected from the wind only by thinly-planted rows of the Scilla Maritima: however, notwithstanding every disadvantage, the harvests are generally satisfactory to the moderate expectations of these rude peasants.

Towards the higher grounds there is a good deal of pasturage, where camels, horses, oxen, sheep, and goats are reared; but the destructive method of the Arabs in impoverishing the land around their dowars, till it becomes exhausted, without any attempt to nourish or assist the soil, is everywhere visible, by the many bare spots whence the tents have been shifted to more fertile situations, which for the same reason soon become, in their turn, deserted also.

I first visited Leptis in May, 1816, to examine into the possibility of embarking the numerous columns lying on its sands, which the Bashaw of Tripoly had offered to His Majesty. The ruins had a very interesting appearance, from the contrast of their fallen grandeur with the mud-built villages of Lebidah and Legatah, and the Nomadic tribes scattered around. The city, with its immediate suburb, occupies a space of about ten thousand yards, the principal part of which is covered by a fine white sand, that, drifting with the wind along the beach, has been arrested in its progress by the ruins, and struck me at the moment as having probably been the means of preserving many specimens of art, which, from the numerous pillars, capitals, cornices, and sculptured fragments strewed around, I could not but suppose to have been extremely valuable, more especially, since having been the birthplace of the Emperor Severus, he might have enriched it with presents; besides which it had been highly favoured for its adherence to the Roman interest during the Jugurthine war. In addition to these circumstances, the fact of Leptis once being sufficiently opulent to render in tribute a talent a day, prompted me, on my arrival at Malta, to recommend it as an eligible field for an extensive excavation.

On my return thither in January, 1817, I was surprised, on riding over the ruins, to find that many of the most valuable columns, which were standing in the preceding May, had either been removed, or were lying broken on the spot, and even most of those still remaining had had their astragal and torus chipped off. I discovered, on inquiry, that a report had been circulated by the Tschaouses on my former visit, of an intention to embark them for England; and as it had long been a quarry whence the Arabs supplied themselves with mill-stones, they had in the interval been busily employed in breaking up the columns for that purpose, providing not only for the present, but also for future supply. This extensive destruction was prompted by the peculiar construction of the Moorish oil-mills, they being built with a circular surface, having a gentle inclination towards the centre, round which a long stone traverses, formed by about one-third of a shaft.

On the 25th, however, having arranged my tents and instruments, I commenced an excavation near the centre of the city with a party of eight Arabs, whom I increased the following day to a hundred; and as they quickly gained the use of the English spade and mattock, the work proceeded with celerity. But I soon had the mortification of perceiving, from numerous local evidences, that Leptis had been completely ravaged in former times, and its public edifices demolished with diligent labour, owing perhaps to the furious bigotry of the Carthaginian bishops, who zealously destroyed the Pagan monuments in every place under their control. Or it might have been partly effected by the vengeance of the Barbarians for the memorable treachery of the Leptitani. From whatever cause it proceeded, the destruction is complete; most of the statues are either broken to pieces, or chipped into shapeless masses, the arabesque ornaments defaced, the acanthus leaves and volutes knocked off the fallen capitals, and even part of the pavements torn up; the massy shafts of the columns alone remaining entire.

With a view of gaining further information, I opened an extensive Necropolis, but with little success. There were neither vases nor lachrymatories, but only a coarse species of amphoræ and some pateræ, with a few coins, neither rare nor handsome, mostly brass, and principally of Severus, Pupienus, Alexander, Julia Mammea, Balbus, and Gordianus Pius. A number of intaglios of poor execution were picked up in different parts, as also some very common Carthaginian medals, but nothing indicating high antiquity or tasteful skill. Willing, however, to make as fair a trial as possible, I continued excavating until the 12th of February, when, having explored the principal Basilica, a triumphal arch, a circus, a peristyleum, and several minor structures, with only a strengthened conviction of the precarious chance of recovering any specimens of art worth the labour and expense of enlarged operations, I determined to desist.

In the course of the excavation I had an opportunity of observing, that the period of the principal grandeur of the city must have been posterior to the Augustan age, and when taste was on the decline; for notwithstanding the valuable materials with which it was constructed, it appears to have been overloaded with indifferent ornament, and several of the mutilated colossal statues I found, were in the very worst style of the Lower Empire. There are also many evidences of the city having been occupied after its first and violent destruction, from several of the walls and towers being built of various architectural fragments confusedly heaped together.

Although there are several exceedingly fine brick and cementitious edifices, most of the walls, arcades, and public buildings, are composed of massy blocks of freestone, and conglomerate, in layers, without cement, or at most with very little. The temples were constructed in a style of the utmost grandeur, adorned with immense columns of the most valuable granites and marbles, the shafts of which consisted of a single piece. Most of these noble ornaments were of the Corinthian order; but I also saw several enormous masses of architecture, ornamented with triglyphs, and two or three cyathiform capitals, which led me to suppose that a Doric temple, of anterior date, had existed there. On a triple plinth near them I observed a species of socte, used in some of these structures as the base of a column, with part of the walls of the Cella, surrounded by a columnar peristyle.

The city was encompassed by strong walls of solid masonry, pierced with magnificent gates, and was ornamented with spacious porticoes, sufficient portions of which still remain to prove their former splendour. It was divided from its principal suburb to the east by a river, the mouth of which forming a spacious basin, was the Cothon, defended at its narrow entrance by two stout fortifications; and branching out from them, may be observed, under water, the remains of two large moles. On the banks of this river, the bed of which is still occupied by a rivulet, are various ruins of aqueducts, and some large reservoirs in excellent preservation. Between the principal cisterns and the torrent to the westward of Leptis, some artificial mounds are constructed across the plain, by which the winter rains were conducted to the reservoirs, and carried clear of the city. On the east bank of the river are remains of a galley-port, and numerous baths, adjacent to a circus, formerly ornamented with obelisks and columns, and above which are vestiges of a theatre. Indeed the whole plain from the Mergip hills to the Cinyphus (now the river Kháhan) exhibits unequivocal proofs of its former population and opulence.

Thus ended my unsuccessful research; but though no works of art were recovered, many of the architectural fragments were moved during the summer down to the beach, by Colonel Warrington, where I called for and embarked them on board a store-ship for England, together with thirty-seven shafts, which formed the principal scope of the expedition, and they are now in the court of the British Museum. Still we were sorry to find that neither the raft-ports nor the hatchways of the Weymouth were capable of admitting three fine Cipolline columns of great magnitude, that, from their extreme beauty and perfection, we had been particularly anxious about.

On his return from a journey into the interior, in search of the ruins of Ghirza, (to which we shall hereafter allude) Captain Smyth observed three hills of moderate size in one of the branches of the Messellata range; which, from their number, appear to answer to the Hills of the Graces, considered by Herodotus as the source of the river Cinyphus. The distance of this range from the sea will not at all correspond (as we have already observed) with the 200 stadia mentioned by Herodotus as the distance of the Hills of the Graces from the coast; but, without relying too much upon their triple form, which might be equally peculiar to other hills, the circumstance of finding in these tumuli the source of the only stream which will answer to the position of the Cinyphus, should, we think, be esteemed as conclusive; and we may hereafter consider the measurements of Herodotus, as given in the passage which we have quoted above, to be decidedly (from whatever cause) erroneous. We may however observe, that we have had, at various times, so many opportunities of admiring the general accuracy of the father of history, that we should rather consider this error to have resulted from some mistake of the numbers, which may have occurred in transcribing the manuscript, than from any incorrectness on the part of Herodotus. We give the remarks of Captain Smyth on this subject in his own words.

From Benioleet I went to the north-eastward, in hopes of finding some remains of Talata, Tenadassa, and Syddemis, which were in the chain of communication with the stations of the Syrtis, Cydamus, and the Tritonis; but I met with only a few dilapidated towers, and some uninteresting ruins, which from the situation were probably those of Mespe. Thence we crossed the Messellata hills, and near the centre of one of the ramifications observed three slight eminences, which I am inclined to think must have been the Tumuli of the Graces of ancient geographers, though, but for the coincidence of the number, I should scarcely have remarked them. They are about 340 feet in height, and nearly five miles from the coast, thus differing in distance from the ancient account of 200 stadia; but as the Cinyphus actually rises here, the early manuscripts may have suffered from bad copyists.

The Cinyphus is now called the Wadie Khàhan, or weak river, in allusion to its sluggish course in summer, though it is still, to a little distance inland, a considerable stream, for this part of the world. Its shrubby banks render the lower part of it extremely picturesque, while both they and the sedgy marshes it has formed towards Tabia point abound with game of all descriptions. Near the high road from Sahal to Zeliten, the river contracts at once: here stood an ancient bridge, of which vestiges remain; and adjacent is a tolerable subterraneous aqueduct, running in the direction of Leptis, with a ventilating aperture, at intervals of about forty yards.

FOOTNOTES:

This is the opinion of Captain Smyth, who examined the remains of Leptis Magna with attention (in the year 1817); and who has obligingly favoured us with the plans and account of it which are given at the end of the chapter.

Nam Leptitani jam inde a principio belli Jugurthini ad Bestiam Consulem et postea Romam miserant, amicitiam, societatemque rogatum. Dein, ubi ea impetrata fuere semper boni, fidelesque mansere; et cuncta a Bestia, Albino, Metelloque imperata gnavitur fecerant.—(Bell. Jugurth. § 77.)

At Gizerichus alia moliri non desiit. Nam, præter Carthaginem, Africæ urbes nudavit omnes . . .—(Procop. Hist. Vandal. à Grotio, Lib. 1. p. 17.)

Questa città (Leptis M.) fu edificata da Romani con mura alte di pietre grosse: la quale fu due volte rovinata da Macomettani, e delle sue pietre e colonne fu edificata Tripoli.—(5ta. parte, p. 72.)

Leo here alludes to the restoration of the city, and not to its first erection by the Phœnicians.

Bacchi (Solomonis frater erat) filios duos regendis Africæ partibus misit Imperator; Pentapoli Cyrum, natu majorem, Tripoli Sergium.—(Procopius, Hist. Vandal, Lib. 2. p. 119.)

Solomon, the uncle of Sergius, was intrusted with the command of the army by Belisarius, when that general left the African coast, and governed with the title of Exarch. After his death at Tebeste, Sergius was appointed by the Emperor Justinian to succeed him, and rendered himself odious by his profligacy and cruelties.—(See Procopius, Hist. Vandal., Lib. 2.)

Now Tibesh, in the kingdom of Algiers.

Such is the substance of this affair as related by Procopius; and we may add, in the words of the eloquent Gibbon, "The arrival of fresh troops, and more skilful commanders, soon checked the insolence of the Moors: seventeen of their princes were slain in the same battle; and the doubtful and transient submission of their tribes was celebrated with lavish applause by the people of Constantinople. Successive inroads had reduced the province of Africa to one-third of the measure of Italy; yet the Roman emperors continued to reign above a century over Carthage, and the fruitful coast of the Mediterranean." The state of Northern Africa, at this period of the empire, is strongly painted in the observations which follow.

"But the victories and the losses of Justinian were alike pernicious to mankind; and such was the desolation of Africa, that in many parts a stranger might wander whole days without meeting the face either of a friend or an enemy. The nation of the Vandals had disappeared; they once amounted to an hundred and sixty thousand warriors, without including the children, the women, or the slaves. Their numbers were infinitely surpassed by the number of the Moorish families extirpated in a relentless war; and the same destruction was retaliated on the Romans and their allies, who perished by the climate, their mutual quarrels, and the rage of the barbarians. When Procopius first landed, he admired the populousness of the cities and country, strenuously exercised in the labours of commerce and agriculture. In less than twenty years, that busy scene was converted into a silent solitude; the wealthy citizens escaped to Sicily and Constantinople; and the secret historian has confidently affirmed, that five millions of Africans were consumed by the wars and government of the Emperor Justinian."

Decline and Fall of the Roman Empire, Vol. vii. p. 353.

Il resto de' diserti di Libia, cio è di Augela fino al Nilo, è habitato d'Arabi et da un popolo detto Levata, che è pure Africano, . . .—(5ta parte, p. 72.)

"The desert which separates Egypt from Lybia" (it is Major Rennell who speaks) "is to be regarded as the proper desert of Lybia: and it may be a question whether the tribe of Levata, although *now* found in the interior of the country, may not have originally inhabited the sea-coast; and that the Greeks denominated Africa (Libya) from them. This was the part of Africa the nearest to Greece, and the first colonised by the Greeks; and it is a known fact, that the Adyrmachidæ and Nasamones, who in the days of Herodotus, inhabited the coast, were at a succeeding period, found in the inland parts about Ammon and Augela. Mr. Park saw a wandering tribe named Lubey, whom he compares, in respect to their habits and mode of life, to gipsies."

Illustrations of Herodotus, (p. 409.)

Tunc Mauri, *Levatæ* appellati, Leptim Magnam (*neque enim longe absunt*) cum exercitu venere, &c.—(Hist. Vandal. ut supra.)

Ήδη γαρ Λιβυη μεν επι Λιβυης λεγεται υπο των πολλων Ελληνων εχειν τουνομα γυναικος αυτοχθονος. (Melp. § με⬜.) It may be at the same time remarked, that some writers have derived the term Libya from the Arabic word لوب (Lūb) which signifies thirst, and might therefore be without impropriety applied to a dry and sultry region. We may add that לביא (Lib⬜a) is the Phœnician, or Hebrew term for a lioness; and Libya is emphatically the country of lions—the "leonum arida nutrix." לובים (Lubīm) is the term used for Libyans in holy writ, and the common burthen of Nubian songs at the present day is—o-sī, o-ēh, to Lūbătŏ—of which we could never gain any other translation from the natives, than that it applied to their own country. Lūbătŏ was occasionally pronounced clearly Nūbătŏ, and it was sometimes impossible to tell which of the two pronunciations was intended.

Bakshees, or Baksheesh, is the Arab term for a gratuity or pecuniary consideration.

Il mio abito Europeo attirò subito lo sguardo del Marabotto, il quale fattosi inanzi, con aria truce, accompagnò il suo gesto minaccioso con parole ch' io non intesi: ma un Nero che aveva accanto, avendole fedelmente tradutte, portavano ch' egli voleva mangiarmi vivo. Il traduttore aggiungeva che il Marabotto ne era capace, perchè questo complimento era stato talvolta fatto da questa gente a qualche Ebreo!—(Viaggio da Tripoli, &c., p. 45).

In the work of Capt. Lyon, in particular, a good deal of curious matter connected with Marábūts will be found.

Εξης δ' εστι ποταμος Κινυφος· και μετα ταυτα διατειχισμα τι ὁ εποιησαν Καρχηδονιοι, γεφυρουντες βαραθρα τινα εις την χωραν ανεχοντα.—(Lib. 17. § 18.)

It must not be forgotten that the geographer is passing from west to east; and we find the remains of the building alluded to above, occurring immediately *after* the river, in travelling in this direction; which answers exactly to the position of Strabo's causeway.

Δια δε αυτων (Macarum) Κινυψ ποταμος, ρεων εκ λοφου καλευμενου Χαριτων, ες θαλασσαν εκδιδοι. ὁ δε λοφος ουτος ὁ Χαριτων δασυς ιδησι εστι, εουσης της αλλης της προκαταλεχθεισης Λιβυης ψιλης· απο θαλασσης δε ες αυτον σταδιοι διηκοσιοι εισι. (Melp. ροε⬜ .)

The Terhoona range is a branch of the Gharian, and may be reckoned, in the part opposite Lebida, to be about eighteen geographical miles from the sea, on the authority of Capt. Lyon's chart.

It will be seen from the account of Lebida annexed, with which we have lately been favoured by Capt. Smyth, that the river actually takes its rise in the low range of hills above mentioned, situated between four and five miles from the coast; so that the distance of Herodotus is much too great.

See Lib. 4. Cap. 3.

In intimo sinu fuit ora Lotophagôn, quos quidam Alachroos dixere, ad Philænorum aras.—(Hist. Nat. Lib. v. c. 4.)

The words of Ptolemy are—Περι αυτον τον ποταμον (Κινυφον) Λοτοφαγοι.

Ejus promontorium est Borion, ab eoque incipiens ora quam Lotophagi tenuisse dicuntur, usque ad Phycunta.—(Lib. i. c. 7.)

Sed litore inter duas Syrtis CCL. M. P. Ibi civitas Oeensis, Cynips fluvius ac regio . . . (Hist. Nat. Lib. v. c. 5.)

After mentioning the Lesser Syrtis, Mela observes—Ultra est Oea oppidum, et Cinyps fluvius per uberrima arva decidens:*tum* Leptis altera, et Syrtis nomine atque ingenio par priori . . .—(De Situ Orbis, Lib. 1. c. 7.)

Αγαθη δε γη και την Ευεσπεριται νεμονται· επ' εκατοστα γαρ επεαν αυτη εωϋτης αριστα ενεικη εκφερει· ἡ δε εν τη Κινυπι επι τριηκοσια. (Melp. ρ4η .)

Scylax calls the region of the Cinyphus χωριον καλον—and Mela describes the river—per uberrima arva decidens. Other authorities may be added to these in support of the fertility of the district.

Libyphœnices vocantur qui Byzacium incolunt.

Plinio dice Libyphœnices vocantur qui Byzacium incolunt. Si tratta dunque di sapere dove abitavano i Libifenicii per sapere il sito della regione Bizacina. Ed eccole una chiarissima risposta di Strabone a questo quesito di antica geografia: Sulla marina che è da Cartagine fino al Cefalo, e fino ai Masselibii è il territorio dei Libifenicii.—(Viaggio da Tripoli, &c. p. 48.)

The Massæsyli seem here to be intended by Signor Della Cella, as will appear from the passage in question.

Ὑπερκειται δε της απο Καρχηδονος παραλιας, μεχρι Κεφαλων και μεχρι της Μασσαισυλιων, ἡ των Λιβοφοινικων γη, μεχρι της των Γαιτουλων ορεινης, ηδε Λιβυκης ουσης. (Lib. 17. § 19.)

The passage which follows from the Second Book of Strabo, fixes the limits which he has assigned to the country of the Byzacii.

Ὑπερ δε ταυτης, και των Συρτεων, Ψυλλους, και Νασαμωνας, και των Γαιτουλων τινας· ειτα Σιντας, και βυζακιους, μεχρι της Καρχηδονιας . . . (Lib. 2. p. 131.)

Πασα δ' ἡ απο Καρχηδονος μεχρι στηλων εστιν ευδαιμων.

Libyphœnices vocantur qui Byzacium incolunt. Ita appellatur regio CCL. M. P. circuitu, fertilitatis eximiæ, &c.—(Nat. Hist. Lib. v. c. 4.)

The interpretation which follows (in this part of Signor Della Cella's work) of a passage which he has quoted from Scylax, and the adoption which he there proposes of the word ποταμος instead of πολις, do not seem to rest, we fear, on any better foundation. (See Viaggio da Tripoli, &c., p. 48—9.)

The concluding words εστι δε ερημος, rather appear to relate to the desert tract between Lebida and Tagiura, than to the country in the neighbourhood of the Cinyphus.

CHAPTER V.

Arrival at Zelīten — Description of the Village and District of that name — Harbour of Zelīten — Remains in its neighbourhood probably those of the Cisternæ Oppidum of Ptolemy — Tomb of the Marábūt Sidy Abd el Salám — Respect shewn to it by our party in passing before it — General appearance of these Structures — Arab credulity and superstition — Leave Zelīten — Remains between it and Selīn — Arrive at Selīn, the Orir, apparently, of Signor Della Cella — Proceed to Zoúia — Ports called by the Arabs Mersa Gusser and Mersa Zoraig — Arrive at Mesurata, the Western Boundary of the Greater Syrtis — Description of the Town and District of Mesurata — Account of them by Leo Africanus — Visit from the Shekh of Mesurata — Splendid Costume and Equipage of the Shekh compared with that of our Bedouin Guide, Shekh Mahommed el Dúbbah — Allusion to the report mentioned at the end of the Third Chapter — Great demand for Medicine at Mesurata — Considerate conduct of Mr. Campbell — Speedy success of his treatment in many difficult cases — Miraculous cure of a young Arab woman by an itinerant Sherīf and Marábūt — Detention of the party at Mesurata — Observations on Cape Mesurata, considered as the Cephalas Promontorium of Strabo — Remarks of Signor Della Cella on this subject — Alterations proposed by that gentleman in the punctuation of a passage in Strabo descriptive of the Promontory — Actual appearance of the Promontory sufficiently consistent with the account of Strabo — Well-founded Remarks of Signor Della Cella on the extension of the Gharian Chain, &c. — Extensive View from the Sand-hills at the back of Mesurata — Singular contrast presented by the view over the dreary wastes of the Syrtis compared with that over the plain of Mesurata — Hot wind, and swarm of locusts accompanying it — Alarm of the Arabs of Mesurata — Precautions adopted by them on the occasion — Destructive consequences (mentioned by Shaw) resulting from the visit of a flight of Locusts which he witnessed — Remarks of Pliny on the same subject — Arrival of the Camels, and departure from Mesurata.

ON our arrival at Zelīten, we found barley and oil in abundance, and much cheaper than in the neighbourhood of Tripoly; we availed ourselves, accordingly, of the favourable state of the market, to replenish our supply of these articles with the produce of the district of Cinyps. Herodotus thought it necessary to observe, in describing the fortunate region here alluded to, that "it *rained* in this part of Libya"—and we had also, in this instance, full reason to acknowledge the accuracy of the father of history: for our stock of provisions was so much damaged by the rain which had attended our passage through the country, that we found it necessary to expose it a second time to the sun, before we ventured to secure it more effectually in the baskets.

The village of Zelīten contains from three to five hundred souls (as Shekh Benzahir, who presides there, informed us); and we were indebted to him, besides, for the honour of a visit, and a present (no less valuable) of some excellent Fezzan dates, which are thought to be superior to those of the country. The *district* of Zelīten, he further informed us, which extends from Wad' el Kháhan to Selin, contains no less than fifteen villages and ten thousand inhabitants. The houses are built with mud and rough stones, the mud, on most occasions, preponderating, as it generally does in Arab buildings; the roofs are formed of mats and the branches of the palm-tree, on which is laid a quantity of earth. The villages of Igsaiba, Fehtir, Irgīg, and Snūd, all smaller than Zelīten, but built after the same fashion, may be said to be appendages to that place. Each of these villages, as well as Zelīten itself, is surrounded by plantations of date-trees and olives, and presents a tolerable show of cultivation. The produce is more than the inhabitants consume, and the overplus, together with straw mats and earthern jars, manufactured in the place, are disposed of to Bedouin traders, or carried to other markets for sale. There are two springs of very good water near Zelīten, which supply a small pond; and in this place the ladies of the place are accustomed to wash and cleanse their wool, their clothes, and, occasionally, themselves, before they fill their jars for home consumption.

The port called Mersa Zelīten is an insignificant cove, that would scarcely afford shelter to a boat. It is formed by a few rocks above water; may be about one hundred yards across, and appears to have no more than five or six feet water in it. Here also are two springs of good water, which would afford a constant supply, if the Arabs would take the trouble of excavating a cistern, and of protecting it from the surf. To the N.E. of the Mersa, at the distance of from half a mile to three-quarters of a mile off shore, the sea broke over sunken rocks: the cliffs are of sand-stone, and about thirty feet in height.

The many ruins which exist in the vicinity of Zelīten, and the frequent appearance of building-stones, and shafts of marble columns, protruding through the mud walls of the village, contribute decidedly to point it out as an ancient site, and it was probably the Cisternæ or Cinsternæ Oppidum of Ptolemy; which is the first town mentioned by this geographer after the Τριηρων ακρον—the Cephalas Promontorium of Strabo—in the tract of country between that point and the Cinyphus.

Among the sand hills which almost surround the village, we found several imperfect ground plans; and near the beach is the tomb of a Marábūt, supported by marble columns, which however are of very trifling dimensions: there also we noticed several fragments of marble columns, and a considerable quantity of pottery and glass. Among the sand hills are likewise some remains of Arab baths, built of stone and cement; and about them are scattered the ruins of walls and buildings, as though the village had once been there, but having been deserted was gradually covered with sand.

Our tents at Zelīten were pitched upon the sand hills close to the tomb of a celebrated Marábūt, called Sidy Abd el Salám, much respected by all the Mahometan population. The Arabs of our escort were particularly desirous that we should show some marks of attention to the remains of this holy personage, by passing his tomb at a slow and solemn pace, and at a respectful distance; and though it may be imagined we had no great faith in the sanctity of this venerated Shekh, and as little in the miracles which were attributed to him, we complied with their pious request. The tombs of such Marábūts as have acquired any tolerable celebrity, present a singular appearance, in the motley collection of votive offerings and deposits which are displayed both within and without the holy structures; and bundles of wood and long grass, ploughs, mats, jars, and shreds of old garments, are seen mingled with rusty firelocks and pistols, saddles, stirrups, and bridles, and chaplets of beads, and rubbish of almost every description.

The more useful offerings of vegetables and fruit may be sometimes observed in the collection; and the appetite of a saint, who has been dead fifty years, is often revived and miraculously exerted on these very tempting occasions. A large portion of food very soon disappears from the board of a living Marábūt, but the heaps which are consumed by a dead one of any celebrity are perfectly astonishing to unbelievers.

The credulity of the Arab has, however, no bounds; and it rather, indeed, appears to increase, in proportion as the marvellous tale which is related is more inconsistent and extravagant.

Marábūts are allowed the most unlimited freedom of access, from the palace and presence of the sovereign, to the tent of the meanest Arab; and their persons are considered as sacred and inviolable, even after the commission of the most unjustifiable outrages. The last-mentioned privilege is not confined to the living; for the tomb of a Marábūt is as inviolable as his person, and affords a sure sanctuary to the worst of criminals, in defiance of law and authority.

To return to our subject, we may remark, in conclusion, that a very considerable part of the population of Zelīten are Jews; and we were informed that the manufactures of the place are chiefly in the hands of these people: we found them uniformly civil, obliging, and industrious, and though much persecuted by the Mahometan inhabitants, they appear to support their ill fortune contentedly.

On the morning of the 18th we left Zelīten, and entered immediately upon an extensive plain, for the most part overrun with squills and brushwood. Two roads cross this plain, one to Mesurata, the other to Benioleed: we took the former, as nearest to the sea; and at the distance of a few miles beyond Zelīten, we observed several scattered heaps of ruins on either side of the road; most of these have been built on artificial mounds, with trenches round them, and appear to have formed parts of a military position; but everything was so much mutilated and buried, that much time would have been necessary to make out their plans, which would scarcely indeed have recompensed the labour of excavation.

At sunset we arrived at Selin, where the tents were pitched near an ancient well, forty feet in depth, and containing a good supply of sweet water. At the distance of about two hundred yards from the well, we perceived upon a hill the remains of what appeared to have been a fort; and many fragments of buildings were discernible here and there in the neighbourhood. This place seems to be the Orir of Dr. Della Cella, but we could perceive no traces of the Mosaic pavement which he mentions, nor anything to mark the spot as the site of an ancient city. The Doctor has fixed upon Orir as the position of Cinsternæ; and the circumstance of its occurring (in passing from west to east) immediately before the promontory which forms the western boundary of the Greater Syrtis, would, in truth, seem to favour the idea. But Zelīten appeared to us more adapted for the site of a city, and the remains of that place had more the character of parts of a town than those which were observable at Selin. We should conceive that the ruins to the eastward of Zelīten were those of a connected series of forts, and that no other buildings had been attached to them than such as are usually found in the neighbourhood of a military position. Cinsternæ, however, was a town of so little importance, that whether its site be fixed at Zelīten or Selin is a matter of very trivial consideration.

On the evening of the succeeding day we reached the little village of Zoúia, which is somewhat resembling, but very superior to, Zelīten. After quitting Selin we had divided our party, and leaving the camels to pursue the direct road, we proceeded along the sand-hills which flank the beach, and arrived at an inconsiderable collection of hovels situated immediately on the coast. This place is called Zoraig, and contains, we were told, about an hundred persons, who cultivate just sufficient ground to supply themselves and their families. They were, however, provided with several wells of good water, which they distributed by means of troughs over the cultivated ground. We here dismounted to partake of some dates and water, which were cordially offered to us by an old man of the village; and we soon learned from him that the Adventure had been there several days, and that a party of the officers had been on shore. Two little ports, if such they may be called, are here formed by reefs of rocks lying off the village, and the natives have dignified them with the titles of Mersa Gusser and Mersa Zoraig.

On the following day we entered Mesurata by a circuitous route shaded thickly with date-trees, and enclosed between well-furnished gardens.

We had now reached the eastern boundary of the cultivated districts, where they terminate on the margin of the Syrtis; and as this was the place where we were to change our camels, we pitched the tents in a garden near the town, and proceeded to make the necessary arrangements.

The town of Mesurata is built with tolerable regularity; its streets cross each other at right angles, and near the centre stands the market-place, which, like most others in this country, is half occupied by a pool of green and stinking water. The houses are only one story high, and are built with rough stones and mud; the roofs are flat, and formed with slight rafters, covered with mats and a quantity of sea-weed, over which is laid a thick coat of mud, smoothed and beat down very carefully. They are fortunate who can mix a little lime with the mud which forms the outer part of their roof; for without this addition it is wholly incapable of resisting the heavy rains which assail it in winter, and a thick muddy stream never fails to find its way, through the numerous mazes of sea-weed and matting, to the luckless inhabitants below: the white-washed walls are in consequence usually marked with long streaks of this penetrating fluid, and present a singularly-variegated appearance. The greater part of the town has been built upon a hard rocky incrustation, about two feet in thickness; the soil beneath is soft and sandy, and, being easily removed, is excavated by the Arabs into storehouses for their corn and dry provisions. Some of these have in the course of time fallen in, and the streets are in such places not very passable.

The extent of the *district* of Mesurata, according to the report of its Shekh, is from Selin to Sooleb, a place in the Syrtis, two days distant to the southward of the town; it consists of the villages of Ghâra, Zoúia, Zoroog, Gusser Hámed, Gezir, &c., and is said to contain 14,000 inhabitants, including those of the town of Mesurata; the population of the five villages which we have just named amounts to about 1250 persons, supposing the estimate of the Shekh to be correct, from whom this statement is derived. The gardens, which extend from Zoúia to Marábūt Bushaifa, produce dates, olives, melons, pomegranates, pumpkins, carrots, onions, turnips, radishes, and a little tobacco and cotton; among these may be mentioned the palma christi, which we frequently observed in this neighbourhood. Many of the gardens are raised from six to eight feet above the road, and are enclosed by mud walls, or by fences of the prickly pear and wild aloe. The dates, which are of several kinds, are in great abundance, and the olives yield a plentiful supply of oil: these, with barley, which is also very abundant, are carried to various markets for sale; for the home-consumption of the place consists chiefly of dates and dúrrah, and the greater part of the barley is exported. The principal manufactures of Mesurata are carpets, the colours of which are very brilliant, straw mats, sacks of goats' hair, and earthen jars. The market is in general well supplied with meat, vegetables, the fruits of the country, oil, manteca, and salt; the latter is procured from some very extensive marshes a few miles to the southward of the town.

Mesurata (or "Mesarata," as some authors write it) has been described by Leo Africanus as "a province on the coast of the Mediterranean, distant about an hundred miles from Tripoly." He states it to have contained many "castles and villages, some on heights, and others in the plain;" and adds that the inhabitants were excessively rich, on account of their having no tribute to pay, and the attention which they bestowed upon commerce. They were in the habit (he continues) of receiving foreign wares, which were brought to them by the Venetian galleys, and of carrying them to Numidia, where they were bartered in exchange for slaves, civet, and musk from Ethiopia; these they carried into Turkey, and made a profit both in going and returning.

In the lifetime of the late Bashaw, Mesurata was in a very disturbed state. The inhabitants had refused to receive Sidy Yusef, and it was only by the assistance of Shekh Haliffe that they were at length reduced to obedience. The place is not now so flourishing as it is stated to have been in the time of Leo, and its commerce appears to be trifling.

Soon after our arrival, the Shekh of Mesurata, Belcázi, came to pay us his visit of ceremony. He was accompanied by Shekh Mahommed el Dúbbah, and attended by a train of mounted Arabs, tolerably well armed with long guns and pistols. The splendid attire of Shekh Belcázi, displayed to advantage by a large and handsome person, threw far into the shade the less imposing costume and figure of his companion. It consisted of three cloth waistcoats, richly embroidered with gold, and a pair of most capacious crimson silk trowsers, bound tight round his waist, which was none of the slenderest, by many an ell of handsome shawl. Over this, notwithstanding the heat of the day, he had thrown, in ample folds, a large white barracan, and above this a heavy red cloth burnoos, the hood of which was pulled over eight or ten yards of muslin rolled round his head as a turban. The eyelids of the Shekh had been carefully painted with the sable powder usually employed for that purpose, and which is considered, even by men, in the regency of Tripoly, to be absolutely requisite on occasions of ceremony. The tips of his fat and gentlemanly-looking fingers were at the same time stained with hénnah; and, as the dye had been recently and copiously applied, would decidedly have made those of Aurora look pale.

While the Shekh had been thus minutely attentive to his own person, that of his horse had been by no means neglected; for his bridle was of crimson silk embroidered with gold, and his scarlet saddle-cloth displayed a broad edging of gold lace: the saddle itself was of rich crimson velvet, and the high back and pummel, which appeared through the saddle-cloth, were also thickly embroidered with gold. A broad band of gold lace was stretched across his chest, and a large and thick tassel of crimson silk and gold (which might have served a Grand Cross of the Bath), together with a numerous collection of charms, were suspended from the neck of the animal. The large gilt Mameluke stirrups, kept in constant motion by the rider, flashed gaily in the beams of the sun, which were glanced off in many a brilliant sparkle from this glittering assemblage of precious metal. If Phœbus himself had appeared in all his splendour, mounted on one of his gayest chariot-horses, he could scarcely have been more an object of admiration and wonder in the eyes of the humble and unassuming crowd of Arabs which had assembled to witness the show, than Shekh Belcázi and his charger were on this occasion.

We dare not guess how the lady of our honest friend the Dúbbah would have supported this splendid exhibition, in which her husband was so completely eclipsed; but we thought that the eyes of Shekh Mahommed himself did occasionally wander to the shining masses by his side, with something like an expression of jealousy. If it were so, however, the glance only found its way through the *corners* of the Dúbbah's orbs of vision; for his head kept its post with becoming solemnity, and was never once turned towards those objects of his envy, to which all other eyes were so fully directed. It must at the same time be allowed, that the toilet of Shekh Mahommed had been much more attended to than usual. He had made a temporary adjournment from his usual *only* garment to a white cotton shirt of very decent exterior, over which he had carefully arranged a clean-looking white barracan; and he had drawn from the innermost recesses of his saddle-bags a new white burnoos of no ordinary texture, which he persuaded himself to substitute for the old and coarse brown one he had hitherto worn on the road. His saddle-case was now observed to be of crimson morocco, a circumstance with which we were not before acquainted; for it had hitherto, on the journey, been turned inside out, or more properly speaking, with the outer side in, to prevent it from being soiled, and from fading in the sun. His saddle-cloth also, which had hitherto consisted of a dirty piece of white flannel, was now of bright scarlet cloth; and, besides the embroidered covers to his silver-embossed pistols, he had carefully suspended from different parts of his body a great variety of little bags, of different colours and sizes: these were the repositories of his powder and ball, and carried tinder, flints and steel, money, nails, and tobacco, with sundry other little matters too numerous to mention. By his side also hung a neat little smàat, or goat skin, with the long black hairs left to ornament and protect the outside; and which, properly speaking, was meant to hold water, but which likewise served indifferently for holding milk, oil, or butter, or any other substance which it might be necessary to carry in it. We should state that, under all this variety of ornament, Shekh Mahommed el Dúbbah sat with dignity upon his mare, a recently-acquired present from the Bashaw, whose spirit had been prudently roused on this occasion by the stimulus of an extra feed of corn. The display of Arab horsemanship which concluded the procession, received additional éclat from this precaution; and the Dúbbah's mare, after manœuvring her head to admiration, first on one side and then on the other, and prancing, and pacing, and rearing, to the delight of the assembled spectators, no sooner felt the angle of the spur assail her sides, than she sprang forward with a bound in advance of the party, and being suddenly pulled up with a powerful bit, was thrown back upon her haunches within a foot of our tent-cords. The old Dúbbah looked round to enjoy the applause which he felt he had deserved, for his horsemanship and his mare, from the crowd who had witnessed the exhibition; and the two Shekhs alighted and entered the tent, each apparently well pleased with himself.

Within they found everything arranged for their reception: the dusty ground had been previously adorned with a mat, over which had been spread some small carpets; and we had taken care to have coffee and sherbet in readiness, which were served up as soon as they were seated. Shekh Belcázi was introduced to our acquaintance by the Dúbbah, who took care at the same time to inform us of his rank and importance; accompanying his harangue with a profusion of fulsome Arab compliments, which were received by Belcázi as a matter of course, and appreciated by us as they deserved. As soon as the usual salutations were over, and the coffee and lemonade had been disposed of (though not before Belcázi had satisfied his curiosity with regard to the several uses of every object in the tent), we began to make arrangements for the number of camels which would be necessary for our journey across the Syrtis. The Shekh of Mesurata undertook to provide them, and freely offered his assistance in any other way in which it might be serviceable to our party.

The camels could not be procured on the moment, but it was settled that Belcázi should let us know the next morning how soon he would be able to collect them. The Dúbbah, in his turn, now began to expatiate upon the attention which *he* would shew us when we reached the district of Syrt, over which he presided as Shekh; and to enumerate the various excellences of the fat sheep and lambs, of the milk, and the butter, and the water we should find there; assuring us that he would consider it his greatest pleasure, as well as duty, to take care that we were well supplied with all these valuable commodities. He then began to state the great advantage of his protection, and how impossible it would have been for us to cross the Syrtis without him. As we suspected that the report which had been mentioned to us by the Consul was invented by our worthy friend the Dúbbah, we took this opportunity of relating it to the Shekh of Mesurata, and of asking his opinion with regard to its probability. Belcázi shook his head, and very confidently assured us that he did not believe there was any foundation for it whatever: it was true, he confessed, that a few years ago such an interruption might easily have occurred; but since the Arab tribes had been reduced by the Bashaw, the communication between Mesurata and Bengazi might be considered as tolerably certain.

Shekh Mahommed, however (whose large and round eyes had been during this discourse very attentively fixed upon those of the Shekh of Mesurata), still insisted upon the existence of this horde of *sbandūt*; and even asserted that he was himself well acquainted with all their favourite haunts and retreats. Some of his party, he added, had tracked their horses' feet from the well which they had recently visited, and had informed him that their troop was very numerous. But he knew, he continued, all the wells which they frequented, and would himself ride before, to reconnoitre the ground when we arrived in the neighbourhood of those places. He then assumed an air of amazing importance, and putting one hand upon the head of a pistol at his side, and stroking with the other his grey bushy beard, bade us not be alarmed at any danger which might threaten us while we were under the protection of the Dúbbah! We were now quite convinced that our valiant old friend had himself been the author of the report, in order, as we then thought, to enhance the value of his protection; and we afterwards discovered the reason why he wished to have an excuse for riding on occasionally in advance of the party. It was, however, not our wish to hurt the old Shekh's feelings by a disclosure of these suspicions, and it was certainly not our policy to do so; we therefore acquiesced in his remarks upon his own importance, and assured him that it was really our firm belief that no *sbandūt* would be daring enough to enter into his presence. After some little further conversation with the Shekhs, from whom we obtained all the information we could, we reminded Belcázi of his promise to collect the camels, which we told him we wished to have as speedily as possible, and he soon after rose to take his leave, and retired with the formidable Dúbbah. On the following morning he sent his son to say that we should have the camels in three or four days, and we took the opportunity of making the youth some few presents, with which he was highly delighted. In the evening we returned Belcázi's visit, and were received with a good deal of that easy politeness, which the better classes of Turks and Arabs know so well (when they choose it) how to practise. We here perceived that the fashions of Tripoly had travelled eastward for green tea was served up with the sherbet instead of coffee, very sweet, and very highly perfumed. On taking our leave, we were again assured by the Shekh that he would send us the camels very shortly; but although we had every reason to be satisfied with Belcázi, so far as professions and civilities extended, we had already seen enough of the Mahometan character to know that his promises should not be depended upon.

We had scarcely been a day at Mesurata before the report of our having a tibeeb (or doctor) in our party soon brought us a multitude of visiters; and the demand for medicine became so extensive, that the contents of twenty medicine-chests, such as that which we had with us, would not have satisfied one-half of the applicants. By far the greater number of those who presented themselves had nothing whatever the matter with them; but there were still many cases of real distress which required and obtained assistance. The most prevalent diseases were those of the eye, and there were many very alarming cases of dysentery; but Mr. Campbell's attention and medical skill soon began to produce very favourable symptoms, and as much of the medicine as could possibly be spared was administered to and distributed amongst those who required it. As is usual, however, in barbarous countries, there were many simple beings whom it was impossible to convince that the powers of medicine are limited, and they were so fully persuaded of Mr. Campbell's omnipotence, that he soon found it useless to deny it. To meet this emergency he found it better to make up some little harmless ingredients for their use, and to tell them that the rest was in the hands of the prophet, who had alone (under Allah) the power to cure them completely. With this declaration, and the medicine together, without which they would by no means have been satisfied, the petitioners used to retire well pleased with their physician, and convinced that the draught or the powders which they had received would infallibly remove their infirmity, however incurable it might be.

A young woman, in the mean time, who resided near the tents, was attacked, after eating a quantity of bazeen, with a violent headache and pain in the stomach; and a celebrated Marábūt, who had lately arrived at Mesurata, was called in to administer his assistance. The holy man did not refuse to comply with the summons; and when he made his appearance at the door of her tent, Mr. Campbell, and such of our party who were near, were led by curiosity to the same place; and taking up, unperceived, an advantageous position, were able to understand, with the assistance of the interpreter, the whole of the conversation which ensued.

The Shereef (for he claimed, or possessed, the distinction) was no sooner made acquainted with the case than he assumed a most mysterious air; and began by declaring to his suffering patient that she was possessed by an *underground spirit*. He then proceeded to state, as the cause of this misfortune, that before doing something (which our party could not distinctly make out) she had omitted to say Bismillah! (in the name of God) a form always used by good and pious Mahometans to draw down a blessing upon whatever they are about to do. This omission (he declared) had been the cause of her dropping some water upon the head of the spirit's child, who was passing beneath her (under ground) at the time; and the justly-enraged gnome had in consequence leaped into her, and was now in the act of tormenting her for the crime. Our party of listeners could hardly contain themselves at this most ingenious discovery of the Shereef; but all the Arabs within the tent believed it most fully, and the poor girl herself began to cry bitterly and to bewail her hard fate and most unlucky omission. The Marábūt, however, now bade her take comfort, and assured her that the case, though undoubtedly a serious one, was not altogether without a remedy. He accordingly called up a severe and commanding look, and, in a tone of authority, ordered the spirit to leave her. As the pain still continued without intermission, it was evident that this personage was not inclined to obey; and the holy man then pronounced him a most obstinate spirit, and told him that he knew of his having entered the woman long before she had sent for his assistance: he added, however, that he was determined to conquer him, and would not quit his patient till morning. At the same time he acknowledged that the task would be difficult, for he could clearly perceive that the woman was wicked: he knew it (he said) by the breadth of her shoulders, and the uncommon blackness of her large rolling eyes, which were even larger and blacker than those of one of his own wives, whom he knew to be a very sinful woman. In the morning it happened that the poor girl was better, and the fame of the Marábūt was widely diffused; but whether her recovery was owing to the holy man's exertions, or to a copious draught of medicine administered by Mr. Campbell, we will leave to the decision of our readers.

During our stay at Mesurata, where we were detained several days, in consequence of the non-appearance of the Shekh's promised camels, we took the opportunity afforded by the delay, of visiting the places of most interest in the neighbourhood.

Bushaifa Bay had been stated by Captain Lautier to afford good anchorage for shipping, and seemed in consequence to call for some examination; but we must confess that it did not appear, upon inspection, to deserve the character which that officer gives it. Of the protection which may be afforded by breakers we cannot venture to speak, Mesurata not boasting so much as a single boat, but it is certain that the land does not give the shelter required, as will be seen by a reference to the chart. On the point of the bay, where is the best landing-place, there has formerly been a fort, which is now entirely destroyed.

As we had arrived on the confines of the Gulf of the greater Syrtis, the position of the promontory, which had been stated by the ancients to form its western extremity, was a most important object of inquiry. Between the town of Mesurata and the sea there is a high range of sand-hills, rising far above the heads of the tallest date-trees about them: and beyond these is a promontory of soft sand-stone, which may be (at a rough estimation) about an hundred feet above the level of the sea. This high land is divided into three distinct heads, or capes, and is described by Captain Lautier as having the appearance (from the sea) of three hills in the form of as many islands. The low ground at the back and to the south-east of these capes is thickly covered with date-trees, but their summits are now bare of wood and destitute of any vegetation: the sand-stone in fact is fast crumbling away, and the height of the promontory is every day diminishing. The appearance of this triple cape coincided so well, in our estimation, with the description given by Strabo of the Cephalas Promontorium, that we have not hesitated to pronounce it the same with that headland. It does not however form the precise point, or western extremity, of the gulf, which is in fact a low rocky projection, scarcely above the level of the sea, about four miles distant from the cape: but this point is too low to be remarked from the sea, and Strabo, when he observed the cape from his vessel, may well be excused for having overlooked it.

The Τριήρων ἄκρον, or Triærorum Promontorium of Ptolemy is no doubt the same with the Cephalas of Strabo; and being laid down a little without the gulf corresponds more exactly with the actual nature of the ground. Strabo certainly describes his promontory as forming the beginning or western extremity of the Syrtis; but the circumstance above mentioned of his having seen it only from the sea, may be easily imagined to have occasioned this little inaccuracy, if such it may indeed be termed.

We are at a loss to imagine what the promontory can be which Signor Della Cella has identified with that of Ptolemy (and which he states to have been *two hours* distant from Mesurata) unless the Cephalas itself be intended, or, in other words, the cape which we have supposed to be the Cephalas. For, with the exception of this, there is no other high land which will in any respect answer to the triple cape of Ptolemy; and this is not more than half an hour's ride from the town, and is not in the route which the army must have taken in marching from Mesurata towards the Syrtis, as will be seen by a reference to the Chart. At the same time, we can neither persuade ourselves that Strabo would have instanced an accidental range of sand-hills as a promontory; nor that the word υψηλη, applied by this geographer to the Cephalas, can be supposed to mean *distant*, or *deep*, instead of high, as Signor Della Cella has imagined; notwithstanding the passage cited from Homer, which the Doctor reads in favour of his argument.

When we consider that the cape which forms the Cephalas Promontorium is, at least, as we have stated, an hundred feet high; and that, from the soft quality of the stone, which is continually crumbling away, it may have been in Strabo's time considerably higher, we may fairly conclude that the term υψηλη (or *high*) is not quite so inapplicable to it as Signor Della Cella has asserted.

It is true that compared with high capes this elevation may appear to be trifling; but it seems quite sufficient when contrasted with the land about it, and particularly with the low and level surface of the Syrtis. The highest parts of the Cape, as we have mentioned above, are not at the present time wooded, whatever they may have been formerly; but the land at its base, to the south and south-east, is thickly covered with date-trees and olives: and, without allowing so much for the changes which time might be supposed to have produced, as would be readily granted to us by the most tenacious of naturalists, we may venture to assert that this cape, under its present appearance, answers sufficiently well to the description of Strabo, to authorize its being identified with the Cephalas.

The observations, however, which Signor Della Cella has made on the map of Northern Africa by Arrowsmith, respecting the extension of the Gharian chain towards the Greater Syrtis, and the omission of the low range which actually branches off from those mountains, are certainly very correct. For a minor branch of the Gharian detaches itself from the chain, and runs down to the sea in the neighbourhood of Lebida; and another part of the same range extends itself from Lebida towards the Syrtis Major, gradually declining as it approaches that place, both of which are omitted in the map to which the Doctor has alluded. The eastern extremity of the Gharian chain appears also to be carried too near to the Greater Syrtis, from no part of which (so far as our experience went) could any portion of this chain be perceived.

We were unable to discover any remains of antiquity at Mesurata; but its remarkable position between the fertile regions of the Cinyphus, and the barren dreary wastes of the Greater Syrtis, cannot fail to make it an object of more than common interest to those who witness the singular contrast.

From the high range of sand-hills, which we have mentioned above, between the town and the sea, an excellent idea may be formed of this striking peculiarity of situation; and we often toiled up their steep and yielding sides to enjoy the singularity of the prospect.

At the foot of these masses, to the southward, and to the westward, are the varied and cultivated lands of Mesurata: there are seen endless groves of palm-trees and olives, among which are scattered numerous villages and gardens, rich tracts of corn land, flocks of sheep and goats, and everywhere a moving and busy population. To the eastward, a tenantless and desolate waste, without a single object rising from its surface, lies stretched in one long, unbroken, line, as far as the eye can range. Not a single tree or shrub is on that side to be seen; not a single house or tent, not a single human being, or animal of any description.

In fact the effect of the Greater Syrtis, from this place, is that of a dreary moor—a wide tract of level, waste land—without anything to distinguish one part of it from another but the windings of a marsh, which threads its dark surface, and is lost in different parts of the unbroken horizon.

Two days before our departure from Mesurata, a strong scirocco wind set in, and brought such myriads of locusts, that the air was literary darkened by them. The inhabitants in consequence remained out all night, keeping up a continued shouting and firing of muskets and pistols, to prevent them from settling on the gardens and cultivated lands. They who were not engaged in this occupation, employed themselves in collecting the locusts which had been beaten down, and carrying them off in baskets as articles of provision: so great was the quantity collected on this occasion, that we observed many asses, heavily laden with these insects, driven into the town and the neighbouring villages. The destruction occasioned by a large swarm of locusts can scarcely be imagined by those who have not witnessed it; and the account which we subjoin of them, extracted from Shaw, may not perhaps be unacceptable to our readers.

After this interesting description, the Doctor proceeds to observe—"The locust, I conjecture, was the *noisome beast*, or the *pernicious destructive animal*, as the original words may be interpreted, which, with the *sword*, the *famine*, and the *pestilence*, made the *four sore judgments* that were threatened against Jerusalem, Ezek. xiv. 21."

"The Jews were allowed to eat them; and indeed when sprinkled with salt, and fried, they are not unlike in taste to our fresh-water cray-fish."

"The Acridophagi, no doubt, were fond of eating them; in so much as they received their name from thence."—He further adds—"The ακριδες, which St. John the Baptist fed upon in the wilderness, were properly locusts; and provided they appeared in the holy land during the spring, as they did in Barbary, it may be presumed that St. John entered upon his mission, and that *the day of his shewing himself unto Israel* (Luke i. 20) was at that season."

Pliny has informed us that the locusts lay their eggs in autumn, which remain all the winter in the fissures of the earth, and come forth in the shape of locusts in the following spring; being, at first, without legs, and obliged to creep upon their wings. He tells us that they invariably choose tracts of level country in which to deposit their eggs, as being most full of crevices and fissures, and hence, if it chance to be a rainy season, the eggs never come to perfection; but, on the contrary, if the early part of the year should be dry, vast numbers of these insects may be expected in the summer ensuing.

Some writers (he adds) are of opinion that locusts breed *twice* in the year, and that they perish as often; the first supply dying in the heat of the summer, and the second immediately succeeding them. The mothers die as soon as they have brought forth their young, by reason of a small worm which breeds about the throat, and ultimately chokes them. The same author informs us that *it is said* there are locusts in India so much as *three* feet in length; and that the people of the country use their legs and thighs for saws, after they are properly dried! Pliny mentions, at the same time, their flight across the sea, over which they are carried by the wind, and where they usually fall, and perish in heaps; although this is not always of necessity the case, as early writers (he says) have remarked, because their wings are wet with the dew; for they have been known to pass over extensive tracts of sea, and will continue their flight for many days without rest. Locusts, he adds, are gifted with the power of foreseeing an approaching famine, and will take the precaution, on such an occasion, of transporting themselves into distant countries. He mentions also the noise which they make with their wings, and that they are sometimes mistaken for flights of strange birds: that they darken the sun in their flight, as if a heavy cloud had passed before it, and spread terror and consternation wherever they make their appearance; eating up everything which comes in their way, and even gnawing the very doors of the houses. Italy, on this writer's authority, was so much infested with locusts from the opposite shores of Africa, that the people of Rome, alarmed at the idea of their producing a famine, had been often obliged to consult the books of the Sibyls, to discover by what means they might avert the wrath of the gods which they considered to be falling upon them. He tells us that in the Cyrenaica there existed a law, obliging the inhabitants, every third year, to wage a regular war with the locusts: on such occasions they were ordered to seek out their nests, to destroy the eggs and the young, and afterwards to proceed to extirpate such as had already come to maturity.

A heavy punishment, at the same time, was inflicted upon those who neglected this useful precaution, as though they had been guilty of an unpardonable crime against their sovereign and their country. In Lemnos, also, there was a measure established to regulate the quantity which each man should kill; and every person was obliged to give in his account to the magistrate, and to produce his measure full of dead locusts.

It may easily be conceived, from these relations, what consternation and dismay is excited among the inhabitants of a cultivated country by the appearance of a large swarm of locusts. The mischief, however, occasioned at Mesurata by those which we have mentioned above, was not by any means so great, we are happy to say, as might have been reasonably expected: and the Arabs of the place were soon as busily employed in eating their formidable invaders, as they had at first been in preserving their crops from experiencing a similar fate.

On the 2nd December, after repeated promises and disappointments, our camels at length arrived; and having made suitable presents to Shekh Belcazi and his son, we prepared to continue our journey. We had few difficulties to encounter in our dealings with the people of Mesurata; and we must confess that we found in their Shekh, notwithstanding his occasional evasions, more openness and honesty than are usually met with in the inhabitants of Mahometan countries.

FOOTNOTES:

Ύεται γαρ δηταυτα της Λιβυης.

The saint and his tomb are thus mentioned by Captain Lyon:—

"This place (Zelīten) is particularly blessed in possessing the remains of a great Marábūt, who is buried in a really handsome mosque, ornamented with minarets and neat cupolas, and whitewashed all over. His descendants are much respected, and are called Weled el Sheikh, sons of the elder; they think themselves authorized to be the most impudent, begging set of people in the whole regency of Tripoly." (P. 335.)

It must be observed, that the opportunity of being buried in a mosque does not offer itself to many Marábūts—their tombs in general are small, insulated buildings, surmounted with a single cupola, having nothing to recommend them, in point of appearance, beyond the neatness and regularity which usually distinguish them. They are commonly built on eminences.

A criminal who may not be forced from a Marábūt, may, however, be starved in his sanctuary; and this is often effected by surrounding the tomb with troops, thus preventing the escape of the prisoner, and the possibility of his being supplied with food. An occurrence, however, took place at Bengazi in the year 1817, which serves to prove that this species of blockade is not always sure to be effectual. Some Arabs of the Zoàsi tribe, who had escaped from Bey Hamed after the massacre of their companions in the castle, took refuge in the tomb of a celebrated Marábūt, situated in the vicinity of the town. The Bey could not venture to force the sanctuary which they had reached, but took every means in his power to prevent their escape, or their communication with any person without. He had closely blockaded the tomb with his troops; and flattered himself that they must shortly perish with hunger, or be reduced to the necessity of surrendering themselves to the soldiers. In either case the object of the Bey would have been accomplished, and he confidently waited the result; while the anxiety of the people and neighbourhood of Bengazi, who pitied the unfortunate fugitives, was raised to the highest pitch. Every one was expecting some horrid catastrophe, for the destruction of the prisoners, by famine or the sword, appeared to be now inevitable; when the timely interference of the departed Marábūt was miraculously exerted in their favour. On the third day after their arrival at the sanctuary, to the astonishment of the assembled spectators, a stream of water was seen to issue from the tomb, and the ground all about it was observed to be strewed with dates and other articles of food for the refugees!!!

It was clear that no other than the Marábūt himself could have afforded this providential supply—(λεγομεν δε τα λεγουσι αυτοι Λιβυες, we tell the tale as it was told to us)—for the place had been watched day and night by the troops, who had been carefully and regularly relieved; and every Arab of Bengazi and the adjacent country can still testify the fact as it is stated!

The same story may be found in the work of Dr. Della Cella, who informs us that the miracle took place during his residence at Bengazi.

Mersa is the Arab term for a port or harbour.

Some account of the government and resources, as well as of the trade, of Mesurata, may be collected from the work of Signor Della Cella, pp. 55, 6, 7.

See Tully's Memoirs, passim.

A coarse brown barracan is on most occasions the only habit of a Bedouin Arab; but as the rainy season was approaching, Shekh Mahommed had allowed himself the additional covering of the old burnoos we have mentioned. Shirts are seldom worn but on gay occasions.

The term applied by the Arabs in the regency of Tripoly to marauders of every description, and which is evidently corrupted from the Italian.

Bazeen (the composition and manufacture of which is well described by Captain Lyon, p. 49) is the common food of the lower classes of Arabs in the regency of Tripoly, and appears to have been a very ancient one; for we find it mentioned by Leo Africanus as being in use among the same people, in his account of Tripoly.—(5ta parte, page 72.)

Dr. Della Cella has confounded the sand-hills with the promontory, the latter of which he asserts is composed entirely of sand; they are however as distinct from each other as sand-stone may be said to be from sand. The sand-hills are, besides, at some distance from the sea, and the promontory immediately upon it.

Il Capo Mesurata, a tre circa leghe di distanza, si mostra sotto l' apparenza di tre monticelli a foggia di tre isolotti.—See Lautier's Memoir, attached to the Viaggio da Tripoli, &c., by Della Cella.

Ειτ' ακρα υψηλη και υλωδης, αρχη της μεγαλης Συρτεως, καλουσι δε Κεφαλας· Lib. 17, § 18.

Dopo *due ore* di cammino giungemmo all' estremità del Promontorio che sporge in tre punte divise da seni di mare: ond' è che il nome di capo Triero con cui è chiamato da Tolommeo ne esprime la forma.—Viaggio da Tripoli, &c., p. 60.

The observations connected with the transposition of the comma recommended by Signor Della Cella, are at the same time, we must confess, rather singular: for it does not clearly appear how the removal of a comma from a place which it never occupied, and the insertion of it in a place where it always existed, can be said to amend a defective passage. A comma is placed after υλωδης, in all the copies of Strabo with which we are acquainted, but none after ακρα although there might be without impropriety; and it seems more consistent with the Doctor's translation to suppose that he meant exactly the contrary of what he has recommended; that is to say, that his real intention was to remove the comma from υλωδης, and place it after ακρα. We might then read, by giving to υψηλη the sense which Signor Della Cella requires for it,—"Then comes the promontory, which forms the *distant* and woody extremity of the Greater Syrtis,"—instead of—"Then (comes) the high and woody promontory, which is the beginning of the Greater Syrtis." We must, however, confess that we do not see any difference in the sense of the passage in question, whether a comma be placed after ακρα or not, provided that after υλωδης be allowed to keep its place: but by the change which we propose, the

Doctor's punctuation will at any rate correspond with his version, which, as it stands, it does not.

We give the observations and the passage together in Signor Della Cella's own words.—"Con questa avvertenza io crederei doversi intendere un passo di Strabone molto diversamente dal penso che gli è dato da tutti i traduttori; parlando del Capo Cefalo, questo geografo così si esprime—ειτ' ακρα υψηλη και υλωδης, ακρη (αρχη of course is intended) της μεγαλης Συρτεως—che tutti traducono—indi (viene) il promontorio alto e selvoso, che è il principio della gran Sirte."

"L'esattezza di questo illustre geografo puo esser salvata *togliendo* la virgola dopo ακρα e *transportandola* dopo υλωδης, e traducendo—quindi viene il promontorio, che forma l' alta e selvosa estremità della gran Sirte— dovendosi riputare quell' alto non all' altezza del capo, che non quadra col vero, ma alla *distanza* che divide l'estremità della gran Sirte dal suo fondo. In questo stesso senso la voce υψηλη trovasi spesso adoperata da Omero per dinotare *gli sfondi del mare nelle terre.*"

. . . ως οτε κυμα ακτη

Εφ' υψηλη οτε κινηστει Νοτος ελθων, &c.—(V. da Tripoli, p. 54.)

Sopra questa osservazione converra correggere la bellissima carta di Arrow-Smith, ove la schiera de' monti del Goriano son disposti in maniera de far credere che tra il capo Mesurata, ove in quella carta si pretendono è la piccola Sirte, vi sia un' ampia e non interrotta pianura. Ora, non solo da questi monti si stacca un ramo che la interrompe, e viene a cadere scosceso sul mare a Lebda; ma di più, il loro prolungamento fino al Capo Mesurata è falso.—(p. 53-4.)

In illustration of these remarks, we need only refer our readers to the chart of the Expedition prefixed, which we may add has been carefully made; but we must observe, in justice to the compilers of those excellent maps which are published in the name of Mr. Arrowsmith, that no blame can be reasonably attached to them, either for the extension or the omission alluded to. They could only avail themselves of the best authorities hitherto existing, and ought not to be made responsible for more than these actually contain.

The rocky land which we have mentioned, and the sea, form the boundaries of the sand-hills to the northward.

The south-eastward would be more correct, for the coast there begins to trend to the southward.

A more comfortless scene can scarcely be imagined than is presented by the opening of this celebrated region, so little known at any period of history. The opinion which the ancients appear to have formed of it may be inferred from the description of Lucan, in his account of Cato's march across it (Pharsalia, book 9.); but it will be seen, as we advance into the regions of the Syrtis, that this description is more poetical than just.

"Those which I saw, ann. 1724 and 1725, were much bigger than our common grasshoppers, and had brown-spotted wings, with legs and bodies of a bright yellow. Their first appearance was towards the latter end of March, the wind having been for some time from the south. In the middle of April their numbers were so vastly increased, that in the heat of the day they formed themselves into large and numerous swarms, flew in the air like a succession of clouds, and, as the prophet Joel expresses it, (ii. 10,) they *darkened the sun*. When the wind blew briskly, so that these swarms were crowded by others, or thrown one upon another, we had a lively idea of that comparison of the Psalmist (Psalm cix. 23), of being *tossed up and down as the locust*. In the month of May, when the ovaries of those insects were ripe and turgid, each of these swarms began gradually to disappear, and retired into the Mettijiah, and other adjacent plains, where they deposited their eggs. These were no sooner hatched, in June, than each of the broods collected itself into a compact body, of a furlong or more in square; and marching afterwards directly forward towards the sea, they let nothing escape them, eating up everything that was green and juicy; not only the lesser kinds of vegetables, but the vine likewise, the fig-tree, the pomegranate, the palm, and the apple-tree—*even all the trees of the field*, (Joel i. 12,)—in doing which *they kept their ranks like men of war*, climbing over, as they advanced, every tree or wall that was in their way; nay, they entered into our very houses and bed-chambers, like *so many thieves*. The inhabitants, to stop their progress, made a variety of pits and trenches all over their fields and gardens, which they filled with water; or else they heaped up therein heath, stubble, and such like combustible matter, which they severally set on fire upon the approach of the locusts. But this was all to no purpose; for the trenches were quickly filled up, and the fires extinguished by infinite swarms succeeding one another; whilst the front was regardless of danger, and the rear pressed on so close that a retreat was altogether impossible. A day or two after one of these broods was in motion, others were already hatched to march and glean after them, gnawing off the very bark and the young branches of such trees as had before escaped with the loss only of their fruit and foliage. So justly have they been compared by the prophet Joel (ii. 3,) to a *great army*; who further observes, that *the land is as the garden of Eden before them, and behind them a desolate wilderness.*"

"Having lived near a month in this manner, like a μυριοστομον ξιφος, or *sword with ten thousand edges*, to which they have been compared, upon the ruin and destruction of every vegetable substance that came in their way, they arrived at their full growth, and threw off their nympha-state, by casting their outward skin. To prepare themselves for this change, they clung by their hinder feet to some bush, twig, or corner of a stone, and immediately, by using an undulating motion, their heads would first break out, and then the rest of their bodies. The whole transformation was performed in seven or eight minutes; after which they lay for a small time in a torpid, and seemingly languishing, condition; but as soon as the sun and the air had hardened their wings, by drying up the moisture that remained upon them, after casting their sloughs, they re-assumed their former voracity, with an addition both of strength and agility. Yet they continued not long in this state before they were entirely dispersed, as their parents were before, after they had laid their eggs; and as the direction of the marches and the flights of them both was always to the northward, and not having strength, as they have sometimes had, to reach the opposite shores of Italy, France, or Spain, it is probable they perished in the sea; a grave which, according to these people, they have in common with other winged creatures."

Psidias apud Boch. Hieroz. par. ii. p. 441.

Diodorus has given a very interesting description of the mode of catching locusts practised by the Acridophagi (or locust-eaters), as well as of the dreadful consequences produced by a too frequent use of them as articles of food.

The time when we observed the swarm of locusts alluded to above, was in the latter end of November; their course, as Dr. Shaw has remarked, was, however, invariably towards the sea, in which myriads of them were lost; and we have never seen a single instance, on other occasions, where they did not take that direction, however far they might have been inland.

Nat. Hist. lib. xi. c. 29.

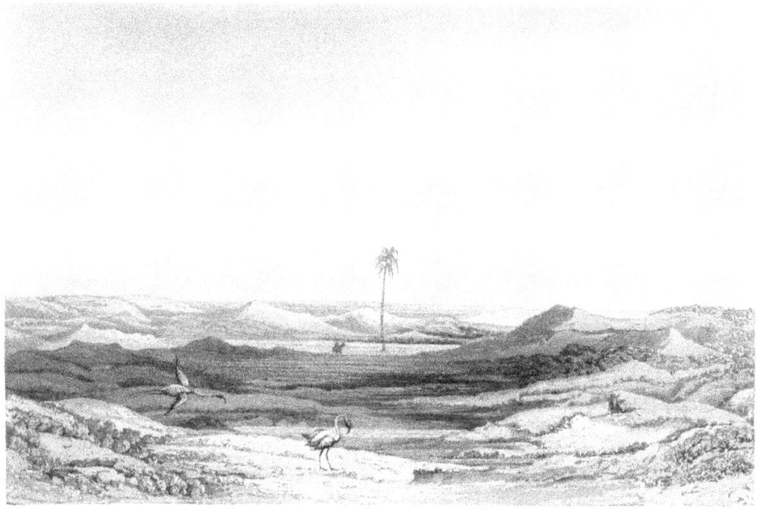

Engraved from a Drawing taken on the spot by H. Beechey.

SOLITARY PALM TREE AT ARAR. REMARKABLE AS BEING THE ONLY TREE FOUND IN THE LYOTIS. *Published March 1827, by John Murray, London.*

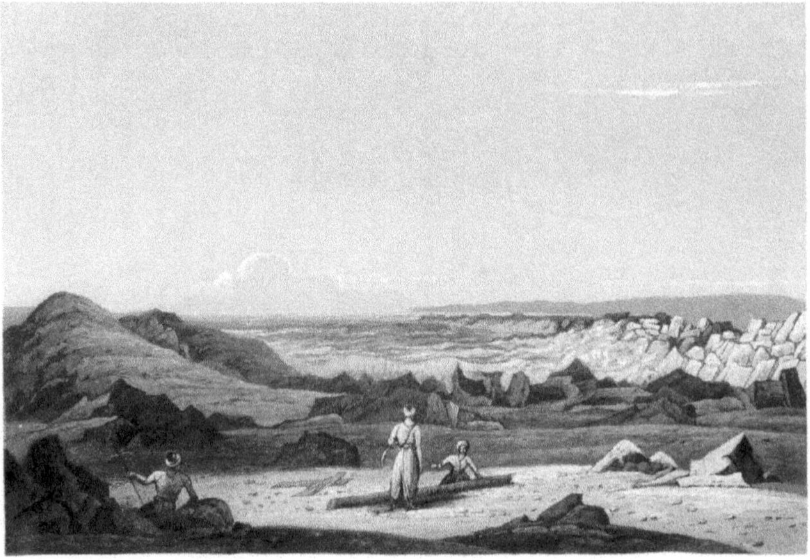

Engraved from a Drawing taken on the spot by H. Beechey.
FORMIDABLE APPEARANCE OF THE COAST AT ZAFFRAN.
Published March 1827, by John Murray, London.

CHAPTER VI.

Entrance of the Syrtis — Extensive Lake, or Marsh, described by Strabo — Remarks of Strabo compared with the actual appearance and extent of the Marsh — Remains considered as those of the ancient Naval Station, described by Strabo, at the Mouth of the Lake — Appearance of another Station more to the northward — Gulf of Zuca — Remarks of Signor Della Cella connected with it — Resemblance of the names Zuchis and Zuca — Non-existence of the Gulf of Zuca in the Greater Syrtis — Error of D'Anville and modern Geographers on this point — Remarks of Signor Della Cella on the terms *Marsh* and *Lake*, as applied to the body of water mentioned by Strabo — Dimensions of the existing Marsh — Alleged danger of crossing it — Insulated spots in several parts of the Marsh, corresponding with the accounts of Strabo — Arrival at Sooleb — Appearance of Pasturage in this neighbourhood — Liberality of Shekh Mahommed — Cause of it ascertained — Sooleb occupies the place assigned in modern charts to the Gulf of Zuca — Continuance of the Marsh — Remains near Mahada called Kusser el Jébbah — Story connected with them related by the Dúbbah — Unwillingness of our Arab Guides to cross the Marsh — Cause of this ascertained — Narrow escape of two of our party — Nature of the soil in this neighbourhood — French Inscription left by the boats of the Chevrette — Another left by the barge of the Adventure — Arrive at Mahàd Hassàn, probably the Turris Hassàn of Edrisi — Remains at Mahàd Hassàn — Arrive at Giraff, where the Marsh terminates altogether — Refractory conduct of our Camel-drivers — Improvement in the appearance of the country — Arrival at Zaffràn — Grateful verdure of its Pasturage — Remains at Zaffràn considered as those of Aspis — Their nature and appearance described — Port called Mersa Zaffràn considered as that of Aspis — Difficulties attending this position — Remains on the Beach — Supposed Date of the Buildings at Zaffràn — Remarks connected with them — Castles mentioned by Leo Africanus — Construction of the Forts at Zaffràn.

ON quitting the groves and gardens of Mesurata for the wilds of the Greater Syrtis, the first object which presents itself, in the level tract of country already mentioned, is the extensive marsh described by Strabo as occurring after the Cephalas Promontorium. It has not now the character of an uninterrupted sheet of water, as it appears to have had when seen by this geographer, but spreads itself in pools over a wide tract of country, and communicates occasionally with the sea. Many of these pools, are, however, some miles in extent, and were they deep enough would deserve the appellation of lakes. When we passed along the marsh the rainy *season* had not commenced although a good deal of rain had fallen, and it is probable that, at the close of it, the greater number of the pools are collected into much larger masses. While at Tripoly, Shekh Mahommed was anxious for our departure chiefly on account of this morass, which he represented as being very dangerous, if not wholly impassable, after the long continuance of heavy rains. The dimensions given by Strabo are three hundred stadia for the length, and seventy for the breadth of the marsh, or lake, which he describes; and these measurements correspond quite sufficiently with the appearance of that which actually exists; its length, from Mesurata to Sooleb, being little less than forty miles, and its breadth, from the sea inland, from nine and ten to fifteen. It does not indeed finish wholly at Sooleb, but is contracted in passing that place, to the narrow limits of two and three miles in width, and then continues as far as Giraff. The great body of the marsh may however be considered as contained between Sooleb and Mesurata; for though it extends much further in length and widens itself again after passing the former place, there is no part where it presents so broad, and uninterrupted a surface, as in the space comprehended within the measurements of Strabo, beginning from the Cephalas Promontorium.

Strabo's lake is stated to have enclosed several islands and to have possessed an υφορμος or naval station, at the point of communication with the Gulf. Several insulated spots are certainly still observable in various parts of the existing marsh; but there are no remains of building which can be attributed to the station mentioned, except those which occur in the neighbourhood of Mesurata. At the distance of about nine miles from that place, are the remains of a kind of causeway of singular construction, extending inland to a length of three hundred and thirty paces from the sea; and forming, with a rising ground on the opposite side of it, what may be called a στομα or communication with the Gulf. The ruins appear to be those of a landing-place; and consist of a long causeway, or terrace, of about ten feet in breadth, which widens itself at regular intervals into squares, from which descend flights of steps on either side of the causeway. One end of it is washed by the sea, which has undermined it considerably, and the whole structure is now little more than a heap of ruins.

If this building have not been a landing-place or quay, we must confess that we know not what use to assign to it; and, admitting it to have been one, it immediately becomes evident that it must have been connected with some station for shipping.

The general character of the land along this part of the coast, which rises higher than the level of the lake or morass, would prevent any communication between the marsh and the sea except in this place and the one which we are about to mention. In this place, particularly, such connexion seems formerly to have existed; for here a passage still remains, through the higher land forming the separation, by means of which the waters of the lake might have emptied themselves into the sea, and on one side of this channel is the structure in question which we have supposed to be a landing place. The small vessels of the ancients might have entered this passage, and have found sufficient shelter behind the high land which formed it; on the inner side of which they might also have been hauled up when the current through the channel was too strong for them to remain afloat.

Nearer to Mesurata, a little to the southward of the Marábūt of Sidy Abou Shaifa, are the remains of what seem to have been a small fort or station: its outer walls enclose a square of about an hundred feet and there are vestiges of smaller walls within, which appear to have divided it into several compartments. On the north-western side there are some small blocks of stone, about two feet square, which seem to have been the abutments of arches formerly supporting the roof of the building; and which are about eight feet distant from each other. These remains, forming at present nothing more than an imperfect ground-plan, are situated on a low rising ground close to the sea; and between them and point Abou Shaifa the lake may have communicated with the gulf a little to the southward of the point. There are also some slight remains of building in the neighbourhood of this place, as well as in that of the causeway, occupying the low range which runs along the coast: but from the presence of the landing-place, at the communication first mentioned, we should be disposed to adopt it in preference to that at Abou Shaifa, as the στομα, or mouth, of the lake mentioned by Strabo.

Signor Della Cella, in stating that the lake or marsh which we have mentioned, is the same with that laid down by D'Anville and other modern geographers, under the title of Gulf of Zuca, or Succa, has instanced the passage above quoted from Strabo in confirmation of this opinion. But the Gulf of Zuca is represented as an inlet, or creek, of not more than four miles across in any part of it; while Strabo's lake is in width more than double that distance, and seems to bear no other resemblance to the gulf than that of having a communication with the sea. If, therefore, the Gulf of Zuca, as D'Anville himself has stated, be actually laid down on the authority of Strabo, we should rather look for its origin in another passage of this geographer which occurs before the one we have quoted. In this passage Strabo describes a Lake Zuchis, to which he attributes the peculiarity of a narrow entrance at the point of communication with the sea; while he merely states, in his description of the lake we have first mentioned, that it emptied itself into the Gulf (of the Greater Syrtis).

The similarity of the names of Zuchis and Zuca and the narrow width which is given to the latter would certainly appear to be in favour of our suggestion; but then the Lake Zuchis is in the *Lesser* Syrtis, near the town of the same name which Strabo has mentioned as being famous for its purple dye and its saltworks; and in pointing it out as that intended by D'Anville, we must suppose that this geographer has confounded the two passages of Strabo, and, consequently, the two lakes, together. As this, however, appears (at least to us) very probable, from the reasons which we have mentioned above, we will submit to our readers the two passages in question, on which our supposition is founded, and proceed to consider the lake first alluded to as wholly distinct from the Gulf of Zuca, to which it has really no sufficient resemblance to authorize us in supposing them to be the same.

We may state at the same time, in positive terms, that no inlet now exists in any part of the Greater Syrtis which resembles the Gulf of Zuca in question; and that it might certainly be altogether expunged from the charts, without the least impropriety; unless indeed its position be shifted from the Greater, to the Gulf of the Lesser, Syrtis.

It must be confessed, at the same time that the reasoning of Signor Della Cella on the words λιμην and υφορμος does not appear to be very satisfactory; for even if we allow that the precise meaning of υφορμος may be open to conjecture, it seems evident that it implied a shelter of some kind for vessels, whether or not it might be considered to mean actually a port; which is the signification that we should be disposed to attach to it in the passage of Strabo in question. We do not, either, see why the word λιμνη in the same passage may not be rendered lake, as well as marsh; for it is certainly used in that sense in many instances as well by Strabo as other Greek writers; and there seems to be no reason why the marsh which we are describing may not have been in Strabo's time a lake, particularly as he mentions it to have had a naval station (υφορμος) at its entrance, which could scarcely have been the case had it been nothing more than a marsh.

As a general description of the marsh above mentioned, we should say that it commences at Mesurata, and extends southward along the coast as far as Giraff; occupying altogether a space of 101 miles by 15, and narrowing towards its southern termination. A small part of the marsh only was covered with water when we crossed it; but from the alternate laminæ of salt and alluvial deposite as well as from the numerous small shells principally of the trochus kind, which cover its surface, it is evident that the sea at times wholly inundates it. Our guides were always desirous that we should not deviate from the track, and were constantly representing to us the danger there was of sinking, with all the usual hyperbole of Arab description. As we suspected, however, that they only made difficulties in order to save themselves the trouble of attending us in our excursions, we paid but little attention to their observations of this nature; and continued to cross the marsh, whenever our duties rendered it necessary that we should examine either the coast or the country beyond it, taking no other precautions than those of keeping in such places as appeared to ourselves to offer the firmest footing. The crusted surface occasionally gave way under our horses' feet, and discovered hollow spaces of various depths underneath, at the bottom of which appeared water: but as none of our party ever sank in very deeply, we concluded that these hollows were too trifling to be dangerous, and continued to cross the marsh wherever it seemed practicable, till experience at length convinced us that a portion of truth was mixed up with the exaggerated accounts of our guides, and induced us to use more precaution.

Many insulated spots, both of earth and of sand, are conspicuous in different parts of the marsh; and most of these places are honoured with a name by their Mahometan visitors or occasional inhabitants. The road, if such we may call it, either winds along the margin of these little islands, or traverses them, when necessary for greater security. The first of these which occurs, after leaving Mesurata, is the little oasis called Towergah; lying out of the track at a distance of seven or eight miles from the coast: it has a village, and a considerable plantation of date-trees.

A little beyond this is said to be another small insulated spot called Wady Halfa, where date-trees are also to be found; but this was not in sight from the immediate neighbourhood of the coast. The surface of the marsh, in the direction of these places, presents a smooth, unvaried level, as far as the eye can reach, wholly destitute of any vegetation; it consists entirely of an incrustation of salt and alluvial deposit. In following the route along the coast, the first rising ground which occurs, of any tolerable dimensions, is Melfa; where are the remains of an old, dilapidated Marábūt, and occasionally a patch of vegetation, affording a scanty supply to a few miserable-looking goats.

To this succeeds Sooleb, which we have already pointed out as the southern limit of the marsh, according to the dimensions given by Strabo; and where that part of the low ground, which could, at any time, be covered with water, is too narrow to interfere with the general character of the geographer's lake. Sooleb has the advantage of some tolerable pasturage, and is in consequence occupied by flocks of sheep and goats, the property of several Arab Shekhs, and which are chiefly tended by negro slaves, who dwell in scattered tents with the animals confided to their charge. The sight of a little vegetation was by no means unwelcome to us after the dismal prospect afforded by the barren flats we had just passed; and the dreary uncultivated wilds of Sooleb assumed, by comparison, some appearance of interest, to which Salisbury plain or Newmarket heath might perhaps be more justly entitled; and which a draught or two of milk, that we were able to procure there, may probably have in some degree contributed to heighten. This refreshment was here more peculiarly welcome, as the water of Sooleb is too bitter, brackish, and stinking, to be drank without the greatest disgust: the purchase of a lamb, also, added meat to our board, which we had not tasted since we left Mesurata. In addition to these luxuries, we received a present from Shekh Mahommed, of a bowl of cuscusu, and another of bazeen; and his liberality was equally extended to the whole of our party.

We were at a loss, when the smoking dishes were ushered into our tent, escorted by no less a person than the Dúbbah himself, to conjecture what could possibly have occurred to occasion this display of Arab munificence; but we soon learnt that Sooleb was the northern limit of the district of Syrt, and that we had entered the territory over which the Dúbbah presided; who had in consequence taken these means of making us acquainted with the circumstance, and of testifying his friendly disposition, together with his magisterial importance.

After quitting Sooleb, which, we may here observe, occupies the place assigned in modern charts to the Gulf of Zuca, we entered again upon marshy ground, and continued our route to Maháda; a tract of rising ground about forty or fifty feet above the level of the marsh, and terminating in a declivity towards the sea, and in perpendicular cliffs on its inland extremities. Near Maháda we perceived the remains described in Della Cella as those of an old castle. They are situated on a spot of rising ground surrounded by a dangerous marsh, and can only be safely approached by following the few narrow tracks winding along the edges of the hollows which abound in it. This building is a *gusser*, or *kusser*, highly venerated by the Arabs of the Syrt, and takes its name of Gusser el Jebha from the son of a celebrated Marábūt, of whom Shekh Mohammed related to us the following story.

Sinessah, a holy man of the neighbouring territory of Esha, possessed of great influence and property, bequeathed to the inhabitants of Esha and Sooleb, some three hundred years since, the privilege of paying no tribute or duty: this charter, we were assured, has continued to the present time, and is said to be still respected by the Bashaw, and to extend itself to the posterity of these people, whether they settle in their native places, or in any other part of the country between Mesurata and Syrt.

Jebha, the son of this celebrated Marábūt, conceived the project of establishing a convenient communication between the two lakes, or marshes, or, more properly speaking, between the two parts of the same marsh, and fixed upon the rising ground which is occupied by the gusser as the spot best qualified for the purpose. He accordingly made known this proposal to his friends, and conducted a little party to establish themselves on the eminence.

But the people of Tówergah, aware of this intention, and jealous of the colony about to be planted by Jebha, stole upon them in the night, and attacking them unexpectedly, massacred the whole of the party. To commemorate the project of the unfortunate Jebha, and the tragical event which attended it, the little structure in question was raised by the people of Esha, and called after the name of their benefactors; while he, and the party which accompanied him, were buried round the consecrated building. Gusser el Jebha consists of three narrow, vaulted chambers, parallel and communicating with each other, and which are entered by a door in the central one.

They are about twenty feet in length, and no more than five in breadth, and are rudely constructed with unhewn stones arranged with tolerable regularity. The cement is mud with a little mixture of lime, and the vaulted ceilings are coated with plaster from the spring of the arch upwards, and ornamented with a pattern raised from the surface; the lower parts of the interior walls are at present wholly bare, and do not appear to have been coated. The outer parts of the building are now a mass of ruin, and the form of the external roof is not to be ascertained; at least we were not able to make it out.

A day or two before our arrival at Jebha, Chaous Mahmoud, one of the Arabs of the Dúbbah's party, had stoutly refused to accompany us across the marsh; but after having been severely reprimanded, and threatened with the loss of his pay, the punishment most dreaded by an Arab, he consented to go, provided we would allow him to leave his own horse with the camels, and take one belonging to our party.

This arrangement being acceded to, we trotted on in advance, telling him to follow as soon as he was mounted; but he continued to busy himself about the saddle and stirrups, making one little difficulty after another, till we were nearly out of sight; and then, mounting the horse which he had exchanged for his own, he galloped round the marsh in another direction, to meet us as we arrived on firmer ground.

On coming up with us he began to make excuses for his conduct, and declared, like a true Arab, that his life was at our service, and that he was ready to risk it for us on all occasions; but his horse, he said, was his friend and companion, and he could not bear the idea of losing him in the marsh, which he was certain he should have done if he had rode him across it in the direction which we had pointed out. His regard for our property had at the same time, he added, prevented him from risking the horse he then rode, and not any regard for his own personal safety, which was at all times indifferent to him in the performance of his duty. Perceiving, however, that this gasconade, delivered with all the vehemence which he could muster for the occasion, was not producing the effect which he desired, he called the Prophet to witness the truth of his assertions, and swore that we had had a most miraculous escape in having been enabled to reach the ground we then stood upon in safety. There was nothing to be said against such solemn asseverations; and we contented ourselves with telling him, in the language of his own religion, that what is destined to happen cannot be averted; that there was no occasion to fear, either for his horse or himself, if the time of their deaths were not come; and that if the fatal hour had really arrived, no precautions whatever could retard it.

At the same time we declared that the marsh, in our opinion, was not so dangerous as he had represented, and that we thought he might cross it, in most directions, without incurring the charge of tempting Providence too far. Mahmoud shook his head as if he did not believe it, but said no more upon the subject; and he perhaps thought we were more obstinate than wise in having so often refused to be regulated by his advice.

Repeated success will, however, at all times give confidence, even under the consciousness of danger; and it is not to be wondered at that we should so often have attempted the passage of the marsh, believing, as we did, that there was little risk in doing so. But an accident which occurred in the neighbourhood of Jebha convinced us that more caution was necessary on these occasions; and we were afterwards surprised, not only at our numerous escapes, but at our want of penetration in not having sooner perceived the danger to which the nature of the marsh had exposed us. It is probable that the frequent attempts of our guides to excuse themselves from any service of difficulty or exertion, had prepared us to distrust them on all subjects equally, and to overlook dangers for no other reason than because they were mentioned to us by them. Truth is so little regarded by an Arab, that when his interest or his comfort will be promoted by a breach of it, he is always prepared with a falsehood; and it is difficult, even for those who are well acquainted with his character, to tell when he is sincere in his assertions. One of two things must necessarily result from this want of proper feeling: they who place too much confidence in Arab sincerity will continually be deceived and imposed upon, or they who distrust it too far will on some occasions be liable to wish that they had been less obstinate in their disbelief.

As two of our party were making their way across the marsh (a few days after the conversation just related) to something which bore the appearance of a ruin, the ground suddenly gave way beneath the feet of the foremost horse, and discovered a hollow of ten or twelve feet in depth, at the bottom of which appeared water. The animal, who was galloping at the time, feeling the insecurity of his footing, sprang violently forward with all the energy of terror, and by this sudden exertion saved himself and his rider from destruction; for it would not have been possible to extricate either from such a place, had there even been more persons at hand to attempt it: the ground continued to crack and break away for some distance farther, as the horse galloped on from the hole, and a large aperture was soon formed in the crusted surface of the marsh as the pieces fell in one after another. The whole extent of the danger was not at first perceived by the rider who had so narrowly escaped; but the person who was following saw the chasm which had been made, and wheeling his horse round in another direction was just in time to avoid plunging into it. As this accident occurred near the middle of the marsh, it was difficult to decide upon the best path to be pursued, the surface being everywhere in appearance the same; but, in order that the weight might be more equally divided, both riders dismounted, and continued to lead their horses till they reached a firmer place. This was however no easy matter; as the poor animals were so terrified with their repeated stumbles, that they could with difficulty be pulled along, and they trembled so violently as to be almost incapable of keeping their legs, for the surface frequently cracked and partially gave way in places which appeared to be secure, and the parties were so often obliged to alter their direction, that they almost despaired of being able to bring off their horses. After much winding and turning, this was, however, at length effected, and both horses and riders were heartily glad to find themselves once more on firm ground. Nothing was said to our guides of this accident, but it served to convince us that their apprehensions of the marsh were not groundless, and we afterwards took the precaution of dismounting when we had occasion to cross any part which was considered to be dangerous. We found on examination that many hollow spaces of considerable depth and extent existed in various parts of the marsh; and that the crust of salt and mud which covered them was sometimes no more than two inches, and an inch and a half, in thickness.

These usually occurred in the most level parts, but as the crust was everywhere in appearance the same, there were no means of ascertaining where they existed, but by breaking the surface which concealed them.

The water contained in these hollows was invariably salt, or very brackish; it was usually clear, and was in some places deep: the depth of mud below the water must also have been sometimes considerable, and the vacant space contained between the outer surface of the marsh and the water was in various instances observed to be as much as twelve and fifteen feet in depth. We had no means of ascertaining the depth of the water in the hollow alluded to above; but the space between its surface and that of the marsh appeared to be more than twelve feet, and, from the sound occasioned by the fall of the pieces into it, its depth could scarcely have been less than six or eight feet. In that part of the marsh which surrounds the Gusser el Jebha the nature of these pits is very apparent; for the ground being unequal, and overgrown with reeds and brushwood, no crust has been formed over them, and their dimensions are therefore easily ascertained. They are here very numerous, and it would be scarcely possible to escape falling into them after dark, as the paths which wind among them are sometimes not two feet in breadth, and the edges of the pits are often concealed by the vegetation which surrounds them; indeed many of these hollows are wholly overgrown, and would not be perceived by a casual observer. In crossing to the Gusser, we could not at first account for the obstinacy of our horses in refusing to quit the path, which to us appeared to wind in a most unnecessary manner, and made our ride five or six times as long as it would have been if we could have crossed to the ruin in a straight direction. But we soon found that the animals were more quick-sighted than ourselves, and that the brushwood through which we attempted to push them concealed pits of the nature already described, from many of which we could in all probability have never been extricated, had we persevered in the attempt to force our horses into them.

In our journey along the beach abreast of Maháda, we passed many fragments of wrecks which the violence of the surf had thrown far upon the shore; and observed a block of marble erected near the sea, with the following inscription:—

LA GABORE DU ROI

LA CHEVRETTE

1821.

LAT. 31° 35', LONG. 13° 18'.

This had evidently been placed by the crew of the Chevrette, which had quitted Tripoly a few months before, to survey the gulf of the Greater Syrtis; and we afterwards learned that one of the boats of this vessel had been round it.

In order to compare longitudes with Captain Gautier who commanded the Chevrette, an able and scientific officer, a base was measured at this place, and reduced to the spot where the block of marble was erected; both were then reduced to the conspicuous position of Gusser el Jebha, and the comparisons were very satisfactory. A few miles farther, we perceived a piece of timber placed upright on the beach, and on examining it found some writing upon it in English, which stated that, on the 24th of October, His Majesty's ship Adventure was lying eighteen miles to the northward of it. This we knew must have been left by the barge of the Adventure, which had been despatched by Captain Smyth, under the command of Mr. Elson, to proceed along the coast as far as it might be practicable; and we were glad to perceive, in these dreary and desolate regions, some traces of our English friends. Our party was soon collected round this old shattered post, and every one employed in searching for more writing, with all the eagerness of an antiquary poring over some valuable inscription. Nothing more was, however, to be discovered, and we took our leave of it with an interest at which we could not help smiling, when we looked at the ragged piece of timber which had excited it. On the evening of this day we pitched the tents at Jereed, a name bestowed by the Arabs upon some low and barren hills of sand-stone, for everything with them has a name: off this place lie some dangerous shoals, which broke, although the sea was tolerably quiet. As the wind was blowing on shore, and the shoals beginning to shew themselves distinctly, we were desirous of remaining a day at Jereed, in order to mark their direction more minutely in the chart, particularly as it appeared, from the erection of the post above mentioned, that Captain Smyth had left the coast; but we found upon inquiry, that our horses would in this event be four days without drinking, and we were consequently obliged to proceed. We continued our route along the base of a low ridge of hills, at the back of which we observed a continuation of the great marsh, which was here very considerably narrowed; and arrived in the evening at Mahad Hassan, a little oasis which rises from the bed of the marsh, and consists of a few hills partially covered with pasturage. In the valleys between these we observed some wild olive-trees, and many remains of buildings were scattered over the ground in all directions. Mahad Hassan is the first place after the long tract of marshy land which has any appearance of an ancient site. Its remains consist of a number of small quadrangular buildings, similar to the fortresses observable at the different stations all the way from this point to Derna. They are in a very dilapidated state, and it is difficult to say for what purpose they were intended. They seem to be too numerous and too close together to have been forts, though their form very closely resembles them; and they are by no means well calculated for dwelling-houses, unless we suppose it to have been necessary that every family should have its castle, unconnected with that of its neighbour, in which it was regularly intrenched. These little structures occupy the plains as well as the rising ground, and are in general from fifty to seventy and a hundred feet square; their height cannot now be ascertained, even from a computation of the quantity of rubbish with which each is surrounded, for the Arabs remove the stones to different places in the neighbourhood to build the rude tombs of their Marábūts and relations; many of which are raised on the site of the buildings themselves, and might sometimes be confounded with the original plan. Shrubs and bushes have overgrown the greater part of these ruins, and rooted themselves firmly in the masses of fallen stones, frequently at the height of twelve and fifteen feet from the ground. None of them are at present more than rude heaps of shattered stones, and the eye in passing over the spot would scarcely detect any regular plan, which is only indeed observable on attentive examination. Among the buildings may be seen a few wells, in one of which we had been told we should probably find a little sweet water, a luxury we had not enjoyed since we left Arár, as the water in the marshy ground is both salt and stinking. We were rather disappointed, however, on reaching it, to find that we had been anticipated by our Arab escort, who had rode on before on pretence of reconnoitring the country, and of endeavouring to procure some provision. It was evident at the same time, by the print of their horses' hoofs, that they had not been contented with allaying their own thirst, but had satisfied also that of their horses, till the last drop of water was expended. At Mahad Hassan we found an Arab tent, and managed to procure a little milk from an old woman who dwelt in it with her two sons. These people were the only living things we had seen, jackalls, gazelles, and water-fowl excepted, since we quitted the little encampment at Sooleb. Sixteen miles south of Mahad Hassan, the marsh finishes at Giraff; we arrived there on the night of the 11th, and pitched the tents upon some sand-hills bordering a plain thickly covered with low brushwood, which extended as far as the eye could reach, and from its green appearance seemed to promise some signs of habitation. Our journey across the marsh had been monotonous and uninteresting in the extreme; no objects had appeared to enliven the scene, and no sounds were heard but the voices of our own camel-drivers, and the tiresome unvaried songs of our Arab escort, which usually consisted of no more than three or four words, repeated eternally without any change of tone, and apparently without the consciousness of the performers themselves.

The only sounds which broke in upon the stillness of the night were the prayers of our friend the Dúbbah as he chanted them at intervals in a low and drousy tone, and the howlings of his namesakes, who prowled about the tents, occasionally mingled with the shriller cries of the jackalls.

We had passed a tolerably comfortable night at Giraff, and were preparing to proceed early on our journey the following morning, when, to our no small surprise, we found that the camel-drivers refused to load their camels, and, on inquiring the cause of this strange behaviour, we were told they would not proceed any farther, unless we paid them their wages each day in advance. As this had not been our agreement with the Shekh of Mesurata, who had hired them for us at that place, we refused to comply with this ill-timed demand, for which there appeared to be no reason whatever. We well knew the impolicy of paying Arabs in advance, which is in fact giving up the best hold which can be acquired upon their conduct; and had the demand been even made with a much better grace, we should not certainly have complied with it. In the present case we refused it most decidedly, and told the mutineers that we should abide by our agreement and expected that they would keep theirs: we added that we were determined at all events to proceed, and that if they persisted in refusing to load the camels we should do so without farther ceremony ourselves. They made no reply, but instead of doing their duty, they all walked away together to a little eminence a few yards distant, where they were presently joined by all our Arab escort, with the exception of the Dúbbah; and began to prime their guns very ceremoniously, charging such of them with ball as did not happen to be already loaded. We took no other notice of this Arab manœuvre than by having our own fire-arms in readiness, and proceeded immediately to load the camels ourselves, in which we were assisted by the Bashaw's Chaous, the Dúbbah all the while recommending us to comply with the demands of the malcontents. This we told him, however, we were determined not to do; and reproached him at the same time with the unfriendly part which he was himself taking on the occasion. It here became evident how little dependence was to be placed upon Shekh Mahommed el Dúbbah and his company, and we were glad to have discovered this circumstance so early, as it might prevent us from relying upon their co-operation, in cases of greater importance. We did not much expect that the Arabs would proceed to extremities, but our party, at all events, was quite as strong as theirs, and we were determined to carry our point. When the Camels were loaded, and we were about to drive them off, the warmth of our opponents had abated; for an Arab very easily makes up his mind to submission when he finds that the chances are not greatly in his favour; and they followed our party without offering further resistance, resuming by degrees their customary occupations. A little beyond Giraff is a small ravine or wady, called Ghebaiba, the banks of which present the only cultivation which is to be found in this neighbourhood; and near it, on a little rising ground, are the remains of some building, too much in ruin to admit of any satisfactory description, and which bears the same name as the wady. As we passed over the plain which occurs after Giraff, the country began to assume a more pleasing aspect. Instead of the dreary, level surface of the marsh over which we had lately travelled, we now passed over a succession of undulating ground, covered with pasturage, among which appeared flocks of sheep and goats, and here and there an Arab tent. But the most welcome objects which this change of soil afforded were the wells of sweet water which presented themselves at Zaffran, near one of which we encamped for the night; and after a few copious draughts, we soon forgot the nauseous flavour of that which we had lately been drinking, which nothing but necessity could have induced any one to swallow. We drew plentifully from the wells, which were very deep, and allowed our horses and camels to drink freely; a luxury which the poor animals had not enjoyed since leaving Mesurata, as their allowance even of the bad water had been necessarily limited, and for the last four days they had been without any. This privation, though not unusual in the Syrtis, was nevertheless severely felt by both horses and camels; and their breath during these intervals, particularly that of the camel, became extremely heated and offensive.

It is in this neighbourhood that we must look for the Aspis of Strabo, which is mentioned by that geographer as occurring *after* the lake, and for a port which he describes as the best in the Syrtis. "After the lake (are his words) is a place (called) Aspis, and a port (which is) the best of those in the Syrtis." The first remains of building which occur after Sooleb (where the great body of the lake has already been said to finish) are those at Mahád Hassan, which is evidently an ancient site. To these remains succeed those of Zaffran, which are more important, and are placed in a much more desirable situation. They occur immediately after Giraff where the marsh finishes altogether, and are situated in a country abounding with pasturage, and furnished with a plentiful supply of sweet water. Zaffrán has been evidently a military station; and it is there that we began to perceive more clearly the nature of those numerous quadrangular buildings which are scattered in all directions over the Syrtis, in passing from Sooleb to Bengazi. These structures may be said to commence at Mahad Hassan; but they assume at Zaffran the appearance of regular forts, and may there be considered as the commencement of a chain of fortified posts extending itself through the whole of the Syrtis. They usually occupy the higher grounds, although some of them are situated in the plains, and are generally so placed as to have been originally seen from each other. Indeed no opportunity appears to have been neglected by the ancients of securing the advantages of pasturage and water which occur in the regions of the Syrtis; wherever these exist we find fortresses erected, or regular stations established, which would materially contribute to facilitate the march of troops and to prevent at the same time the predatory incursions of the Arabs and the establishment of their tribes in these desirable positions.

If it be considered necessary to fix the sight of the τοπος Ασπις at the *first* place where remains of ancient building are found, after the lake which is laid down by Strabo, we must place it at Mahad Hassan; but if it must be identified with the port mentioned with it, which does not seem, indeed, to be necessary, we are then obliged to fix it at the first place where a port is to be met with, after the termination of the marsh, and this will bring us to Mersa Zaffran. The little port of this name is the first which occurs in passing eastward from the Cephalas Promontorium, and the remains of building which are found there, on the beach, will authorize the conclusion that it has been used as such by the ancients.

Its present appearance will however by no means entitle it to the distinction of καλλιστος, (bestowed by Strabo upon Aspis, or the port which succeeds it); for the Gulf of Syrtis, though ill supplied with conveniences of this nature, has certainly ports of more consideration than Mersa Zaffran.

We must at the same time recollect that the space required for the vessels of the ancients was much less than would be necessary for those of the present day, and the depth of water required for them comparatively inconsiderable. The port at Zaffran is also much less than formerly, and, like that at Lebida, nearly filled up with sand; so that although it cannot now be considered as a good one (nor, indeed, in the present acceptation of the term, as any port at all) it may certainly have afforded very good shelter and accommodation for vessels such as those of the ancients. The remains on the beach are constructed with larger stones than are usually employed in the Syrtis, and, from what we could perceive of them, for the tops only appear above the sand, have been built with more than common attention to workmanship and regularity. Traces of building may also be observed for nearly a mile from the Mersa to the eastward, and the whole place is strewed with fragments of pottery. Several stone troughs are lying on the beach, some of them in an unfinished state; they do not appear to have been intended for sarcophagi, as their lengths vary from five to eight feet; while their breadth remains nearly the same, or from fifteen to eighteen inches. Had our time and means allowed it we should have remained a few days to excavate at Mersa Zaffran, and we had marked it as one of the places to be examined on our return: there is little to remove but sand, and it is by no means improbable that the results of excavation at this place would be interesting. As Mersa Zaffran appears to have been used as a port by the ancients, and is the first which occurs after the marsh, we may fairly consider it as that mentioned by Strabo with Aspis; and the remains at Zaffran are probably those of Aspis itself, which we may conclude to have been a military post from the nature of the buildings which are found there; although the word τοπος applied to it by Strabo, does not necessarily imply any idea of fortification. No place worth selecting for any advantages which it might afford could, however, have been secure without some fortification; and accordingly we find every desirable position in the Syrtis provided with forts for its defence, which ensured, at once, the possession of the local advantages and a communication with the adjacent inhabited places.

It is difficult to fix any precise date to these buildings, but we may perhaps conclude, with some appearance of reason, that the greater number of them were erected by the Romans under the emperors, who possessed, at various times, the whole of the north coast of Africa, and kept open an extensive communication along the shores of the Mediterranean, as well as with some parts of the interior. The quadrangular form of these structures is the same as that used by the Romans in their stations and encampments; and the small number of troops which was allotted by the empire for the defence of Africa, made it peculiarly necessary that their garrisons should be well intrenched. It has been calculated that a square of seven hundred yards was sufficient, according to the Roman method of encampment, for containing a body of twenty thousand men; and a square of one hundred feet would, at that rate, suffice for the accommodation of nine hundred and fifty. The habitable parts of the forts above mentioned very rarely exceeded a square of that size, and this portion of the structure, in by far the greater number of them, seldom amounted to sixty feet. As the nature of the country rendered it necessary to lay up stores of provision, a part of each fortress must have been set aside for that purpose, and it is probable that the greater number of the forts did not contain more than from fifty to two hundred men. The most perfect of those now remaining may perhaps have been constructed in the time of the emperor Justinian, when the victories of Belisarius and Solomon had restored the Roman authority in Africa: for it would then have been advisable to secure, by means of forts, the advantages which arms had obtained. The privations which were experienced by the army of Marcus Cato, in its march across the regions of the Syrtis, make it appear extremely probable that no stations or resting-places, had at that time been erected within their limits; and we may perhaps also infer that the fortresses of Euphrantas and Automala were not then available as places of accommodation. Should this have been the case, some of the forts and stations now existing, in various parts of the country in question, may be reasonably attributed to the well-founded policy of the emperors Augustus and Hadrian.

A regular and uninterrupted communication was, under these princes, beginning to be firmly established with all parts of the Roman empire; and the intercourse which then existed between the eastern and western parts of Northern Africa was much greater than that which had obtained under the governments of the Greeks and Carthaginians. The numerous native tribes who inhabited the coast were perpetually at variance with their foreign invaders, and ever ready to avail themselves of the slightest opportunity of harassing their oppressors, or of recovering their ancient inheritance. It must also be observed, that, however worthless and insignificant the regions of the Syrtis might possibly appear, to the inhabitants of more favoured countries, there are parts of them which must always have been eagerly coveted by the wanderers of the desert which bounds them to the southward; since the advantages which they are occasionally found to afford, though consisting merely in a little fresh water, and a few spots of scanty vegetation, would naturally be objects of great attraction to those who had seldom the opportunity of finding either. From the sudden, but unskilful, attacks of these people, the forts and stations of the Syrtis would have been sufficient defence; and they would also have been more convenient for the troops than the usual Roman encampment, greatly contributing at the same time, to facilitate the communication of one part of the country with another, by ensuring a good supply of water, and serving as depôts for stores and provisions. We must not, however, venture decidedly to assert, that the Syrtis was unprovided with buildings of this nature before the occupation of the country by the Romans; for, without mentioning those of Euphrantas and Automala, we find that castles were in use among the natives of Northern Africa before that period; and if they are known to have been previously erected in other parts of the coast, they might equally have existed in the Syrtis.

Many buildings of this nature appear to have remained in a tenable state long after the conquest of Africa by the Mahometans; for they are frequently mentioned by Arab writers as having been occupied by the natives; and wells still continued to be found within the works, which could not be approached without the consent of the garrison.

An instance in point may here be given from Leo Africanus, who tells us that three castles were accidentally discovered, far in the desert of Libya, about eighteen years before the time when he related the following story:— "The guide of a caravan (whose name was Hámar) had missed the usual track, in consequence of a complaint in his eyes; and there being no other person in the whole caravan who knew the road they ought to take but himself, he went on, upon his camel, in advance of the party, and at every mile they made he caused a handful of sand to be presented to him, which he smelt, and then continued his journey. In this manner the caravan continued to advance till they came within forty miles of the castles above mentioned, near which there were five or six little hamlets, and a profusion of excellent dates. The guide then addressed himself to those who were about him, and assured them that they were in the neighbourhood of some inhabited place, but few of the party believed what he said, for as they were at least four hundred and eighty miles from Egypt, it was imagined, if indeed the assertion should be true, that they must have moved back upon Augela."

"On the third day, however, after this notice, they came in sight of the three castles above mentioned; and the people of the place, surprised and alarmed at the appearance of so many strangers, retreated to the castles, where they shut themselves up, and refused to supply the caravan with water, of which they were greatly in need. As the wells were within the fortifications, there was nothing left for the caravan, under these adverse circumstances, but to carry the forts, and to supply themselves by force, or to continue their journey across the desert, at the risk, perhaps the certainty, of perishing with thirst. They soon determined to make an attack upon the castles, which, after a slight engagement, they succeeded in carrying; and having obtained from the wells as much water as was necessary, they proceeded on their route across the desert."

In many of the forts which we visited in the Syrtis, one or two, and sometimes more, wells were still visible within the works (although, for the most part, they were filled up with mud and sand, or with the rubbish of the fallen materials of the buildings); and it is probable that all of them were originally provided with a convenience so essential to the garrison. In some cases we found wells decidedly without the works, in places which appeared to be wholly undefended; except we may suppose them to have been within range of the archers and slingers from the walls, which did not always appear to have been the case.

In such instances, however, we must not conclude that there were originally no wells within the forts, because none are found there at present; for a single century of neglect would in many cases be sufficient to account for the disappearance of a well altogether.

We may observe with regard to the structure of these forts, that some of them have the habitable part of the building (which is always of a quadrangular form, and placed in the centre) surrounded by a double wall of very solid work; leaving a space between the walls, of ten, twenty, and thirty feet, sometimes of more, in which wells are occasionally found, and which may have served for the accommodation of the horses, sheep, or cattle of the garrison. Others have been built in one solid mass, with sloping sides, resembling the base of a pyramid, having only a square space left in the centre for the accommodation of the troops and the stowage of stores and provision. On these there is always a platform, and sometimes two, the sides of which form a glacis at a slope of from thirty to forty-five degrees, some of them being steeper than others: it seems probable that a parapet originally existed on the platforms of some of the forts, behind which the troops might more securely encounter their enemies; but on most of them there are now no traces of any defence of this nature, and the platform is left exposed. The lower platform is usually raised about ten and fifteen feet from the ground, and the upper one about eight or twelve feet above that. Trenches are rarely seen round the last mentioned buildings, but those enclosed within walls usually possessed that additional defence. Both are constructed with stone found in the neighbourhood, generally without any cement, particularly the sloping ones, although a very good cement may sometimes be observed in them: the most considerable forts are built with large and regularly-shaped stones, while the more unimportant are composed of stones of unequal forms and sizes, care being always taken, however, to leave a smooth surface on the slope of the glacis, in order to make the ascent more difficult. If we suppose that the greater number of these fortresses were built as defences against the attacks of the predatory natives, and not to resist the regular siege of a disciplined army, it may certainly be allowed that they were well calculated to afford security to their garrisons on such occasions; but their resources must soon have been exhausted by a continued blockade, the space enclosed being inadequate to contain many stores or much provision. As, however, there could scarcely have been any accommodation for horses or cattle in the pyramidal-shaped forts, which are by far the most numerous, more provision might certainly have been stowed in them than would at first sight be imagined. From the extreme height of the habitable part of these buildings in proportion to its breadth, we may conclude that it possessed an upper story, or, it may be, two; for otherwise a great portion of space would be thrown away: this fact, however, from their ruined state, could not be properly ascertained.

The roofs were most probably arched, for no wood is to be found in the Syrtis, and large blocks of stone could not always be procured, and would at any rate have been less convenient to employ than the small ones, which might be used in the arches. From the circumstance of finding no aperture in the sides of the buildings, we may conclude that the light was admitted from above; and it is by no means improbable that a space was left uncovered in the centre for that purpose, this mode of building being common in hot climates, and it would at all times have been easy to guard against the inconvenience of rain, as the surface exposed would have been inconsiderable.

No appearance of doors, or of apertures of any kind, is observable in the sides of these structures; and they must either have been entered from the top, or by some subterranean communication. There are instances still remaining, in the eastern parts of the Syrtis, of fortresses more difficult of access than these, where they who entered have evidently been drawn up with ropes by the persons already stationed above; and we may conclude, as no traces of any subterranean entrance were discernible in the forts, which we have just described, that they were entered in a similar manner. In the walled forts we found entrances to the *outer* works by means of gates, but could in no instance discover any door in the habitable part.

We often wished for an opportunity of excavating some of these buildings, that we might be enabled to give their plans more correctly; but, as it was important to secure the coast-line before the rainy season set in, we did not think ourselves justified in delaying the advance of the party any longer than was necessary for the attainment of that object.

As a general remark, we may here observe, that, in passing from west to east of the Greater Syrtis, the fortresses were found to be more perfect as we advanced towards the Cyrenaica; their interest may be said to begin at Zaffran, to increase at Medīnét Sultàn, and to continue, from thence, in almost a regular progression, to become stronger at every step that is made towards Bengazi.

FOOTNOTES:

Εισπλεοντι δη την μεγαλην Συρτιν, ενδεξια μετα τας Κεφαλας, εστι λιμνη τριακοσίων που σταδιων το μηκος, εβδομηκοντα δε το πλατος, εκδιδουσα εις τον κολπον, εχουσα και νησια και υφορμον προ του στοματος.—Lib. 17, § 20.

The measurements are taken roughly, on account of the ruined state of the structure.

No part of this land can properly be called high—but only by comparison with the lower level of the marsh.

It was not, however, necessary, in places of this kind, that the vessels should be drawn upon shore; for υφορμος is the term here employed by Strabo, and the ορμοι, or υφορμοι, were somewhat similar to our own docks, and consisted of walls parallel with each other, between which vessels would be perfectly secure from wind and waves, as well as from the effects of strong current.

Μετα δε την Συρτιν (the Lesser Syrtis is here meant,) Ζουχις εστι λιμνη σταδιων τετρακοσιων, στενον εχουσα εισπλουν, και παρ' αυτην πολις ομωνυμος πορφυροβαφεια εχουσα και ταριχειας παντοδαπας·—(Lib. 17, § 18.)

D'Anville's words are these—"Strabon parle d'un grand lac debouchant dans la Syrte, et ce lac forme une *saline* dont l'entrée est nommée la *Succa*."—(Géog. Ancienne, tom. 3, p. 70.)

The circumstance of there being saltworks in the Mesurata lake, as well as in that of the Lesser Syrtis, will tend to strengthen the idea of their having been confounded.

We even fear that to make the reasoning of Signor Della Cella at all consistent with itself, we must be obliged to suppose that he has again stated exactly the contrary of what he appears to have intended. His words are, "Quanto alla stazione che rimaneva probabilmente alla sua imboccatura (meaning the mouth of the lake, or marsh in question). Non può realmente dirsi che fosse *porto*, servendosi Strabone della voce υφορμον per *porto* e non di λιμνη (λιμην is intended) la qual voce malamente trovasi tradutta da Buonacciuoli per *molo*. Cosi passo e passo a conto di Strabone si è fatto un porto e non è tosto mancato che le ha guarnito di molo." (p. 75-6.) As υφορμον, and not λιμην, is the word used by Strabo in the passage in question, the deduction of Signor Della Cella may scarcely be made without reversing the words as we have stated.

Strabo distinguishes between λιμην and υφορμος in the following passage—speaking of the coast of the Cyrenaica from Apollonia to the Catabathmos—ου πανυ ευπαραπλους και γαρ λιμενες ολιγοι και υφορμοι και κατοικιαι και υδρειαι.—(Lib. 17, § 22.)

Arar occurs before Melfa; but, though a good deal above the level of the marsh, it cannot well be considered as an island, but is rather a continuation of the little range of high land which we have mentioned as running along the coast in the neighbourhood of the causeway. It consists wholly of heaps of sand, overspread occasionally with vegetation, and is remarkable as possessing a tall and solitary date-tree, the only one to be met with on the coast of the Syrtis, in a tract of more than four hundred miles.

The noxious qualities of the night air in these swampy regions were occasionally severely felt by our party; one of our servants was seized with a fever while at Sooleb, and we were apprehensive that he would not be able to proceed for some days; but after being bled rather copiously he found himself better, and was the next day in condition to travel with the camels. The atmosphere after sunset was always very chilly in the Syrtis, and there was usually a heavy deposit of dew; a very offensive smell was also experienced in many parts of the marsh.

Gusser is a term indiscriminately applied by the Arabs to ruins of every description.

Monsieur Lautier has some remarks upon this part of the gulf, which do not appear to be very intelligible.—See the account of his voyage in Della Cella, p. 216. These observations are alluded to in the hydrographic remarks attached to the journal.

Edrisi has mentioned a tower called Hassān, which he places at four days' journey from the western point of the Syrtis—and Mahād Hassān is four days' journey from Mesurata, at the rate of between thirteen and fourteen geographical miles per day.

We have already stated that Shekh Mahommed was called el Dúbbah, or the Hyæna.

The camel has been known to go as much as ten days without water, but they suffer very much from an abstinence of three and four days.

Μετα δε την λιμνην τοπος εστιν Ασπις, και λιμην καλλιστος των εν τῇ Συρτει.—Lib. 17, p. 836.

Buildings of the same nature are also found in the Cyrenaica.

Aspis is laid down in Ptolemy on the western side of the gulf, at about sixty miles within the promontory of Triæorium; but this distance would only bring us within nine miles of Jaireed, and we have already stated that Mahād Hassān is the first place in the Syrtis (travelling eastward) which can be considered as an ancient site. Strabo's lake finishes at Sooleb, but there are no remains of building in the neighbourhood of that place, nor between it and Mahād Hassān.

The naval station above mentioned, at the junction of Strabo's lake with the sea, is not styled λιμην, but υφορμος; and we may conclude from this circumstance that it was formed by art, and not by any of those peculiarities of coast which usually constitute a fort.

It is formed by a rocky projection, which appeared to have been partly natural and partly artificial; and though its inconsiderable size would not allow vessels in it to ride clear of the surf in a gale of wind, yet in moderate weather there would be quite sufficient shelter for them to load and unload; and in the event of a gale they might easily have been hauled up on the beach.—See the plan of Mersa Zaffrān annexed.

The tower of Euphrantas is however stated to have been a boundary fort under the Ptolemies; and the fortress of Automala, at the bottom of the gulf, is mentioned by Diodorus to have been in existence before the occupation of Cyrene by the first of those princes.—See Strabo, lib. 17, and Diod., lib. 20.

"With regard to Egypt, Africa, and Spain, (says Gibbon, in describing the distribution of the Roman forces,) as they were far removed from any important scene of war, a single legion maintained the domestic tranquillity of these great provinces."

"We may compute (says the same writer) that the legion, which was itself a body of six thousand eight hundred and thirty-one Romans, might, with its attendant auxiliaries, amount to about twelve thousand five hundred men."

Λιβυων δε τοις ες πυργους και φρουρια (ἁ πολλα ην εν τῇ χωρα) καταφευγουσιν.—Appian Hist. de rebus Punicis, lib. viii. p. 101.

Diodorus also speaks of their castles near the watering-places.—Lib. iii. p. 128.

Τοις δε δυνασταις αυτων πολεις μεν το συνολον ουχ υπαρχουσι, πυργοι δε πλησιον των υδατων, εις ους αποτιθενται τα πλεοναζοντα της ωφηλειας.

Leo Africanus in Ramusio, quinta parte.

Arched roofs are also common in the forts of the Cyrenaica; but the sides both of the upper and lower stories, which fronted the centre, were probably left open, after the manner of galleries.

CHAPTER VII.

Remarks on the City of Sort, or Sert, of Edrisi and other Arab Geographers — Description of it by Leo Africanus — Position of Sert, on the Authority of Abulfeda — Zaffrān considered as Asna — Remarks of Major Rennell on these Places — Remains at Medīnét Sultàn considered as those of Sort — Columns and other Remains described by Signor Della Cella, in the Neighbourhood of Zaffrān — Train of Argument adopted by the Doctor on this Occasion — Remarks of the same Writer on the Tower of Euphrantas, and the Town of Charax, as laid down by Strabo — Nature of the Inscriptions on the Columns alluded to by Signor Della Cella — Formidable Appearance of the Coast at Zaffrān — General Appearance of the Country in its Neighbourhood — Species of Crocus abounding there — Obliging Treatment of our Party by the Arabs of Zaffrān — Arrival at Medīnét Sultàn — Description of its Remains — Further Remarks on the Tower of Euphrantas — Arrival at Nehīm — Aukward Situation of Shekh Mahommed el Dúbbah — Visit of the Dúbbah to our Tent — Object of it discovered — Departure of Shekh Mahommed, well pleased with the result of his Visit.

IT is in the neighbourhood of Zaffran (if the measurements of Edrisi be correct) that we must look for the remains of the city of Sort or Sert. They are placed by this geographer at two hundred and thirty Arabic, or two hundred and forty-six geographic, miles from Tripoly: at least such is the distance given in the gross; for the detail (as Major Rennell has already observed) allows no more than two hundred and ten Arabic miles, or two hundred and twenty-two geographic.

The first distance, of two hundred and forty-six geographic miles, would carry us seven miles beyond Zaffran, and within three of Jedeed, which is ten miles to the eastward of Zaffran.

The distance in detail, or two hundred and twenty-two geographical miles, would bring us within two miles of Jiraff, and fourteen beyond Mahad Hassan; while the number of days allotted by Edrisi, for the journey in question from Tripoly to Sort, which is eleven, would give a distance (on the computation of Major Rennell) of two hundred geographic miles only; and this would bring us within six miles of Mahad Hassan, that is, six miles to the westward of that place. These measurements, considered with reference to the places enumerated, would induce us to place the city of Sort either at Mahad Hassan, or at Zaffran, or perhaps in the neighbourhood of Jedeed; for it is at these places that the greatest assemblage of ruins may be observed.

To the westward of Mahad Hassan is the marsh, and at Jiraff there are nothing but sand-hills. Between Jedeed and Shuaisha there are a good many scattered ground-plans, apparently of slightly-built dwelling-houses (which seem to be those pointed out by Signor Della Cella as the remains of the Charax of Strabo,) and many insulated forts, and other scattered remains of building, may be observed on the road from Jedeed to Medīnét Sultàn.

It appears, on the authority of Leo Africanus, that there was nothing more remaining, in his time, of the city of Sort (or, as he writes it, Sert,) than a few inconsiderable vestiges of the walls; and, if this statement is to be taken literally, it will scarcely be possible to fix the site of the town with any accuracy in a tract of country where ruins abound.

We will content ourselves with repeating, that it may either be placed (upon the authority of the measurements stated above) at Mahad Hassan, at Zaffran, or in the neighbourhood of Jedeed; but if we are to fix it on the authority of Abulfeda, we must remove it further eastward, to the neighbourhood of Medīnét Sultàn, which is the spot we should ourselves prefer for it.

Abulfeda, in mentioning the remains of the city of Sort, informs us that on the *west* of them is a Gulf called Rodaik, or Rodakiah, (apparently the same) says Major Rennell (with the Zadic Sinus of Edrisi) near which stands the town of Asna, one hundred and two Arabic miles, or one hundred and eight geographic, to the south-east of the Promontory of Kanem.

The Promontory of Kanem may be considered as the western extremity of the Greater Syrtis (say the Cephalas Promontorium in the neighbourhood of Mesurata); and a distance of one hundred and eight geographical miles from Mesurata would bring us within five miles of Zaffran, that is, five miles to the west of it; for Zaffran is one hundred and thirteen miles from Mesurata. According to this measurement, we should be induced to place Asna at Zaffran, in the absence of any ruins, as we have stated above, between that place and Mahad Hassan.

The town of Asna is laid down by Edrisi at forty-six Arabic miles from the city of Sort; and this distance added to the hundred and eight above stated would bring us to the neighbourhood of Medinet Sultàn, which is one hundred and fifty-one geographic miles from Mesurata. If we suppose, with Major Rennell, that forty-six has here been substituted for twenty-six, the latter measurement would bring us to Shuaisha, where there are certainly, as we have already stated, some inconsiderable remains, but not apparently those of a town. About two miles south-east of Medinet Sultàn are decided remains, of an ancient town, called Medina, (the city) which from the circumstance we are about to mention, we should be inclined to suggest as the most eligible position (at least in our opinion) for the city of Sort.

The distance of Asna from the western point of the Syrtis, as given by Abulfeda, is found to correspond sufficiently well with that of Zaffran from Mesurata. Sort is stated to be situated to the eastward of Asna, at a distance of forty-six Roman miles from that place, according to the testimony of Edrisi; and the distance of Zaffran from Medina (forty-seven M. P.) corresponds very well with this statement, the latter place being, at the same time, to the eastward of the former.

We may add that the term Sort, or Sert, is not known at the present day to the Arabs as applied to any city or town; but is merely used to designate the tract of country which lies between Sooleb and Barca. The ruins of Medina are situated within this territory; and supposing them to be actually the remains of Sort, we may imagine that when this city lost its former name, it continued to be distinguished as *the* city, (the Medina) of the district to which its name of Sort had been transferred.

This arrangement will place the city of Sort at least forty miles to the eastward of its position according to the measurements above stated from Edrisi: but a short distance in reckoning is always preferable to a long one, and we should on that account prefer taking the distance of Sort from Asna to reckoning it from Tripoly as above. For the same reason the measurement of Abulfeda, from the Promontory of Kanem to Asna, is more likely to be correct than that of Edrisi from Tripoly to the city of Sort.

The Gulf of Rodaik (or Rodakiah) might have served to elucidate this question had there been anything like it remaining; but it will be seen, on a reference to the chart, that there is no appearance on this part of the coast which can at all be considered as a gulf; and this will of course equally apply to the Sinus Zadic of Edrisi.

We will not at present pursue this subject further, but leaving our readers to judge, from the data already given, how far we may be authorized in placing the city of Sort in the position we have ventured to suggest for it, we will proceed to notice some remains which are found in the neighbourhood of Zaffran.

In traversing this part of the Syrtis, Signor Della Cella discovered a square column of tolerable height and placed upon a pedestal. It was composed, he says, of sandstone, but so corroded by time that the characters which entirely covered its four sides had become altogether unintelligible. An hour afterwards he arrived at a second, and, after a similar interval, at a third of these erections, all equally covered with writing and so much decayed that, what with the little time which he had at his command, and the state of ruin in which the pillars were found, he could not succeed in putting together a single word of their inscriptions. "Opposite to the first of these columns" (he adds) "on the part next the sea, rise the remains of a tower surmounted with a cupola, and this spot is called Elbenia."

The Doctor confesses himself at a loss to decide for what purpose these pillars could have been erected; but suggests that, supposing Zaffran to be Aspis, the ancient tower with a cupola which is near it, and, "as Strabo says, συνεχης to Aspis," must inevitably be the πυργος, or tower named Euphrantas of that geographer. From this conclusion he is induced to suspect that, as the tower of Euphrantas was the boundary of the Cyrenaic and Carthaginian territory under the Ptolemies, the three pillars above mentioned were erected to mark the limits of those countries, as well as to record other matters which (he says) were usually engraved by the ancients on objects of this nature.

Finding his courage rise at this happy coincidence of ancient with what he terms modern geography, Signor Della Cella now assumes a more decided tone, and taking boldly for granted what he has just advanced on supposition, proceeds to deduce from it an unqualified conclusion; and this leads him into his favourite practice of scepticism, for which his deeply-rooted antipathy to all commentators and editors seems to have given him a most decided partiality.

"Encouraged by this coincidence," (are the Doctor's own words) "in my opinion, so plausible, of ancient and modern geography, I no longer hesitate to believe that the ancient ruins which we met with on the road, after three hours' journey from Elbenia, point out the spot which is called, by Strabo, Charax."

Without attempting to give the least description of these ruins, or any explanation of the reasons why he thinks they are those of Charax, the Doctor all at once proceeds to criticise the passage in Strabo, and to offer a new reading for the approbation of his friend, the professor, on the subject of the silphium and the liquor which was extracted from it. We do not pretend to any skill in logic, but the train of argument here adopted by Signor Della Cella does certainly appear to us a little extraordinary: it seems to run thus—"If Zaffran be Aspis, the tower with a cupola must be the tower of Euphrantas; and, as the tower of Euphrantas was a boundary under the Ptolemies, the three square pillars with the illegible inscriptions are also boundaries; and the ruins which are met with three hours afterwards are those of Charax, which Strabo says was used by the Carthaginians for a fair, at which the juice of the silphium was exchanged for wine; and, as I read in this passage, juice of the silphium, instead of juice and silphium; or, as Buonacciuoli very badly translates it, 'il belgioino e il silfio.'—You will agree with me (he concludes, addressing the professor) in this little alteration in the text of the Grecian geographer."

He then leaves the subject, records another march through a very hot day, and describes a visit with which he was honoured by the Bey in his tent, and the excellent supper which he made off an ostrich's egg, which His Highness in his munificence had presented him with. The supper and the chapter finish together, and the Doctor goes to sleep, without further discussion, as soon as the meal is over.

The position of Zaffran, with respect to the marsh, and to the port which bears its name, will perhaps authorize us to consider it as the Aspis of Strabo; and we have already stated the reasons why we think it not improbable that it may be: but the necessity for placing Charax and the tower of Euphrantas in the positions assigned to them by Signor Della Cella, does not seem, in our opinion, to be quite so great as the Doctor has imagined. For the tower surmounted with a cupola, which he has supposed to be the same with the tower of Euphrantas, has no pretensions whatever to half the antiquity which it would be necessary in that case to assign to it: it is in fact nothing more than a rudely-formed Arab building, and never could, at any time, have aspired to the title of tower, had it even been built under the dynasty of the Ptolemies. It appears to have been a dwelling-house, somewhat resembling the tomb of a Marábūt; but being situated on the top of a range of hills overlooking the road, it appears more important from below than could well be imagined by those who might only have examined it closely; and it is probable that the view of it which Signor Della Cella obtained, and which suggested to him the analogy between it and the tower of Euphrantas, was from the road in the plain below. It is certainly somewhat singular that, in a place where several ancient forts may be observed, the Doctor should have pitched upon an Arab building as the boundary of the Cyrenaic and Carthaginian territory; but had he even been willing to adopt one of the forts as the tower, it would have been difficult to select any one from the number which had more claim than the rest to that distinction; and there does not, in fact, appear to be any building at Zaffran sufficiently conspicuous to be considered as the structure in question.

It seems to us that the tower of Euphrantas should be looked for in some commanding situation, which either occasioned its being built, or selected as a boundary for the kingdoms we have mentioned; and there seems to be no more reason for placing it at Zaffran than at Medīnet Sultàn, where there are also many forts; except that the term συνεχης, (following upon, or succeeding to,) which Strabo uses to point out its position, would induce us to place it as soon after Aspis as circumstances would seem to allow. At all events, we do not hesitate in rejecting the "torre sormontata da una cupola" as the tower of Euphrantas; and we should much rather, if it be necessary to place this structure at Zaffran, select for its representative one of the fortresses already mentioned, than any building like that which is suggested by Signor Della Cella, were it even of ancient construction.

There is another building which stands in a conspicuous position on the same range of hills where the Doctor's tower is situated, and to which it is difficult to assign any use, unless we suppose it to have been a sepulchral or other monument, built as a conspicuous object merely. It occupies a square of about twenty feet, and could have been little more at any time than a mass of solid stone and cement, the space which is left in the centre being not more than four or five feet square, and without any apparent communication with the exterior. The height of the whole building appears to have been about thirty feet, but little more than the basement upon which it has been raised now remains; and this estimation is made from a computation of the quantity of fallen materials, and from the probable proportion of the height with the breadth given. The basement itself is six feet in height, and composed of well-shaped stones, some of which are five feet long, and from twelve to sixteen inches in height and thickness: above this no more than three feet of the superstructure now remain in any part; but the base of a pilaster, which still appears in one of the angles, proves that the exterior at least has been constructed with some attention to architectural ornament. The outer part only of this structure is *built*, the whole of the interior, with the exception of the space mentioned in the centre, having been filled up with unshaped stones deeply bedded in cement, the proportion of which is much greater than that of the rubble thrown into it.

Were it not that the base of the remaining pilaster appears to be a Saracenic imitation of the Greek, we should be disposed to allow a greater antiquity to the building in question than it seems to us from this circumstance to possess: for the stones employed in it are of good size, very regularly placed, and well finished, and the cement which has been used is excellent. Attached to this tower, for such it may be called, although it never could have been employed for military purposes, are the remains of a subterranean storehouse for grain, the roof of which is raised about a foot from the ground above it and composed of cement: between this and the tower there is a sort of well, which appears to be the entrance to the storehouse, but which was too much encumbered with rubbish to allow of our descending into it. Some traces of walls attached to the roof of the storehouse may be seen in the ground-plan annexed, but we could not determine whether either these, or the souterrain itself, were originally attached to the building.

No architectural remains could be perceived among the fallen ruins of the tower by which we might have been enabled to fix the time of its erection with more precision; and the base of the pilaster which we have mentioned at the angle of the building, is the only evidence of this nature which we could obtain.

To us this structure appears to be Saracenic; but if others should be disposed to think differently, and to adopt it as the tower of Euphrantas, the circumstance of its having (at least in our opinion) been built as an object merely without any other apparent use, might perhaps be considered by some persons, to favour the idea; and we are a little surprised that Signor Della Cella did not adopt it in preference to the building which he has pointed out.

With regard to the columns with the illegible inscriptions, which the Doctor supposes to have been boundaries; we know of no other objects which will at all answer to his description but those at Hámed Garoosh; and our guides, as well as the Arabs of the place, were obstinate in persisting that there were no others of any kind.

The columns at this place are "tolerably high," and they are also quadrangular, and have the advantage of a pedestal, as the Doctor has remarked of his boundary stones. But then they are not of sandstone, nor of any stone at all, that is, not of any blocks of stone, but merely of small irregular fragments of stone, put together with cement, with which they are cased, and which gives them the appearance at a little distance of being formed of a single piece. Then, instead of one, there are two upon one pedestal, and unless we suppose that the Doctor saw them in one direction only, when the two were in one, it is not easy to account for this difference between his description and the reality. The characters which are upon them do certainly coincide with those mentioned by Signor Della Cella, so far as the circumstance of their being wholly illegible is concerned; for they consist altogether of unmeaning scrawls, and of some of those marks which are used by the Arabs to distinguish their particular tribes, and have been scratched for the amusement of those who may from time to time have stopped to rest themselves in the shade which the pillars afforded.

It will be seen by the drawing of them, that these pillars are of different sizes, although they may, perhaps, have been once of equal height; and we will not venture to hazard any conjecture with regard to the purpose for which they may have been erected: they cannot be seen from the sea-shore, or the lower road, although they are but a short distance from both; for notwithstanding they are placed on a ridge of hills, they are so situated in the hollow in which they stand, as to be indistinguishable from below. In rejecting, however, the "torre sormontata da una cupola" as the boundary established in the time of the Ptolemies, we may, perhaps, at the same time, dispense with the columns which Signor Della Cella has imagined to regulate the division; and it will not in that case be of any great importance whether the square pillars at Hamed Garoosh be or be not the same as those which the Doctor has mentioned. For our own part we see no building whatever in this neighbourhood, which answers to our idea of the tower of Euphrantas, either with regard to its nature or position; and as we find other buildings to the eastward of Zaffran which seem to us better calculated for boundary towers, we are content to take a more extended sense of the term employed by Strabo (συνεχης) than Signor Della Cella thinks it prudent to adopt.

We cannot take our leave of Zaffran without noticing the very singular and formidable appearance of the beach at this place and its neighbourhood; and had we not ourselves beheld the extraordinary scene which it presented, we should scarcely have believed it possible that the force of the sea could, under any circumstances, have raised the large blocks of stone which are piled up on this part of the coast. The occasional regularity in which these are heaped one above another, induced us, on the first view of them, to imagine that they had been intentionally placed there for the purpose of a breakwater; but the long extent of the ranges soon proved the improbability of this supposition and the idea was dismissed as heartily as it had been entertained. Heaps of sand and sea-weed are thrown up with these blocks of stone, and the roar and confusion which a moderate gale of wind here occasions, are such as in other places will seldom be found to accompany the most violent weather.

The general appearance of Zaffran is however by no means unpleasing, although it is destitute, like the rest of the Syrtis, of the advantages afforded by trees. The monotony of the flat and marshy surface, so predominant in other parts, is here broken by hills which are covered with verdure and overspread with a variety of flowers; some of the valleys are partially cultivated, and the flocks of sheep and goats which are scattered over the higher grounds, together with the tents of the Arabs who inhabit the place, give an appearance of cheerfulness and comfort to the scene which contrast renders doubly agreeable.

The water which is found here, and which is excellent and plentiful, contributes at the same time in no small degree to increase the attractions of the place; and though the claims of Zaffran might be humble, were it placed in a more favoured country, we may venture to affirm that no traveller who reaches it will ever be disposed to analyze too minutely its pretensions to actual beauty.

Zaffran is a place of some note in the district of Syrt; it affords excellent pasturage, and furnishes large supplies of corn, wool, and manteca. The name which it bears would lead us to imagine that this place has been originally famous for its saffron; Zaffran is the Arab term by which that plant is distinguished, and we know that the northern coast of Africa has been noted for the excellence of the saffron which it produced. We could not, however, perceive any traces of the plant properly so called; but the whole neighbourhood of Zaffran is overspread with a species of crocus from which saffron might very possibly be extracted.

The best saffron of our own times is that which is made from the crocus, by selecting the pistils and carefully drying them in a kiln; and the colour of the plant which we saw was well calculated to suggest the idea that it might be usefully employed in a similar way: it is a bulb, with a flower somewhat larger than the crocus, and grows to a height of four or five inches. We had collected a few specimens, but the nature of our journey did not allow of our stopping to have them properly dried, and we afterwards found, on unpacking them at Bengazi, that the damp had destroyed them, together with some others which we had collected in passing through the Syrtis.

The inhabitants of Zaffran are Bedouins, as are also all those of the other parts of the Syrtis; for there is not a single inhabited town or village to be found between Mesurata and Bengazi. We found them hospitable and obliging, and never entered one of their tents without receiving a cordial reception: their simple fare of milk and dates was always freely offered, and our horses were regaled with a feed of corn which they usually found very acceptable. Fresh milk was not always to be had, but they were never without a good supply of léban (sour milk, or more properly butter-milk), and we were seldom unwilling to alight from our saddles to take a draught of this patriarchal beverage, which a long day's hard riding through a country without roads, and under the influence of an African sun, made infinitely more palatable than will easily be imagined by those who can spare it for their pigs.

We were often much amused on these occasions with the surprise which our appearance created, and at the contest between ill-repressed curiosity and the respect which our Arab friends were desirous of shewing to their guests.

This struggle usually lasted till we had finished our repast, and our hosts would then begin to draw a little nearer to the mats which they had spread upon the ground for our seats; the women to examine our dress more minutely, and the men to handle our sabres and fire-arms.

The white linen of which our turbans and under garments were composed excited the greatest admiration in the former, while our double-barrelled guns, and pocket-pistols with stop-locks, were the objects of attraction to the latter. In a very short time the reserve of both sexes would begin to wear away very rapidly, and the whole family of our host would crowd round us indiscriminately each trying to be heard above the other: one question after another poured in upon us from all sides, and either nobody waited for an answer, or the answer was given by half a dozen of the family at once, each expressing a different opinion from that of his neighbour. At length, when no satisfactory conclusion could be formed upon the subject of their inquiry, they would wait to have the question formally answered by ourselves; and the real use of every object which excited their curiosity was generally so different from all those which they had assigned to it, that the whole party, then waiting in silent expectation for the result, would burst out all at once into the loudest exclamations of surprise, and sometimes into fits of laughter, which laid them rolling on the ground, and left them scarcely strength to rise when we got up to take our leave.

Among the numerous objects of attraction, our compass, telescopes, and watches, excited universal admiration; and the reason why the hands of the latter should move round of themselves, and why the needle of the compass should always turn to the northward, must have been canvassed among them for many months afterwards.

Why a man or a camel could be seen distinctly through a tube, when they could scarcely be seen at all, at the same distance, without it, will afford equal matter for speculation: and the next European who may visit the tents of our friends will probably hear an account of these wonders so much disfigured by misrepresentation, and so much exaggerated by the enthusiasm of Arab fancy, as will lead him to doubt whether they ever saw what they are describing, or to believe that they are telling him some whimsical story which has no better foundation than those of the Hundred and one Nights or the description of a Mahommedan Paradise.

We found the men of Zaffran active, healthy, and well made, and the women pretty and well-behaved; the dress of the former consists merely of a coarse baracan, with a red cap, and sandals of camel's hide.

The women wore a loose cotton shirt under the baracan, and instead of the sandals were furnished with laced boots. They had as usual a profusion of rude ornaments, and charms to avert the evil eye, and were not at all anxious to keep their faces veiled or to avoid the society of strangers. A small looking-glass and a few strings of beads were received with delight by the fairer part of this community, and a knife, with a few flints, and some powder, were accepted very thankfully by the men.

Our Chaous, who sometimes attended on these occasions, never omitted an opportunity of displaying his own knowledge, and took a large share in the explanation of the different objects of attraction. He never omitted to beg for an exhibition of our chronometer, that he might have an opportunity of descanting upon the manner in which we regulated it, which he used to say was done by *weighing the sun*; and poor Sala, our attendant on such occasions, was always called upon to produce the quicksilver used for the artificial horizon, which never failed to excite the astonishment and delight which our dilettante Chaous had anticipated.

Having purchased a supply of corn for our horses, which is here deposited, as is usual in Northern Africa, in cisterns or storehouses which have been excavated by the ancients, we left Zaffran, and continued our journey to Jedeed, where the tents were pitched for the night. This mode of preserving corn is frequently alluded to by ancient writers, and Varro has asserted that wheat thus preserved will keep for fifty years, and millet for more than a hundred.

From Jedeed we proceeded on to Shuaisha, passing by Bennet Hadeed and Hamed Garoosh, where are the remains of some forts, and a building called by the natives Rumīa (or Christian), but which has nothing to mark it as such, nor anything to recommend it to further notice. The country from Zaffràn to Hamed Garoosh becomes gradually higher, and in the valleys is well cultivated. We noticed many flocks of sheep and goats, some oxen and camels, and found in all parts hares, plovers, quails, curlews, wild-ducks, a few snipes, and a multitude of jackalls, which latter were indeed, throughout the journey, our constant companions. The evening setting in stormy, with heavy rains, we were very late in reaching our tents, and having passed unexamined some part of the coast, we remained at Shuaisha the whole of the following day (the 16th) in order to complete it. Between Jedeed and Shuaisha the coast is formed in small bays, and has some sunken rocks very close in shore: at about a quarter of a mile from the latter place, to the westward, we found the remains of a building shewing itself through the side of the cliff which covered it; its height from the foundation was about twenty-five feet, but its plan could not of course be obtained without previous excavation. At nine o'clock, on the 17th, we left Shuaisha, passed Marábut Duscarga (the remains of an old fort), and in seven hours reached Medīnet Sultàn, where we found a good supply of sweet water.

Medīnet Sultàn has been an important military position, as the remains of several strongly-built fortresses still remaining there attest; these buildings, like those at Zaffràn, are quadrangular, and the foundations of strong walls, communicating with the forts, are seen to cross them in various directions.

The plans of the buildings are more perfect than those of Zaffràn, and are upon a larger scale; those of the walls, however, could not be determined, and would require, from their ruined state, a very long and attentive examination, before their original dimensions and precise points of contact could be ascertained. We have given the plans of two of the forts, one of which, though apparently very perfect, is unprovided with any visible entrance. Two gates will be observed in the outer works of the other, although none is apparent in the habitable part of the building, which constitutes the most important part of it.

Within a square, or rather quadrangular, inclosure, attached to another of the same size, is a subterranean storehouse, or reservoir, which has been first excavated in the soil, then formed with rough stones, and lastly coated with an excellent cement, which is still in a very perfect state. The descent to this souterain is by a square well of trifling depth, which was so much overgrown and encumbered, as not to be immediately perceived. Having with us the means of procuring a light, we succeeded, without much trouble, in descending into the chambers which are excavated on each side of it, and in procuring the plan which appears in the plates. We were in hopes to have found some inscription on the walls, which we have already described as being very perfect, but nothing appeared but a few rude and unimportant Arab scrawls. In the neighbourhood of the military position, which we have noticed above, are the remains of the town already mentioned, called Medīna, where there are a number of wells and tanks in very good preservation; but the buildings above ground are in so mutilated and ruinous a state, as to render any satisfactory plan of them impossible, without a great deal of previous excavation.

So little is mentioned by any writer (with whose works we ourselves are acquainted) of the buildings contained in the Syrtis, that it will for the most part be difficult to assign any other name to the remains of forts and towns at present existing there, than those by which the Arabs of the country now distinguish them. Charax is pointed out by Strabo as occurring after the tower of Euphrantas; but before the position of this town can be ascertained, it will be necessary to decide upon that of the tower itself, which, in a country presenting a continued chain of forts from one extremity to the other, is by no means very easily established. The Philæni villa is also offered to our notice; but its position must depend upon that of the Philænean altars, which we are told by Pliny were merely of sand, and which we know were not remaining in the time of Strabo.

Were it not that a more eligible position for the tower of Euphrantas occurs further eastward, at a place called Bengerwàd, in the neighbourhood of Houdea, we should have been inclined to adopt Medīnet Sultàn as a port where the tower might very well be looked for; and the circumstance of its being nearer to Zaffràn (which we have already given our reasons for identifying with Aspis) would certainly point it out as the more eligible position of the two, so far as the meaning of the term συνεχης may be concerned. But the local advantages which the tower we shall hereafter mention at Bengerwàd possesses (considered both as a boundary fortress, and as a very conspicuous object), would certainly induce us to give a greater latitude to the term in question, than we should, under other circumstances, have ventured to allow; and we have accordingly given this fortress the preference in fixing the position of the tower of Euphrantas, or rather in suggesting a position for it which there is so little authority for fixing with accuracy .

At Medīnet Sultàn there is a sandy bay in which boats might find shelter with particular winds; and a lake commences here, apparently deep, which communicates with the sea in two places, and extends itself along the coast to the eastward. We narrowly examined the points of communication, in expectation of finding a passage through them by which small vessels might have entered the lake; it being probable, from its vicinity to the ruins abovementioned, that the lake might have been used as a port. But the nature of the beach without, which was altogether stony, running out into dangerous shallows impracticable for vessels of any kind, rendered the existence of such a passage impossible. The coast between this place and Garoosh is high, and the land terminates towards the sea in cliffs, with a low sandy beach, and rocky points at the foot of them; but from the wady eastward it lowers again, and is marked only by sand-hills. Upon the lake we noticed a great many flamingoes, with red bills and legs; the head and neck were white, the primary feathers of the wings black, and crimson in the inside; the secondaries and tertials were grey, and the under coverts crimson: several coveys of snipes and curlews were also observed along the lake, which, as well as all other lakes and marshes in the Syrtis, is salt and unfit for use. On leaving Medīnet Sultàn we continued our route along this low and marshy ground, which extends itself as far as Nehīm, where our tents were pitched for the night, near two wells of excellent water. There were no remains of building that we could perceive along this track, with the exception of a few stones on two little eminences, which had been rudely put together for Marábut tombs. We learnt also from Shekh Mahommed, that the country inland was equally devoid of interest, and unoccupied by buildings of any kind. At Nehīm there is a sandy bay, into which ships might send their boats, with almost all winds, for water, at three wells which are situated near the beach.

At Hámmah also, a bay a few miles farther eastward, water may be procured almost at all times, the sea being rendered smooth by a shoal which stretches itself across the entrance of the bay. The two bays may be known by a promontory situated nearly midway between them, on which there are some ruins of an ancient fort which formerly overlooked the cliff, but these are now too much fallen to be perceived from the sea.

While we were pitching the tents, and all hands were employed, some of our horses got loose, and Shekh Mahommed el Dúbbah, who had just come up with us on his trusty mare, was violently assailed by them on all sides. He called out most lustily for help, and in the mean time exhibited uncommonly good horsemanship; wheeling about rapidly in all directions, and making his mare kick out in the intervals, to the no small amusement of our whole party, who were at first too much overcome by laughter to give him any effectual assistance.

As the attack however began to grow serious, from the number and impetuosity of our valiant Shekh's assailants, we soon recovered ourselves sufficiently to make a diversion in his favour, and eventually to secure all the horses, though not before the Dúbbah was quite out of breath, and had broken his gun in his defence.

The next morning he entered our tent with the fragments of his ill-fated weapon in his hand; and after he had squatted himself down as usual, and paid his two or three customary salams, and a variety of fulsome compliments, which always preceded any request he had to make, he began to expatiate upon his rencontre of the preceding evening, and the address which he had shewn on the occasion: he concluded by holding forth the shattered remains of his béndikah (musket), and observing that the Dúbbah had now nothing to defend himself with in case of an attack from the formidable bands of robbers which he had always asserted to be lying in wait for us. As we had no time to spend in trifling, and were not inclined to take the hint by presenting him with one of our muskets, we suddenly changed the subject, to the discomfiture of his hopes, and began to make inquiries about the camels which he was to provide us with at Boosaida, where we expected to arrive the next day. He replied that he had already given directions about them, but that he thought it would be better that he should proceed on in advance of the party, to make arrangements for their being in readiness on our arrival; he proposed in the mean time to leave his eldest son as his *locum tenens*, who had lately come from the eastward to pay his respects to his father.

This proposal being agreed to, we remained silent for a few moments, in expectation that he would rise and leave the tent; we were however disappointed, for the Dúbbah kept his post, and it was evident that he had something more to ask. The customary toll of a little brown sugar had already been allowed and accepted; for Shekh Mahommed, though old, had not yet lost his relish for sweets, and we usually indulged him when he visited our tent with a few spoonfuls of his favorite dainty. His approbation had also been extended, as usual, to the knives, pens, and pencils, pocket-pistols, and powder-flasks, and other little things usually lying about the tent, without any of them having been offered to him: yet he still remained sitting, to our great annoyance; for besides taking up our time, as we thought, very unnecessarily, he was all the while colonizing our carpets and mats with the fleas and other animals which escaped from his baracan; and this article of his dress (which indeed was generally his only one) was at all times sufficiently well provided with these residents to allow of very extensive emigration. At last our patience was exhausted, and our complaisance very nearly so; the watch was pulled out, and when we had expressed our surprise that it should be so much later than we had imagined, we ventured to ask of our white-bearded visitor if it would not be better that he should set out in advance, as he had himself so very prudently suggested. Upon this the Shekh rose, to our great delight, and after paying his adieus with the air of a man who was wholly occupied with other reflections, he took the Doctor aside, and with a significant half-smile upon his countenance, begged he would furnish him with the exhilarating medicine which he had promised him on a former occasion. The secret was disclosed which had so baffled our penetration; for the Dúbbah confessed that as he was going home, from which he had been some time absent, he was particularly desirous of assuming an animated and youthful appearance in the presence of his young and handsome wife, who, he was fearful, he said, had already began to fancy him a little too old for her. He described this girl, to whom he had lately been married, as uncommonly pretty and only sixteen years of age; and concluded by saying he did not despair, Imsh Allah (please God), that with the Doctor's assistance, he might yet contrive to make himself agreeable to her! Our chagrin was now succeeded by a violent fit of laughter, which we freely indulged in at the old Shekh's expense, and which he bore very goodnaturedly: the Doctor was not long in preparing the draught; and the Dúbbah had no sooner deposited it in his old leathern pouch, as safely as a glass phial could conveniently be put up with flints and steel, musket balls, old nails and horse-shoes, which were usually observed to be assembled there, than he mounted the gallant mare who had so well conducted herself the night before, and brandishing his stirrups, rode off at full gallop, well pleased with the result of his long-winded visit, and anticipating all the wonderful effects of the cordial which the Doctor had so considerately bestowed upon him.

FOOTNOTES:

In this neighbourhood we must look for the Macomades Syrtis of the Itinerary.

Serte (says Leo) è una città antica, edificata, come alcuni vogliono, da gli Egitti, e secondo altri dai Romani, benchè siano alcuni da oppinione che ella fosse edificata da gli Africani. Come si fu, hora è rovinata, e credesi che la distrussero i Mahumettani; ancor che Ibnu Rachik, historico, dice dai Romani; ne altro in lei si vede fuori che qualche picciolo vestigio delle mura.—(L. Afr. in Ram., 5ta parte.)

If Mahād Hassān may be taken as the *Turris Hasan* (or Cosr Asan) of Edrisi, with which it appears to correspond, we may fairly venture, perhaps, to place Asna at Zaffrān, that place being thirty M. P. from Hasān, on the testimony of the Arab geographer, and Zaffrān thirty geographic miles from Mahād Hassān. The wells of Zaffrān are, at the same time, on the beach, as those are said to be which Edrisi has mentioned at Asna.

Medīna is the Arabic term for a city, and Medīnet Sultàn, as it is termed by the Arabs, may be translated, royal city, or city of more than ordinary distinction.

The remains of Medīnet Sultàn are on a larger scale than those of Medīna, and might on that account have been termed Sultàn; but they are rather those of an important military station than of a city, and we prefer taking Medīna as the position of Sort for this reason.

Viaggio da Tripoli, &c., p. 77, 78.

We subjoin a few of these characteristic marks, with the names of the tribe, to which they belong, attached. Some of them, it will be seen, resemble Greek letters, and when they are well cut, have a very knowing appearance.

Mogharbé, Ouarghir, Wéled Sulimàn, Orfilli, Wéled Ben-Miriam,

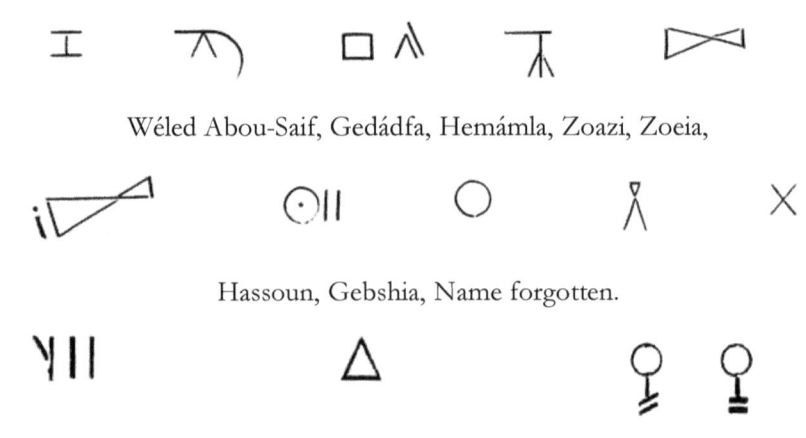

Wéled Abou-Saif, Gedádfa, Hemámla, Zoazi, Zoeia,

Hassoun, Gebshia, Name forgotten.

The drawing annexed will give some idea of the manner in which these blocks are disposed.

The dangerous peculiarities of the Gulfs of Syrtis are frequently noticed by the ancients; but the following passage from Sallust seems to allude more particularly to the powerful action of the surf, so conspicuous in the instance which we have just described.

Nam ubi mare magnum esse, et sævire ventis cœpit, limum, Arenamq: et *saxa ingentia fluctus* trahunt; ita facies locorum cum ventis simul mutatur. Syrtes ab tractu nominatæ.—(Bell. Jugurth., p. 78.)

The saffron of the Gharian mountains has been described by Leo Africanus as the best in the world.

Shaw observes that this expression is used in the neighbourhood of Tunis, and indeed it is very common among the Arab tribes in general.

"Quidam granaria habent sub terris, speluncas, quos vocant σειρους, ut in Cappadocia ac Thracia. Alii, ut in Hispania citeriore, puteos, ut in agro Carthaginiensi et Oscensi. Horum solum paleis substernunt: et curant ne humor aut aer tangere possit, nisi cum promitur ad usum. Quo enim spiritus non pervenit, ibi non oritur curculio. Sic conditum triticum manet vel annos quinquaginta: milium vero plus annos centum."—(De Re Rustica, i. 57.)

See also Cæsar (de Bell. Afric., cap. 25). "Est in Africa consuetudo incolarum, ut, in agris, et in omnibus fere villis, sub terra specus, condendi frumenti gratia, clam habeant, atque id propter bella maxime, hostiumque subitum adventum præssarent."

The Φιλαινου κωμη (of Ptolemy) υφ' ην οι ομωνυμοι βωμοι, οριον Αφρικης—between which and Charax, his φαραξ κωμη, Ptolemy has however laid down some inconsiderable places.

Ου γαρ νυν όι φιλαινων μενουσι βωμοι αλλ' ό τοπος μετειληφε την προσηγωριαν·—(Lib. iii. p. 171.)

In intimo sinu fuit ora Lotophagon, quos quidam Alachroas dixere, ad Philænorum Aras: ex harena sunt eæ.—(Nat. Hist., lib. v. c. 5.)

It must be recollected that Strabo has described the tower of Euphrantas as *contiguous to*, or *immediately succeeding*, the port of Aspis, for so we must translate συνεχης, if we take it in its strict and literal sense.

Among the several towers which present themselves at Medīna Sultàn, there is no one which could be pointed out as more conspicuous in position than another; and were the tower of Euphrantas to be fixed at this place, it would scarcely be possible to select one of them as its probable representative.

CHAPTER VIII.

Leave Nehīm — Arrive at Boosaida — Shekh Hamed Shakshak — Return of Shekh Mahommed — Revival of the Report above mentioned — Motive for renewing it — Discharge our Mesurata Camel-drivers — Treaty with the Dúbbah for others — Interested Conduct of Shekh Mahommed — Commencement of another Salt-Lake at Sharfa — Easy mode of shifting Quarters practised by the Arabs — Their manner of travelling — Termination of the Lake — Arrive at Shegga — Remains of Forts observed there — Other Remains in its Neighbourhood — Abundant Pasturage at Shegga — Fortress of Bengerwàd — Peculiarities of its Position — Bengerwàd considered as the Castle of Euphrantas — Objections to this Supposition — Reasons in favour of it — Leave Wady Shegga — Cross a Tract of Red Sand — Spacious Bay at Ras Howeijah — Good Anchorage probably found there — Remains of an ancient Town near Ras Howeijah considered as those of Charax — Trade of Charax alluded to, as mentioned by Strabo — Further Reasons for placing the Tower of Euphrantas at Bengerwàd — Allusion to the Barter of Silphium at Charax — Emendation of Strabo's Text proposed by Signor Della Cella — Arrive at Hudīa — Alleged Origin of this Name as applied to the Place in question — Hudīa lately infested by a formidable Band of Robbers — Precautions of our Arab Escort to prevent any Attack — Rigorous Measures of Mahommed Bey apparently very necessary — Remarkable Hill of Gypsum at Hudīa — Celebration of Christmas-day by our Party at Hudīa — Fortress at Mahirīga — Arrival of a Party of Pilgrims from the Westward — Disturbance at Linoof — Apparent Causes of it — Ill-behaviour of the Dúbbah — His sudden change of Conduct, and artful Manœuvres — Remarks on Arab Character — Satisfactory Termination of the Disturbance — Arrival at Mukhtàr, the Boundary of the Districts of Syrt and Barka.

ON quitting Nehīm we proceeded along the edge of a marsh which commences there, extending itself for several miles parallel with the beach, from which it is separated by sand-hills, and in the evening arrived at Boosaida. The whole of this tract (from Nehīm to Boosaida) is very flat and uninteresting, and we could perceive no remains there of any kind. At Boosaida may be observed the ground-plans of small walls, apparently those of dwelling-houses, between where our tents the spot were pitched and the sea; the remains are however so few and inconsiderable, and so much mixed with stones belonging to the soil, as to be wholly without any interest.

The country at Boosaida is somewhat hilly, and overrun with grass and brushwood, a small part only being planted with barley. The few Bedouins who inhabit it appear to have no other occupation than that of tending their camels, sheep, and goats; and the women are chiefly occupied in curing skins for containing water and manteca, which is done by means of certain roots found in great quantities in the neighbourhood. The Shekh, or principal man of the place, was named Hamed Shakshak, who, in order to ensure our being well supplied, for we ought not to suspect so obliging a personage of any less praiseworthy motive, took care to usurp the sole right and privilege of furnishing us himself with whatever we wished to purchase; never forgetting, however, in the excess of his zeal, to put a most unconscionable price upon everything. So careful had this considerate person been in his manœuvres, that we could not get even a draught of milk from the women in other tents, without promising to keep it secret from Hamed Shakshak. As we had no wish to embroil the honest inhabitants with their Shekh, we thought it better to take no notice of this proceeding, especially as the time we had to remain at Boosaida was short, and our demands were not likely to be very great.

It was here that our agreement with the Mesurata camel-drivers finished; and the day after our arrival we were rejoined by our friend the Dúbbah, who had left us, as before stated, to make arrangements for furnishing us with others. He entered our tent with three large ostrich eggs wrapped up very carefully in the folds of his baracan, (for this garment may be considered as a general envelope for everything which an Arab thinks worthy of a cover,) and having unfolded them, one by one, laid them down very solemnly and ceremoniously, and with the greatest air of consequence imaginable, on the mat upon which we were sitting. All this was of course intended to enhance the value of the present, and we received it accordingly with all due acknowledgments. The prelude being over, Shekh Mahommed assumed a very mysterious air, and drew a little closer towards us; then lowering his voice, which was not usually one of the most gentle, he began to inform us (looking occasionally round the tent, as if he feared to be overheard from without) that a large troop of marauding Arabs were then at Kebrīt, having recently arrived there from the neighbourhood of Cairo, and that they were lying in wait for our party. There could be no doubt, he added, of the truth of this statement, for one of his own sons had just arrived from Cairo himself! On our asking him whether this son had actually seen the Arabs in question, he replied that, as yet, no person had seen them, but that the prints of horses' feet, to the number of sixty, had been observed about the wells near Kebrīt, and that there could be no doubt whatever of the sinister intentions of the party. "But fear nothing," continued the Shekh, with an air of greater importance, "while the Dúbbah is your friend and conductor; for I will myself," said he, "go on in advance, and if I find the tracks of hostile horses about the wells, woe be to the rascals upon their backs!" We had been trying very hard, during this important communication, to keep as solemn a face as we could, but the concluding bravado of old Shekh Mahommed rendered all our best efforts unavailing; and we fairly laughed out, in spite of ourselves, to the great discomposure of our valiant protector. The old Shekh had often talked of similar interruptions which were to be expected upon the road, but we could not, at first, upon the present occasion, perceive his actual motive for introducing the subject so formally and circumstantially. The next day, however, we found there had been a competition between the Dúbbah and our Mesurata camel-drivers, who were desirous of accompanying us to Bengazi, and whom for their good conduct on most occasions we should have been very willing to retain in our service. At any rate, we wished the competition to continue till we had concluded our bargain with one of the parties, as we knew that we should otherwise be exposed to the extortion which is almost invariably practised by an Arab when he knows there is no alternative but to accept his proposals. Both parties, however, knew that we must, under any circumstances, continue our route; and that it would not be possible for us to do so without camels, whether we advanced or returned. For this reason we had never made any positive promise that we would take the Dúbbah's camels at Boosaida, and we had never given any notice to the camel-drivers of Mesurata that we should not continue them if they wished to proceed with us farther.

Having reason to believe that his Mesurata rivals were willing to go on with us to Bengazi, Shekh Mahommed now brought forward his story of the robbers to deter them from accompanying us any farther; for in the event of our being surprised and overpowered, they would themselves have lost their camels as well as all they had with them. Whether this story, which the Dúbbah had taken care to have generally circulated, really frightened the men of Mesurata, or whether they thought it imprudent to make an enemy of the old Shekh at a distance from their own country, and in a part of his own, did not very clearly appear; but they soon after came to us, and declined proceeding any farther, alleging, at the same time, that Shekh Mahommed had already engaged camels for us from his own people in the neighbourhood, and that we should therefore have no occasion for theirs. We told them that we had as yet made no bargain with the Dúbbah, and that although we might wish to give him an opportunity, as our friend and conductor, of making a fair profit of his camels, we should certainly not accept them if we found that his demands were unreasonable. Finding, however, that the men were really unwilling to go on, under any circumstances, though they would not state precisely the grounds of their objection, we settled our accounts with them, giving each a few piastres in addition to what had been agreed for, as an acknowledgment of their good behaviour, and they shortly after set out on their return to Mesurata. Before their departure, however, we sent for Shekh Mahommed, and told him the number of camels we should have occasion for; stating, at the same time, the sum we intended to pay him for them, to which, after some little parley, he consented. The next morning he made his appearance in our tent, and said that the camels would be brought to us immediately, but that the men whom they belonged to, on estimating the weight of our baggage, had refused to carry it so long a journey, unless we would consent to take twenty-five instead of eighteen camels, (the number we had mentioned to him on the preceding evening,) and which was fully sufficient for the whole of our baggage. To this proposal, however, we gave a very decided negative, and a long parley, ensued in which the Dúbbah went through the whole gamut of Arab vociferation, accompanying each tone with its appropriate gestures, and expressing himself with an energy which almost amounted to frenzy. The whole strength of the Dúbbah's lungs, with all his powers of gesticulation, were, however, unable to convince us that his proposal was a reasonable one; although it must be confessed, in justice to his logic, that no poissard ever screamed louder, and that the most accomplished Neapolitan buffoon could not have surpassed him in vehemence and variety of gesture.

The result was that we could come to no satisfactory terms; for the Dúbbah was aware that our old camel-drivers were gone, and thought we had no alternative but to comply with his demands: he concluded by declaring, in the name of the Prophet, that we should either have none at all, or else take the whole number of camels which he had proposed, and went out of the tent as he delivered his final resolve, fully satisfied that we should soon call him back and agree to his unreasonable terms.

Had we done so he would soon have found some excuse for increasing the number still further, and we should in all probability not have been able to get away without twice as many camels as we had any occasion for.

We were, however, determined not to submit to this imposition while any means remained of avoiding it; and Shekh Mahommed had no sooner left the tent than we ordered two horses to be saddled immediately, and despatched one of our party, accompanied by the Chaous, to bring back the Mesurata camel-drivers, who we knew could not have been far advanced on their journey. The old Shekh now imagined that we were going to send express to Tripoly to complain of his conduct to the Bashaw; although such an embassy, had we waited for the reply, must have detained us much longer than it would have been advisable to delay the expedition for any point so comparatively trifling. As he had however fallen into this error, and was evidently much disturbed at the idea, we did not of course undeceive him; and when he had most solemnly promised to abide by our decision on the subject in dispute, he begged that we would allow him to recall the two horsemen, who had already made some little progress: no sooner had he obtained our permission to do so than he mounted his mare in all speed, which he had contrived to have saddled in the interval, and riding after the envoys as fast as he could gallop, overtook them as they were nearly out of sight. By this time the day was half gone, and our departure was consequently deferred till the following one, which, as the weather turned out, saved us a good wetting. We left Boosaida on the morning of the 22nd, and passing through Sharfa, stopped for the night at Shedgane, having only made good twelve miles, in consequence of the delays occasioned by the young camels which the Dúbbah had provided for us, which were continually throwing off their loads. The ground was besides so full of holes, made by the Jerboa, that both horses and camels were continually tripping.

At Sharfa commences another salt lake which extends to Houeijah, a remarkable promontory, taking the appearance at a distance of a castle in ruins, and which may possibly be the cape called Liconda. Between the lake and the sea is a narrow slip of land occupied by a party of Arabs, who were so completely concealed among the hills, that we were close upon them before we were aware that any living soul was in the neighbourhood. The cattle of this place were closely attended by the men, to prevent their ranging on the heights, and, consequently, becoming visible to those who might be passing; a manœuvre which they probably had adopted from supposing us to be some of the Bashaw's people, whose observation they hoped by such means to elude, and thus escape the payment of the tribute which in the event of their discovery would have been exacted from them by the soldiers of His Highness. We were however received by these people very kindly, and they brought us out milk and dried dates, unasked for; in return for these attentions, we gave the men some gunpowder, with which they were highly delighted, and presented the women with some strings of beads of different colours, which were accepted with many smiles of acknowledgment.

So well practised are the Arabs in eluding observation, from the nature of the wandering life which they lead, and the little security which there is for property in the country they inhabit, that even those who are well acquainted with their usual haunts are often unable to find them; and strangers might often pass within a hundred yards of their tents, without suspecting there was a soul in the neighbourhood. As the whole property of a wandering Arab consists in his flocks and cattle, and the few little articles contained in his tent, he has very little trouble in moving, and half an hour after he has determined to leave the place of his residence, no traces will remain of his late habitation, but the ashes scattered about the hole in the earth which served his whole family for a fire-place. His sheep and cattle are collected without difficulty at the sound of his voice, or that of some part of his family, while his tent, in the mean time, with all its contents, the chief of which are his wives and his children, are packed up in a few minutes on the backs of his camels, and ready to move on with the rest. If he is not pressed for time, the women often walk with the older children, and assist in driving the cattle; and should he have no camels, which is very often the case, both women and children are loaded to the utmost of their strength with such articles as cannot be transported in other ways. But neither women nor children on these fatiguing occasions exhibit any signs of discontent or uneasiness; the length of their journey and the weight of their burdens are borne with the greatest cheerfulness; and the whole is considered as a matter of course, which their habits of life have accustomed them to expect, and to support without any other effects than the temporary fatigue of the exertion. If the journey should be long, the tent is seldom unpacked till they have arrived at the place of their destination, and the whole party sleep very soundly on the ground, in the midst of their sheep and cattle, till the first appearance of day-light summons them to rise and take up their burdens, which have probably in the mean time been usefully employed in affording them the luxury of a pillow.

On quitting the hills among which our late acquaintance were encamped, we passed along the track of Ras Houeijah (the promontory above mentioned), and were detained some time in consequence of the lake having terminated in a swamp, which extended to the sea, and in which our horses sank so deep as to render great caution necessary. The land at the back of the marsh rises tolerably high, and was better peopled than any part we had yet seen in the district of Syrt. At about one o'clock we reached Wady Shegga, a large fiumara so called, and having procured some brackish water a little way up it, continued our route till we reached some Arab tents, where we halted for the night. At Shegga we found the remains of some forts, strongly and regularly built, and of the same quadrangular form with those which we have already described. On a large mound of rubbish we also observed a Marábut, rudely built with the stones of fallen structures about it. In a valley belonging to the chain of hills which runs at the back of Shegga are considerable traces of small buildings, rudely put together with the unshaped stones of the soil. They consist principally of strait lines and parts of squares, built with very little regularity, and occupying both sides of the valley. Traces of walls may also be still observed across the valley, which is furrowed and torn up by the passage of torrents rushing down in the rainy season from the hills, but which seems to have formerly contained much more building than can be perceived in it at present. The rain seems to have been also a principal agent in destroying the buildings on the sides of the valley; but the loss which has been sustained is scarcely to be regretted; since neither these structures, nor those which occupied the centre of the valley, could ever have been of any importance, although they have certainly been very numerous. Before the entrance of the valley, near the forts which have been mentioned, are also seen traces of building, but which do not seem to have been much more important than those which we have just alluded to. On the whole, nothing more can well be collected from these remains, than that the place has been formerly the site of a small town, which must always have been a very miserable one. There is however a good deal of pasturage in the neighbourhood, occasioned by the plentiful supply of water from the hills, and we found ourselves surrounded on all sides by flocks of sheep and goats, among which were also a good many camels.

At about two miles' distance from the remains above described (to the eastward) is a very remarkable projection of a high cliff into the sea, on which has been built a strong and very conspicuous fortress, constructed with large stones regularly shaped and put together. The greater part of this building, owing to the cliff having given way, is tumbled in ruins about the beach, and though little of the ground plan now remaining can be satisfactorily made out, yet it may well be inferred, from an inspection of the whole, that this fortress has been one of considerable strength. It commands an extensive view, on both sides, over the sea, and overlooks many remains of building which are scattered about the plain at the back of it. At the foot of the eminence on which the fortress has been built, is a ravine, which must at times be the bed of a considerable torrent, and which, crossing the plain from the mountains by which it is bounded, empties itself into the sea at the base of the fort. The mountains, which here run parallel with the beach, approach at the same time so closely to the sea, that the plain which intervenes might be easily defended by means of the ravine just described. Along this ravine are traces of strong walls which have been constructed on both sides of it, and have formerly extended from the sea to the foot of the hills; and which must in their perfect state have formed, together with the ravine, a very effectual barrier to the pass.

Such advantages of situation could not well have been overlooked by the ancients; and there is little doubt that this position was originally one of importance. It appears so well calculated, both by nature and art, for the establishment of a boundary line, that we have little hesitation in supposing the remains above mentioned to have at some period defended the limits of the states of Cyrene and Carthage; and it is accordingly here that we should feel most inclined to fix the site of the Castle of Euphrantes. The distance of this fort from Zaffràn, considered as Aspis, does indeed seem too great for the literal meaning of Strabo's term συνεχης: but then the circumstance of its uniting a strong boundary line with a very conspicuous position, seems to make this place so very eligible a site for the castle in question, that we cannot refrain from pointing it out to our readers as the spot of all others which we could most wish should prove to be really such. We know the πυργος Ευφραντας to have been a boundary tower, since it is expressly said by Strabo to have been the limits of Carthage and Cyrene under the Ptolemies; so far therefore the resemblance between this fort and that of Strabo appears to be sufficiently complete. Again, amongst all the fortresses with which the Syrtis is filled, two only are mentioned in ancient history *by name*, those of Euphrantas and Automala; and it would seem probable, from this circumstance (at least it appears so to us), that these castles should have been distinguished from others by conspicuous positions. Of all the positions occupied by forts between Zaffràn and the point to which we are arrived, there is no one which can be materially distinguished from another but that of Bengerwàd, which we have just been describing; and this is so remarkably conspicuous a position, from the height of the eminence and its almost insulated situation on the beach, that must have been at all times an object of importance from the sea, and could not fail to have been noticed by Strabo in his passage along this part of the coast. It is probable that the position of the Philænean Altars was not sufficiently well calculated by nature for a boundary; and that this circumstance, rather than the desire of increasing his territory in so unprofitable a district, induced one of the Ptolemies to remove the line of separation further westward to the castle of Euphrantas. In passing along the coast, in a westerly direction, from the sandy tract where the monuments of the Philæni might be looked for, had they still been in existence, the most eligible situation which would present itself for a boundary post is certainly that of Bengerwàd; and this, as we have stated, is so extremely well calculated for such a purpose, that we can scarcely suppose it could have been overlooked by the king of Egypt when he fixed the new limits of his dominions.

It will be unnecessary to trouble our readers with any protracted discussion of a point which admits of no positive proof; and we will leave others to decide, without further remark, how far the meaning of the term employed by Strabo (συνεχης) may be extended, in consideration of the reasons which we have alleged.

On leaving Wady Shegga we passed over a tract of red sand collected in little hillocks about the plain, which were, however, as well as the spaces between them, occasionally covered with vegetation. We here saw some gazelles, hares, and jackalls, and a good many jerboas, and fired at a snake about six feet in length, which the Arabs told us swelled out when much irritated, and was very venomous; he however escaped slightly grazed into a hole in the sand. This was the only snake of any size which we had seen in the Syrtis; it was of a very dark colour, and about as thick as a man's wrist.

Immediately behind the promontory which we have mentioned above, is a small sandy bay which the Arabs call a port, and which might in former days have served as a landing-place for boats. This Ràs (or head land), with Ràs Houeijah, forms a spacious bay, in which good anchorage might probably be found close up under the western shore. After passing Bengerwàd the coast gets lower, and the road leads along an uninteresting flat between it and the hills.

Five miles from the Ràs, upon a sandy point, are the remains of a small fort, and about three-quarters of a mile inland of it are several large mounds of sand and rubbish, through which appear occasionally parts of the walls and ground plans of houses. These are evidently the remains of an ancient town, and the houses have here been more concentrated than those of any town which we have observed in the Syrtis; but they are now in so very incumbered a state, that we could form no correct idea either of their number or of their plans. It is probable also that excavation would here be uninteresting, as the hand of time seems to have been fully as much concerned in the destruction of this place as that of its most inveterate enemies. Considerable traces of building may be observed all the way from these remains to the wells at Hudea, and indeed all the way from Bengerwàd; and immediately about the wells the ground plans become more regular, as well as more numerous. There is no doubt that the greater part of this tract has been formerly inhabited, but the mounds which we have mentioned seem to us more characteristic of a town than any of the other remains; and we will venture to suggest them as those of Charax, described by Strabo as a trading frontier-town, resorted to by the people both of Carthage and Cyrene. It was at Charax that the Carthaginians exchanged their wine for the silphium, and the liquor which was extracted from it, (so we translate the passage, reversing the order); neither of which, from the value attached to these commodities, were allowed to be exported from the Cyrenaica by individuals; and were consequently disposed of with great caution and secrecy to the traders of Carthage who assembled at Charax to treat for them.

As the identity of the fortress at Bengerwàd with the tower of Euphrantas may scarcely, perhaps, be considered as decidedly established; it will probably here appear strange that we should point out the vicinity of the ruins above mentioned to Bengerwàd as one of the reasons why we imagine them to be those of Charax.

But whether the tower of Euphrantas be placed at Bengerwàd or not, we cannot consider that place as any other than a boundary; and as Charax was evidently a frontier-town, and must be looked for somewhere in this neighbourhood, we may assume the vicinity of the remains in question to the only spot which we have met with which may decidedly be termed a boundary, as a reason why they are probably those of Charax. This once allowed, it will be the more readily admitted that the ruin at Bengerwàd is very likely to be that of the tower of Euphrantas; for Charax, as before stated, is the first place which is mentioned by Strabo after that fortress, and may therefore be identified with the first town to be met with in passing from the tower to the westward. Here is however nothing *certain* but the existence of a boundary, and that of a town a little to the westward of it; and it remains to be determined how far the facts which we have stated may be received as proofs of the positions which have been suggested for the tower of Euphrantas and the trading town of Charax, both of which must be looked for between Aspis and the bottom of the gulf, and to the westward of the Philænean altars and the fortress of Automala.

In alluding to the sale of the silphium at Charax, which he places as we have already stated at Zaffràn, Signor Della Cella has indulged himself in his favourite practice of emendation, and has proposed a new reading in the passage of Strabo which mentions this town and its commerce.

"I will not speak to you of the silphium (says the Doctor) till I arrive in the place which produces it . . . but I cannot conceal from you that I have allowed myself to read, in translating this passage of Strabo, οπον του σίλφιου, juice of the silphium, instead of οπον και σίλφιον, juice and silphium." "We know that from this plant, peculiar to the soil of the Cyrenaica, the Cyreneans extracted a most valuable liquid which was particularly celebrated in those times. The juice of this plant alone was sold on account of the state, and it was of this liquid only that the contraband trade consisted which is mentioned by Strabo, and was carried on between the Cyreneans and Carthaginians. If you will only reflect now (continues Signor Della Cella, addressing himself as usual to his friend the Professor) that the Cyrenean liquid is very often used by Strabo, and others of the ancients, as a synonymous term for the silphium, you will agree with me in the trifling alteration which is thus effected in the text of the Grecian geographer."

We must confess that the substituting the word *of* for *and*, and a genitive case for an accusative, appears to us to be hazarding more than would be ventured upon by critics and commentators in general; and it is to be feared, at the same time, that there is scarcely more reason for the changes here proposed than there has been hesitation in suggesting them. For the plant called silphium was as much an article of commerce as the liquid which was extracted from it, and we find them again mentioned as two distinct things in the very next page to the passage of Strabo which Signor Della Cella is so desirous of emending. Pliny also distinguishes them by separate names, calling the extract "laser," and the plant "laserpitium;" and many other authorities might be adduced to the same effect: so that we may perhaps allow the passage of Strabo to remain in the state in which it usually appears, without any detriment to its genuine and proper signification.

For ourselves, we are content to believe that the plant laserpitium, or silphium, was really sold, or rather bartered, at Charax, as well as the liquor which was extracted from it. We will however agree with Signor Della Cella in deferring any further remarks on the silphium till we find ourselves in the country which produced it; and will in the mean time proceed with our journey along the shores of the Syrtis.

Soon after passing the several mounds which we have suggested as the probable remains of Charax, we arrived at the wells of Hudīa; a name which the Arabs suppose to have been given to this place in consequence of the bad water usually found there, and which they consider to be only fit for Jews; the Arab term for a Jew being Hudi, and the Jews themselves little esteemed by Mahometans.

We will not however venture to attribute this origin to the term by which the place is distinguished, although it is by no means improbable that the name may have a reference to the persecuted people who are here so contemptuously alluded to. We know that the Jews were formerly very numerous in the Pentapolis, and we find them described by Procopius as having once inhabited the country on its western extremity. Hudīa may in such case be the last settlement they possessed in this neighbourhood, and the place may very probably have received its appellation from that circumstance.

There being no other resting-place at less than a whole day's journey from Hudia, we pitched our tents for the night near the wells above mentioned; about which we observed considerable remains of building, of which nothing however now remains but the ground-plans.

Hudīa was a few years ago so much infested by parties of marauding Arabs, that although they had been completely destroyed or dispersed by the vigorous measures of the Bashaw, yet the dread which had been created by their former depredations still continued to be felt in the place which was once the scene of them. Decoy-fires were carefully placed by our Arab escort, in various directions, at the suggestion of Shekh Mahommed, and that worthy personage could not resist from bestowing a few hearty curses on poor Morzouk, our watch-dog, who he said was too fond of barking. He related to us, looking round every now and then as he spoke, the massacre which was made among the robbers by Mahommed Bey, the eldest son of the reigning Bashaw, and which the number of piles of stones, which marked the graves of these unfortunate people, too evidently proved to have been very extensive. It appears, however, to have been very necessary; and the consequence is, that the route is now safe which was before its perpetration impassable.

Mahometan policy considers only the end without caring for the means which may be used for its accomplishment, and the most summary mode of getting rid of obnoxious persons is usually considered by Mussulmen as the best. If we did not approve this indiscriminate slaughter, we certainly experienced the advantages which resulted from it, and we slept much more quietly among the tombs of the robbers than we should probably have been allowed to do had they never been occupied.

At Hudīa there is a remarkable hill, through which gypsum protrudes itself in almost every part; it terminates in a conical mound of pure gypsum, so smooth as to have the appearance of ice, the diameter of the cone, at its base, being about thirty feet. We found the valleys between the hills very fertile, producing, among other flowers, a variety of wild geraniums, singularly mixed with a species of leek, which flourishes there in great abundance. The water was collected in a hollow between the hills, and having lately received a fresh supply from the rains, was found to be tolerably sweet. Neither its flavour nor its clearness were however much improved by the provident cares of our Arab conductors, who began to wash their caps and baracans in it before we were aware of their intentions; and it may readily be supposed that these articles of dress, which were almost the only ones that our friends possessed, and which had certainly not been washed since they left Tripoly, could not be particularly clean.

With this water, however, we managed to commemorate Christmas day, which occurred while we were at Hudīa, in a much better manner (so far as conviviality was concerned) than we should have been able to do, had it fallen a few days later, in the barren, rocky country which ensued, where no water is to be found at all. It may be imagined by some that conviviality and dirty water are by no means compatible with each other; but when the necessaries of life become luxuries they will always be appreciated as such; and there are many occasions on which they who might think it impossible to make merry without wine, would feel themselves both able and willing to do so in a good hearty draught of muddy water.

Our route on the following day lay over a barren and rugged country, which continues all the way from Hudīa to the confines of Barca, where the soil begins gradually to assume a better appearance. In the afternoon, as we passed Mahirīga, we observed the remains of a quadrangular building occupying the summit of a low range of hills which lay between our road and the sea. On a closer examination, we found it to be different in plan from any building which we had hitherto met with. At each of the angles there is a circular turret, sloping down from the top, and becoming considerably wider at the base. The sides of this building are constructed with well-shaped stones of four and five feet in length, closely fitted together, and fastened with an excellent cement; but the turrets were found to be built of much smaller stones, not shaped or put together with the same attention to regularity, and proved on near inspection to be built *on* to the outer walls and not into them. They may therefore be considered as forming no part of the original plan, and have probably been added at some early period by the Arabs. No traces remain of the external roof of this building, but part of an arched roof is still visible on the ground-floor within, which, from its inferior workmanship, we should be inclined to attribute to the same period at which the turrets were added. Traces of walls are also seen in the inside of the building, which have formerly divided it into chambers; they are composed of very small stones and appear to be of later work than the exterior. This fortress, for such it has originally been, is surrounded by a wall of four feet in thickness, enclosing an area of twenty five feet between it and the outer wall of the building, but there is no appearance of any trench. The enclosed space is entered by a single gate in the wall which surrounds it, but no appearance whatever of any entrance is observable in the walls of the building; and we must therefore conclude that there was some subterranean communication with it from without, or that they who entered were drawn up with ropes by persons already stationed in the fortress; as we have already observed to be the case in other fortified buildings in the Syrtis. There are traces of other walls about this building in different directions, and the whole brow of the hill on which it stands appears to have been formerly enclosed; below this, to the northward, is a well, built in the soil, of not more than two feet square, which is now filled up with rubbish to within five feet of the surface, and near it are traces of another well, and some large building-stones apparently little out of their places.

The present height of the turrets and outer walls of the fort are about fifteen feet; and were it not for the dilapidated condition of the former, the entrance would not be easy without a ladder.

In a ravine at Mahirīga we found some very good water, which was particularly acceptable to a party of pilgrims from the westward, by whom we were joined, on their journey to Mecca. They took up their abode at night near our tents; and after repeating with great solemnity the proper number of prayers, made themselves very comfortable round a large fire, which the chilness of the nights began to render very necessary; and which was the more severely felt from being contrasted with the sultry heat of the day, occasioned by a parching southerly wind.

After consuming with excellent appetites whatever they could procure from our tents, they would lay themselves down in a circle round the fire, with their feet as close to it as they could bear, and sleep very soundly without any other covering than their bernusse, till the next hour appointed for the performance of their customary devotions. They were not the least discouraged by the length of the journey before them, or the difficulties and privations which they would necessarily have to encounter; but we uniformely found them contented and cheerful, always offering their assistance, unasked for, to our people, whenever it seemed to be necessary. Some of them continued with us as far as Bengazi, and appeared to be very grateful for the few piastres which we gave them there, to assist in supporting them on the road to the Holy City.

We found a few Arabs who possessed some sheep and goats in the neighbourhood of Mahiriga; but we could not prevail upon them to part with a single animal from their flocks, although they knew we were wholly without meat, and would themselves have been delighted to obtain the money which they would have had in exchange for it. We could not at the time account for this obstinate refusal; but circumstances soon after convinced us that it was owing to the intrigues of the Dúbbah.

We continued to travel after leaving Mahiriga over a country equally barren and uninteresting with that to the westward of it, and arrived at night at Linoof.

Early the next morning, as we were making the customary preparations for continuing our journey, we perceived that our new camel-drivers had all assembled together, and on being told to bring the camels as usual, not one of them stirred from his place, the whole party exclaming in concert, in no very conciliatory tones, hàt el flūs, hàt el flūs, give us the money. Here was evidently one of those concerted manœuvres which Arabs of all classes are so skilful in practising; but we were at a loss to conjecture its real cause, which is generally very different from the apparent one. At Boosaida, where the camels were hired, we had arranged with the Dúbbah that they should be paid for on arriving at Bengazi; and the camel-drivers themselves, who (with the exception of one) were all his own relations, had certainly understood and agreed to this arrangement. But they were now in a place which was too well adapted to their views to be passed without inventing some scheme for extorting money, a practice which is seldom omitted by an Arab when he thinks there is a proper opportunity for making such an attempt.

A more dreary and barren spot could scarcely have been anywhere found than that which our friends here selected; it was at least two days' journey from any encampment, and wholly without produce of any kind; if we except the rocks and stones of the soil, and the jackalls and hyænas which sheltered themselves among them. It was imagined that being here without any resource, unable to procure either provisions or water, and far from any inhabited place, we should necessarily be induced to comply with whatever demands it might be advisable to make on the occasion. They could not really have been anxious about their money; for they had seen the former camel-drivers punctually paid, and well pleased with the additional gratification which their general good conduct had induced us to make them. But the opportunity was too tempting, and they could not find it in their hearts to pass it over. It is true that had we paid them every day, the supply of money which we had brought with us from Tripoly, for the expenses of the road, would not certainly have lasted us to Bengazi; and there were no means of obtaining any more till our arrival at that place, where we had an order from the Bashaw on the Governor of the town. Neither the camel-drivers, however, or their relation the Dúbbah, were at all aware of the present slenderness of our supply; and it was not because they doubted our ability to pay them that they got up the scene which was acted at Linoof, but because they thought the opportunity too good to be lost, of getting what money from us they could. Whatever may have been their object, we were determined not to comply with it, and accordingly told them that although we should not have had the least objection to comply with their proposal, had they made it in a more proper manner, yet the insubordination and the insolence which they had displayed upon the occasion had determined us at all events to reject it. We reminded them also of the understanding with which they were hired at Boosaida, to which none of their party could plead ignorance, and declared that we should certainly abide by it, whatever they might imagine to the contrary.

In order however to leave open a door for reconciliation, we told them at the same time that their treatment depended upon themselves; and that if they brought the camels immediately and conducted themselves well for the future, we would pass over their conduct on this occasion, and make them some little present at Bengazi, in addition to the hire of their camels, as they had seen us do to the men of Mesurata. All we could with propriety concede was, however, of no avail; the men positively refused to bring the camels, and we as positively refusing to be imposed upon, they all began to drive them away, and then ranging themselves in a row, unslung their muskets from their shoulders and began hammering their flints, and priming them afresh; looking all the time as fierce and as formidable as they could, as if they were resolved to carry their point at all risks. A very little will convert a quarrel into a fray, and it was certainly not our interest to begin one; we were determined, however, not to be bullied, and as fire-arms had now been brought forward as arguments, we were not long in producing our own. We told our opponents, at the same time that we had no wish to hurt any one of them, that we were quite determined we would not be dictated to; and that if they persisted in not bringing the camels, we should despatch one of our party, accompanied by the chaous, to procure others from the Arabs of Barca; and in case they refused to supply them, to proceed on with all speed to Bengazi, where the Bey would not fail to provide them with as many as we had occasion for. In the mean time, we said, we should load our own horses, and go back to the Arab tents at Mahiriga, where we should at least procure water, and would subsist on our remaining stock of rice till the messengers returned with the camels. We now threatened the Dúbbah with reporting his conduct to the Bashaw, who he very well knew was our friend; but he appeared not to mind what we said, and did not offer to interest himself in our behalf. Our refractory camel-drivers still refused to bring their camels, although they did not attempt to proceed further on the offensive than the hammering and priming above mentioned; and nothing seemed left for us, but to put our proposed plan into execution, however ill-timed the delay might be to us, and however unpleasant might be the annoyances which we should probably have been exposed to from the Arabs to whose encampment we must remove, while at variance with the Dúbbah and his relations. As there was, however, no alternative but submission to the mutineers, or the immediate adoption of some plan like that we have mentioned, we made up our minds at once upon the occasion; and having concerted arrangements for despatching two of our party to Bengazi, we were proceeding to put them in execution, when matters began to assume a different aspect, and our project very happily was rendered unnecessary.

The Dúbbah was the first who began to relent; he had probably been reflecting upon our threat of reporting his conduct, and he very well knew what an unfavourable footing he would stand upon with the Bashaw, if he ventured so decidedly to disobey the injunctions he had received from him when he was directed to conduct us to Bengazi. He now came out of his tent, and going first to one of his party and then to another, pretended that he was using all the means in his power to induce them to relinquish their demands, and to bring their camels to be loaded as usual; whereas one single word from him would, at any time of the dispute, have been sufficient to put an end to it altogether.

This farce was kept up, however, with all due solemnity; and as an opening was now made towards accommodation, we left Shekh Mahommed to manage matters in his own way, without letting him know we saw through his manœuvres. It must be allowed, at the same time, that the acting on both sides was excellent: some pretended they were weighing the Dúbbah's arguments very gravely, while others made a show of not listening to them at all, and walked away towards their camels as if to drive them away, the old Shekh following closely, and holding them by the baracan, while he went through all the manual of pantomimic persuasion. At last he made his appearance in our servants' tent, and told them very gravely that he had succeeded in appeasing the malcontents, who had now agreed to drop their demands, and to bring their camels to be loaded. He then went through a long string of arguments which he had been obliged to use to induce them to make these concessions, but all of which had proved unavailing; and he promised at last (he majestically asserted) laying his hand at the same time on his breast, to be answerable for the money himself! Nothing, however, would do, till he fortunately bethought himself of offering *in pledge* the new gold-lace crimson burnoose, which His Highness the Bashaw had presented him with on his departure from Tripoly! All eyes, he observed, were fixed on it, as he drew this precious object out of the bag; and when he unfolded the eloquent garment, and displayed all the logic contained in its rich folds, they had not a word more left to say on the subject, but consented immediately to receive it in pawn, and to abide by whatever he should decide.

It is scarcely possible for those who have had no dealings with Arabs, to imagine all the trouble and exertions which they will give themselves in getting up a performance of this nature; the whole piece too is in general so naturally acted, that if the spectators had no cause for suspicion, they would seldom perceive that the acting was overdone, which is almost invariably the case in some part or other of the play. We had been much accustomed to scenes of the kind, but till the time when the Dúbbah began to interfere, we never suspected that the parties were not in earnest, although it was clear that they acted in concert. The good-humour with which an Arab will bear his disappointment, when nothing after all is gained by his stratagem, is another very prominent feature in his character. He never appears to regret the trouble he has taken; though it may have cost him whole days to plan his manœuvre, and a great deal of personal exertion to put it in execution. He bears no ill will to the persons who may have detected him; but will relate the whole thing as an excellent plot, immediately after its failure, and commend the penetration of those who have baffled his best efforts to deceive them.

It was not worth our while to undeceive the old Shekh, by letting him know that we saw through the whole of this manœuvre, and he continued to give himself great credit for the mode in which he had terminated it; he really believed that he had greatly ingratiated himself with our party by having *pawned* the new gold laced burnoose above mentioned to extricate us from our *hazardous situation*, and took every opportunity of making some pompous allusion to the liberal part which he had acted. The camel-drivers returned to their duty as usual, and we continued our journey to Muktahr, where we arrived on the same day at sunset, just as if nothing had happened.

FOOTNOTES:

A great quantity of broken pottery was found at this place, and red earthen jars were observed protruding through the sides of the cliff where it had fallen away; the floor and two sides of a chamber, coated with excellent cement, were also remarked in the side of the cliff near the sea; the other parts had fallen away with the rock, and were scattered in ruin on the beach, which was thickly strewed with remains of the fortress.

We have already stated, on the authority of Pliny, that the Philænean Altars were of sand; and as they must be looked for in this neighbourhood, we have supposed them to have been erected in the sandy tract which we shall shortly mention in our progress eastward from Bengerwàd. For had they been raised on a spot where other materials could have been easily obtained, it is not probable that any so unstable as sand would have been used for the commemoration of so noble an action as that which occasioned their erection.

Ειτ' αλλος τοπος Χαραξ καλουμενος—ω εμπορειω εχρωντο Καρχηδονιοι κομιζοντες οινον, αντιφορτιζομενοι δε οπον και σιλφιον παρα των εκ Κυρηνης λαθρα παρακομιζοντων·—Lib. xvii. p. 688.

For, after mentioning Charax, Strabo adds—ειθ' οἱ φιλαινων βομοι, και μετα τουτους Αυτομαλα φρουριον, φυλακην εχον, ιδρυμενον κατα τον μυχον του κολπου παντος· Here we find the fortress of Automala placed in the innermost recess of the gulf, which is much farther to the eastward than the point to which we are at present arrived.

Page 79, Italian edition.

Ομορει δε τη Κυρηναια ἡ το σιλφιον φερουσα, και τον οπον τον Κυρεναιον, ον εκφερει το σιλφιον οπισθεν·—Lib. xvii. p. 837.

Pliny's words are—Ab his proximum dicetur auctoritate clarissimum laserpitium, quod Græci vocant silphion, in Cyrenaica provincia repertum: cujus succum vocant laser, magnificum in usu medicamentisque, &c.—(Hist. Nat., lib. xix. c. 3.)

De Ædificiis, lib. v. p. 110-11. Par. fol. 1663.

CHAPTER IX.

Barren and desolate appearance of the Country in the Neighbourhood of Muktáhr — Sulphur Mines at Kebrīt — Extensive Marsh near Muktáhr — Arrive at Sachrīn, the southernmost Point of the Gulf — Singularly desolate and comfortless Appearance of it — Examination of the Coast from the Heights of Jerīa — Extreme Difference of its Outline from that laid down in modern Charts — Suggested Causes of this Error — Accumulation of Sand on the Beach in this Neighbourhood — Alarm of Signor Della Cella in passing it — Causes of this Accumulation considered — Character of the Country at the Bottom of the Gulf — Observations of Signor Della Cella respecting it — Allusion of the Doctor to the Expedition of the Psylli — Remarks on the Latitude of this part of the Gulf — Monuments of the Philæni — Record of their Patriotism by Sallust — Various Positions of the Philænian Altars by the Ancients — Boreum Promontorium and Oppidum of Cellarius — Suggested Causes of their Position by this Author in the Bottom of the Gulf — Observations on the Nature of the Soil of the Greater Syrtis — Allusion to the March of Cato across it — Island called Bushaifa at the Bottom of the Gulf — Gradual Improvement in the Appearance of the Country — Arrival at Braiga — Remains observed there — Harbour of Braiga — Heaps of Sulphur lying on the Beach there for Embarkation — Salt Lake and Marsh at Braiga below the Level of the Sea — Well-constructed Forts at Braiga — Braiga considered as the Site of Automala — Contest between the Avarice and Conscience of the Dúbbah — Its Termination in Favour of the latter — Arrival at Tabilba — Excavations and Remains there — Tabilba considered as the Maritimæ Stationes of Ptolemy — Arrive at Ain Agàn — Chain of Salt Lakes and Marshes said to extend two Days to the South-eastward — Island of Gàra, probably the Gaia of Ptolemy — Wells of Sweet Water, Two Miles to the North-east of Shiebah — Abduction of a Lamb from an Arab Shepherd by our Party — Consequences of this Measure — Departure of the Dúbbah in search of his Camels — Arrival at Carcora — Two Boat Coves observed there — Springs of Fresh Water within a few feet of a Salt Water Lake — Arrive at Ghimēnes — Forts and Remains there — Excavated Tombs in the Neighbourhood — Change of Weather experienced — Wasted Condition of our Horses from Fatigue and want of Water — Hardy Constitution of the Barbary Horses — Treatment of them by the Arabs — Improved Appearance of the Country in approaching Bengazi — Singular Fences of Stone generally adopted in this part of the Country — Causes of their Erection — Position of Bengazi — Fertile Appearance of the Country about it — Arrival at Bengazi — Friendly

Reception of our Party by Signor Rossoni, the British Resident there — Establish ourselves in the Town for the rainy Season.

THE country which we travelled over after quitting Linoof was stony and perfectly barren: no living creature made its appearance there, with the exception of a single hyæna, and a species of wild bull which the Arabs call Bograh-wash, both of which ran off on perceiving us. Our route for the last two days had been over the rocky ground a little inland, but the coast between Hudīa and Muktahr is low, with sand-hills here and there almost the whole way; and has many small bays formed between very low rocky flats, which are in most parts not more than a foot above water.

Muktahr is the boundary of the districts of Syrt and Barca, the line being marked by small piles of loose stones; and from here there is a road branching off to some sulphur-mines called Kebrīt, which are situated a day and a half to the southward. The sulphur is brought on camels from these mines to Braiga, where vessels occasionally arrive to receive it; and it is probably from that circumstance that the part of the gulf in this neighbourhood is called by the Arabs, Giun el Kebrit (Gulf of Sulphur). Near Muktahr is a remarkable table-hill called Jebbel Allah, and an extensive salt lake (Esubbah Muktahr), along the edge of which we passed for a few miles, and then crossing a ridge called Jerīa, proceeded on a few miles further to Sachrīn, where we pitched the tents for the night.

We had now arrived at the most southern point of the Gulf of Syrtis, and few parts of the world will be found to present so truly desolate and wretched an appearance as its shores in this neighbourhood exhibit. Marsh, sand, and barren rocks, alone meet the eye; and not a single human being, or a trace of vegetation, are to be met with in any direction. The stillness of the nights which we passed in this dreary tract of country was not even broken by the howlings of our old friends the jackalls and hyænas, which prowled about our tents in other parts of the Syrtis; and it seemed as if all the animated part of creation had agreed in the utter hopelessness of inhabiting it to any advantage.

Sachrīn may be said to be the bottom of the gulf, and it was here more particularly desirable to ascertain the exact form assumed by the coast in terminating this extensive bay. We proceeded therefore, early on the morning after our arrival here, to the high land which we have mentioned at Jerīa, for the purpose of comparing the actual form of the gulf at this point with that which is assigned to it by the geographers who have hitherto described it. A thick mist for some time concealed every part, but it cleared off before noon, and we had then an extensive view of the whole line of coast. We had the various charts before us, and the opportunity which now offered itself was as favourable as could possibly be wished. But how different was the form which now presented itself to our observation, from that which appeared in the authorities which we were enabled to compare with it. Instead of the narrow and cuneiform inlet in which the gulf has in modern charts been made to terminate, we saw a wide extent of coast, sweeping due east and west, with as little variation as possible; and in the place of the numerous ports and sinuosities which appeared in the maps before us, we saw a shore but very slightly indented, which offered no possible security to vessels of any description.

The chart ascribed to Ptolemy is the only one we are acquainted with which approaches to something like the actual form of the coast; and every step which modern geographers have receded from this outline has been a step farther from the truth.

It is difficult to say on what authorities the narrow inlet was originally introduced which terminates the gulf in the charts above mentioned; unless, indeed, the terms which have been used by ancient geographers, in describing this part of the Greater Syrtis, may be supposed to have occasioned the idea. The castle of Automala is mentioned by Strabo as situated in the *innermost recess* of the gulf. And Pliny speaks of the coast inhabited by the Lotophagi (which he places in the Greater Syrtis) as being equally in the *innermost* part of the bay. It may be possible that these terms have induced the more recent geographers to consider the gulf as terminating in an inlet, and to hazard, on their authority, the introduction of that which is now in question in the absence of any accurate survey. If such meaning can be supposed to have been extracted from the term used by Strabo, his authority might certainly have been safely relied upon by those who employed it on this occasion without any reproach to their caution; since this geographer himself visited the coast in a vessel, and may therefore be supposed to have seen what he described. However this may be, we can positively assert that no inlet whatever exists in the Gulf of Syrtis; and that the direction of the coast at the bottom of the gulf is, as nearly as possible, due east and west for a whole day's journey together; turning afterwards to the northward so slightly, that this difference is scarcely perceptible to the eye. A large tract of quick sand is also laid down by many in this part of the Gulf of Syrtis; but we have traversed the sand and the sand-hills which are found here, on horseback, in almost every direction, and may safely affirm that they afford as good a footing as any dry sand or sand heaps can be supposed to present. If any other authority may be acceptable in proof of the extreme dryness of the sand in this neighbourhood, we have only to cite that of Doctor Della Cella to put everything like scepticism on this point at rest. "Woe be to us," exclaims this gentleman, (in describing the sandy tract here alluded to) "if a sirocco, or southerly wind, had unhappily overtaken us in this place, the whole army would have been buried beneath the sands which the action of the winds here raised up in waves no less formidable than those of the sea!" Now if anything like moisture had really existed in the formidable particles which caused the Doctor such alarm, he might have looked in defiance at every point of the compass, without anticipating, with so much well-described horror, the fatal consequences which would have resulted to himself and the whole army, had the wind been unfortunately to the southward.

The anticipation of this premature burial was occasioned by the passage of Signor Della Cella and the army over a long range of sand-hills thrown up on the beach in this neighbourhood; and which are supposed by the Doctor to have been blown there from the Great Desert to the southward. Of this latter circumstance we have certainly some doubt; and can more readily imagine the "seven hours and a half of real misery" endured by our traveller, "under the influence of a burning sun," in passing the sand-hills here mentioned, than we can suppose these unwelcome impediments themselves to have travelled from the desert in the interior. For all the sand-hills which encumber the beach in these parts, as well as all others which we recollect to have seen in the Syrtis, are, in our opinion, blown up from the beach itself, and not from the desert to the southward.

The tract of country, at the same time, which intervenes between these sand-hills and the desert is perfectly clear from any encumbrance of the kind; which could scarcely be the case if the masses on the beach had passed over it in their passage from the Sahara; but Signor Della Cella is further confirmed in his opinion by the circumstance of his not having been able to perceive, though he looked, he says, very attentively, any chain of high land in the interior, between the sand-hills which he mentions and the desert. "In the tract of country which lies at the bottom of the gulf" he saw nothing whatever but sand, and no hills whatever but sand-hills.

From this circumstance the Doctor derives a new proof that the sand-hills have travelled from the southward; and in further proof of the non-existence of any chain of hills in this quarter, he has instanced the passage of northerly winds from the Mediterranean, to find their equilibrium in the southern regions of Africa; which passage they could not have effected, he supposes, if they had had a chain of hills to get over in their journey! The Doctor then proceeds to relate the expedition of the Psylli, as recorded by Herodotus, in further support of his position; but in telling us that when these unfortunate gentlemen arrived on the confines of the desert, they were all of them buried in the sands which there assailed them, he does not express the surprise which might be expected at their not having met with a similar accident long before they arrived at that point; for this misfortune might assuredly have happened with equal probability before they set out on their journey to the southward, if the whole of the country, as we are informed by the Doctor, consisted of nothing else, from the desert to the sea, but the formidable red sand which at last put an end to them. The fact is, however, that the "ampia depressione" which is stated by Signor Della Cella to exist between the bottom of the gulf and the great desert, is unfortunately interrupted by a chain of hills, a little inland, of at least four or five hundred feet in height; and we will venture to assert that, in the whole of the tract which has here been described by the Doctor, there is no part where high land does not intervene between the sand-hills and the desert alluded to. We are sorry to place so substantial an impediment in the way of the northerly wind, which the Doctor imagines could not go to the southward to gain its equilibrium if such a bar were placed in its route; but if the whole country from the sea to the Niger were never again to be refreshed with this desirable breeze, we must still be obliged to leave our hills where we saw them in spite of so severe a misfortune. In stating that the level supposed to exist between the bottom of the Gulf of Syrtis and the great desert is not uninterrupted by hills, we must also observe that these hills are not of sand, and that a great portion of marshy and stony land is mingled with the sand which the Doctor states to be exclusively found there. We must at the same time remark, that the only part where the sand is red is in the neighbourhood of the sulphur mines; and this peculiarity may be considered as wholly occasioned by the nature of the soil where it is found. It is besides of so fine a texture as to partake more of the nature of dust than of desert sand, which is neither so red nor so light. It is not raised up in large heaps like the sand on the beach, but scattered over the surface in little hillocks, on which a scanty vegetation is occasionally observable. In fact this substance has no resemblance whatever either to the sand on the beach or to that of the desert, and it ceases altogether with the soil which occasions it. How Signor Della Cella could have confounded it with the sand heaps thrown up on the beach we are at a loss to imagine; for these are considerably whiter than the desert sand, while the light powder in question is considerably redder. Besides, the sand-hills continue long after this substance has ceased to appear; and in the parts where they are found in the greatest masses there is not a particle of red sand to be seen. At the same time that we differ on this point with Signor Della Cella, we must also confess that his conjecture with respect to the extension of the gulf to the southward is not better founded than his remarks on the extension of the sand. For it is somewhat remarkable, that while the shape of the bottom of the gulf has been so very incorrectly laid down in modern charts as it is found to have been, the latitude which has been assigned to it by the same authorities is as near the truth as possible; and we may safely affirm that the most southern part of the Gulf of Syrtis does not approach at all nearer to the desert than it is made to do in the charts alluded to by

Signor Della Cella, notwithstanding the confidence with which the Doctor maintains a contrary opinion, on the authority of his friend Captain Lautier.

It is somewhere at the bottom of the Syrtis that we must have looked for the monuments erected to the Philæni, had they still been in existence; it appears however, as we have before mentioned, on the authority of Strabo, that they were no longer extant in the time of that geographer. But if the pillars have disappeared which marked the spot where the brothers were interred, the record of their patriotism still exists in the pages of history; and the account which has been given of this disinterested sacrifice by Sallust may not perhaps be unacceptable to the reader. "At the time (says that historian) when the Carthaginians ruled over a great part of Africa, the people of Cyrene were also powerful and opulent. A sandy plain was on the frontiers of the two countries, the surface of which was uniform and unbroken, and neither mountain nor river appeared in it, by which the boundary of these kingdoms might be determined; a circumstance which occasioned many frequent and bloody wars between them. After various alternate successes and defeats, they entered into the following agreement; that certain persons deputed by each state should leave their home on an appointed day, and that the place where the parties might meet should be considered as the boundary of the kingdoms."

"Two brothers, named Philæni, were appointed on the part of Carthage, who contrived to travel faster than the deputies from Cyrene, but whether this was occasioned by accident, or the indolence of the Cyreneans, I have not been able (says the historian) to ascertain."

"Stormy weather (he adds) might undoubtedly occasion delays in such a country, as well as it is known to do at sea: for when violent winds prevail in level and barren tracts, the sand which is raised by them is driven so forcibly into the faces and eyes of those who cross them, that their progress is considerably impeded. So soon as the people of Cyrene were aware of the ground which they had lost, and reflected on the punishment which would await them, in consequence, on their return, they began to accuse the Carthaginians of having set out before the appointed time; and when a dispute arose on the subject, they determined to brave everything rather than return home defeated. In this state of affairs, the Carthaginians desired the Greeks to name some conditions of accommodation; and when the latter proposed that the deputies from Carthage should either be buried on the spot which they claimed as the boundary, or allow them to advance as far as they chose on the same conditions, the Philæni immediately accepted the terms, and giving themselves up to the service of their country, were buried alive on the spot where the dispute had occurred. On the same spot two altars were consecrated to their memory by the people of Carthage, and other honours were also decreed to them at home."

In the old map of Peutinger (as we have stated above) we find the Philænean altars placed much farther to the westward in the neighbourhood of the little Syrtis; but the authorities of Ptolemy, Strabo, Pliny, and Mela, are sufficient to fix them in the Greater Syrtis; and as they are expressly stated by Strabo (lib. 17) to have occurred before Automala, in passing from west to east, we must suppose them to have existed somewhere in the tract of country just described, since the fortress of Automala is laid down by that geographer in the bottom of the gulf. There is a difficulty in reconciling the accounts of Pliny and Mela on this point; for the Philænean altars are mentioned by the former of these writers as placed on the eastern boundary of the country of the Lotophagi, which he lays down in the bottom of the gulf. Mela may be understood to assign the same position to the altars (although something appears wanting in the text in this part to connect the two sentences together); but then he makes the country of the Lotophagi commence at the Borion (Boreum) Promontorium, and finish at the promontory of Phycus (answering to Ras Sem), and this will place the Lotophagi far in the Cyrenaica, and out of the Gulf of Syrtis altogether, which finishes at the Boreum Promontorium.

It seems to be with the intention of reconciling these accounts in some degree, that Cellarius has placed a Boreum Promontorium and Oppidum in the bottom of the gulf. And he is indeed somewhat justified in doing so, by the position assigned to a city called Boreum (βοϱιον) by Procopius, which is mentioned by that writer as the most western city of the Pentapolis, and distant about four days from Augila. This is the city which we have mentioned, in speaking of Hudīa, as having been inhabited by Jews of the Cyrenaica; it was exempt from the payment of tribute and duties, and was fortified at the same time with the adjacent country, by the command of the emperor Justinian. But the Borion Promontorium is at the same time mentioned by Pliny as the eastern extremity of the Gulf of Syrtis, as which it is also considered by Ptolemy and Strabo; so that except we may allow that there were two places of this name, we can see no mode of reconciling so many contradictory statements. This accommodation, as we have mentioned above, appears to have been intended by Cellarius, who has marked one of his promontories at the eastern boundary of the gulf, and placed the other at the bottom of it.

We cannot quit this subject without observing that the idea which appears to have been entertained by the ancients of the soil of the Greater Syrtis, is not confirmed by an inspection of the country in question. Cato is described by Strabo as having marched his army across the Syrtis through deep and burning sands, and Lucan has given so exaggerated an account of the same march, as to make his description almost wholly poetical. Sallust also, in his account of the Philæni, describes the "level and sandy plain, in which these monuments were erected, without either river or mountain by which they might be distinguished". But there is no sandy plain of this description in the bottom of the Syrtis; and, although there is no river, there are certainly mountains, if hills of solid stone, of from four to six hundred feet in height, may be entitled to that distinction.

It is true that the chain of hills at the bottom of the gulf run in an east and westerly direction, and might not, on that account, be well calculated for objects by which limits in the same direction might be ascertained; but the account given by Sallust would lead us to imagine (as it seems to have done Signor Della Cella) that the place was without any inequalities of this nature whatever.

Again, if it be true that Cato marched his army over the sand-hills which appear to have been so laboriously traversed by the army which the doctor accompanied, it was certainly no very good proof of the patriot's generalship; for, with the exception of one place, where the passage is occasionally impeded by marshy ground, reaching close up to the foot of the sand-hills on the beach, there could have been no occasion for crossing the sand at all, since the country to the southward of it is clear . The same may be said of the whole tract of country in general, where sand-hills are found in the Syrtis and Cyrenaica; the sand-heaps being confined to the beach alone, and not overspreading the whole face of the soil. Indeed, after passing the bottom of the gulf, the country at the back of the sand-hills becomes very capable of cultivation, and affords, in many places, an excellent pasturage. So that if we should consider the Syrtis in general as a large unbroken body of sand, which the ancients seem mostly to have done, we should certainly form a very wrong idea of the nature of the country in question.

North-west of Sachreen, which may be considered as the bottom of the gulf, at about a mile and a quarter from the shore, is a small islet called Bushaifa, with breakers east and west of it; and to the southward is a large marsh, with a ruin on a small rising ground inland of it: from here a valley extends eastward between the high land to the southward and some sand-hills on the coast. The road lies tolerably close along the sides of these sand-heaps, which in some places rise abruptly from the edge of the marsh, leaving a very narrow path between the two. It was probably here that Signor Della Cella and the army which he accompanied chose the passage over the sand-hills in preference to that along the marsh at the foot of them; or it may be possible that the water of the marsh reached too close to the sand-hills when they passed, to allow of any choice of road at all. We however found the path at the foot of the sand-hills very practicable, although we were occasionally obliged to pass singly along it. Had these sand-hills been capable of suddenly detaching large masses from their summits or sides, we might occasionally perhaps have been buried *pro tempore* under their weight, and might, in some places, have experienced considerable difficulty in extricating ourselves at all; but we must confess that we did not anticipate any very fatal effects from the action of southerly winds; nor did we believe it very probable that an avalanche of sand would seize the precise moment in which we were passing under it to precipitate itself upon our heads. Two hours, we should imagine, would fully suffice for the accomplishment of the passage between the marsh and the sand-hills, at any season in which it might be practicable; and if double that time be allowed for the passage over the hills in question, when that below might be impassable from the rise of the water in the marsh, we should conclude it would be amply sufficient. As there is no other part of the gulf in which it could, at any time, be absolutely necessary to pass over the sand-hills at all, we are at a loss to imagine why the army of the Bey, and that of his Roman predecessor, should have given themselves so much trouble in crossing them. Immediately after the marsh commences pasture land, and after five hours' journey from Sachreen, we arrived at a place called Gartubbah, where we found some Arab tents, and established ourselves for the night.

The next morning we proceeded on to Braiga, where we were led to expect, from the report of our Arab guides, that we should find a harbour full as good as that of Tripoly. Braiga has been a strongly-fortified post, as appears from the remains of several well-constructed and spacious castles which have been erected there. On the western point of the bay which constitutes the mersa (or harbour) is some tolerably high land, on which one of the forts has formerly stood; but which is now so much destroyed and encumbered with rubbish, as to offer little interest on examination. Along the same range of hills are other remains of building, originally connected with this fort, part of which we were induced to excavate, but found the chamber which we cleared to have been merely a storehouse for grain, or a reservoir for preserving water. It had been excavated in the rock, on the top of the range, and may be considered as offering an excellent example of the durable quality of the cement employed by the Romans in its formation: for the stone in which it had been excavated had crumbled away, and left the cement with which the interior had been coated standing upright in its original position, in defiance of the storms of wind and rain which must have frequently assailed it from the sea.

We found some Greek and Roman characters traced in the interior, and the representation of a ship and a palm-tree, of which copies will be found annexed, together with plans of the forts and of the chamber excavated. The surface of the cement on which these objects had been sketched was as smooth and as perfect as it could have been at any time, and we were in hopes, when we first saw the drawings, that others would be found on further excavation, and probably some inscription in Greek or Latin, by which we might have dated these productions. No other drawings or letters however were found, and we were obliged to content ourselves with taking copies of those described, and in making the plan of the chamber.

The ground about this excavation, and, indeed, along the whole range, was strewed with fragments of pottery and glass, among which we found a brass coin of Augustus Cæsar in a very tolerable state of preservation. While the excavations were going on in this quarter (for the outer wall of one of the forts was also cleared a few feet, in order to obtain the measurements of the gateway by which it had been entered) the plan of the harbour had been completed, as far as it was possible without boats, and the reefs were set down by bearings and estimated distance. The best landing for boats was found to be under the high point which we have mentioned to the westward, on which the fort excavated had been built; and on the beach at this angle were several heaps of sulphur, collected in equal-sized masses for embarkation, which had been brought on camels from the mines to the southward, and were said to belong to Mahommed Ali, the Pasha of Egypt. South-west of this point there is a large salt lake and marsh, which are evidently below the level of the sea, as we perceived a stream of salt water oozing from out a porous part of the rock on the seaside, about eight feet above the level of the lake, and running into it. The land at the east and western extremities of the lake is so low, as to render it very probable that it may once have communicated with the sea, and that the point on which the fort stands may have been an island. If there should prove to be sufficient water in the harbour of Braiga, it is probable that good anchorage would be found there, with all winds, behind reefs of breakers extending across the mouth of it: it may be easily distinguished by the very high sand-hills at the back of it, and by the ruin on the rocky point mentioned at its western extremity. Among these sand-hills are some wells, in which the water, though several hundred feet above the level of the sea, is perfectly brackish. Beyond them to the southward is a hilly country covered with verdure, in which a number of camels were feeding, and numerous flocks of sheep and goats; but although we found ourselves in the midst of such plenty, we were unable to purchase a single sheep, in consequence of our friend the Dúbbah's manœuvres. At Gartubbah, which possessed the same advantages, we were equally unable to succeed in a similar attempt. Among the green hills just mentioned are several ruins of forts, of the same quadrangular form as usual, and which have been built with large stones very regularly shaped; so that Braiga may be considered as a military station, and must have certainly been one of importance. If it be necessary to give it an ancient name, we should consider it as the site of

Automala, which was also a military station, according to the account of Strabo.

Automala, it is true, has been laid down by this geographer at the innermost part of the gulf, which must be taken as the most southern point of it; and the coast had already begun to bend to the northward before we arrived at Braiga. But a place which would answer to the description here given of Automala, could scarcely have disappeared altogether; and there is no place of any kind at the bottom of the gulf before the occurrence of Braiga. The coin of Augustus, which was found among the ruins of Braiga, would afford some proof of its having existed in the time of that emperor, and the form and solidity of the buildings which are found there sufficiently point it out as a fortified position. No fortified place is however mentioned to have existed in this neighbourhood, except Automala; and if Braiga may not be considered as the remains of that fortress, it has been wholly overlooked by the ancient authorities, and we know of no name which can be properly bestowed upon it.

We should be the more inclined to consider the fortifications of Braiga as those which are mentioned at Automala, from the circumstance of their vicinity to other remains, which answer extremely well to those of the *maritimæ stationes* laid down in the map of Ptolemy. In this map, the stations are placed a little to the northward of Automala, with no other place intervening; and the position of Braiga with regard to Tabilba, which answers precisely to the *maritimæ stationes*, is exactly that assigned to Automala in the order here adopted by Ptolemy.

Sachreen may undoubtedly be considered as the extremity of the gulf in its present state; but a place which was only twenty miles distant from it might well have been said to be situated in this recess, by a person who viewed it from the sea, particularly when the outline of this part of the gulf is considered at the same time. Braiga, from the sea, must have, besides, been at all times very conspicuous; and we can scarcely imagine that the fort which stands so high above the beach there would have been unnoticed by Strabo, had it existed in his time, which we may suppose with probability that it did. He has, however, noticed only Automala; and it remains to be considered how far we are really authorized in assuming these places as the same, upon the data already before the reader.

Before we left Braiga, one of the Arabs of the place brought a present of five lambs to the tents, and gave them in charge to Shekh Mahommed el Dúbbah, who, thinking that this would prove a most excellent opportunity of showing his generosity to the best advantage, as well as his extraordinary influence with the Arabs of the place, in being able to procure sheep when we could not purchase them at all, made his appearance with great ceremony at the entrance of our tent, with two of the lambs above mentioned. After many compliments and professions of service, he offered the two lambs as a present from himself, and begged we would do him the favour to accept them. As we had lately found reason to be much dissatisfied with the Dúbbah's conduct, we did not choose to be under an obligation to him; and having given him to understand the reason of our refusal, declined accepting the lambs as a present, but offered at the same time to purchase them. The old Shekh looked disconcerted, as we intended he should be, and slowly retired from the tent. And now began a parley between his avarice and his conscience, which terminated at length in favour of the latter; for, though not very tender on most occasions, this inward monitor of our worthy conductor would not allow him to receive money for what he knew was already our own, although it did not object to let him take the credit of presenting it to us. The result was, that he soon after paid us a second visit, bringing with him the two lambs as before, but which he now acknowledged were intended as presents to us, instead of to himself, as he assured us he had imagined: he informed us, at the same time, that the Arab who brought them was a shepherd belonging to the Bashaw, who wished to shew us what attentions were in his power, and had presented us with the best that he had. The other three lambs, he said, were really intended for him; but we afterwards found, from the shepherd in question, that the whole number had been presented to us. We also discovered that the reason why we could not, on many occasions, procure sheep or goats from the Arab tents which we passed on our journey, at which we had often been surprised, was because two of our party, followers of the Dúbbah, had usually gone before on pretence of reconnoitring, and had strictly enjoined the Arabs not to sell us anything whatever. We afterwards recollected, in confirmation of this manœuvre, that the only times when we had been able to purchase sheep were those at which we had accidentally been in advance of this worthy couple; and the Arabs we chanced to meet seldom failed on these occasions to ask us, of their own accord, whether we did not want a sheep or a goat, some butter, manteca, or other articles of provision, which they would have been able to furnish us with, and which they would, in fact, have been glad to dispose of. We could assign no other motive for this conduct on the part of our Arab guides, than the wish of making us as dependent as possible upon themselves, that they might either have an opportunity of showing their influence, or of planning with more effect some scheme to impose upon us. Yet the very same people who would take so much trouble to forward their own interested views, at the expense of another, would in all probability consider themselves greatly to blame, or at any rate highly disgraced, if they suffered a hungry traveller, of whatever creed or nation, to leave their own tents unsatisfied, should he apply to them for relief. But such is the inconsistency of Arab character; and it may perhaps be said, that he who should consider them as a generous nation, because they practised this species of hospitality, would be as much deceived in his opinion of them, as he would be who should imagine that they have no liberal feelings, because they are well skilled in selfish tricks and manœuvres.

On leaving Braiga, we travelled over a hilly country to the eastward, and passed two interesting ruins of ancient forts, of which we contrived to obtain plans. About noon we halted near a bold rocky promontory, called by the Arabs Tabilba, on which are the remains of a castle. On a hill just above it are the ruins of a very strong fortification, which was connected with the castle by a wall of five feet in thickness carried quite round the precipice on which it stood. This was defended on the inland side by a fosse of thirty feet in width excavated in the solid rock; and the rubbish extracted from it was piled up to form a bank on the outer side. On the beach are the remains of a wall remarkably well constructed, or it never could so long have resisted the violence of the surf which beats against it. It appears to have formed part of a landing-place or quay which has originally been built in its immediate neighbourhood. The interior of the rock on which the castle stands has been excavated into numerous galleries and chambers, which seem to have answered the purpose of barracks. Some of these are very spacious and very well finished; but the dash of the sea, which now washes through the exterior chambers, has completely destroyed their surface, and has left them in parts so little foundation as to render it very dangerous to enter them. In fact, the base of the rock in which these excavations have been made is perforated like a honeycomb by the continual action of the sea, which now washes through the hollows with a roar which may be heard at a considerable distance, and must in stormy weather be tremendous. In one of the chambers were several Greek inscriptions which have been written with ink on the walls; but they are now so indistinct, that we could not succeed in copying more than a few words of one of them.

They are written in what may be called the running-hand of the Greeks of the Roman Empire, and it is probable that one much accustomed to this character might succeed, with the assistance of a strong and steady light, and the frequent application of water to the inscriptions, in making out more than we were able to do with the little time we had at our disposal, and the light we were able to procure. In other parts of the rock were excavated tombs, some of which were entered by a quadrangular well, in the manner of those common in Egypt. We found nothing in any of them but scattered bones, from which we were not able to ascertain the mode of burial adopted. There can be no doubt that great part of the rock just described has already been washed away by the sea, which has here gained considerably on the land; and several wells are now observable some feet under water, which were of course originally above its level.

In the wall fronting the south, we observed part of an arch protruding itself from among the rubbish which encumbered it; and found, on clearing it, that it had been constructed without a key-stone, of square blocks, arranged so as to touch each other at the bottom, and having the interstices above filled up with good cement, which appeared to be more durable than the stone. We found other examples of arches so constructed in different parts of the Syrtis and Cyrenaica. The appearance of the top of the arch just described had given us hopes of discovering an entrance to some part of the fortification through the wall in which it was formed; but we found to our disappointment, on clearing it from the rubbish, that what we thought would prove the entrance extended no more than three feet from the external surface; and that all farther advance was prevented by a solid wall built across it, which appeared to be part of the original structure. Among the rubbish we found a silver coin, and several copper ones, so corroded that it was impossible to ascertain their antiquity.

We should willingly have given a much longer time to the examination of the ruins at Tabilba than the few hours we were enabled to bestow upon it; but the lateness of the season left us no choice on the subject, and we had already spent more time at Braiga than we could well afford to employ in such researches. It must however be confessed, that if we had doubted the probability of being able to return and examine them with greater minuteness, we might have been tempted to stay longer at many places in the Syrtis than we should perhaps have been authorized in doing.

We have no hesitation in supposing Tabilba to be the site of the *maritimæ stationes* of Ptolemy. Its position corresponds so well with that assigned to the naval stations in question, and its remains are so well calculated to induce the belief that they have originally been appropriated to the defence and accommodation of a considerable number of men, that we cannot be sceptical on the occasion. On either side of the promontory on which the castle has been built is a small sandy bay, neither of which at present affords any shelter for vessels, but from which the galleys of the ancients might have been easily drawn up on the beach, when it might not have been practicable for them to keep the sea.

This mode of sheltering their vessels was common to the Greeks and Romans, to whom a port, such as in our days would be considered a good one, appears to have been by no means necessary. We are told indeed by Strabo, that this part of the coast was very sparingly provided with ports and watering-places, and the harbour which he calls the best in the Syrtis is now no harbour at all. Mersa Braiga is in fact the only port in the gulf which can at all be considered as such, in our estimation of the term; and here the shelter is only afforded by breakers, and could not prevent the small vessels of the ancients from being driven on shore in stormy weather.

On the day after our arrival at Tabilba we continued our journey along the coast, and proceeded to Ain Agàn, passing two ruins of forts conspicuously situated on the hills. The beach in this neighbourhood presents a very dreary prospect; but the scene is much improved after passing the wady, and the country then begins to be cultivated. Many flocks of sheep and goats soon presented themselves to our view, and tents were scattered about in all directions. We procured from the Arabs here a scanty supply of corn for our horses, of which the poor animals stood very much in need; but we were obliged to apply for it in a more decided tone than we had hitherto found it necessary to assume on such occasions, as the Arabs, though they had plenty, were not very willing to part with it. There are some wells of brackish water at Ain Agàn, which is however the best that this neighbourhood affords, and we were glad to fill all our water-skins with it before we proceeded any farther.

A few miles from Ain Agàn is a remarkable hill, called Aàlum Limàrish, the summit of which overlooks an extensive tract of country, and Mersa Braiga may be plainly distinguished from it. To the southward of Aàlum Limàrish we observed a chain of lakes and swamps, which the Chaous informed us extended two days to the south-eastward. They communicated with the wady at Ain Agàn, and might once have joined the sea; the water in them is quite brackish.

To seaward we observed an island about a mile in length, with breakers east and west of it extending a considerable distance; from which we may infer that it was once much larger. The Arab name for this island (which is Gàra) too much resembles that of Gaia, one of those laid down by Ptolemy, to leave much doubt of their being the same. Gàra is situated farther to the north eastward than the island which we allude to in the map of Ptolemy, and is besides nearer the coast; but the similarity of the names cannot here be overlooked, and we do not hesitate to identify it with Gaia. At about a mile from the shore, nearly opposite Aàlum Limarish, is a remarkably white rock, about forty feet high, and steep on all sides; it has breakers scattered about it, and should not be closely approached till better known: beyond this rock, which is called Ishaifa, we perceived the sea breaking heavily over another rock, as much as four miles from the shore, which extends itself in reefs towards Gàra. There are two other islands laid down by Ptolemy in the Gulf of the Greater Syrtis; but one of these is placed in the neighbourhood of Aspis, where we could perceive nothing whatever like an island, and the other is laid down so far in the centre of the Gulf, that we could not certainly have seen it had it been still in existence. On coming abreast of Gàra, which lies about six miles off shore, we had a good opportunity of observing it with our glasses; it appeared to be covered with verdure, and we thought we perceived some appearances of building upon it; it rises in white cliffs from the sea, in some parts very abruptly, but the table-land on their summits was green when we passed it. It was in vain that we longed for some means of crossing over to this island, for there is not a boat or a vessel of any description to be found from one end of the Gulf of Syrtis to the other; but we consoled ourselves with the idea that it would be visited by the officers of the Adventure, which we afterwards found to have been the case. In passing by Ain Agàn, the Shekh of the place paid us a visit; but as we found that we could obtain no information from him, and he soon discovered that there was little chance of getting any bàkshis from us, the visit was not of very long duration. From Aàlum Limàrish to Sheibah, the country is much encumbered with sand-hills, which are however partially covered with vegetation; and finding we made but little progress in passing among them, we kept along the beach, which is hard and level as far as Rhout el Assoud, so called from its dark colour. Near Sheibah we found the water tasted very strong of sulphur, besides being brackish and stinking, but among some sand-hills two miles beyond it there were several wells of sweet water; a circumstance which it is essential to know, as the water of Sheibah can scarcely be called drinkable, and there is no other but that just alluded to at less than two days from the place.

On our way to Rhout el Assoud we passed several flocks of sheep, but could not persuade the shepherd to part with a single one. As we were now heartily tired of being so often refused what there seemed to be no sufficient reason for withholding, we told the man that we should act as the Bashaw's people would on similar occasions, if he did not think more considerately on the subject; which was as much as to say, that if he would not part with his sheep voluntarily, we should certainly make bold to take it without his leave; the only difference being, that His Highness's people would have taken the animal without paying for it, while we were quite ready to pay the full price of it. But the Arab, who had evidently been tampered with by the Dúbbah, was steady in his decided refusal; and we were too hungry to wait very long in endeavouring to reason him out of his obstinacy. Besides, we had already proposed an alternative, and could not with credit avoid putting our threat in execution. As neither our dignity, therefore, nor our appetites, would allow us to discuss with our obstinate Arab friend the propriety or impropriety of eating his mutton against his will, we judged it better to dispense with all such logical minutiæ on a subject where the parties were not likely to agree, and, dropping the argument, we took up the sheep, and tendered the money we had offered for it. Our opponent, however, was still as obstinate as before in refusing to take our piastres, though he saw a fat sheep take its departure from his flock, and occupy a position upon our Chaous's shoulders, while nothing remained to him in lieu of it. We had no doubt, on our leaving him, that he would change his mind before long, and told him, in consequence, where we meant to pitch our tents, that he might come for his money at his own leisure and convenience. But the sheep was killed and eat, at least a good part of it, and still no shepherd appeared; and we went to sleep in full assurance that he would come the next morning before the camels were loaded. During the night our Arab watch-dog kept up a continual barking, very much to the annoyance of old Shekh Mahommed, who was always rejoiced to have any opportunity of finding fault with poor Morzouk, whom he frequently honoured with the titles of useless cur, noisy rascal, and other equally flattering appellations. Our whole party, however, were too much tired with the day's exertions to pay any particular attention to this warning; and indeed it must be said that our shaggy young guardian was too much in the habit of employing his nights in barking merely for his private amusement, to render any further notice of him absolutely necessary, than that of lifting up occasionally the canvass of the tent to throw a stick or a stone at him, accompanied in general with some little verbal admonition. No one, however, was kept awake on this occasion, so far as we have been able to learn, but old Shekh Mahommed el Dúbbah; and we have reason to believe that his opinion of Morzouk's sagacity was not quite so indifferent after this night's alarm, as it had been before its occurrence; for the first thing which he discovered on turning out in the morning, which he usually did very early, was that three of his camels were missing; and on summoning his people, and searching everywhere in the neighbourhood, no traces whatever could be seen of them, but the track of their footsteps in the sand, with those of a man in their company.

It was impossible not to laugh when the fact became current that some of the Dúbbah's camels had been stolen, and we really believe that every individual of our party, with the exception of himself and his sons, were wicked enough to enjoy the circumstance, and to consider it as an excellent joke. No sooner were the traces observed by the Dúbbah of the man's footsteps who had carried off his camels, than he knew them to be those, at least so he declared, of our obstinate friend the shepherd above mentioned. The man certainly never made his appearance again while we remained in the neighbourhood, and it is probable that he took this summary process of paying himself for the sheep which had been so unceremoniously transferred from his flock to our kitchen kettle.

Three camels were no doubt something more than a fair remuneration for the loss of a single sheep; but then something was to be allowed for the risk of the raid, and everybody owned that the camels had been lifted in a very neat and expeditious manner, such as would not have disgraced the keenest moss-trooper on record in the annals of Border exploits. The animals had perhaps been supposed to be ours; or it may be that the reaver was not particular as to property, and had merely contented himself with taking as much as he could carry off, without reference to the doctrine of retribution. Be this as it may, the visitation had in reality fallen upon the head of the proper person; for had it not been for the intrigues of the Dúbbah, our obstinate friend would have been happy to sell us as many sheep as we might have required of him; and we were all too well convinced of this circumstance to regret the loss which the old Shekh had sustained.

Our stock of provisions, both for ourselves and our horses, was by this time so much diminished, that we had (we know not whether to say luckily or unluckily) no absolute occasion for the camels which were missing; and the remaining ones had little more to carry, in addition to their former loads, than a collection of empty baskets and boxes, which could now only serve to feed the flames or the camels themselves. There was in consequence no occasion for delaying our advance, by seeking to replace the loss sustained; and we continued to move on as usual, with no other motive for discontent than the absence of old Shekh Mahommed, whom we sadly longed to plague on his indifference to the summons which had been so loudly and unceasingly given him by the *"useless* cur Morzouk, who *always* barked without the slightest occasion." But the Dúbbah had taken horse before the camels were loaded, and was following the tracks of his lost animals as fast as he could spur his old mare.

At a short distance from Rhout el Assoud, we observed, to the north eastward, about a mile distant from the shore, six rocks connected by breakers, under which there appeared to be good anchorage for small vessels: the coast opposite them is low, and formed in shallow sandy bays, some of which have rocks extending across their entrance, and would afford protection for boats. At night we halted at Shohàn, without having seen a single living object during the day. On a hill near Shohàn are the remains of a Maràbut, overlooking a large plain covered with brushwood. From this hill we could perceive the ruins of two forts situated upon eminences to the south eastward. On the following day, after travelling eight hours along a plain, bounded by marsh and sand-hills towards the sea, we reached Carcora, where we hoped to find the place described by Captain Lautier on the north side of the bay, in which he states that he discovered an ancient well containing many Greek inscriptions. All our researches, however, on this point were unavailing; and the Arabs we met with about Carcora were all positive in affirming that no such well existed. We had the more reason to regret our failure, as the inscriptions (should they have turned out to be legible) would most probably have given us names and dates which might have been essentially useful to us, and could scarcely have failed of being interesting. There are at Carcora two coves which would serve for boats; they may be known by some high sand-hills lying between them, and by two ruins situated upon the hills inland nearly abreast of them. With the exception of these coves, there is nothing whatever of any interest on the coast between Carcora and Bengazi. Inland, however, there are many ruins of ancient forts, and considerable remains of building, which become more numerous and interesting as they approach Bengazi. At Ghimenes, which is a day's journey to the northward of Carcora, there are several interesting remains of ancient forts; some of which are altogether on a different plan from those which have been already described. They are built of large unequal-sized stones, put together without any cement, and made to fit one into another in the manner which has been called Cyclopian. Their form is a square, with the angles rounded off, and some of them are filled up with earth, well-beaten down, to within six or eight feet of the top; the upper part of the wall being left as a parapet to the terrace, which is formed by the earth heaped within it.

In the centre of the terrace we sometimes found the foundations of building, as if chambers had been erected upon it; the roofs of which, in that case, must have been higher than the outer walls which formed the parapet; and a space seems always to have been left between these central buildings and the parapet, in which the garrison placed themselves when employed in defending the fort. An opening like a window was observed in the parapet of one of the Cyclopian castles at Ghimenes, which might have been used for drawing up those who entered the fort, as there was no other mode of entrance whatever. In fact there could scarcely have been any communication between the upper and lower parts of these erections; for the whole space between the walls was filled up with earth in the manner already related, to within a few feet of the top. We noticed near most of them a small rising ground, with one or two wells in it, having remains of building about it; they were generally within fifty yards of the fort, by which they were commanded.

The castles have most of them been surrounded with a trench, on the outer side of which there is generally a low wall strongly built with large stones. Some of the trenches which have been excavated in the solid rock of the soil are of considerable depth and width; and in one instance, occurring between Ghimenes and Bengazi, we observed chambers excavated in the sides of the trench, as we find to be the case in that which surrounds the second pyramid, and which is equally formed in the rocky soil on which the building stands, although of course on a much larger scale. The trench of the fort here alluded to is about five-and-twenty feet in width, and its depth about fifteen; the fort itself is an hundred and twenty-five feet in length, and ninety in width, of a quadrangular form, and in the centre of each of its sides is a quadrangular projection, sloping outwards from the top, of twenty feet in length by twelve, which appears to have served both as a tower and a buttress.

The measurements are here given in the rough, but they will be found in detail by a reference to the ground-plan and elevation No. 9, in the plate containing the details of some of the forts which have been noticed in the course of the journey.

In some instances we found wells in the trenches surrounding the forts, at others, within the outer walls; and more frequently without the forts altogether, among traces of building in their immediate vicinity. The remains of building last mentioned were sometimes very considerable; but the ground-plans alone of these are now extant, from which little more may be collected than that the chambers were built in squares, ranged in line with some attention to regularity, though differing a good deal in size. Tombs are occasionally found excavated in the neighbourhood of such forts as are built on a rocky soil; but we never were fortunate enough to find any thing in them which could point out decidedly the mode of burial which had been adopted. Some of these were entered by wells of different depths, and others by approaches cut in the rock, sloping down from the upper part of the door, like those in front of the Kings' tombs at Thebes.

The remains about Ghimenes and Imshaila may answer to those of the Diachersis Præsidium of Ptolemy; but we are not aware of any remains which may be pointed out on the coast as those of the Turris Herculis, or of the Diarrhœa Portus, of this geographer.

When we had arrived within a day's journey of Bengazi, the weather, which had hitherto been very fine for the time of year, began to show that the rainy season had commenced in good earnest, and we congratulated ourselves in having escaped it so long; for had the bad weather overtaken us sooner, it would effectually have put an end to our researches, and obliged us to advance as fast as possible upon Bengazi, the only place which could have sheltered us between Mesurata and Derna. Indeed, it would have been difficult to make any progress at all; for the ravines would, in a few hours, have assumed the form of torrents, and the marshy ground have become everywhere dangerous, and in most places wholly impassable; our camels besides would have fallen every moment under their loads, as they cannot keep their feet in slippery weather, and some of our horses would certainly have sunk under the exertions which would have been necessary to overcome these additional disadvantages. As it was, we had been obliged to lead two of the horses for several days before our arrival at Bengazi, and it would indeed be thought extraordinary, by those accustomed only to the horses of Europe, that any of them arrived there at all after the fatigues and privations which they had endured. They had all of them been rode through the whole of the day, over a country without any roads, for more than two months successively, exposed to the heat of the sun during the day, and without any shelter from the cold and damp of the night; while at the same time, instead of having any extra allowance to enable them to support this exertion, they were often left, unavoidably, for more than four-and-twenty hours, without anything whatever to eat or drink, and on one occasion were as much as four days without a drop of water of any kind. It may therefore be readily imagined that they were not in very excellent condition before half the journey had been accomplished, and indeed it was distressing to see the wasted carcasses which most of them presented on arriving in the neighbourhood of Bengazi; but we may venture to say that few, if any, European horses, under similar circumstances, would have survived the journey which they performed at all; much less have displayed the activity and spirit which never left them, under so much fatigue and privation.

We were often amused, in spite of his forlorn condition, with the spirit exerted on all occasions by an old white horse, which was rode by one of our servants; he had belonged for many years to a soldier of the Bashaw, and his face was well known to all the Arabs of Bengazi, as a constant appendage to the army which came there occasionally to collect the tribute. This fine-spirited animal, before the journey was half over, had scarcely a leg to stand upon, yet he never for a moment forgot his military habits, and would arch his neck, and curvet, and throw himself back on his haunches at the slightest application of the spur. No fatigue or exhaustion could ever make him forget that he had once been a charger of some consideration: even in walking he would lift up his legs, and step out, with all the parade and importance of a horse trained at Astley's or the Circus; throwing his head about, at the same time, from one side to the other, as if he took a delight in displaying his long mane, and shewing himself off to advantage.

It may well be supposed that no exertions of our own were at any time wanting to procure food and water for the weary animals who had so amply deserved them; but we could only carry a certain portion of corn with us from Tripoly, and when this was exhausted we were obliged to depend upon occasional supplies from the Arab tents we met with in our route, and the scanty pasturage which the Syrtis afforded.

The distance at which some of the wells were placed from each other was the occasion of our being often without water; and our horses, though suffering greatly from thirst, would frequently refuse to drink the water which we were glad to drink ourselves, when it chanced to be more than usually brackish.

It often happened when they had been long without water, or were more than ordinarily fatigued with the day's exertions, that some of them would refuse to eat at all, though they had been without food the whole of the day, as well as all the night which preceded it.

They were never in the habit of being fed more than once a day, which was in the evening, when we stopped for the night; so that if they refused to eat their corn at that time, or before starting the next morning, it was more than probable that they would get nothing till the tents were pitched again, after sunset, on the evening succeeding. Under these circumstances they would perhaps have to trot hard the whole day, and occasionally to gallop, when we were pressed for time; sometimes along the loose sand on the beach, and at others up and down hill in every direction, wherever there was anything to examine: all this often happened during a hot southerly wind, and under a burning sun, which kept them in a continual fever, without their appearing to sustain any particular inconvenience, or to be more than usually exhausted at night.

The habit of feeding horses only once a day is common in Africa under the most favourable circumstances. Their meal is after sunset, and before their corn is given them they are generally allowed to drink as much as they like. After this they get neither corn nor water till the same time on the following day. Some of the Arabs make a constant practice of obliging their horses to go two days without drinking, in order to accustom them to support with a better grace the privations they must occasionally be exposed to in the desert; a mode of training which would probably have the same effect on our English horses as that which is said to have resulted from the well-known experiment of the Frenchman, who had just contrived to make his horse do without food, when he was unluckily prevented by the death of the animal from availing himself of so important an advantage.

A few weeks' repose in a comfortable stable at Bengazi was, however, sufficient to restore most of our horses to their former strength and condition; and they afterwards carried us in very good style over the steep woody hills and rugged passes of the Cyrenaica.

From Carcora to Bengazi the country improves at every step, and we soon found ourselves surrounded by extensive crops of barley and abundance of excellent pasturage: this increase of produce was naturally attended by a corresponding increase of population, and numerous flocks and herds were everywhere seen where the soil was not appropriated to cultivation. A great part of the country from Ghimenes to Bengazi is encumbered by blocks of stone, placed upright in long lines, which are crossed at right angles by others, so as to form a complete labyrinth of inclosures. This peculiarity appears to be occasioned by the nature of the soil, which, although rich and excellent, is covered everywhere with a surface of stone of various thickness, which it is of course necessary to break up and remove, in order to cultivate the soil beneath it. To move the blocks, which are taken up altogether from the ground, would be an endless and perhaps a superfluous labour; and they have accordingly been ranged in the manner we have mentioned, serving at the same time as boundaries to property and as impediments to the approach of an enemy. Before we were well acquainted with the nature of these inclosures, we thought to pass in a straight line across them to the several ruins which attracted our attention; but after leaping our horses over some of them, and making them scramble over others, we soon found the labour was endless; and that the longest way about, as the old proverb teaches us, was in reality the shortest way home. Instead of attempting, in consequence, to advance any farther in a direct line to the object of our inquiry, we sought for some path between the walls which might lead us as near to it as possible. After some little trouble, we discovered that long alleys were occasionally left in different directions, serving as roads to the places of greatest resort. These we afterwards found it most advisable to follow, though they did not lead us quite in the direction we wished; and having got as near to our object as they could carry us, we had seldom many walls to scramble over before we reached the place where it stood. It is probable that some of these walls are of very considerable antiquity; for the soil in this neighbourhood could not at any time have been cultivated without removing the crust of stone from its surface; but we could not discover any inscriptions upon them, though we often examined them with the hope of being able to do so. We observed that in the vicinity of the forts the walls were usually placed much closer together, and the inclosures were in consequence smaller than in other parts.

The extensive plain in which the town of Bengazi is situated, is bounded to the southward by the range of high land, on whose summit Cyrene once stood so conspicuously; and the whole of the plain at the foot of this range is covered with vegetation from the hills to the sea. The sight, we believe, was refreshing to all parties; for our very horses and camels appeared to partake of the pleasure which we could not avoid feeling ourselves in contemplating so agreeable a scene. One of our party was dispatched in advance to Bengazi, accompanied by the Bashaw's Chaous, to apprize the British resident of our approach, and to concert with him such measures as might be necessary for our accommodation in the town, where the violence and long duration of the winter-rains would oblige us, we well knew, to remain for some time. It was night before they reached the salt lake by which Bengazi is nearly surrounded, and which it was necessary to cross before they entered the town; the rains which had already fallen had swelled it more than the Chaous had anticipated, and the darkness of the night rendered it difficult for him to find the spot at which it was necessary to ford it. After wandering about the banks for some little time in uncertainty, and trying several plans without success, they at length reached the opposite shore; though not before their horses had plunged into several holes, from which they could only extricate themselves by swimming. On the following day our whole party arrived at Bengazi, and were received with every mark of attention and politeness by Signor Rossoni, the British Vice-Consul, to whom the necessary instructions from Mr. Consul Warrington had already been forwarded. We found that Signor Rossoni was already in treaty for the house of an Arab Shekh, one of the best which the place afforded, and only waited our arrival to arrange the terms on which we were willing to take it: these were soon settled, and we took possession of our new abode the day after our arrival in the town, and began to make ourselves as comfortable as circumstances would allow, under the disadvantages of a rainy winter, at Bengazi.

Bengazi is allowed to have been built upon the site once occupied by the town of Berenice, the most western city of the Pentapolis; but before we proceed to describe this part of the Cyrenaica, it will be proper to look back upon the tract of country already before the reader, and, in taking a general view of the gulf and shores of the Greater Syrtis, to bring together some of the most prominent remarks of ancient writers respecting it.

FOOTNOTES:

In this neighbourhood was the cave of the formidable Lamia, so much dreaded by the children of the ancients. It is described by Diodorus as situated in a deep valley formed in the rocks which occur soon after Automala; that is, in passing from east to west, for such was the course of the army of Ophellas, which is stated by the historian to have passed it in their route to join the forces of the tyrant Agathocles. The account which he gives of this afflicted royal lady, whose misfortunes at length rendered her so savage and remorseless, is such as to render it probable (if the story may be relied upon) that she really at one time existed in this part of Africa. At least the mode in which the fabulous parts of her history are accounted for appears to be sufficiently rational, and the place of her residence is very decidedly pointed out.—(See Diod. lib. xx. p. 753—4.)

Ιδρυμενον κατα τον μυχον του κολπου παντος·—Lib. xvii. p. 836.

In *intimo sinu* fuit ora Lotophagon, &c.—Nat. Hist. lib. v. cap. 5.

Ho pure fatto attenzione in tutti questi giorni se scorgera, *anche in distanza, alcuna schiera di monti che da ponente si protendesse al levante,* onde riconoscere se la giogaia dell' Atlante realmente si prolonga ne' monti della Cirenaica, o bensì se rimpetto al Golfo della Gran Sirte fosse interrotta. Ma nulla ho osservato che possa confermare questa prolungazione. (P. 91), Ital. edition.

. . . Giacchè in quest' ultimo recinto del Mediterraneo non *ho visto che sabbie ne altri monti che di sabbie*. (P. 92.)

The Psylli we are told by Pliny, on the authority of Agatharcides, were so called from their King Psyllus, whose tomb is said to have been somewhere in the Greater Syrtis. They were remarkable for their power of charming serpents; and possessed some innate quality of body which was considered to be destructive to these reptiles; so much so that the very smell of them was supposed to lull a serpent asleep. They had a singular custom of exposing their children to the most venomous kinds of serpents, in order to convince themselves of their legitimacy. If the serpents, on whom the trial was made, did not fly from the children exposed to them, it was concluded to be a proof of decided illegitimacy, since the animals, they imagined, could not avoid doing so, had the infants been really descended from this gifted tribe.

It has been observed by other writers, that the Psylli merely cured the bite of serpents by sucking the poison from the wound, and that they were therefore more indebted for their reputation to their courage, than to any peculiar qualification of nature.

Ed io inclino tanto più a credere quest' ampia depressione di suolo giungere fino al gran deserto, poichè per quanto posso congetturare dal cammino fatto non sarebbe improbabile che l'estremità del golfo si prolungasse assai più a mezzodì di quel che trovasi nelle migliori carte, nelle quali non saprei sopra qual fondamento è stata stabilita. È per me di qualche peso la relazione del Cap. Lautier, il quale non navigò certamente oltre il 30° 27' 11" di latitudine, ma da questo punto non iscoprì il fondo del golfo, nè v' era apparenza di prossimità al continente. Ho ferma credenza che migliori osservazioni confermeranno questa mia congettura.—(p. 94.)

For Strabo tells us (lib. iii. p. 171), in alluding to the custom practised by the ancients, of erecting columns on particular occasions, that the monuments raised to the memory of the Philæni were situated nearly midway in the Syrtis—at least, such is the sense in which we must take this passage, to make it at all consistent with the position allotted to the Philænean altars in the seventeenth book. Although we may certainly read in the passage we are about to quote, above mentioned, "midway in the country *between* the *Syrtes*"—for the Syrtes are here mentioned in the plural—and this circumstance would otherwise rather tend to confirm the position of the altars in the table of Peutinger (as mentioned by Cellarius, lib. iv. cap. 3, sec. 3.) which is between the two Gulfs of Syrtis. "At, in

Peutingeriana tabula vetusta, (says Cellarius) redactæ hæ aræ sunt fere ad minorem Syrtim, ut dubitare possis de situ et positione ex tot auctoribus jam descripta." Strabo's words are—και ὁι φιλαινων λεγομενοι βωμοι, κατα μεσην, που, την μεταξυ των Συρτεων γην.

Bell. Jugurth. (79.)

Major Rennell has observed on this subject—"At the date of Hannibal's expedition to Italy, B. C. 217, the Carthaginian empire extended eastward to the Philænean altars, which stood at the south-east extremity of the Greater Syrtis. The story of the Philæni, as it is told, is in some points very improbable. It is said that the parties set out from their respective capitals, Carthage and Cyrene, and met at the place where the altars afterwards stood. Now the altars were situated at about seven-ninths of the way from Carthage towards Cyrene; and the deception would have been too gross had it been pretended that the Carthaginian party had travelled seven parts in the nine, while the Cyrenean party had travelled no more than two such parts of the way. Would either party have trusted the other with the adjustment of the time of setting out? Perhaps they mutually set out at the opposite extremes of the territory in dispute, and not from their respective capitals."

That is, if we may read the passage in the third book of Strabo, quoted above, in the sense which we imagine he intended; if not, he contradicts himself.

Ειθ' οι φιλαινων βωμοι και μετα τουτους Αυτομαλα φρουριον, φυλακην εχον, ιδρυμενον κατα τον μυχον του κολπου παντος.—Lib. xvii.

We have adopted the positions assigned by Strabo to these places, as being more exactly defined; and because it may be presumed that he saw the objects which he describes, with the exception of the altars of the Philæni, which he has stated to have been no longer extant in his time.

Nat. Hist. lib. v. cap. 5.

Ejus promontorium est Borion, ab eoque incipiens ora quam Lotophagi tenuisse dicuntur, usque ad Phycunta (et id promontorium est) importuoso litore pertinet. Aræ ipsæ nomen ex Philænis fratribus traxere, qui contra Cyrenaicos missi, &c.—De Situ Orbis, lib. i. cap. vii.

Vide Procopius (De Ædificiis, lib. v.)

. . . ωδευσε δε πεζος εν αμμω βαθεια και καυμασι.—Lib. xvii. p. 836.

Pharsalia, lib. ix.

Ager in medio arenosus, una specie; neque flumen, neque mons erat, qui finis eorum discerneret, &c.—(Bell. Jugurth. 79.)

The water is, however, more frequently found among the sand on the beach than elsewhere; but it scarcely seems necessary that the whole extent of the sand-hills should be traversed by the army on this account. Their guides must have known where the water was to be found, without the necessity of traversing so many miles of sand-heaps in search of it.

We have already assumed that the greater number of the forts in the Syrtis have, in our opinion, been constructed by the Romans.

A few miles inland of Braiga, at a place called Attallàt, are the remains of a castle, whose outer walls are still standing to a considerable height; it is a quadrangular building, surrounded by a trench; and within it we observed the remains of an arch constructed without a key-stone, in the manner of one at Tabilba, which we shall allude to in describing that place.

Αυτομαλα φρουριον, φυλακην εχον, &c.

It appears, upon the authority of Diodorus Siculus, that the fortress of Automala was already erected when Cyrene was first occupied by the troops of Ptolemy Lagus: for the army which was led by his general Ophellas to the assistance of the tyrant Agathocles, then at war with the Carthaginians, pitched their tents, we are told, in the neighbourhood of Automala, having consumed eighteen days in their march to that fortress from the Cyrenaica.

Οκτω και δεκα μεν ουν ημερας οδοιπορησαντες, και διελθοντες σταδιους τρισκιλιους, κατεσκηνωσαν περι Αυτομαλας.—Lib. xx. p. 753-4.

If it could be positively ascertained from what point of the Cyrenaica the army of Ophellas set out on their journey across the Syrtis, we should have the position of Automala sufficiently well ascertained; but the historian merely states, that when everything was prepared for the expedition, Ophellas set his army in motion, without mentioning the precise point from which they set out, and that the distance which they accomplished in eighteen days, as far as Automala, was three thousand stadia. Had there been any point in the bottom of the gulf which could be decidedly fixed upon as the μυχος, or innermost recess of it, in which Strabo has placed Automala, there would be no occasion for any other evidence of its position; but the coast is so straight at the bottom of the gulf, that it is not possible to fix with accuracy upon any one point which may be taken as the μυχος in question. Sachreen is certainly the most southern point, but the difference of latitude between this place and the other parts of the coast which form the bottom of the gulf is so trifling, that it can scarcely be said to amount to anything at all.

Braiga is the nearest place to Sachreen where any remains are found which will answer to Automala, and that is twenty miles distant from it, in making the circuit of the coast.

It may be added, that the forts in the neighbourhood of Braiga and Tabilba, erected among the hills a little inland, are very interesting, and much more perfect than usual. A fortnight or three weeks might be very profitably and agreeably spent in making out the interior ground-plans of these buildings.

Εχει δε το μεταξὺ διαστημα και λιμενες ου πολλους, υδρεια δε σπανια.—Lib. xvii. p. 836.

That of Aspis—καλλιστος των εν τη Συρτει.

It must be observed, that an old wicker-basket is by no means an unsavoury dish for a hungry camel, and the animals in question had already dined off much tougher materials; for the date-stones which we had occasionally given them, in the absence of other tenderer meat, were eaten up with a relish which left little room for doubting the speedy disappearance of hampers and baskets, whenever we might afford to serve them up as entremets.

Nel fondo di questo seno v' ha un pozzo di acqua dolce, ove si attinge a una grandissima profondità, sopratutto in estate. È rotondo, con una scalinata interna, per la quale vi si puo facilmente discendere. Ad ogni dieci scalini vi si trovano scolpite inscrizione in Greco. Furono impiegate nel mese di Settembre ottanta tre braccia di corda per attignerle l' acqua.—(Della Cella: Viaggio da Tripoli, &c. p. 220-21.)

At the foot of the sand-hills at Carcora there are some springs of fresh water, remarkably sweet and good, within a few feet of an extensive salt-marsh, and on the same level with it. The circumstance is worthy of remark, although there are other instances of similar occurrences.

The horses, when we stopped, were ranged in a line along a thick cord, to which their fore legs were fastened; and a smaller cord was passed from this to one of their hind legs, to prevent them from kicking one another.

*CHART Shewing the difference between the coastlines as delineated in former charts and that obtained by the late Survey the shaded line representing the latter made in 1821 & 1822. By Capt*ⁿ*. F. W. Beechey R.N.*

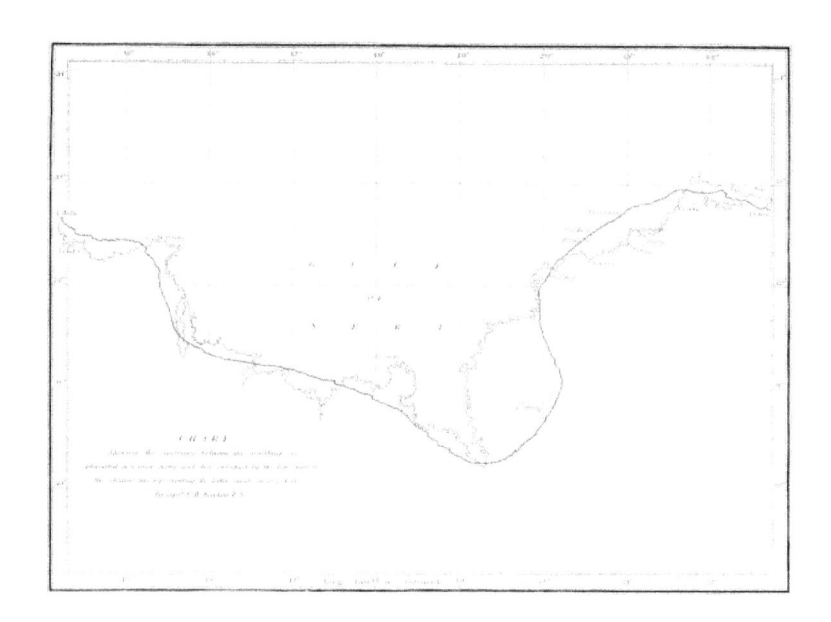

J. & C. Walker Published as the act directs, April 1827, by J. Murray,
Sculp*t*. Albemarle S*t*. London.

CHAPTER X.

OBSERVATIONS ON THE GULF AND SHORES OF THE GREATER SYRTIS.

The Dimensions of the Gulf, according to Ancient Writers, considered, and compared with those resulting from the Observations of the Expedition — Difference in the Statements of the several Writers quoted — Reasons why a Difference may be expected in their Accounts — Observations of Major Rennell on the Measurements of the Ancients — Ptolemy's Outline of the Gulf more correct than any hitherto given — Number of Square Miles of Error in modern Charts of the Greater Syrtis — The Ideas of Ancient Writers (Herodotus excepted) with respect to the Nature and Resources of the Syrtis (the *Territory*, not the *Gulf* of the Greater Syrtis is here meant) more erroneous than the Dimensions which have been assigned to the Gulf itself — The General Character of the Syrtis not that of a Sandy Plain — Incorrectness of the Arab Accounts of what is termed by them the Desert of Barka — Account of Herodotus considered — Apparent Accuracy of his Statements — Inferences drawn from them — Ancient Accounts of the *Gulf* of the Greater Syrtis, dimensions excepted, very correct — Accumulation of Soil on the Shores of the Gulf accounted for — Apparent Elevation of the General Level of the Syrtis — Advance of the Sea on the Northern Coast of Africa — Appearance of the Coast at Alexandria and Carthage consistent with that of the Shores of the Greater Syrtis and Cyrenaica — Observations of Major Rennell and Dr. Shaw on the Elevation of the Coast of Tunis, and the Advance of the Sea in that quarter — Observations of Lucan on the Level of the Greater Syrtis — Dangers of the Navigation of the Gulf of Syrtis considered — Inset into the Gulf still existing to a great extent — Flux and Reflux of the Sea mentioned by Strabo and Mela considered — Remarks on the Derivation of the term *Syrtis*.

IN considering the dimensions which have come down to us of the Greater Syrtis, those allotted to it by Strabo (in the seventeenth book) are so singularly inconsistent with each other, that there appears to be no possible mode of reconciling the measurements he has given of its diameter, with those which he has in the same place ascribed to its circumference, without material alterations in the text. "The circumference of the Greater Syrtis" (observes the geographer) "is about nine hundred and thirty stadia; and its diameter, at the bottom of the Gulf, is one thousand five hundred stadia: the breadth of the entrance (or mouth) is about the same:" that is, about fifteen hundred stadia. Here we have a circumference considerably less than its diameter, and no way of getting rid of a difficulty so formidable to mathematicians, without making such decided alterations in the text as no sober-minded editor would hazard. Various readings have been given, by different commentators, of this passage; but it will be useless to compare their several merits; since both the measurements in question will be found to be no less inconsistent with the truth than they have been seen to be with each other. For the actual circumference of the gulf of the Greater Syrtis may be estimated at four hundred and twenty-two geographic miles, and its diameter at two hundred and forty-six: so that it would be necessary to alter both the circumference and diameter given by Strabo before any use could be made of his dimensions; and then the measurements must be taken on the authority of the commentators, since they would be no longer those of the geographer. In short, the difficulty appears to be scarcely surmountable; for though it is evident that the passage is not as Strabo left it, we have no sufficient data for deciding what it really was originally. The measurements given by Pliny are somewhat nearer the truth; indeed his diameter of the gulf may be considered as remarkably accurate; for it is stated at three hundred and thirteen Roman miles, equal to two hundred and forty-eight and a quarter geographic miles, and there is consequently no more than two miles and a quarter difference between these dimensions and the actual diameter. His circumference, however, is not by any means so accurate; it is given at six hundred and twenty-five Roman miles, which are equal to four hundred and ninety-four geographic miles, and will therefore leave a difference of seventy-two geographic miles between this measurement of the circuit and the actual one. The difference also exists on the wrong side; that is to say, the whole distance of Pliny is not only much more than the actual distance by observations, but much more than the actual road-distance, which is the longest which can be allowed. The diameter of the gulf, already stated, of this author, will be found to coincide remarkably well with the measurement which may be deduced from the distance he has given us in another place, between the cities of Leptis Magna and Berenice, of three hundred and eighty-five Roman miles: for the distance between Lebida (Leptis Magna) and Mesurata, the western extremity of the gulf, may be reckoned at fifty-eight geographic miles, equal to seventy-three Roman miles; so that this being deducted from the whole distance given, of three hundred and eighty-five M. P. we shall have a remainder of three hundred and twelve of the same for the distance between Mesurata and Bengazi, leaving a difference of only one mile between the diameter of the gulf thus deduced and that above stated of three hundred and thirteen. But although we may infer, from the coincidence of the two measurements, that the three hundred and twelve miles in question may be taken as distance *across* the gulf, they are by no means stated to be such in the text; and if they had chanced to coincide with the circumference instead of the diameter of the gulf, they might just as well have been taken for the road-distance between Mesurata and Bengazi; the measurements which we find in the Itinerary of Antoninus, of the distance between Leptis Magna and Berenice, come nearer to the actual road-distance between these places, by one hundred and thirty Roman miles, than that which is obtained by adding the seventy-three miles between Lebida and Mesurata to the circumference of the gulf given by Pliny; for the whole distance of the Itinerary from Leptis to Berenice is not estimated at more than five hundred and sixty-eight Roman miles, while those above mentioned being added together would make no less than six hundred and ninety-eight. So that the circumference of the gulf which may be deduced from the Itinerary differs only from the actual circuit by road-distance in thirty-seven Roman miles, or twenty-nine and a half geographic.

But instead of being surprized at the differences which obtain between the measurements which have descended to us from the ancients, we ought rather, perhaps, to wonder that they do not differ even more than they are usually found to do from each other. It is true that abundant materials were furnished to the early geographers, by the numerous military and naval expeditions which enterprizing or ambitious states had fitted out for the purposes of conquest or discovery; but the maps and charts which resulted from them were laid down without the aid of astronomy; and the distances between the places described in them were either measured or computed along the roads which the armies traversed, or deduced from the track of vessels along the coast. Major Rennell has observed, that the difference which will generally be found between the measurements of Eratosthenes and Strabo, and those which appear in modern geography, will be that which exists between the measure of a *direct* line, drawn from one place to another, and that of the *road* distance between them. "Nothing can speak more strongly to this point," (says the well-informed and intelligent writer here quoted,) "than the circumstance of Strabo's giving the number of stades in Nearchus's coasting navigation for the lengths of the coasts of Persia and Caramania."

In fact it was not till the time of Ptolemy that geography began to be placed upon that solid basis on which it now stands so conspicuously; and it certainly appears somewhat singular, that the writers on this subject who flourished between the time of Hipparchus and that of the Alexandrian geographer (among whom were Strabo and Pliny,) should not have availed themselves of the discoveries of the former to check the measurements which appear in their works. Various errors have been pointed out in the geography of Ptolemy; but as it can scarcely be supposed that he had sufficient observations to regulate the position of all the places which he has laid down, we ought not to be surprized at this circumstance. His outline of the Gulf of Syrtis, though it cannot be called correct, is notwithstanding more so than those which have since been given of it; and the prolongation of the gulf at its southern extremity, so erroneously marked in modern charts, as well as the inlet called the Gulf of Zuca, which we have stated does not exist, are neither of them laid down in it at all. It may therefore be said, that the true character of the gulf is much better preserved in the loose outline of Ptolemy than in any other of which we are aware. Whatever may be the reasons which have induced modern geographers to introduce into the Gulf of Syrtis the errors which we have alluded to, it is certain that the best chart which they have hitherto produced of it must undergo a correction of ninety miles in longitude, and upwards of thirty miles in latitude, that is to say, it must part with nearly six thousand square miles of ground, before it will be consistent with the truth.

Should we pass from the measurements to the general character of the Syrtis, we shall find that if the ancient authorities have erred in their dimensions of it, they have been no less deceived with regard to its nature and resources. The whole country from Bengazi to Mesurata appears to have been generally considered by the writers of antiquity as a dreary tract of sand, without water or vegetation, and swarming with venomous serpents. But we have already shewn that there are spots in this tract where vegetation is very luxuriant, and where water may be readily procured; and although the extent of marshy ground is in many places considerable, yet the proportions between the barren and the productive parts of the Syrtis are not so little in favour of the latter as appears to have been generally imagined. The whole tract is so thinly inhabited, that a very trifling portion of it only is cultivated; but this circumstance is owing more to the character of the Bedouins who frequent it, and to the government to which they are subjected, than to the incapacity of the soil itself.

The Bedouin, though active, is far from industrious; and if he can gain a livelihood from the flocks which he possesses, he will seldom trouble himself to cultivate even the most productive soil; indeed, if he were to do so, he has in general no security that any part of the produce or the profits of it would be his own. His tent and flocks may be removed at a few minutes' notice, but his crop of corn or vegetables could not be so disposed of; and they who came as his friends, for the purpose of collecting tribute, or as enemies, for the purpose of spoliation, would take care to be with him before his crops were cut, and make sure of the object of their visit. We remember asking an Arab, in the district of Syrt, why his tribe would not trouble themselves to dig a few more wells in a place which they frequented, where there was plenty of water, at no great depth from the surface of the soil: his answer was that, if they were to do so, the Bashaw's troops who collected the tribute would more easily overtake them, when they chose to run away, than if the supply of water were more scanty: for without a good supply of water the troops could not advance more than a short distance into the interior, and would consequently be less likely to overtake them in their flight. This reason was sufficient in his opinion to account for the circumstance; but it is probable that, if there were no grounds for apprehension on this head, neither our friend himself, nor any Arab of his tribe, would have had resolution enough to sink a single well, however much they might chance to be in want of it; and that they would have preferred removing their whole establishment to another place, which might be better provided with water, to the trouble of digging for it where they were.

It is not only in the works of early writers that we find the nature of the Syrtis misunderstood; for the whole of the space between Mesurata and Alexandria is described by Leo Africanus (under the title of Barca), as "a wild and desert country, where there is neither water nor land capable of cultivation." He allows, however, that the country was inhabited, *after* the occupation of Africa by the Arabs, though not before that period; and tells us, that the most powerful among the Mahometan invaders possessed themselves of the fertile parts of the coast, leaving the others only the desert for their abode, exposed to all the miseries and privations attendant on it: for this desert, he continues, is far removed from any habitation, and nothing is produced there whatever. So that if these poor people would have a supply of grain, or of any other articles necessary to their existence, they are obliged to pledge their children to the Sicilians who visit the coast; who on providing them with these things, which they bring with them from Sicily, carry off the children they have received. Here we have the whole of the Syrtis and Cyrenaica described as a desert tract of country; and although the same author states, that "Sert was an ancient city, built, as some think, by the Egyptians, and, as others believe, by the Romans," he informs us that the country in which it was situated was uninhabited, from Mesurata to Alexandria, before the arrival of the Mahometans in Africa.

It must, however, be confessed, that the half-starved Musselmen with whom he has peopled it were scarcely more deserving of our commisseration than the "vastæ Nasamon populator Syrtis," or any other of the very respectable personages of antiquity who are said to have inhabited this coast. The Sicilians were most probably aware of the character of their customers before they exacted from them the hostages above described; for Leo goes on to say, that these Arabs were the greatest thieves and the most treacherous people to be found in the whole world. They ranged the country round, as far as Numidia, attacking and plundering the poor pilgrims who were unfortunate enough to meet them; and not contented with taking from them everything that was to be found upon their persons, they made them swallow a quantity of hot milk, and then shook them about till it acted as an emetic, so violently as to leave nothing whatever on the stomach.

This was done lest the poor unhappy patients, to whom the medicine was administered, should have taken the precaution of swallowing their money to prevent its being taken from them by their assailants. "Perciocché dubitano queste bestie (says our indignant author) che i viandanti, come s'appressano a quel diserto, inghiottino i danari perchè non gli siano trovati adosso."

It appears to be chiefly from Leo Africanus that modern historians have derived the very unfavourable idea of what they term the district and desert of Barca. Yet the whole of the Cyrenaica is comprehended within the limits which they assign to it; and the authority of Herodotus (without citing any other) would be amply sufficient to prove that this tract of country, not only was no desert, but was at all times remarkable for its fertility.

We find on the same authority, that the Libyans (or Africans) who inhabited, at an early period, the southern shores of the Mediterranean, were divided into pastoral and agricultural tribes; and that the former, most of whom were inhabitants of Barca, were by no means in the miserable condition in which they have been by some represented.

They are described by Herodotus as living on flesh and milk; and the prejudice which they entertained for what Englishmen would term cow-beef, could scarcely have existed among a people who were scantily provided with the necessaries of life.

With regard to the present inhabitants of the district of Barca (we mean the part of it comprehended in the Syrtis and Cyrenaica), we should certainly call them a healthy and good-looking race; and not at all the ugly, meagre, grim-visaged people, which they have been described to be in some of our best received accounts of them. We allude in particular to the Bedouin (or wandering) tribes, which are those more immediately in question; and who are generally a finer people, both in character and appearance, than what are termed the more civilized inhabitants of Arab cities. Whatever may be the descent of the present inhabitants of this part of Africa, they appear to lead exactly the same kind of life, and to have as nearly as possible the same resources, as the early possessors of the regions which they occupy.

The penetration of Herodotus has not failed to discover among the African tribes which he enumerates, that they were a very healthy race of people; and the practice of cautery, still adopted by their Mahometan successors, and to which he is uncertain whether or not to attribute the healthy appearance of the Libyans, is mentioned by this author as one of their peculiarities.

No allusion is made by Herodotus to the parched and barren sandy soil which later writers have bestowed upon the country in question, described by Leo Africanus as a region "dove non si trova ne acqua ne terreno da cultivare;" and we may safely affirm that the impression left upon our minds of this part of the coast and its inhabitants (after reading the account of Herodotus) would be much more consistent with the appearance and peculiarities of both, in their actual state, than that which would result from the descriptions of any succeeding writer.

The parts which are nearest the sea he describes as inhabited by Nomadic, or pastoral tribes; and the inference is, that where there are flocks and shepherds, there is also pasturage and water. The country inland of these, and immediately adjoining them, he states to be abounding with wild beasts; and for these animals, also, more shelter and moisture is necessary than could be afforded them in the burning sands of a desert: we may therefore conclude that the parts where they are found would most probably contain caves, or woods, which might serve them as habitations and places of retreat and security. This tract we should consequently imagine to be wild and stony, unadapted to cultivation, and affording little or no pasturage, but certainly not wholly of sand, or altogether unprovided with water. The third region, mentioned by Herodotus as succeeding to the two before enumerated, and placed farther inland than either, is the sandy tract of country usually, though not necessarily, implied by the term desert, in which there is neither water, nor vegetation of any kind; nothing, in fact, by which life could be sustained. This tract he merely states to be a long ridge of sand, extending itself from Egypt to the pillars of Hercules. It is but justice to state, in confirmation of the account here submitted to us by the father of history, whose veracity has been so much called in question, that (so far as our own experience, and that of the Arabs whom we have questioned on the subject, has enabled us to judge) it is perfectly consistent with the truth. What was beyond the sandy desert was little known to Herodotus, and must not therefore be adverted to in considering this description.

With regard to the water afforded by the Syrtis, we find the Psylli inhabiting a tract of country inland of that possessed by the Nasamones, who occupied the south-eastern coast of the Gulf; these people must therefore have been provided with water, though they were nearer to the sandy desert than the Nasamones; and if we are told that, in consequence of their supplies being dried up, they were compelled to emigrate, and perished in their journey to the southward, we must at the same time conclude that, previous to this accident, they had water enough to support them at home, though it might not have been very plentiful. On the whole, we may observe, without entering further into this subject, that the district of Barca, including all the country between Mesurata and Alexandria, neither is, nor ever was, so destitute and barren as it has been represented; that the part of it which constitutes the Cyrenaica is capable of the highest degree of cultivation, and that many parts of the Syrtis afford excellent pasturage, while some of it is not only adapted to cultivation, but does actually produce good crops of barley and dhurra. We may remark, at the same time, that the proportion of sand which is actually to be found in the Syrtis will by no means authorize us to call it a sandy region, and that the proportion of water which it actually possesses will not justify us in asserting that it is unprovided with that necessary. We may observe, too, that the number of serpents and venomous reptiles, so freely bestowed upon the Syrtis by Roman writers, and by others who flourished after the occupation of Northern Africa by Roman colonies, appears to be greatly exaggerated: that it possesses, in fact, no terrors peculiar to itself, at least, not that we are acquainted with; and no difficulties which may not be readily surmounted by those who are acquainted with the nature of the country, and will adopt the precautions which are necessary.

From the regions of the Greater Syrtis let us pass to the Gulf itself; and of this we may remark, that the accounts which have come down to us of its peculiarities do certainly appear to be much better founded than those which we possess of the country along its shores. Herodotus, although he has minutely described the people who inhabited the coasts of the Syrtes, has left no account of the Gulfs; but we learn from Strabo, that the dangers which presented themselves to navigators, in the Gulfs both of the Greater and Lesser Syrtis, were occasioned by the frequent occurrence of banks and shallows, formed by the flux and reflux of the sea, on which vessels were continually striking, and it rarely happened that any of them were got off. "For this reason," he adds, "it was usual to keep away from the coast, in order to avoid being embayed."

What we must here understand by the flux and reflux of the sea, is not (we should imagine) the usual action of the tides, which is very trifling in the Mediterranean, compared with that which is observable in other seas; but the inset occasioned by violent winds blowing for any long continuance on shore, and the subsequent reaction of the sea in regaining its original level.

As northerly winds are very prevalent, and very strong on this coast, which fronts the widest part of the Mediterranean, they might no doubt occasion the accumulation of soil alluded to in this passage of Strabo; and we certainly find that a great part of the coast is so exceedingly shallow as to make the landing very hazardous and difficult. It is probable, also, that this accumulation of soil has raised the level of the low lands in the Greater and

Lesser Syrtes much above what it formerly was, and that both these regions were once covered with water to a greater depth than at present.

We have already observed that the sea appears to have made great advances on the whole line of coast of Northern Africa; and this fact seems to be proved from the circumstance of our finding the remains of ancient towns, along its shores, at present under water to a considerable extent. We may now pass in boats over the ruins of the northern part of Alexandria, (as many travellers of our time can testify); and remains of the city of Carthage, "for the space of three furlongs in length, and half a furlong, or more, in breadth," are well known (on the authority of Shaw) to be at the present day "entirely under water." In the intermediate space, we may instance the maritime towns of the Cyrenaica, where the sea has made considerable advances; those parts of the Greater Syrtis which are not exposed to the accumulation of sand, and the town of modern Tripoly, the northern part of which (as we have already stated in the words of Leo Africanus) appears to have been in his time under water.

This rise in the level of the Mediterranean could scarcely fail to have occasioned an overflow in the low grounds of the Syrtie, to a much greater extent than formerly, if it had not been accompanied by, at least, a proportionate accumulation of soil: but it will rather appear that in these regions the land may be said to have advanced upon the sea; since we find their ancient ports now filled up with sand, their lakes to have taken the character of marshes, and their quicksands (if ever they had any) to have become solid and firm.

To these remarks we may add the observations of Major Rennell, on the actual and former state of the Lake Tritonis and the Lesser Syrtis, which we will give in the author's own words.

"From the authorities which we shall presently adduce, we can suppose no other than that this Syrtis" (the Gulf of the Lesser Syrtis) "did once enter much deeper into the land; and that it even formed a junction with the Lake Lowdeah within it—the Tritonis Palus of the ancients. Otherwise we must not only reject the reports of Herodotus and Ptolemy, but that of Scylax also, the writer of a periplus, and who ought to have known the truth." Again, after a learned and ingenious discussion—"In effect the ancients, as Dr. Shaw justly observes (p. 213), seem to have described this quarter from report, or uncertain information only; and therefore we can hardly expect consistent, much more critical, descriptions. They appear, however, to have furnished us with very good grounds for believing that the Syrtis and Lake Tritonis communicated in former times; and that the communication continued even to the time of Ptolemy. We think it equally probable that the river Triton flowed into the lake, and that the island called by some Triton, by Herodotus, Phla, together with the temple of Minerva, (in which the Triton is said to have deposited Jason's tripod) was situated near the mouth of it: moreover, that the island in question is now a part of the sandy plain in which the rivulet of Hammah, the supposed river of Triton, loses itself. For it appears to us that the difference between the present state of things, at this place, and the ancient description of the lake and Syrtis, may be reconciled, by merely adverting to the changes that have taken place on other sandy shores; and more particularly at the head of a gulf where the tide exerts its greatest power of casting up the sand to a higher point. That which has happened at the head of the Red Sea may be adduced in point; and, as the shore of the Syrtis is much flatter than the other, the operation has probably gone on with greater rapidity."

Lucan (as Major Rennell has justly observed) "appears to believe that the bottom of the Syrtis" (that is, the Greater Syrtis) "was growing firmer, and the water shallower; and surmises that it may hereafter become dry and solid." "What changes" (he continues), "in point of form and extent, they may have undergone, or if any, we know not: but it is certain they have hitherto preserved their original properties."

We insert below the lines of Lucan alluded to, from Rowe's translation.

It will be seen that the principal danger of the Syrtes, according to the passage above quoted from Strabo, consisted in the difficulty of what is termed by seamen working off a lee-shore, for which the vessels of the ancients were very ill adapted; and we can readily believe, from what we have seen of the coast, that (under the influence of the heavy surf which rolls over the shallows when the wind blows strongly on shore) few vessels which chanced to strike could escape. The inset into the gulf, at the same time, being great, (when the north and east winds blow strongly against the coast,) it must have been extremely difficult for vessels of this description to avoid being drawn into its vortex; and indeed we may observe that few ships will, at the present day, sail from Bengazi, westward, when the wind is blowing strongly into the gulf, on account of this consequent indraught.

"The improved state of navigation" (Major Rennell very justly observes) "has, however, stripped the Syrtes of the greatest part of their terrors;" and it is probable that the report of them which we shall have from Captain Smyth will in consequence prove to be much less formidable than the accounts which have descended to us from the ancients.

It appears, from Mela, that the Syrtes were not only considered to be dangerous on account of the frequent occurrence of shoals, but more so in consequence of the flux and reflux of the sea which we have already mentioned above. This rise and fall (as we have stated) can scarcely have been the customary motion of the tides; but it may reasonably be supposed that the reaction of such a body of water as must (under the influence of violent and continued winds) have been driven over the low lands of the Greater Syrtis, was occasionally very considerable. This may have been the reflux (we imagine) alluded to; while the inset into the Gulf, caused by strong winds blowing into it, may have been the rise which is mentioned as the flux.

Of the indraught in question there can be no doubt; indeed, we may remark that a rise of this nature is more or less observable in gulfs in general; and when we consider that an unbroken sweep of level ground, very slightly raised above the surface of the sea, will be found extending itself on the western coast of the Greater Syrtis for the space of a hundred miles in length, and occasionally as much as fifteen in breadth, we may easily allow that the reflux of the water, driven over a tract of such dimensions, may well be considered as formidable.

It appears to be from the effect of the flux and reflux alluded to, that the names by which the Gulfs of Syrtis are distinguished have been derived; that is, if we may suppose them to be of Greek origin, as Sallust and others have asserted.

Cellarius has, however, been censured by Signor Della Cella for having ventured to adopt this derivation, and for "not knowing that Sert meant desert in Arabic, and that this name is still preserved in the bottom of the (Greater) Syrtis." But were we even to agree with Dr. Della Cella, that the district called Syrt is a desert, (which our friend Shekh Mahommed, who lives there, with many others, very comfortably, would be very unwilling, and very ungrateful to allow,) there does not appear to be any reason why the regions in question should be particularly distinguished as deserts, when the country which bounds them to the southward, and which is much more entitled to the appellation of desert than they are, was never called Syrtis either by ancients or moderns. The term existed, it is evident, in the age of Scylax and Herodotus, both of whom we find to have used it; but, in enumerating the several tribes which inhabited the shores of these gulfs, it by no means appears (as we have stated above) that the latter of these writers meant to characterise their country as a desert, or that he was aware of any such meaning implied by the term in question, Syrtis. If, therefore, we suppose the word to be of oriental origin, we should rather look beyond the language of the Arabs for its root; and as the Phœnicians were well acquainted with these shores at a very early period of history, we might suppose, with some appearance of probability, that the term has originated with them. As the peculiarities of the Gulfs of Syrtis appear to be more striking than those of the territory within them, it is also probable that the country would have been named from them, and not the gulfs from the country; particularly as the Phœnicians were a naval nation, and may be supposed (at the early period to which we allude) to have been better acquainted with the Gulfs than with the country here in question.

The Phœnician (or Hebrew) words from which the term Syrtis might originate, are probably the roots of the Arab phrase Sahara (صحرا), to which Signor Della Cella appears to allude; but instead of applying them to the country of the Syrtis, as expressive of its barren and desolate appearance, we should rather apply them to the Gulfs themselves, as expressive of the violent storms of wind which are known to prevail in them, and of the agitation and confusion resulting from their influence.

The terms to which we allude are the Hebrew words Saar (סַעַר), or Saàrat (סְעָרַת), signifying whirlwind, or tempest; and the root Sàar (סָעַר), from which they spring, expressive of agitation and disturbance; Soarah (סֹעֲרָה), tempest-tossed, is also another derivative of Sàar.

We have very slender pretensions to any skill in Hebrew, and merely offer the above suggestions for the consideration of those who may be inclined to reject the Greek origin of the term Syrtis; which, for our own part, we are very well contented to allow, on the authority of the writers already quoted, and on inspection of one of the places in question. It may be possible, however, that some Phœnician term, like those we have instanced, may have descended from that people to the Greeks, and afterwards through the latter to the Romans, who may have looked for the origin of it in some word of the Greek language which appeared to them expressive of the qualities of the Gulfs, without considering that the Greeks might themselves have received it from others.

FOOTNOTES:

The stade of Strabo has been estimated by Major Rennell, in his admirable treatise on the itinerary stade of the Greeks, at 700 to a geographical degree; and 930 stades will, on this computation, be equal to 100½ Roman miles, or 80☐ geographic miles. While the dimensions of the diameter, 1500 stades, will be equal to 162½ Roman miles, or $128^{57}/_{100}$ geographic.

The geographical and Roman miles differ (says Shaw, on the authority of D'Anville) as 60 is to 75½, that is, 60 geographical miles and 75½ Roman miles are equal to one degree of a great circle. The Roman mile is consequently one-fifth less than a geographic mile.—Vol. i. p. 30.

Ἡ δε μεγαλη Συρτις τον μεν κυκλον εχει σταδιων εννακοσιων τριακοντα που· την δ' επι τον μυχον διαμετρον χιλιων πεντακοσιων· τοσουτον δε που και το του στοματος πλατος.—Lib. xvii. p. 385.

In the second book, however, the measurements given by Strabo are more consistent; for he tells us that the circumference of the Greater Syrtis is (according to Eratosthenes) five thousand stadia, or $428^{45}/_{100}$ geographic mile; and its depth, from the Hesperides to Automala, and the limits of the Cyrenaica, one thousand eight hundred, or $154^{29}/_{100}$ geographic miles. Others, he adds, make the circumference four thousand stadia, $342^{88}/_{100}$ geographic miles; and the depth one thousand five hundred stadia, or $128^{57}/_{100}$ geographic miles; the same, he says, as the breadth of the gulf at its mouth.—Lib. xi. p. 123.

At the rate of 700 stades to a degree.

This estimate of the circumference is deduced from the camel-track, corrected by observations; and the accuracy to which this mode of computation may be brought by care and attention, and by making the proper allowances, will be seen in the examples which we shall hereafter submit of it.

If, however, we take the measurements just quoted from the second book of Strabo, as those which he intended to be received in the present case, we shall find that the $428^{45}/_{100}$ miles, resulting from the 5000 stadia of Eratosthenes, come very near the truth. The other measurements, however, are far from correct. It will be observed that the diameter given in this place is the same with that mentioned in the second book (1500 stadia).

Inde Syrtis Major, circuitu DCXXV. aditu autem, CCCXIII. M. Passuum.—Nat. Hist. lib. v. cap. 4.

Nec procul ante Oppidum (Berenice) fluvius Lethon, lucus sacer, ubi Hesperidum horti memorantur. Abest a Lepti CCCLXXXV. M. P.—(Lib. v. cap. 5.)

Sesostris is said to have recorded his march in maps, and to have given copies of them not only to the Egyptians, but to the remote and uninformed inhabitants of Scythia, who viewed them with the greatest astonishment. The expeditions of Alexander furnished the materials for an interesting survey, a copy of which was given to Patroclus the geographer; it was from the work of Patroclus that Eratosthenes derived his principal materials in constructing the Oriental part of his map of the world, and it is frequently quoted both by Strabo and Pliny.

Many tolerably accurate surveys resulted from the conquests of the Romans; and we learn from Vegetius that their generals were always furnished with the maps of the provinces which were to be the scenes of their operations. Julius Cæsar ordered a general survey to be made of the whole empire, which occupied twenty-five years; and the Itinerary of Antonine, as well as that which was constructed in the reign of Theodosius the Great, commonly called the Peutingerian table, are well known as valuable authorities.

"The expedition of Alexander" (says Major Rennell, in the preliminary remarks attached to his Illustrations of Herodotus,) "besides the *éclat* of the military history belonging to it, furnished in Greece and Egypt an *epoch* of geographical improvement and correction, which may not unaptly be compared with that of the discoveries of the Portuguese along the coasts of Africa and India; or of that of the present time, in which geography has been improved in every quarter of the globe."

"To a philosopher," (observes the same author,) "the changes in the comparative state of nations, in different ages of the world, are very striking, and lead one to reflect what may be the future state of some *now* obscure corner of New Holland or of North America; since our own island was known only for its tin-mines by the most celebrated of ancient nations, whose descendants, in turn, rank no higher with us than as dealers in figs and currants!"

"Variations ever did and ever will exist (continues the Major) on computed distances; instances of which existed on our own public roads previous to their improvement, and which do yet exist on many of the cross-roads." "It is probable," he adds, "that Herodotus, Xenophon, Nearchus, Strabo, &c., all intended the same stade, but may have given occasion to different results, by reporting the numbers on the judgment of different persons."

Hipparchus of Nicæa ("who can never," says Pliny, "be sufficiently commended,") appears to have been the first who united geography with astronomy, by determining the position of some of the places which he described, according to their *latitude* and *longitude*. He died about one hundred and twenty-five years before Christ, and his important discoveries remained neglected, or at least unapplied, for nearly three hundred years, till they were adopted by Ptolemy in his Geographical Treatise.

See Ptolemy, Geog. lib. i. c. 4, and Pliny, Nat. Hist., lib. ii. c. 12—26.

―――― Una campagna diserta et aspera, dove non si trova nè acqua nè terreno da coltivare.—(Leo Afr. in Ram. 5ᵗᵃ parte, p. 72.)

Prima che gli Arabi venissero in Africa fu il detto diserto dishabitato: ma poi che, &c.

There can be no doubt that the desert of Barca, here described, is the whole tract of country bordering on the Mediterranean, from Mesurata to Alexandria; for, after having described Mesurata as situated on the coast, the author proceeds to observe—"This desert (that of Barca) begins from the confines of the district of Mesurata, and extends itself eastward as far as the confines of Alexandria, a space of about one thousand three hundred miles in length, and about two hundred in breadth." The dimensions of Barca here given appear to be as singular as the description already noticed of it which follows; for besides that the length is much too great, the two hundred miles of breadth which is allotted to it would carry us far to the southward of Augila, into the desert of Libya, which does not seem, from other passages, to have been intended by Leo. We were ourselves, at one time, in passing along the eastern side of the Gulf of Syrtis, only four days' journey from Augila; and it then bore to the eastward of the south; so that it could not be anything like two hundred miles from the coast, even reckoning from the most northern part of the Cyrenaica.

The place mentioned by Strabo in the following passage, as being *four* days' easy journey from the bottom of the Syrtis, could scarcely be any other than Augila.

Τεταρταιους μεν ουν φασιν απο του μυχου της μεγαλης Συρτεως τους κατ' αυτο μαλακως βαδιζοντας ως επι χειμερινας ανατολας αφικνεισθαι. Εστι δε ο τοπος ουτος εμφερης τω Αμμονι, φοινικοτροφος τε και ευυδρος.—Lib. xvii. p. 838.

Procopius also (de Ædificiis, lib. v.) makes Augila *four* days' journey from Borium, (the Borium *Oppidum*, at the bottom of the Gulf.)

Ουτο μεν μεχρι της Τριτωνιδος λιμνης απ' Αιγυπτου νομαδες εισι κρεοφαγοι τε και γαλακτοποται Λιβυες· και θηλεων τε βοων ουτοι γευομενοι, &c.— Melp. ρπϛ .

Melp. ρπζ.—Sallust has observed of this coast and its inhabitants:—

"Mare sævum, importuosum. Ager frugum fertilis, bonus pecori, arbori infecundus: cœlo, terraque penuria aquarum: genus hominum salubri corpore, velox, patiens laborum: plerosque senectus dissolvit, nisi qui ferro, aut a bestiis interiere. Nam morbus haud sæpe quenquam superat, ad hoc malefici generis plurima animalia."—(Bell. Jugurth. § 17.)

This account agrees very well with that of Herodotus; but the description which Sallust afterwards gives of the country where the Philænean altars were placed, conveys too much the idea of a flat sandy plain.

That is, on the surface; for in most sandy deserts water may be found by digging.

Ουτοι μεν όι παραθαλασσιοι των Νομαδων λιβυων ειρεαται. υπερ δε τουτων, ες μεσογαιαν, η θηριωδης εστι λιβυη· υπερ δε της θηριωδεος οφρυη ψαμμης κατηκει, παρατεινουσα απο Θηβεων των Αιγυπτιεων επι Ηρακληιας στηλας. (Melp. ρπα .)

Strabo seems to place the Nasamones farther inland, whither they were probably driven by the Cyreneans subsequent to the account of Herodotus.

Την δε υπερκειμενην εν βαθει χωραν της Συρτεως και της Κυρηναιας κατεχουσιν Οἱ Λιβυες παραλυπρον και αυχμηραν· πρωτον μεν Οἱ Νασαμωνες, επειτα ψυλλοι και τινες γαιτουλοι, επειτα Γαραμαντες· (Lib. 17. p. 838.)

The want of accurate information which has hitherto obtained, respecting the Gulf and the Shores of the Greater Syrtis, has not only occasioned their being incorrectly laid down in modern maps, but has necessarily subjected the observations of modern writers upon them to errors which would not otherwise have been made.

In alluding to the breadth across the mouth of the Greater Syrtis, Major Rennell has remarked as follows:—

"Scylax reckons it a passage of three days and nights across its mouth; which, however, measures no more than one hundred and eighty geographic miles on the best modern maps. This allows about sixty miles for each day and night collectively."

But the actual distance across the Gulf, from Mesurata to Bengazi, is two hundred and forty-six geographic miles, instead of one hundred and eighty, and this would give a rate of eighty-six miles per day (considered as twenty-four hours).

Again—the same author observes—"Strabo says that Cato had ten thousand men, which he divided into separate bodies, that they might more conveniently obtain supplies of water in that arid region. That they marched on foot, and completed the tour of the Syrtis from Berenice in thirty days. Those who examine the distance will find that the rate of marching was eleven and a half geographic miles in direct distance, or about one mile above the mean of ordinary marches, which is 10.6."

But as the circumference of the Greater Syrtis is ascertained (as above stated) to be four hundred and twenty-two geographic miles, it will follow that the rate of marching must here have been, in actual distance, about fourteen geographic miles for each day.

Ἡ χαλεποτης δε και ταυτης της Συρτεως, και της μικρας, οτι πολλακου τεναγωδης εστιν ὁ βυθος, κατα τας αμπωτεις και τας πλημμυριδας, συμβαινει τισιν εμπιπτειν εις τα βραχη και καθιζειν· σπανιον δ' ειναι το σωζομενον σκαφος. Διοπερ πορρωθεν τον παραπλουν ποιουνται, φυλαττομενοι μη εμπεσοιεν εις τους κολπους υπ' ανεμων αφυλακτοι ληφθεντες. (Lib. 17. § 20.)

The word σκαφος here used, though it means literally *boat*, appears to be applied in this passage to vessels in general.

Travels in Barbary, vol. i. p. 164.

Major Rennell has noticed a parallel instance in our own country. "There can be no doubt" (he observes) "of the increase of the Goodwin (sand) at the present moment, and of its slow progression towards the state of firm land. Let those who doubt the facts here set forth attend to the changes at Ephesus, at Myriandrus, in the Gulf of Issus, and various other places."

In a note the author adds, "possibly with an exception to Scylax as a professed guide to others. The observations of Polybius would probably, had they come down to us, have saved us much conjecture."

When Nature's hand the first formation tried,
When seas from land she did at first divide,
The Syrts, nor quite of sea nor land bereft,
A mingled mass uncertain still she left;
For nor the land with seas is quite o'erspread,
Nor sink the waters deep their oozy bed,
Nor earth defends its shore, nor lifts aloft its head.
The site with neither and with each complies—
Doubtful and inaccessible it lies;
Or 'tis a sea with shallows bank'd around,
Or 'tis a broken land with waters drown'd;
Here shores advanced o'er Neptune's rule we find,
And there an inland ocean lags behind.
* * * * * *
Perhaps, when first the world and time began,
Here swelling tides and plenteous waters ran;
But long confining on the burning zone,
The sinking seas have felt the neighb'ring sun:
Still by degrees we see how they decay,
And scarce resist the thirsty god of day.
Perhaps in distant ages 'twill be found,

When future suns have run the burning round,

These Syrts shall all be dry and solid ground:

Small are the depths their scanty waves retain,

And earth grows daily on the yielding main.—(Pharsalia, Book 9.)

It here seems evident, that the Gulfs of Syrtis in Lucan's time were believed to be growing shallower, and the land advancing upon the sea. This is certainly consistent with the present appearance of the Greater Syrtis (as contrasted with the accounts of the ancients respecting it,) and, from all that we have been able to learn, of the Lesser Syrtis also. It must, however, be recollected, that this accumulation of soil is only observable in the low grounds, where the sand is constantly heaped up by the sea; for in other parts (as we have already stated) the sea has gained upon the land. The advance of the sea, which may be considered to be equally certain with that of the land, will serve to prove how rapidly the soil must have been accumulating in the lower parts of the Syrtis; since there is reason to believe that (notwithstanding the rise of the Mediterranean on these shores) they were formerly covered with a greater body of water than at present.

We allude here to the vessels of the country, which we were told at Bengazi usually gave the Gulf a wide birth; thus realising, in modern days, what Strabo mentions of the vessels of the ancients.

——— importuosus atq. atrox, et ob vadorum frequentium brevia, magisq. etiam ob alternos motus pelagi affluentis ac refluentis infestus. (De Situ Orbis. Lib. 1. c. 7.) This is said of the Lesser Syrtis, but the Greater Syrtis is stated, immediately afterwards, to be nomine atque ingenio par priori. Pliny also mentions both these peculiarities very briefly but decidedly; he speaks of both Gulfs as being *vadoso* ac *reciproco* mari diros. (Lib. v. c. 4.)

From συρειν, to draw, or drag along. Sallust's words are "Syrtes ab tractu nominatæ." Shaw has quoted Solinus, c. 6, and Dionysius Periegetes, 1. 198, as suggesting the same derivation. As if (he adds) "a συρω, quod in accessu et recessu arenam et cœnum ad se trahit et congerit." (Vid. Eustath. Comm.) Travels in Barbary, vol. 1. p. 211.

Viaggio da Tripoli, &c. p. 62.

Plan of the PORT *and* NEIGHBOURHOOD of BENGAZI BY *Capt*ⁿ. *F. W. Beechey R.N.*

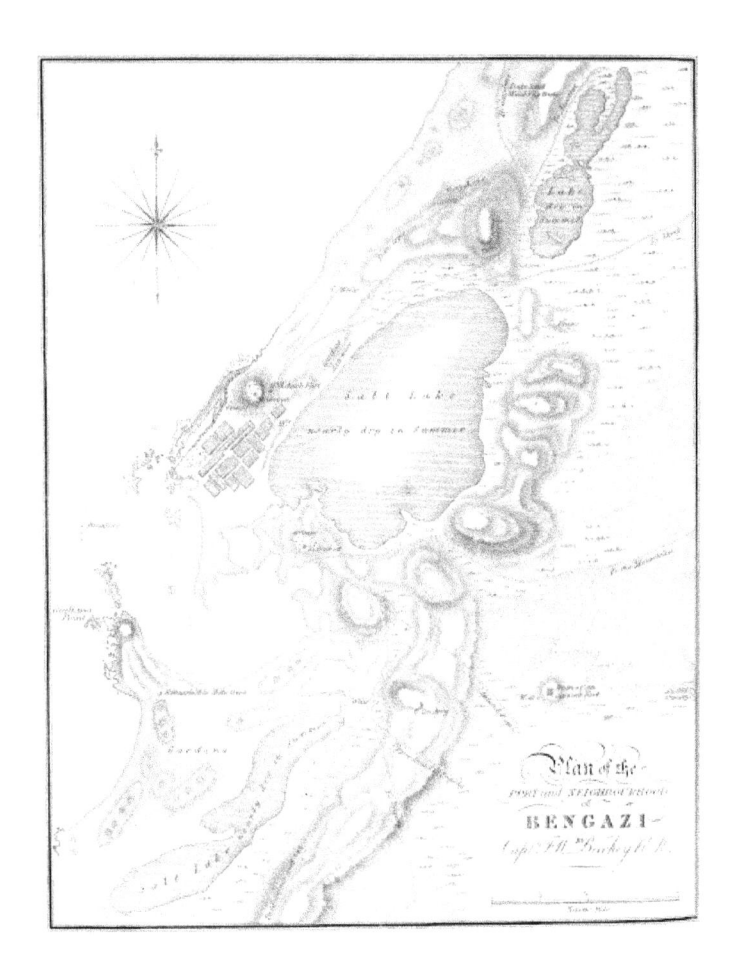

J. & C. Walker　　　　　　Published as the act directs, April 1827, by J. Murray,
Sculp‎ᵗ.　　　　　　　　　　　　　　　　　　　　　　Albemarle S‎ᵗ. London.

CHAPTER XI.

The Rainy Season sets in at Bengazi towards the middle of January, and continues with little interruption till the beginning of March — Miserable Condition of the Town during that period — Construction of the Houses — Improvidence of the Arabs — Dirty state of the Streets — Swarms of insects which infest them — Position of Bengazi — Description of its Harbour — Castle of the Bey — Visit to Bey Halîl — Friendly Reception of our Party by his Excellency — Occupations and arrangements during the Rainy Season — The Shekh el Belad Mahommed — Jews of Bengazi — Trade of the Town — Produce of the Environs — Wretched state of the Bullock Vessels — Mahometan Inhabitants of Bengazi — Alarm of the Lower Classes during our residence there — Confusion resulting from it — Mob collected at our door on this occasion — Narrow Escape of Mr. Giacomo Rossoni — Friendly Conduct of our Mahometan Acquaintance — Parley with the Arabs — Dispersion of the Mob — Prejudices of the Arabs respecting the Treatment of Diseases — Fatal Effects of this species of Folly at Bengazi — Prevalent Diseases in Bengazi and its vicinity — Singular cause of Alarm among a Party of Arab Shekhs — Arab notions of decorum and propriety contrasted with those of European Nations — Bengazi supposed to occupy the Site of Berenice and Hesperis — Existing Remains there — Little regard manifested by Turks and Arabs for the relics of Antiquity — Probable Limits of Berenice — Quarries, and singular Chasms in its Neighbourhood — Gardens of Hesperides — Position of the Gardens according to Scylax, Pliny, and Ptolemy — Conjectures of Gosselin and others respecting them — Circumstances which appear to favour our position of the Gardens — Lakes and Subterranean Caverns in the Neighbourhood of Bengazi, (or Berenice) — Concealed Body of Water observed in one of the latter — Examination of the Caverns — Remarks of the Bey respecting it — The Subterranean Stream in question considered as the River Lathon, or Lethe — Testimonies of the Ancients on this point — Supposed Communication of the Subterranean Stream with the Lake adjoining the Harbour of Bengazi — Signification of the term *Lathon* alluded to — Further Remarks in confirmation of our suggested Position of the River, and of its probable Communication with the Lake above mentioned — Remarks of Strabo and Cellarius on the subject — Temple of Venus, and Lake Tritonis of Strabo — Remarks on the name *Berenice* — Total ignorance of the Arabs of Bengazi with respect to the former celebrity of their City — Pleasing little Fable of Kazwini, on the changes which take place in the Nature and Appearance of Places, and the little knowledge which remains, after a lapse of time, of their former Condition, even on the spots where they existed.

ON the 12th of January our whole party arrived at Bengazi, having employed on the journey two months and seven days from the time of our departure from Tripoly. Shortly after our arrival, the heavy rains commenced, and continued with little interruption, until the beginning of March, accompanied with constant gales of wind from the north-east and north-west. The state of the town during this period may truly be said to have been miserable; the houses being chiefly put together with mud, were continually giving way, and falling in; and we were frequently apprized of occurrences of this nature, in our own immediate neighbourhood, by the shrieks and cries of women, whose families had been sufferers on some of these occasions.

The streets during part of the time were literally converted into rivers; the market was without supplies, owing to the impossibility of driving cattle into the town; and the number of sheep and goats which perished in the neighbourhood of Bengazi, from the extreme inclemency of the weather, amounted (we were informed) to several thousands. For ourselves, we were fortunate in having one room in our house which was capable of resisting the rain, the terrace on its roof having been cemented by one of the Beys, who had occupied it a short time before; and this, we really believe, was the only room in the town which could be fairly considered weather-proof. The court-yard round which our apartments were built (if they may be dignified with so imposing an appellation) assumed for a long time the appearance of a pond, and a narrow space was only left here and there on its borders, by which we could pass from one room to another.

From the state of our own house, which we have already said might be considered as the best in the town, the condition of other parts of Bengazi, during the rains, may be in some measure imagined; although it will scarcely be possible for the inhabitants of civilized countries, unacquainted with the nature of Arab towns, to conceive half the wretchedness and the utter want of comfort which they present on similar occasions.

The houses of Bengazi are built after the usual manner of Arab buildings, that is to say, with rough and unequally-shaped stones, put together with mud instead of mortar; they generally consist of a ground floor only, built round a square court-yard, which is exposed to the weather, and into which the doors of the chambers open, which seldom communicate with each other: the court is not paved, and in houses of more than ordinary consequence, there is sometimes a well in the centre. The roofs are flat, and are formed of rafters (chiefly of young pine-trees from the neighbouring forests) over which are laid mats, and on these there is generally a quantity of sea-weed, or other vegetable rubbish; over the whole is spread a thick stratum of mud, which is beat down as hard as Arab laziness will admit of at the time when the terrace is made.

They who can afford it (and there are very few so fortunate) spread a preparation of lime over the mud; which, as the cement is usually well made, forms a surface impervious to the weather, while the coating remains in good condition.

The rain which falls is in these cases highly beneficial, since it is carried off by spouts into some general reservoir, or is collected in large earthern jars for the daily consumption of the house. By far the greater number of houses are, however, unprovided with any defence of this nature; and if the precaution of beating down the mud which forms the terrace, sufficiently hard to make the water run off, be not adopted at the commencement of the rains, it is more than probable, that the whole of the building so neglected will disappear before the season is over. As the religion and the laziness of an Arab equally prompt him to depend more upon the interference of Providence, than upon any exertions of his own, this precaution is often neglected; and after having borne, with exemplary patience, all the dirt and inconvenience occasioned by the passage of the rain through the mud over his head, he is roused from his lethargy by the screams of his wife and children, alarmed, or badly wounded by the fall of the roof, or by some serious accident from a similar cause, by which he is a sufferer himself. Many persons were severely wounded at Bengazi in the winter during which we were confined there; and it is probable, that there are accidents in the town every year, occasioned by similar neglect.

When a house falls, it is generally left in a state of rubbish and ruin, and the survivors of the family remove to another spot without troubling themselves further about it: the consequence is, that the streets are often nearly blocked up by mounds of this nature disposed in various parts of them; which form in the winter-time heaps of mud and mire, and, in the dry weather, scatter thick clouds of light dust in the faces and eyes of the passengers.

As these masses of rubbish also serve at the same time as general receptacles for the superfluities of the city, groups of half-famished dogs and myriads of flies are invariably collected about them; in the midst of which are seen lying very contentedly, or rolling about for diversion, swarms of little naked children, regardless of either, which one might almost fancy were actually produced by the fertilizing qualities of these heaps of putrid matter, as the monsters of old are asserted to have been from the slime and the mud of the Nile. There is, however, nothing singular or peculiar to Bengazi in the scene which we have just described;

for every Arab town and village will be found, more or less, to present to us a similar spectacle. Filth and dust, and swarms of insects of every description, must inevitably be the consequences of this continued neglect; and we accordingly find that these several annoyances, together with the scattered groups of lean dogs and naked children, form the principal characteristics (in the estimation of their European visitors) of these enviable places of abode. We say, in the opinion of the natives of Europe, because an Arab or a Moor sees nothing remarkable in any of the objects here alluded to, and would consider it a mark of affectation or effeminacy to be annoyed at any similar objects or inconveniences.

In addition to the nuisances already enumerated, the open spaces in Bengazi are usually ornamented by pools of stagnant, putrid water; and that which is in the market-place is rendered more particularly offensive, from the circumstance of its being the common receptacle of the offal and blood of the animals which are killed there, and which may truly be said to realize the words of the poet in "making the green one red." It may readily be imagined, that in the heat of the summer these places are not very wholesome, and they are probably often the causes of fevers, especially during the prevalence of southerly winds. That these sinks of corruption should ever be bathing-places will not perhaps be so easily conceived; but they are nevertheless often used for such purpose; and the children of the town will very frequently adjourn from the dust-heaps already described, to cool themselves (we cannot in conscience say to clean themselves) in the green and red pools here alluded to. With so many objects to attract and encourage them, it is not to be wondered at, that Bengazi is proverbial for flies; and every part of the town, both within and without the houses, may truly be said to swarm with them. Among the various annoyances with which the place abounds, these are, perhaps, the most serious of any; or, at all events, they are those from which it is least possible to escape; there is, in fact, no chance of avoiding them; they follow you everywhere from place to place, settle on every part of the arms, legs, and body, which the heat of the weather obliges you to leave uncovered; creep obstinately into the corners of the eyes, and up the nostrils, into the hollows of the ears, and the corners of the mouth when it is closed, and often fly down the throat, nearly choking you, when it is open; at meals every part of the dishes and their contents are covered as soon as they are produced, and every fluid becomes a trap for as many of these insects as can crowd themselves over its surface. In short, there is literally no riding or walking, no reading or writing, or eating or resting one's-self, in any part of Bengazi in comfort for them; and if at night they take up their accustomed position on the ceiling, and give place to the fleas and mosquitos, the first dawn of morning finds them on the wing, and all alive to recommence their operations. They are at the same time so watchful, and so quick in their motions, that it is difficult to succeed in killing any of them; we often caught thirty or forty fleas in a morning on turning down the bed-clothes with a little attention, and as many during the day on different parts of our dress, particularly about the legs and ancles; but the whole collection of flies which we could kill in a week would scarcely amount to this number; unless we except those which were caught in the traps which we were usually in the habit of setting for them. All hot climates are more or less subject to these nuisances; but it is probable that no place on earth will be found to abound more in flies than Bengazi; we might perhaps say, that few places could be mentioned where so many of them will at any time be observed.

The situation of Bengazi is, however, much better than so filthy a town may be said to deserve. It is built on the coast, close to the sea, at the extremity of a beautiful fertile plain, extending itself to the foot of a long chain of mountains about fourteen miles distant (in this part) to the south-eastward. Plentiful crops of corn and vegetables are afforded to the town by the cultivated lands in the neighbourhood, and the supplies of beef and mutton are in general very regular and abundant. The harbour of Bengazi appears to have been formerly capable of containing good-sized vessels, and, even in the recollection of some of the present inhabitants, the Bashaw's ships were accustomed to lay, where now only boats can be accommodated.

At present it can only be entered by small vessels, drawing seven or eight feet water, and that merely in moderate weather. It is well protected from the sea by reefs of rocks, between which the entrance is so narrow as to render a pilot necessary.

There seems to be little doubt that the harbour originally communicated at all times with the lake to the southward of the town, as it does at the present day in the rainy season; but owing to the accumulation of sand from the sea, and of alluvial deposite from the lake, the communication is now, during the summer months, wholly interrupted. At the entrance of the port is the castle of the Bey of Bengazi, constructed on the ruins of an ancient building, part of which is still visible at the base of the castle next the sea. The existing structure is built with small stones and mud, so slightly, that when the Adventure made its appearance before it, the Bey requested Captain Smyth would dispense with the usual salute, as he feared the concussion would otherwise bring down a part of the walls. Its form is square, with a round tower at each of three angles; the fourth, which fronts the entrance of the harbour, being occupied by a pile of building, appropriated to the harem of his excellency.

If the gallantry of Mahometans has been doubted or denied, here is surely a proof of its existence; for the angle given up to the service of the ladies is almost the only one which could prove of any annoyance to vessels entering the harbour; and, while the three turrets mentioned are provided with guns, this angle is left without any. The fair inhabitants of the harem are in consequence favoured with a view of the "dark blue main," and the grated windows of their apartments command at the same time a view of the entrance to the harbour.

The cool sea-breeze enters freely, and the ladies may sit with the lattice spread open to enjoy it, without incurring the danger of meeting the gaze of any vulgar or sacrilegious eye. The dashing of the waters against the base of the castle may also serve to lull them to sleep; but candour, at the same time, obliges us to state, that it may also serve to waken them rather too abruptly on no very distant occasion. Were it not that the lower part of the structure is (as we have before mentioned) ancient, and consequently strongly built, the interruption to which we allude would have happened long before now; and Neptune, as if encouraged by the daily glances of so many soft dark eyes, would have washed away the barrier which so cruelly interposed itself, and carried off the lovely inhabitants of the harem to enliven his submarine *soirées*.

Besides the harem of the Bey, the castle contains the officers and chaouses of his household, and a numerous body of troops might be lodged within the limits of its walls. In time of trouble, it is the only place to which he could retreat with any safety, and it forms the only ornament and the only protection which the town of Bengazi possesses.

The Bey, whose name is Halīl, was once fortunate enough to possess a daughter of the Bashaw as his wife, a circumstance which secured for him a good deal of influence (or at least a great portion of the royal favour) during the life of his consort. He was not, however, destined to enjoy his good fortune long, for the princess died a short time before our arrival at Tripoly, and with her highness departed that portion of influence which Bey Halīl through her means had obtained. The profits arising from the government of Bengazi would have been sufficient to enrich its possessor, had he been allowed to enjoy them; but the demands which were continually made upon him by the Bashaw became so heavy after the death of his wife, that the surplus was very inconsiderable. Besides this, the collection of the tribute from the Bedouin tribes in the neighbourhood was often attended with difficulty, and must have made the receipts uncertain; but no allowance is made in Mahometan countries for casualties of this description; the will of a superior is a law, and his demands must be punctually complied with, (whatever may be the means of satisfying them,) if the office, and often the life of the person upon whom they may be made, are valued by him. The consequence is, that extortion in the heads of departments is the cause of extortion in subalterns; and he who has no power to avail himself of tyranny, is generally doomed to be the sufferer himself, for not being able to do more than his resources will allow him to accomplish. Many a well-meaning man who would have acted with propriety, had the alternative been less severe, is thus obliged to commit acts of cruelty and injustice which his nature would not have inclined him to; the force of habit and example at length subdues his better feelings, and necessity is so often made the excuse for tyrannical conduct, that it not only becomes a plea where it actually obtains, but is urged as such eventually on occasions where no necessity really exists, to justify private acts of caprice and oppression, which have themselves only resulted from the long-indulged habit of executing similar outrages for others.

The Bey having been officially apprized of our arrival, and that we were desirous of paying our respects to him, appointed a day to receive us; and when the time arrived we proceeded to the castle, accompanied by Signor Rossoni, the British vice-consul at Bengazi, and his brother, Mr. Giacomo Rossoni. We found the Bey in a plain whitewashed room of unimposing dimensions, but cool and tolerably clean, seated upon cushions spread round a niche which had been formed in the wall for the purpose. On each side of this recess, or alcove, were ranged the principal officers of the household, the chaouses, and several shekhs; other parts of the room were occupied by slaves and persons of inferior condition. There was much less ceremony in the court of Bey Halīl than in that of the Bashaw at Tripoly, and the conversation appeared to have been pretty general before we entered the apartment in which he received us.

The hum of voices subsided all at once as we made our appearance, and every person's eyes seemed determined to exert themselves in proportion as his tongue was laid under restraint; for the steady gaze of all present was fixed upon our party as we took up our stations near the Bey. We found his excellency a good-looking, well-formed man, who, apparently from inactivity and good living, had attained to that state of dignified *embonpoint* at which persons of inferior consideration in Mahometan countries are very seldom destined to arrive. A Georgian by birth, Bey Halīl possessed strongly the Asiatic cast of countenance and features, and an expression of unassumed and unreserved goodnature gave a pleasing character to his sharp, black eyes. His reception of our party was in unison with his appearance; and the formal inclination of the head, usually made by Mahometans to strangers whom they honour with their notice, gave place to a hearty English shake of the hand; while a cordial *Bon giorno! Ti sta bono?* was substituted for the grave and ceremonious *salam*, which, whenever it is offered by the faithful to unbelievers, is almost invariably dictated by politeness or policy merely.

Near the Bey stood his secretary, Hashi (whose pale and thin countenance, and weak, inflamed eyes, appeared to testify that his place was no sinecure); and two of his head chaouses, one a native of Constantinople, a short, corpulent, sleepy-looking personage; the other a tall, raw-boned, hard-featured Arab, who had shewn great bravery and activity in petty wars with the Bedouin tribes, and whose shattered hand bore testimony to his exploits.

Several persons came in from time to time, and having kissed his excellency's hand, and made the appropriate salams, squatted themselves down in different parts of the room, according to their rank and station, and began with great attention their survey of our party.

The objects of the expedition had in all probability been made known to the Bey before our arrival; but we thought it proper to state them in general terms to his excellency, through the medium of Mr. Giacomo Rossoni, in his official character of interpreter.

This was no sooner done than the eyes of the spectators, which had hitherto been actively employed, were relieved for a short time by their organs of speech, exerted in ill-suppressed whispers. From their gestures, and a word or two which we caught *en passant*, we could perceive that very few of the Arabs assembled believed a single word of our statement, (so far, at least, as the motives for the expedition were concerned;) for they could not at all imagine why persons should be commissioned to make researches of such a nature as those which they had just heard proposed, where money was not in fact the real object of inquiry.

His excellency the Bey, though he received the statement graciously, and offered his assistance very freely in facilitating the operations of the mission, was scarcely himself convinced of the sanity of a government which could concern itself with science and research, particularly if no considerable *pecuniary* equivalent was likely to result to His Majesty's treasury for the expenses incurred by its expeditions.

We had brought with us several papers for Bey Halīl from the Bashaw, all of which, when presented (with the exception of one), he put into the hands of his secretary Hashi, his excellency not being himself quite *au fait* at deciphering the contents of his letters. The paper retained was the teskeré from the Bashaw (already mentioned) for five hundred dollars; and it is probable that the frequent arrival of similar orders had rendered their appearance so familiar to Bey Halil, that he was able to distinguish them without the assistance of his secretary, though he could not read a word of other matter.

A slight change of countenance, when he first cast his eyes upon the teskeré, was, however, the only visible effect which it produced on the exterior of the Bey of Bengazi; and his good breeding did not allow him to manifest in any other way that our visit was not in all respects perfectly agreeable to him. We may add, that the sum was punctually paid to us, after some little (possibly unavoidable) delay, by the hands of secretary Hashi; and the credit of his excellency was in no other way diminished, than by the discharge of the five hundred dollars at several times, instead of being made at one payment. Had we known at Tripoly so much of the Bey's private history, as we have already stated above, this teskeré might have been spared him; for we should certainly not have been induced to accept any order upon him, however trifling, could we have supposed that its payment might be inconvenient.

Soon after we left the coast of Africa, Bey Halil was removed from the government of Bengazi, and it is probable that he had reason to rejoice at his dismissal; for had he remained there much longer than he did, the continued demands for money and cargoes, so unmercifully made upon him by his Highness, could scarcely have failed to ruin him. In addition to these, he had sustained a considerable loss in the capture of one of the vessels which he had freighted, by the Greeks, as we were informed, at Bengazi; and also in the destruction of the jewels and wardrobe of his wife, which the Bashaw had ordered to be burnt (it was said) after the death of that unfortunate princess.

In compliance, we presume, with the practice of the court of Tripoly, tea was served to us with the sherbet, instead of coffee, at the interviews we had with Bey Halil; as we have already mentioned it to have been in that with the Shekh of Mesurata.

In the course of our first visit, we took occasion to mention to his excellency the careless manner in which Shekh Mahommed el Dúbbah had fulfilled the injunctions of the Bashaw; and to enumerate a few of the impositions, the unnecessary delays, and privations, to which we had in consequence been subjected; acquainting him at the same with the loss of property which we had sustained, from the thievish disposition of the Dúbbah's people. We hoped by this complaint to get back a pocket compass, and some other articles which we could ill spare, which had been stolen from our tents on the journey across the Syrtis. Bey Halil was, however, either unwilling or unable to assist us in the matter; and after shrugging up his shoulders in dignified silence (as if he had expected nothing less), he summed up the whole of his displeasure in the single exclamation of—Arab! By which he seemed to imply, that, as one of that race, the Shekh could not be other than a rogue.

Unsatisfactory as this administration of justice may appear, it did not seem probable that we should obtain any other; and having one means of punishment, at least, in our own hands (that of mulcting the Shekh, whom we had not fully paid, to the amount of the property stolen), we did not press the subject any further with his excellency; and after having made known to him our intention of remaining during the rainy season in Bengazi, and of proceeding afterwards to the eastward, we concluded by requesting his assistance and protection, in furtherance of the remaining objects of the mission, and took our leave under the most decided and friendly assurances of having everything arranged as we could wish.

As soon as this visit of ceremony was over, we began to employ our time, which, on account of the heavy rains, was necessarily passed in doors, in putting together the materials which we had collected on our route, in making some arrangements for improving the condition of our horses, of which they stood much in need, and in preparing provisions and other necessaries which were required for our journey to the eastward. In these pursuits we were materially assisted by the vice-consul and his brother, Mr. Giacomo Rossoni, to both of whom our thanks are particularly due, as well on these as on many other occasions. Our time, though we passed it as agreeably as we could, nevertheless often hung very heavy on our hands; and we soon found that Bengazi was a residence which we should quit with very little regret. There is not a single place of public resort or amusement in any part of this gloomy abode: its inhabitants idle or sleep away the greater part of their time, without appearing to entertain the slightest desire of improving their comfortless and miserable condition, or of enlivening the monotony of their pursuits. Turkish towns are not in general remarkable for gaiety, and we did not expect to find theatres or assembly-rooms; but there is usually a good deal of amusement to be derived from occasional visits to the coffee-shops and bazaars, and not unfrequently some useful information. These resources, however, were not afforded us at Bengazi; for there is nothing of the kind there that we felt an inclination to visit a second time. Strangers who arrive there may indeed find a shelter from the weather, in a place well known to Mahometans as the Fundook, a temporary place of reception and partial accommodation. We once, and once only, took occasion to visit this place; and on entering it through the aperture of a broken door, we found ourselves in a long arched room, in which there was scarcely sufficient light to show us where to place our feet, a precaution which was nevertheless highly essential. Here we perceived the remains of a charcoal fire, which had been kindled on the well-smoked capital of a marble column, and a greasy Arab stretched close to it on the ground, snoring amid the folds of his barracan. The building itself was of some antiquity, though not apparently older than the worst time of the lower empire, the roof being supported upon small columns of execrable taste, and the other parts of the building in no better style. The exterior had undergone some repair from time to time, but no attention whatever had been paid to the chamber within, not even that of removing the dirt and filth which was collected there; and the consequence was, that the level of the floor reached two-thirds of the way up the columns. We need scarcely add, that whatever attractions this place may have had for an Arab, it had little allurement for us; and we should have laid ourselves down, without the least hesitation, to pass a rainy night in the street, rather than subject ourselves to the punishment of taking shelter for an hour under its roof.

The house in which we had taken up our abode was the property of the Shekh el Belad, a very worthy person, much respected by all who knew him: he soon made us acquainted with the principal people of the town, from whom we collected what little information they could afford us, respecting the country, and the several objects of our mission. We were informed that Bengazi contained about two thousand inhabitants, a large proportion of which were Jews and negro slaves; but the number of persons residing in the town is continually varying, owing to the circumstance of many persons removing to the country, whenever the weather permits, where they establish themselves in tents, or in huts made of palm-branches and dhurra-stalks. The Jews of Bengazi are a persecuted race, but uniformly steady in their pursuit after riches: as is usually the case in Mahometan countries, they are (with the few exceptions we shall presently mention) the principal merchants and tradesmen of the place; and their well-directed and unremitted industry alone enables them to meet the heavy exactions which are made upon their purses and property by the adherents to the religion of the Prophet. Their houses are generally cleaner and better furnished than those of most of the Mahometans, and we never entered any of them without finding the whole family employed in some useful occupation.

We found them invariably civil and obliging, and apparently contented with their condition; which proves how much habit will reconcile us to evils, which, to those not inured to them, would be intolerable. The "fierce impatience" which formerly characterized the Jews of the Cyrenaica has disappeared with the probability of its being successfully exerted; and poverty is now almost the only evil to which they will not quietly submit. The trade of Bengazi is not, however, wholly confined to the Jews; for, besides the Bey himself, who may be considered as the first merchant, there are several other very respectable Mahometan traders; the Bazaar, notwithstanding, presents little more than the articles in greatest request among the Bedouins; amongst which may be seen bundles of rusty nails, horse-shoes, musket-balls, and large flints, which form the chief objects of their visits, and are exposed for sale, on boards, at the doors of a few of the most industrious Arab inhabitants of the town, and bargained for with as much seriousness and vehemence, as if they were the most costly goods. The produce of the interior consists chiefly in corn, wool, and manteca, with which the merchants freight the different foreign vessels which purposely touch at Bengazi. This is done in preference to employing the small vessels of the country; first, because the foreign vessels are much better navigated, and secondly, because in sailing under European colours they are less liable to molestation from the Greeks. Besides these articles, oxen are well known to constitute a great portion of the trade of Bengazi, and many vessels are kept constantly employed in transporting them to Malta and other places during the summer months. If the wind prove favourable, and the passage be quickly made, the profits to all parties are great; but it sometimes happens that, from violent or contrary winds, or from the vessel being ill calculated for the cargo, and more frequently from there being too great a number of these poor animals crowded inconsiderately together, that so many oxen die from thirst and suffocation, from bruises, and occasionally from drowning, as to render the profits of the voyage very trifling.

The cattle are chiefly driven from the neighbourhood of Cyrene, where their original cost is from six to eight dollars a head; some expenses, of course, are incurred on the road, but these are amply covered by the price of ten and thirteen dollars, at which sum the oxen are furnished to the captains of the bullock-vessels: the master, again, being fully compensated by a contract of about eighteen dollars a head at Malta.

The prospect of fine weather very often induces the captain to take on board as many as there is standing-room for in his vessel, on both upper and lower deck, in both of which the poor animals are jammed as close as they can possibly be stowed. The sufferings of the oxen in hot and oppressive weather, taken at once from the invigorating atmosphere of their native mountains, and exposed to the thick and almost suffocating steam (proceeding from their own bodies) which they must necessarily breathe in the place of their confinement, will be more easily deplored than described. So oppressive is the heat, on many occasions, in the lower deck of the bullock-vessels, that the men employed to look after the unfortunate animals can scarcely stay more than ten minutes there, except immediately under the hatchways; and such of the oxen as chance, from their situation, or other causes, to be more affected by the closeness of the atmosphere than the rest, are obliged to be dragged up continually to the deck above, to prevent them from dying of suffocation.

We are sorry to say that our own experience enables us to speak decidedly on these points; for as there was no other vessel in the harbour of Bengazi, when we left the coast, than a bullock-vessel, and no other expected to arrive, we were obliged to take a passage in the only one of them then remaining. As we experienced, nearly the whole voyage, the most provoking calms, our passage was an unusually long one; and independently of the extreme inconvenience (to use the mildest term) which we experienced ourselves, we had to witness a scene of suffering which we shall never forget, and which we would willingly have gone through much more than we experienced to have avoided. It is indeed scarcely possible to conceive that human nature could be really so degraded from its rank in creation, as it appears to be in the persons of those who form the crew of a bullock-vessel.

And yet many of them are not, on other occasions, cruel men—but the constant habit of witnessing and inflicting sufferings, which they seem to think matters of course, has so blunted their kinder feelings in the discharge of this particular duty, that one might almost blush (on witnessing their conduct) at being classed in the same species with them. The horrors of slave-ships are happily for the most part abolished, through the humanity and the influence of Englishmen; and if the government of Malta were acquainted with the horrors of bullock-vessels, they would surely take means to prevent the recurrence of them. Let us hope that some Martin may arise in the Mediterranean who will exert himself in bringing this about; we will answer for it, he will never sit down to a piece of beef without feelings of more than usual satisfaction.

Among the persons to whom we were introduced by Shekh Mahommed, there were several whose good sense and good feeling would have done credit to a more civilized people; and the time which we spent in their society was often very agreeably passed. They were able to afford us a good deal of information respecting the country to the eastward, and in the interior, which we afterwards found very useful; but they were generally shy in giving an opinion upon affairs of a political nature. They would, however, talk freely of the exploits of Mahommed Bey, who was so instrumental in reducing the country to its present state of tranquillity; and whose sanguinary measures alone procured for Bengazi the security which it now enjoys. We often conversed on the subject of the existing war with the Greeks, and they manifested at all times extreme curiosity to know what part we should take, in the event of the arrival of any Greek vessel off their port. Our answers were always satisfactory to them; and a report of the English being favorably inclined towards the Porte having by some means reached them, we were in subsequent interviews addressed as Sahab, or ally.

This confidence in our intentions was not, however, so strongly felt among the lower classes of people; at least it did not appear to have been so on the occasion which we are about to mention.

Some vague reports of the successes of the Greeks, and their merciless treatment of the prisoners which they had taken, having reached the people of Bengazi, they became, on a sudden, uncommonly nervous, and were in momentary apprehension of an invasion, and of an indiscriminate slaughter of themselves and their families. The appearance of the Adventure, about this time, on their coast, which had not been visited by a man-of-war for a long time before, together with the arrival, soon after, of our party, whose real objects were for the most part unintelligible to them, added to the circumstance of their having seen us employed in making plans and drawings of their fort and harbour, all contributed to strengthen their suspicions and their fears; and they soon began to consider our residence among them as, in some way, connected with the Greeks. While their minds were thus prepared, it unluckily happened one evening just before sunset, that some hard clouds had formed themselves on the horizon, into shapes which they conceived to resemble ships under sail; the appearance soon excited the greatest alarm, and many an eager eye was fixed upon the formidable armada which imagination had suggested to the terrified Arabs. Before they could be satisfied that there was no foundation for their fears, it was too dark to distinguish anything more; and the greatest confusion very shortly prevailed in every part of Bengazi. The men now began to prepare their fire-arms, and the signal to assemble was everywhere repeated; the women and children running about in the greatest terror, calling out that the Christians were coming to murder them!

The disturbance was not long unknown to our party, for our door shortly became the centre of confusion; a mob of Arabs was very soon collected about it, who manifested the most hostile feeling, and the street rang with invectives against the Nasáras. It would have gone hard with any Christian who had been found unarmed in the streets at this moment; for even Giacomo Rossoni (the brother of the Consul), who was a great favorite with the Arabs, and who chanced to be out just before, very narrowly escaped with his life in making his way to take refuge in our house. We had every desire to act as conciliatory a part as possible, but finding our doors assailed in the manner described, we armed ourselves, with the intention of defending the house to the last, should the Arabs proceed to extremities. At this difficult moment Shekh Mahommed and his brothers, accompanied by some of our other Arab friends, made their way through the mob and arrived just in time to prevent an immediate attack upon our quarters; and we afterwards learnt that one of the Shekh's brothers had been felled to the ground, for his remonstrances in our favour, before he could reach our door. A parley was now begun with great vehemence on both sides; but before any measures could be determined upon, an alarm was excited that the Greeks might be landing while this discussion was pending, and the whole party of rioters hurried down to the beach, leaving none but the women and children in the town. Muskets were now discharged in various directions, without any person knowing what they were firing at, and the whole strength of the place was drawn up on the beach in momentary expectation of being attacked by the invaders. At length, after a lapse of several hours, they conceived that sufficient time had been given for the approach of the vessels, if Bengazi had been really their object; and after inquiring of one another what grounds there had been for all the disturbance they had been making, without any one being able to give a satisfactory answer, the whole party retired very quietly to their houses, and nothing more was ever heard of the formidable invasion which had excited such alarm and confusion. In the mean time Signor Giacomo, who had been some time in our house, became anxious to relieve his family from the apprehensions which they could not but have entertained for his safety; but his European dress being likely to attract attention, and expose him to danger or insult, we offered our services to accompany him; and on reaching his house in safety, he learnt that the Consul had been obliged to shut himself up with his family, and that they had been in the greatest alarm for him. Thus ended a panic which arose from the most trifling circumstance, threw the whole town into serious confusion, and threatened the lives of all the Christians in the place, without having the slightest foundation.

It was singular to observe, during the whole of this affair, the total want of system and discipline which prevailed; each person hurrying he hardly knew where, because he saw others in motion, and leaving his home, with his family and property, at the mercy of any one who might invade it. A handful of men might have taken the whole town, which was left for several hours without any defence, and carried off their plunder beyond the reach of pursuit before the inhabitants knew they had been there. This was the only molestation we ever met with from the people of Bengazi; and, to do them justice, we must allow that it proceeded rather from their ignorance and their fears, than from any decided hostility or ill-will towards ourselves. On all other occasions we found them civil and obliging, and usually inclined to be of service to us when they could. With regard to the manners and customs of the people of Bengazi, we saw nothing in which they differed materially from those of Arabs in general; and it would merely be repeating what has been often observed by others, were we to give any detailed description of them. It is well known what reliance is placed by the Arab on the efficacy, we may say, the infallibility of charms and family nostrums, and how much they are averse to calling in medical aid till they have repeatedly tried their own remedies without success. We saw a lamentable instance of this adherence to popular prejudice and superstition, in the case of an interesting girl of Bengazi, the daughter of one of the Arabs of the town. As Mr. Campbell was standing at the door of our house, in company with some others of our party, an old woman hurried towards him, and eagerly seizing both his hands, conjured him to come and visit her daughter, who she said was very ill with a swelling in the throat. Mr. Campbell immediately complied with her request, and accompanied her, together with one or two of the other officers, to the house where the patient was lying. On entering they found the poor girl we have mentioned, extended upon the floor, in a state of delirium, while her sister, on her knees by her side, was endeavouring by means of a fan to keep away the myriads of flies from her face, with which the room as usual abounded. Her throat was soon found to be so much ulcerated and swelled, as almost to prevent respiration; and it seemed but too evident that the hand of death was already lying heavily upon her. She had been ill for nine days with a typhus fever, and the usual charms and remedies had been employed by her parents, who only came to Mr. Campbell for advice when all their own prescriptions had failed. The violence of the fever had now subsided, leaving the unhappy girl in a state of exhaustion, and a mortification appeared to have taken place. Every means were of course resorted to which our medicine-chest afforded, and every possible attention was paid to the comfort of the patient; but all our care was unavailing; the disease was too far advanced to be subdued by medical skill, and the poor girl shortly expired, a victim rather to ignorance and superstition, than to any fatal symptoms in the disease itself, had the proper remedies been applied in time.

Through a similar infatuation, the son of our worthy landlord, Shekh Mahommed, who was in other respects a very sensible man, had nearly fallen a victim to the prejudices of his father. He had, unknown to us, been for many days dangerously ill of a fever; during which time his father kept him shut up in a dark, close room, and almost smothered him with blankets. When we heard of the circumstance, Mr. Campbell immediately offered his advice and assistance; but both were civilly declined, the good Shekh observing, at the same time, that if it were the will of God that his favourite son should die, no exertions of any one could save him, and he himself had only to submit, without repining, to the visitation which heaven had been pleased to bring upon him. We, however, at last succeeded in prevailing upon him to accept of Mr. Campbell's mediation, and, in the course of a few weeks, we are happy to state, the boy completely recovered. Some other cures which Mr. Campbell was enabled to make at length gained him a great reputation, and some of the operations to which he had recourse at once delighted and astonished the Arabs.

A man much emaciated, who had been long afflicted with the dropsy, was persuaded to submit to the operation of tapping; and when his numerous Arab friends, who had assembled to witness the ceremony, saw the water streaming out from the abdomen, they were unable to restrain the loud expression of their surprise at the sight; and lifting up their hands and eyes to Heaven, called Allah to witness that the *tibeeb* was a most extraordinary man!

Dysentery and liver complaints were very common in Bengazi, but we did not observe so many cases of ophthalmia as we had found at Tripoly and Mesurata. Cutaneous diseases of the most virulent kind were very prevalent, as well among the people of the town, as among the Bedouin tribes in the neighbourhood; indeed, we found that these disorders prevailed more or less in every part of the northern coast of Africa which we visited. The inhabitants of the Cyrenaica suppose them to be chiefly occasioned by handling their cattle, but it is probable that unwholesome food and water, to which they may be occasionally subjected, and the little use which they make of the latter for external purposes, contribute more effectually to engender and encourage these diseases, than the circumstances to which they attribute them.

Among the numerous instances, which we observed during our stay at Bengazi, illustrative of Arab character and prejudices, we may notice one which occurred in the skeefa (or entrance-hall) of our house, where a *select party* of the inhabitants of the town usually assembled themselves when the weather permitted. On this occasion, the women of England formed the principal subject of conversation, and the reports of their beauty, which had reached some of our visitors, appeared to have made a great impression in their favour. One of our party then produced a miniature from his pocket, which chanced to be the resemblance of a very pretty girl; and he roundly asserted, as he handed it to the company, that every woman in England was as handsome. We have already observed, that the subject was a very pretty girl; and they who are unacquainted with the force of custom and prejudice, will hardly conceive that an object so pleasing could be the cause of a moment's alarm. But truth obliges us to add, that the first Arab of our party, who was favoured with a sight of the lady in question, started back in dismay and confusion; and all his worthy countrymen who cast their eyes upon the picture, withdrew them, on the instant, in the greatest alarm, exhibiting the strongest symptoms of astonishment and shame. The fact was, that the young lady who had caused so much confusion, was unluckily painted in a low evening dress; and her face was only shaded by the luxuriant auburn curls, which fell in ringlets over her forehead and temples.

There was nothing, it will be thought, so extremely alarming in this partial exhibition of female beauty; and the favoured inhabitants of less decorous, and more civilized countries, would scarcely dream of being shocked at a similar spectacle. But to men who inhabit those regions of delicacy, where even *one* eye of a female must never be seen stealing out from the sanctuary of her veil, the sudden apparition of a sparkling pair of those luminaries is not a vision of ordinary occurrence. At the same time, the alarm of the worthy Shekhs assembled, which the bright eyes and *naked* face (as they termed it) of our fair young countrywoman had so suddenly excited, was in no way diminished by the heinous exposure of a snowy neck and a well-turned pair of shoulders; and had they been placed in the situation of Yusuf, when the lovely Zuleika presented herself in all her charms as a suitor for the young Hebrew's love, or in the more embarrassing dilemma of the Phrygian shepherd-prince, when three immortal beauties stood revealed before his sight, they could scarcely have felt or expressed more confusion. Every Arab, who saw the picture, actually blushed and hid his face with his hands; exclaming—w'Allah harám—(by Heaven 'tis a sin) to look upon such an exposure of female charms!

It is, no doubt, very gratifying, in these ages of assurance, to witness so unequivocal a display of genuine modesty; and we confess that we ought not to have laughed so heartily as we did at this laudable expression of it in our guests: but it certainly did appear to us somewhat ridiculous to see men, with long beards, who had each of them two or three wives, so completely discomfited at the sight of a rosy-faced girl. At the same time, we must allow that we have also our prejudices; and it is probable, that the appearance of a young Arab damsel, with her veiled face and naked legs and feet, in the midst of a party of Englishmen, might occasion no trifling confusion; scarcely less, perhaps, than that which was occasioned by the display of the fair face and neck above mentioned. It was some time before our worthy Arab friends recovered from the serious shock which their modesty had sustained; but as modesty (for what reason we will not pretend to determine) is by no means an unconquerable feeling, we prevailed upon the blushing Shekhs, when the first impression had subsided, to take a second look at the picture; declaring, that there was nothing in so innocent a display at which the most correct of true believers need be shocked. We will not venture to say that they were quite of our opinion; but it is certain that their curiosity (at least we suppose it to have been that) very soon got the better of their scruples; and we even think, that some of them might actually have been persuaded to trust themselves in those sinful regions where a pretty face and figure may be looked at and admired without any very serious breach of decorum. As for Shekh Mahommed, he had so far recovered himself as to put the object of his former confusion into his pocket, though merely to show it (as he said) to his wives; and was hardy enough to keep it three or four days, before he returned it to its owner.

With respect to the Arab women, we will venture to say (though we do not think that modesty is their predominant quality) that no consideration could induce them to dress themselves in the manner which caused such astonishment to our acquaintance: and they would certainly not believe that the ladies of Europe, to whom such costume is familiar, would object to appear in the presence of the other sex without their shoes and stockings. As for dancing with men, and taking them by the hand, it would be looked upon as the last stage of effrontery and indelicacy; yet their own familiar dance is at the same time of such a nature that no modest women of Europe could look at it. It would be a curious experiment in natural history to see which of the ladies would require most persuasion; the Arab to appear in public without any veil, or the Englishwoman without shoes and stockings. There can be no question which of the two is most civilized; yet, we own, we cannot see that it is at all more indecent to appear in public with the legs and feet uncovered, than it is to expose the face, arms, and neck; or that it is really more modest to cover the face than to leave it in its natural state. Of the two, we should certainly think it more modest to cover the face than the feet; yet we know that the practice of going without a veil is adopted by the most refined nations of the globe, and that the habit of wearing it is by no means inconsistent with levity and want of proper feeling.

To return to our description of the town; we have already stated, that Bengazi may be considered as occupying the site of the Berenice of the Ptolemies, and of the Hesperis of earlier times; but very few remains now appear above ground to interest the sculptor, the architect, or the antiquary. Berenice has, in fact, disappeared from the beautiful plain on which it stood, and a miserable, dirty, Arab town has reared itself on its ruins, or rather on the soil which covers its ruins, for all its interest is now under ground.

The erection of Bengazi on the site of the ancient town, rather than the effects of time, or of hostile violence, appears to have been chiefly the cause of the total disappearance of the latter; for the stones of which the buildings were originally composed being too large for the purposes of the Arabs, are broken up into small pieces before they are used in modern structures, and generally before they are removed from the places in which they are dug up. Many a noble frieze and cornice, and many a well-proportioned capital has been crushed under the hammer of these barbarians; so that, even were there not a single house in Bengazi which has not been composed of ancient materials, yet there is nothing of architecture in any of them at present to fix, and scarcely to arrest, the attention. We were ourselves just too late to save from the hammer several portions of a large and well-executed Ionic entablature, which a worthy Arab Shekh had caused to be excavated and brought into his court-yard, to form part of a house which he was building without the town, and which was carefully beat to pieces by his servants and slaves before it was bedded in the mud which received it. Very extensive remains of building are still found about Bengazi, at the depth of a foot or two from the surface of the plain; and whenever a house is intended to be erected, the projector of it has nothing more to do, in order to obtain materials for building it, than to send a few men to excavate in the neighbourhood, and with them a camel, or two or three asses, to transport what is dug up to the spot which has been fixed upon for the house. If the fragments which are found should prove too large for removal (which is generally the case) they are broken into smaller pieces, without the least hesitation or concern, till they are reduced to a convenient size for loading, and are afterwards broken again into still smaller pieces, as occasion may require, on the place where the house is built. Many valuable remains of antiquity must have disappeared in this way, but it is probable, at the same time, that many still exist to reward the expense of excavation; and we have little doubt, that statues and inscriptions, numerous fragments of architecture, and good collections of coins and gems, might still be obtained within the distance of half a mile round Bengazi. On the beach to the northward and to the north-eastward of the town, where a bank of twenty and thirty feet (more or less) is formed of the rubbish of one of the ancient cities, coins and gems are continually washed down in rainy weather; and the inhabitants of Bengazi repair in crowds to the beach, after storms, and sift the earth which falls away from the cliff, disposing of whatever they may find to the few Europeans of the place.

When we reflect that Berenice flourished under Justinian, and that its walls underwent a thorough repair in the reign of that Emperor, it will be thought somewhat singular, that both the town and its walls should have disappeared so completely as they have done. We have already mentioned the disappearance of the city, and it may here be observed, that scarcely a vestige of its walls now remains above the surface of the plain, and that it would not be possible to decide its precise limits, without a great deal of previous excavation. It is probable, however, that Berenice did not extend beyond the actual limits of Bengazi; for the salt-water lake to the southward of the town would prevent its going farther in that direction, and the ground to the eastward is in most parts so low as to be frequently overflowed by the sea, which oozes through the sand heaped upon the beach in that direction.

From the circumstance of the water in Bengazi being brackish, it is probable that the ancient town was furnished with an aqueduct from some springs of sweet water, about half a mile distant from it to the eastward;

and the existence of remains of ancient reservoirs, or cisterns, with troughs, constructed of stone, leading into them, still observable on the beach where the coins and gems are collected, would seem, in some degree, to favour this supposition.

On first discovering the quarries from which the city of Berenice, and probably that of Hesperis also, have been constructed, we flattered ourselves that we should have found them full of excavated tombs, which are usually formed in similar situations, when the quarries are not far from the town: but two or three chambers only appeared, which did not seem to us to have been intended for places of burial, and the tombs of both cities must be looked for in the plain, under the soil or the sand which now conceals them.

The trees and shrubs which are growing in the quarries we allude to, and have rooted themselves, at the same time, in the sides of the rocks which they are formed in, give these places a very wild and picturesque appearance, not unworthy of the pencil of Salvator; and, had not our time been fully occupied in research, when the weather allowed us to ramble, we should have been glad to have made some sketches of them. The caper plant is found there in great abundance, and spreads itself, like ivy, over the steep sides of the rocks, hanging down in the most luxuriant and beautiful clusters.

In speaking of the steep rocks in which these quarries are formed, we must state, that they do not rise above the surface of the plain, but are sunk down, perpendicularly, to a considerable depth, so as not to be visible till they are closely approached. Besides the quarries here mentioned, some very singular pits or chasms, of natural formation, are found in the neighbourhood of Bengazi: they consist of a level surface of excellent soil, of several hundred feet in extent, inclosed within steep, and for the most part perpendicular, sides of solid rock, rising sometimes to a height of sixty or seventy feet, or more, before they reach the level of the plain in which they are situated. The soil at the bottom of these chasms appears to have been washed down from the plain above by the heavy winter rains, and is frequently cultivated by the Arabs; so that a person, in walking over the country where they exist, comes suddenly upon a beautiful orchard or garden, blooming in secret, and in the greatest luxuriance, at a considerable depth beneath his feet, and defended on all sides by walls of solid rocks, so as to be at first sight apparently inaccessible. The effect of these secluded little spots, protected, as it were, from the intrusion of mankind by the steepness and the depth of the barriers which inclose them, is singular and pleasing in the extreme: they reminded us of some of those secluded retreats which we read of in fairy legends and tales, and we could almost fancy ourselves, as we looked down upon them, in the situation of some of those favoured knights and princes, the heroes of our earlier days, who have been permitted to wander over the boundaries of reality into regions shut out from the rest of mankind.

It was impossible to walk round the edge of these precipices, looking everywhere for some part less abrupt than the rest, by which we might descend into the gardens beneath, without calling to mind the description given by Scylax of the far-famed garden of the Hesperides.

This celebrated retreat is stated by Scylax to have been an inclosed spot of about one-fifth of a British mile across, each way, filled with thickly-planted fruit-trees of various kinds, and *inaccessible* on all sides. It was situated (on the authority of the same writer) at six hundred and twenty stadia (or fifty geographical miles) from the *Port of Barce*; and this distance agrees precisely with that of the places here alluded to from Ptolemeta, the port intended by Scylax, as will be seen by a reference to the chart. The testimony of Pliny is also very decided in fixing the site of the Hesperides in the neighbourhood of Berenice. "Not far" (he says) "from the city" (Berenice is here meant) "is the river Lethon, and the sacred grove where the gardens of the Hesperides are said to be situated." Ptolemy also may be supposed to intend the same position, when he informs us, that the garden was to the westward of the people of Barca; or, what is the same thing, that the Barcitæ were to the eastward of the garden of Hesperides.

The name, indeed, itself of Hesperides would induce us to place the Garden, so called, in the vicinity of Bengazi; for the Hesperides were the early inhabitants of that part of the Cyrenaica, and Hesperis, as we have already stated, was the ancient name of the city of Berenice, on the site of which Bengazi is built, and which was probably so called by the Greeks, from the circumstance of its being the most western city of the district.

It has been supposed by Gosselin and others, that those celebrated gardens of early times (for they are frequently mentioned in the plural) were nothing more than some of those Oases, or verdant islands, "which reared their heads amid the sandy desert;" and, in the absence of positive local information, the conjecture was sufficiently reasonable.

The accounts which have come down to us of the *desert of Barca*, from the pens of the Arab Historians, would lead us to suppose that the country so called (which included not only the territory in question, with the whole of the Pentapolis and Cyrenaica, but also the whole tract of coast between Tripoly and Alexandria) was little more than a barren tract of sand, scarcely capable of cultivation. Under such an impression, we can readily imagine that modern writers might be easily deceived; and when it was necessary to fix the site of groves and gardens in the country so erroneously described, we may certainly justify them in looking for such places in the only parts of a sandy desert where luxuriant vegetation is found, the Oases, or verdant islands alluded to. "Objects here presented themselves" (says the learned and ingenious Author of the Discoveries and Travels in Africa, in speaking of the western coast of that country, where the Hesperides have by some writers been placed) "which acted powerfully on the exalted and poetical imaginations of the ancients. They were particularly struck by those Oases, or verdant islands, which reared their heads amid the sandy desert. Hence, doubtless, were drawn those brilliant pictures of the Hesperian gardens, the Fortunate Islands, the Islands of the Blest, which are painted in such glowing colours, and form the gayest part of ancient mythology. The precise position of these celebrated spots has been a subject of eager and doubtful inquiry. The chief difficulty is, that there are different points of the continent in which they seem to be fixed with almost equal precision. In fact, it seems clearly shewn, by some learned writers, that this variety of position is referrible, not to any precise geographical *data*, but to the operation of certain secret propensities that are deeply lodged in the human breast."

"There arises involuntarily in the heart of man a longing after forms of being, fairer and happier than any presented by the world before him—bright scenes which he seeks and never finds, in the circuit of real existence. But imagination easily creates them in that dim boundary which separates the known from the unknown world. In the first discoverers of any such region, novelty usually produces an exalted state of the imagination and passions; under the influence of which every object is painted in higher colours than those of nature. Nor does the illusion cease, when a fuller examination proves that, in the place thus assigned, no such beings or objects exist. The human heart, while it remains possible, still clings to its fond chimeras: it quickly transfers them to the yet unknown region beyond; and, when driven from thence, discovers still another more remote in which they can take refuge. Thus we find these fairy spots successively retreating before the progress of discovery; yet finding still, in the farthest advance which ancient knowledge ever made, some remoter extremity to which they can fly."

"The first position of the Hesperian gardens" (continues our author) "appears to have been at the western extremity of Libya, then the farthest boundary, upon that side, of ancient knowledge. The spectacle which it often presented, a circuit of blooming verdure amid the desert, was calculated to make a powerful impression on Grecian fancy, and to suggest the idea of quite a terrestrial paradise. It excited also the image of islands, which ever after adhered to these visionary creations. As the first spot became frequented, it was soon stripped of its fabled beauty. So pleasing an idea, however, was not to be easily relinquished. Another place was quickly found for it; and every traveller, as he discovered a new portion of that fertile and beautiful coast, fondly imagined that he had at length arrived at the long-sought-for Islands of the Blest. At length, when the continent had been sought in vain, they were transferred to the ocean beyond, which the original idea of islands rendered an easy step. Those of the Canaries having never been passed, nor even fully explored, continued always to be the Fortunate Islands, not from any peculiar felicity of soil and climate, but merely because distance and imperfect knowledge left full scope to poetical fancy. Hence we find Horace painting their felicity in the most glowing colours, and viewing them as a refuge still left for mortals, from that troubled and imperfect enjoyment which they were doomed to experience in every other portion of the globe." (Murray's Account of Africa, vol. i. chap. 1.)

Nothing is more just than the picture of human nature here presented to us by the intelligent writer just quoted; and it must be confessed that the position of the Hesperian gardens has been fixed by different authors in so many parts of the coast of Africa, that we may scarcely hope to reconcile statements so opposite.

The legends connected with these celebrated places are at the same time so wild and extravagant, as well as so discordant with each other, that we might often be tempted to consider the gardens themselves as fabulous and imaginary spots, existing only in the creative brain of the poet and the mythologist, and nowhere to be found in reality.

We should not, however, say, from our view of the subject, that "the variety of position" assigned to the gardens of the Hesperides "is referrible to no precise geographical *data*:" the details which we have already quoted from Scylax are too minute to be wholly rejected; and the position of the gardens, as laid down by Ptolemy and Pliny, coincides with that assigned to them by Scylax.

We have shewn, at the same time, that the nature of the ground in the neighbourhood of Berenice (or Bengazi) is consistent with the account of Scylax; and that places like those which he has so minutely described are actually to be found in the territory where he has laid down the gardens. This singular formation, so far as we have seen, is also peculiar to the country in question; and we know of no other part of the coast of northern Africa where the same peculiarities of soil are observable. We do not mean to point out any *one* of these subterranean gardens as that which is described in the passage above quoted from Scylax; for we know of no one which will correspond in point of extent to the garden which this author has mentioned: all those which we saw were considerably less than the fifth of a mile in diameter (the measurement given by Scylax); and the places of this nature which would best agree with the dimensions in question, are now filled with water sufficiently fresh to be drinkable, and take the form of romantic little lakes.

Scarcely any two of the gardens we met with were, however, of the same depth or extent; and we have no reason to conclude that because we saw none which were large enough to be fixed upon for the garden of the Hesperides, as it is described in the statement of Scylax, there is therefore no place of the dimensions required among those which escaped our notice—particularly as the singular formation we allude to continues to the foot of the Cyrenaic chain, which is fourteen miles distant, in the nearest part, from Bengazi. When we consider that the places in question are all of them sunk below the surface of the soil, and that the face of the country in which they are found is overspread with brushwood, and nowhere perfectly level, it will not be thought extraordinary if some of them should have escaped us in a diligent and frequently-repeated search. At any rate, under the circumstances which are already before the reader, it will not be thought a visionary or hastily formed assumption, if we say that the position of these celebrated spots, "long the subject of eager and doubtful inquiry," may be laid down with some probability in the neighbourhood of the town of Bengazi. The remarkable peculiarities of this part of northern Africa correspond (in our opinion) sufficiently well with the authorities already quoted, to authorize the conclusion we have drawn from an inspection of the place; and to induce us to place the gardens of the Hesperides in some one, or more, of the places described, rather than in any of the Oases of the desert, as suggested by Monsieur Gosselin and others. It seems probable that there were more than one garden of this name; but they could scarcely have been all of them so large as that mentioned by Scylax; and the greater number of those which we were able to discover were considerably smaller in all their dimensions, as we have already stated above.

It has been mentioned that some of the chasms above described have assumed the form of lakes; the sides of which are perpendicular, like those of the gardens, and the water in most of them appears to be very deep. In some of these lakes the water rises nearly to the edge of the precipice which incloses them, and in others is as much as twenty feet below it. They are no doubt much fuller after the rainy season than at other times of the year, and the water is then sweeter than ordinary. Besides these, there are also several subterranean caves in the neighbourhood of Bengazi. One of these, at the depth of about eighty feet from the surface of the plain, contains a large body of fresh water, which is said to run very far into the bowels of the earth, or rather of the rock which overshadows it. On descending into this cave, we found that it widened out into a spacious chamber, the sides of which had evidently been, in many places, shaped with the chisel, and rose perpendicularly to a considerable height. Our progress was soon stopped, as we were advancing into the cave, by the body of water we have mentioned; which, notwithstanding the lights we procured, was scarcely visible through the thick gloom which surrounded us. We found the water shallow at the edge, but it soon became gradually too deep to be practicable; we were also unable to discover any end to it, and a stone thrown as far as we could send it, fell into the water without striking. We had, however, seen enough to excite our curiosity very strongly, and we determined to return, at some early opportunity, with a boat and a good store of torches, intending to go as far along this subterranean stream as the height of the rock would allow us.

On mentioning our visit and our intentions to Bey Halil, he informed us that he had himself paid a visit to the place, in company with a chaous of his suite; and that he had carried with him a small boat in which he embarked with the chaous, and proceeded a considerable distance. They became, at length, afraid of not finding their way back, and put about to return as they came, having found (as he said) on sounding, that the depth of the water was in some parts as much as thirty feet. This account naturally made us more anxious than ever to put our intentions in execution; but no boat could then be found in the harbour sufficiently small for our purpose, and we were obliged to defer our subterranean voyage; determining, however, that if we could not find a portable boat on our return from Cyrene, we would contrive to put together some pieces of timber, and prosecute our researches on a raft, after the example of Sindbad the sailor.

But, alas! who can say that to-morrow is his own?—and who is there who makes the most of to-day? If we had constructed our raft before we moved farther eastward, instead of waiting for the chance of a boat when we came back, we should in all probability have been able to ascertain the extent of this mysterious river. As it was, we were obliged, by circumstances which we could neither control nor foresee, to leave the coast of Africa before we had completed our researches in the city and neighbourhood of Cyrene; and the short time which we had at our command on returning to Bengazi was insufficient (under the pressure of other occupations) for accomplishing this object of our wishes.

The disappointment here alluded to was only one among many others which we experienced, in consequence of our hasty and unexpected return; but it was one which we regretted more, perhaps, than it deserved; for mystery will always add a charm to inquiry, which further investigation might probably remove, but which will continue to preserve its powers of fascination while the uncertainty remains which created it.

We are too well acquainted with the talent of amplification so generally possessed by Turks and Arabs of all classes, to rely implicitly upon the truth of every part of the above-mentioned narrative related to us by the Bey of Bengazi: there is, however, no reason, of which we are aware, connected with the nature of the place, which militates against its probability; and we submit it accordingly, as we received it, to our readers, in the absence of more decided information.

We have already wandered into the regions of fable in speaking of the Gardens of the Hesperides; and before we retrace our steps, we must be permitted to linger for a while on the borders of the mysterious, hidden stream above-mentioned.

The Lethe, or Lathon, (for it is no less a stream to which we are going to call the attention of our readers,) is laid down by geographers in the neighbourhood of the gardens, and close to the city of the Hesperides.

Strabo makes the Lathon flow into the harbour of the Hesperides, and Ptolemy also lays down the same river between Berenice and Arsinoe; Pliny describes the Lathon as situated in the neighbourhood of Berenice, and Scylax places a river (which he calls Ecceus, Εκκειος) in a similar situation. The river Lethe is supposed to have lost itself underground, and to re-appear (like the Niger) in another place; and the point to which we would call the attention of the reader is—whether the subterranean stream above-mentioned, which certainly may be said to lose itself underground, be the source of the Lethe, or Lathon, in question? and whether a small spring, which runs into the lake near the town of Bengazi, may be supposed to be the re-appearance of the same river, in the place so decidedly assigned to it by Strabo—the port of the Hesperides, or, which is the same, of Berenice.

The circumstance of finding a subterranean stream in this neighbourhood, between the mountains and the lake which joins the Harbour of Bengazi, would certainly appear to favour the conclusion, that the course of the stream was towards the lake, that is to say, from the higher ground to the lower. And although the mere discovery of a small stream of fresh water emptying itself into the lake here alluded to, does not by any means tend to confirm the existence of a communication between it and the subterranean stream in question; yet there is no proof (at least, not that we are aware of) that one of these is not connected with the other. At the same time we may add, that if it were really ascertained that no connexion existed between the two, such a circumstance would not be considered as proving that the ancients did not suppose that they communicated. It was believed by the Greeks (or, at any rate, it was asserted by them) that the Alpheus communicated with the fountain of Arethusa, and that anything thrown into the former at Elis would re-appear on the waters of the latter in Sicily.

Other instances might be mentioned of similar extravagancies, which are considered by the moderns as poetical inventions, and never received as historical facts. The disappearance of the Lathon, and its subsequent rise, might have been equally a poetical fiction; but when we find, in the country in which it was placed, a large body of water which actually loses itself, we are naturally led to believe one part of the assertion, and to seek to identify the actual subterranean stream with that which is said to have existed. On a reference to the authority of geographers and historians, we find a river called Lathon laid down very clearly in the place where this body of water is found, and we remark that the name which they apply to the river signifies *hidden* or *concealed*. So far there is a probability that the Lathon of the ancients and the subterranean stream in the neighbourhood of Bengazi may be one and the same river.

Again, we are told, on the authority of Strabo, that the Lathon discharged itself into the Harbour of the Hesperides; and we find a small spring actually running into the lake which is connected with the harbour in question; and which might, from the position of the subterranean spring between it and the mountains to the southward of it, have received at least a portion of the waters, which lose themselves in a place where the level is higher. When we find that the Lathon (or hidden stream) of Bengazi is *directly* between the mountains and the harbour, it becomes the more probable that such a communication may have existed; and whether the little spring which runs into the lake be a continuation of the Lathon or not, there appears to be quite sufficient reason for believing that the ancients might have imagined it was. If we consider how trifling are the existing remains of the Ilissus, the Simois, the Scamander, and other rivers, to which we have been in the habit of attaching importance, we must not be surprised to find a celebrated stream dwindled down into a very insignificant one. The changes which a lapse of nearly two thousand years may be supposed to have occasioned on the northern coast of Africa, are fully sufficient to have reduced the river Lathon to the spring which now flows into the Lake of Bengazi.

The lake itself is salt, and in the summer is nearly dry; while the small stream in question takes its rise within a few yards of the lake, and running along a channel of inconsiderable breadth, bordered with reeds and rushes, might be mistaken by a common observer for an inroad of the lake into the sandy soil which bounds it.

On tasting it, however, we found its waters to be fresh, and the current which is formed by its passage into the lake is very evident on the slightest examination.

If we may suppose this little stream to be all that now remains of the celebrated River of Oblivion, we shall be enabled to throw light upon a passage in Strabo which has hitherto been the subject of much discussion.

It has been questioned by commentators, whether Strabo intended to make the river Lathon discharge itself into the *lake*, or into the *port* of the Hesperides; and the near resemblance which the words λιμην (limen) and λιμνη (limne), the former of which means a port, and the latter a lake, do certainly bear to each other, will allow of their being confounded in transcribing, by the mere transposition of a single letter. Without reference to the authority of the most approved manuscripts, we may observe, on that only of local inspection, that either of these words would be correct. It has already been stated that the Harbour of Bengazi communicates with a salt-water lake, and it is probable that in Strabo's time the vessels of the ancients might have passed from one into the other. The harbour and the lake might in that event be considered without any impropriety as the same. It is into this lake that the small stream discharges itself which we have alluded to above, and if we can suppose it to be the remains of the Lathon, the statement of Strabo may be considered as confirmed by the actual appearance of the place. If, however, we are disposed to be sceptical on this point, we must give up the river altogether, or, at least, we must give up the re-appearance of it in the lake and in the Harbour of Hesperis, or Berenice; for no other spring, that we are aware of, flows either into one or the other. It is probable that λιμην was the word used by Strabo, and it seems also probable that he intended to imply, that the harbour and the lake he calls Tritonis, on which stood the temple of Venus, were the same; at least, in reading the whole of the passage together, we can scarcely divest ourselves of this idea.

It may be, however, that the nature of the place, rather than the construction of the passage in question, has in fact suggested this reading to us: for on the borders of the lake, which still communicates with the Harbour of Bengazi, is a spot of rising ground, nearly insulated in winter, on which are the remains of ancient building; and which, at the time when the harbour was deeper, and the lake itself practicable for vessels, must have been (occasionally, at least) completely surrounded with water. Here then might have stood the temple of Venus mentioned in the passage above, and the introduction of the word μαλιστα by Strabo (taken in the sense of *mostly*, or *generally*), in speaking of the island in question, would seem to confirm this position.

Berenice (he tells us) is placed on the Point of Pseudopenias, near a certain lake called Tritonis, in which there is *mostly* an island (εν ἡ μαλιστα νησιον εστι), with a temple upon it dedicated to Venus. We may remark, in support of this supposition, that it is probable, from the position of the rising ground alluded to, that it was not at all times surrounded by water; and that it was only in the winter season, or at times when the sea advanced farther than ordinary, that it was completely an island.

We may suppose, in receiving this island as the one mentioned by Strabo, that the circumstance just stated was alluded to by the geographer, when he informs us that there was *usually* an island in the lake; but we do not mean to insist upon this reading of the passage in question, and will confess, that it would probably never have suggested itself to us had we never visited Bengazi; it must therefore be left to the discretion of our readers, to adopt it or not, as it may seem to deserve, on a reference to the local peculiarities we have mentioned.

With regard to the name of Tritonis, bestowed upon the lake in this passage, it is difficult to say whether the lake which Strabo mentions was actually called by that name; or whether the geographer has confounded it with the Tritonis Palus (the Lake Lowdeah of Shaw), situated in the Lesser Syrtis, and which also contained an island, according to Herodotus.

But whatever may have been the proper name of the lake at Berenice which we seek to identify with the Tritonis of Strabo, it appears to us to answer remarkably well to the lake of that name which he mentions. We will therefore suggest, that the Tritonis in question and the lake which now communicates with the Harbour of Bengazi, are one and the same lake: that it was originally deep enough to admit the vessels of the ancients, and to have formed occasionally the island containing the temple of Venus, on the spot of rising ground already pointed out, where remains of ancient building are still observable: that a small spring of fresh water runs into the same lake which may possibly be the remains of the Lathon of Strabo, at its point of re-appearance and communication with the Harbour of the Hesperides; and that the subterranean stream in the cavern between the lake and the mountains, which we have mentioned above, may also be the source of this river. When we add, that the gardens upon which we have remarked, are probably some of those called the Gardens of the Hesperides, we have pointed out all that now occurs to us of any interest in the neighbourhood of the town of Bengazi; and we submit these suggestions to the judgment of others better qualified than ourselves to decide the points in question.

It appears to have been from Berenice, the daughter of Magas, who was married to Ptolemy Philadelphus, that the city of Hesperis changed its ancient name into that which afterwards distinguished it. But the name of Berenicidæ, which seems to have been conferred upon the inhabitants of this part of the Cyrenaica, was not by any means generally adopted; for we find that these people continued notwithstanding to be called by their former appellation of Hesperides. It is, however, somewhat singular that Pomponius Mela, who flourished towards the middle of the first century, and nearly a hundred years after the extinction of the dynasty of the Lagides, should have mentioned this city under its ancient name of Hesperis only; while he gives its Ptolemaic name, Arsinoe, to Teuchira, and distinguishes the port of Barca by its appellation of Ptolemais. Yet the name of Berenice continued to be used by other writers long after the age of Mela; and Pliny, who flourished nearly at the same time with this geographer, mentions the city of the Hesperides by that title. It is probable that a name of such poetical celebrity as that which gave place to Berenice was not easily laid aside by the lovers of literature; and we find that Ptolemy thought it necessary, an hundred years after Mela, to add, when he speaks of the city of Berenice, that it was the same with that of Hesperis, or, as he writes it, Hesperides; from which we may infer that the ancient name of the place still continued to be better known than the modern one. But alas for the glories of Hesperis and Berenice! both names have passed away from the scene of their renown; and the present inhabitants of the miserable dirty village, (for we can scarcely call it a town,) which has reared itself on the ruins of these cities, have no idea that Bengazi did not always occupy the place which it has usurped on the soil of the Hesperides.

The Arab who now gathers his corn, or his fruit, in some one, perhaps, of those gardens so celebrated in the annals of antiquity, dreams of nothing whatever connected with it beyond the profits which he hopes from its produce. He knows nothing of the stream or the properties of the Lethe; and the powerful influence of the River of Oblivion seems to have been so often, and so successfully exerted, as to have drowned at length even the recollection of itself.

FOOTNOTES:

On these terraces barley and grass are frequently seen growing, and goats feeding very contentedly.

This idea is so strongly rooted in Mahometans of all classes and descriptions, as to have called forth the animadversions of writers of their own persuasion. We find the following remarks on the subject, in the Account of Egypt by Abd-Allatif, which we give in the French version of Silvestre de Lacy.

"Quand il ont aperçu des monumens d'une grandeur colossale, l'aspect de ces monumens leur a inspiré la terreur; ils se sont fait des idées sottes et fausses de la nature de ces restes de l'antiquité. Comme toutes les pensées de ces gens là n'étoient occupées que de l'objet unique de leurs vœux, et de la seule chose qui eût des charmes pour leurs cœurs, je veux dire de l'or et de l'argent, ils ont éprouvé ce qu'un poëte a dit d'un buveur:"

"Tout ce qu'il aperçoit lui paroît un gobelet; quand il voit quelqu'un, il croit toujours voir celui qui verse à boire."

"Ainsi tout ce qui paroissoit désigner quelque chose été, à leurs yeux, le signal d'un trésor caché: ils n'ont pas pu voir une ouverture pratiquée dans une montagne sans s'imaginer que c'étoit un chemin qui conduisoit à quelque riche dépôt; une statue colossale a été pour eux le gardien de l'argent déposé à ses pieds, et le vengeur implacable de toute entreprise formée contre la sûreté de ce dépôt. Ils ont donc eu recours à toutes sortes d'artifices pour détruire ces statues et les dégrader; ils en ont mutilé les figures, comme des gens qui espéroient par-là atteindre leur but, et qui craignoient, en les attaquant ouvertement, de s'attirer leur propre ruine: ne doutant point que ce ne fussent autant de coffres forts remplis de sommes immenses; ils se sont aussi enfoncés dans les fentes des montagnes, semblable aux voleurs qui pénètrent dans les maisons par toute autre voie que par les portes, et qui saisissent avidement une occasion inconnue à tout autre qu' à eux."—(Rél. d'Egypte, p. 197.)

In this passage it clearly appears how much credulity and superstition was mixed up with the idea in question; and these exist in conjunction with it, to the present day, among the various Arab tribes of Asia and Africa, and in a great degree among the Turks.

As the Dúbbah had sworn that neither himself nor his people knew anything of the articles which we had lost, we never got them back again; although one of his own party afterwards confessed that they had stolen all that was missing. Shekh Mahommed did not hesitate to take a false oath—but he had too great a value for what he thought his character, to confess that he had deliberately perjured himself. At Malta we heard that a heavy fine of sheep and camels had been levied upon him by the Bashaw, for his disgraceful behaviour and wilful disobedience of his Highness's most positive orders.

The Shekh el Belad Mahommed was nearly related to Shekh Belcazi, from whom we had received so much civility at Mesurata—he had two brothers also in Bengazi, both of whom were shekhs and merchants.

Signor Della Cella has mentioned five thousand as the number of inhabitants in Bengazi; but this statement appears to be overrated, as well as that of the number of Jews residing in the town, which, he tells us, amounts to half the population.

"This fierce impatience of the dominion of Rome continued, on the part of the Jews, from the reign of Nero to that of Antoninus Pius."—(Gibbon, vol. ii. p. 384.)

"In Cyrene the Jews massacred two hundred and twenty thousand Greeks; in Cyprus two hundred and forty thousand; in Egypt a very great multitude."—(See Dion Cassius, as cited by Gibbon.)

Among the most conspicuous of these was Hassan Larkoum, to whom we had brought a letter of recommendation from the ex-minister at Tripoly, Mahommed D'Ghies, and who treated us with the greatest civility and attention.

It was curious to observe the singular mixture of feeling displayed by some of the crew of our vessel—after deliberately inflicting the most cruel treatment on some unfortunate, groaning animal, we often heard a man exclaim, when he had finished his task, "Poverino! so ben che tu patisci!" and he would then hurry on to inflict the same cruelties on some other wretched object of his care.

Previously to these measures, the town was constantly subject to the attacks of the neighbouring tribes of marauding Arabs, who, as occasion offered, made incursions into it without ceremony, and retired with their plunder into the interior. The garrison and citizens opposed them as well as they could, and many a desperate skirmish frequently ensued; but as Bengazi is unprovided with walls, it was difficult to prevent a surprise, and the people lived in continual fear. Mahommed Bey began by building a round fort on the sandy tract to the eastward of the town, and then collecting his forces, carried the war into their territory, and after making severe examples of the most refractory, succeeded in reducing the Bedouins to subjection.

About the same time some high poles had been erected by our party, on the sand hills to the eastward of the town, as objects from which to take angles for the survey; and these were now considered to have been placed there as signals to regulate the motions of the enemy's fleet.

The Arab term for all who profess Christianity.

Tibeeb is the common Arab term for a doctor.

Several quarts of water were taken from this poor man, who, when he left our house, was scarcely distinguishable as the same person who had entered it, having diminished so much in size after the operation. He was, in fact, materially relieved, and continued to improve daily in health; till one day, after washing his shirt, he put it on, as the quickest way of drying it, a custom not uncommon among the Arabs, and caught so bad a cold in consequence, that all the doctor's exertions were afterwards unable to save him.

Yusuf and Zuleika are the Mahometan names of Joseph and Potiphar's wife.

An excellent collection of these remains of Grecian art has been recently sold for a considerable sum, by a relation of the Vice-Consul of Bengazi, who had not been many years resident there.

Six thousand dollars, as we were informed.

These would however serve equally for the reception of rain water, which falls in abundance at Bengazi during the winter.

In one of these quarries a large portion of the rock, shaped into a quadrangular form, has been insulated from the rest to serve the purpose of a tomb, after the manner of those at Ptolemeta.

Two stadia is the length and breadth given by Scylax, which, taken as the *mean* Grecian stades of Major Rennell, of about ten to a British mile, would give the measurement here stated.

Nec procul ante oppidum fluvius Lethon, lucus sacer, ubi Hesperidum Horti memorantur.—(Nat. Hist., lib. v. c. 5.) Again, in the same book, Berenice—quondam vocata Hesperidum, &c.

Βαρκιται απο ανατολων του κηπου των Ἑσπερίδων.

Βερενικη ἡ και Ἑσπερίδες.—(Ptol. Geogr.): and as Stephanus describes it, in the singular, Ἑσπερις, πολις Λιβυης, ἡ νον Βερονίκη.

Geographie Ancienne; Murray's account of Discoveries and Travels in Africa, &c.

Gosselin and Malte Brun.

Strabo, 1.—Plutarch in Sertorio—Horat. 4. od. 8. v. 27. Epod. 16. Pliny 6—6. C. 31-2.

Signor Della Cella has supposed that the passage of Scylax refers to the *elevated* parts of the Cyrenaica, and places his gardens of Hesperides in the mountains; but we think that a review of the passage in question, combined with the local information which we have been able to collect on the subject, will authorize us to doubt this position.

Here Lethe's streams, from secret springs below,
Rise to the light; here heavily, and slow,

The silent, dull, forgetful waters flow.

(Rowe's Lucan, book ix. p. 209.)

Lucan places his Lethe and Hesperian Gardens in the neighbourhood of the Lake Tritonis, in the Lesser Syrtis; but the western part of the Cyrenaica is the most approved position for both. See also Solinus on this point.

Εστι δε και λιμνη Ἑσπεριδων, και ποταμος εμβαλλει Λαθων. (Lib. 17. p. 836.)

Some of the Commentators read λιμνη Ἑσπεριδων, and Cellarius says on this subject—"Est et de exitu fluminis dubitatio, in quod se infundat, in mare an in lacum. Straboni est λιμην Ἑσπεριδων, in quem Lathon effluit. Vetus autem interpres iterum dissentit, et quasi λιμνη legerit, *lacus* vertit *Hesperidum*. Videant (he adds) quibus vel regionem cognoscendi, vel inspiciendi antiquos codices, facultas est." (Lib. iv. c. ii.)

Εστι δε ακρα λεγομενη Ψευδοπενιας, εφ' ης ἡ Βερενικη την θησιν εχει, παρα λιμνην τινα Τριτωνιδα, εν ἡ μαλιστα νησιον εστι, και ιερον Αφροδιτης εν αυτω· εστι δε και λιμην Εσπεριδων, και ποταμος εμβαλλει Λαθων.

We have already assumed, upon reasonable grounds, that this was probably the case in earlier times.

Βερενικιδαι απο Βερενικες της Μαγας θυγατερος, γυναικος δε και Πτολεμαιου, ωνομαθησαν Βερενικιδαι ὁι δημοται. (Steph. Byzant. v.)

Urbes Hesperia, Apollonia, Ptolemais, Arsinoe, atque (unde terris nomen est) ipsa Cyrene. (De Situ Orbis, Lib. i. c. 8.)

Βερενικη, ἡ και Ἑσπεριδες.

The name of Berenice is mentioned by Edrisi as remaining in his time in this part of Africa; but we never could find any traces of the name, though we often inquired for it of the Arabs of the country, as well as of the inhabitants of Bengazi.

The changes which time may be supposed to effect in the character and appearance of a country, are well expressed in the following little fable of Kazwini, translated from the Arabic by Silvestre de Sacy.

"I passed by a very large and populous city, and inquired of one of its inhabitants by whom it was founded. Oh, replied the man, this is a very ancient city! we have no idea how long it may have been in existence; and our ancestors were on this point as ignorant as ourselves. In visiting the same place five hundred years afterwards, I could not perceive a single trace of the city; and asked of a countryman, whom I saw cutting clover, where it stood, and how long it had been destroyed. What nonsense are you asking me? said the person whom I addressed: these lands have never been any otherwise than you see them. Why, returned I, was there not formerly here a magnificent and populous city?—We have never seen one, replied the man, and our fathers have never mentioned to us anything of the kind."

"Five hundred years afterwards, as I passed by the spot, I found that the sea had covered it; and, perceiving on the beach a party of fishermen, I asked them how long it had been overflowed."

"It is strange, answered they, that a person of your appearance should ask us such a question as this; for the place has been at all times exactly as it is now. What, said I, was there not at one time dry land in the spot where the sea is at present?—Certainly not, that we know of, answered the fishermen, and we never heard our fathers speak of any such circumstance."

"Again, I passed by the place, after a similar lapse of time,—the sea had disappeared—and I inquired of a man whom I met at what period this change had taken place. He made me the same answer as the others had done before—and, at length, on returning once more to the place, after the lapse of another five hundred years, I found that it was occupied by a flourishing city, more populous, and more rich in magnificent buildings, than that which I had formerly seen! When I inquired of its inhabitants concerning its origin, I was told that it lost itself in the darkness of antiquity! We have not the least idea, they said, when it was founded, and our forefathers knew no more of its origin than ourselves!"—(Chréstomathie Arabe, vol. iii. p. 419.)

Plan *of the* REMAINS *of* TAUCRA, Or TEUCHIRA; BY *Capt^(n).* F. W. *Beechey* R.N.

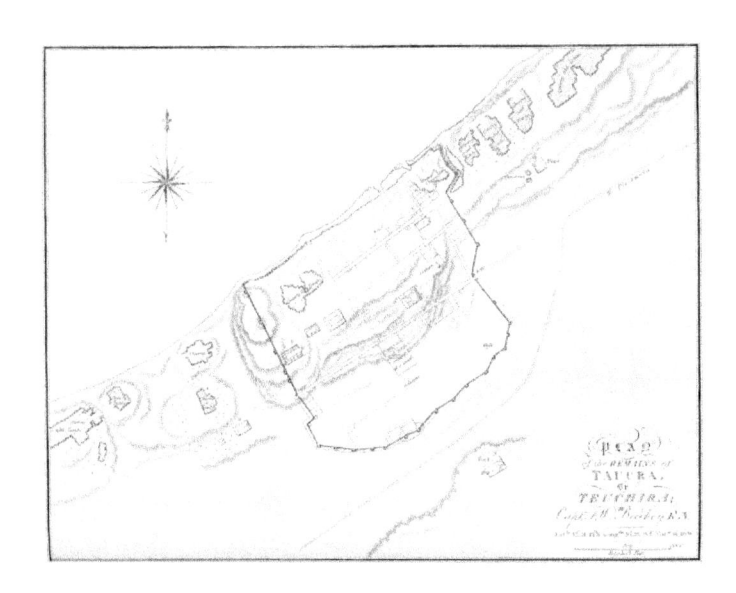

J. & C. Walker   Published as the act directs, April 1827, by J. Murray,
Sculp^t.   Albemarle S^t. London.

Plan *of the RUINS and ENVIRONS of* PTOLEMETA, *now called* DOLMEITA. BY *Capt^r. F. W. Beechey* R.N.

J. & C. Walker Sculpt.

Published as the act directs, April 1827, by J. Murray, Albemarle St. London.

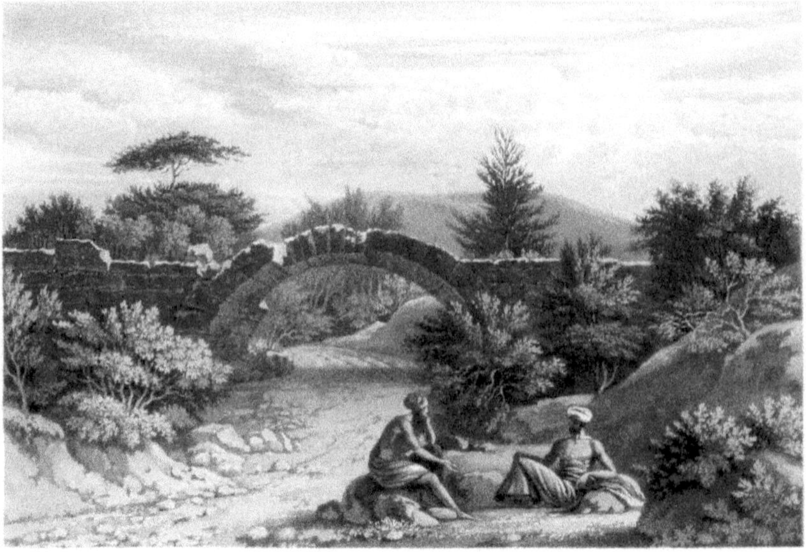

Engraved from a Drawing taken on the spot by H. Beechey. REMAINS OF AN ANCIENT BRIDGE AT PTOLEMETA. THROWN ACROSS THE BED OF A TORRENT. *Published March 1827, by John Murray, London.*

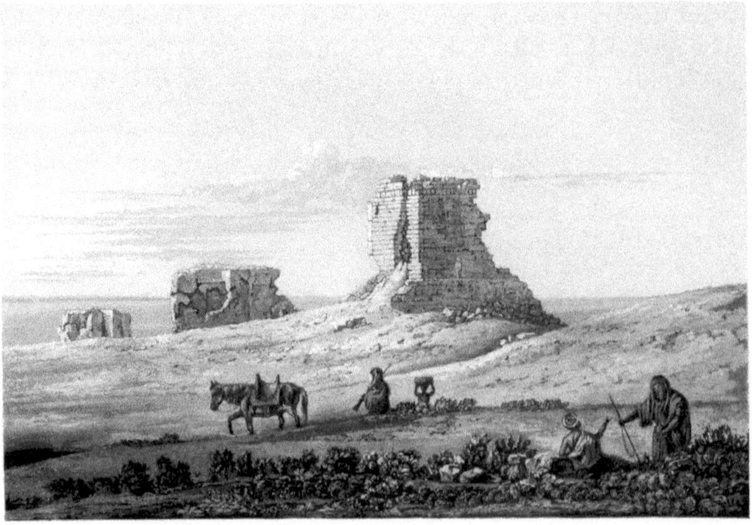

Engraved from a Drawing taken on the spot by H. Beechey. REMAINS OF AN ANCIENT MAUSOLEUM AT PTOLEMETA. *Published March 1827, by John Murray, London.*

Drawn by H. Beechey. Engraved by E. Pinden.

REMAINS OF AN IONIC BUILDING AT PTOLEMETA. *Published March 1827, by John Murray, London.*

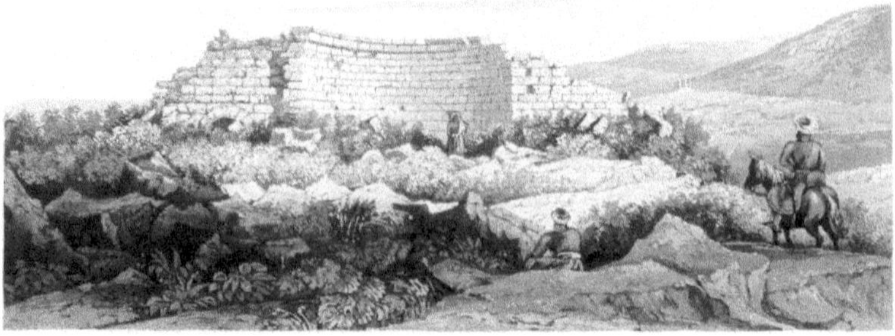

Engraved from a Drawing taken on the spot by H. Beechey. REMAINS OF A CHRISTIAN CHURCH AT PTOLEMETA. *Published March 1827, by John Murray, London.*

CHAPTER XII.

Remarks on the Soil of Bengazi and the Country in its Neighbourhood — Distinction of Sex in the Palm-tree, &c., noticed by the Ancients and by Mahometan Writers — Persian Anecdote of a Love-sick Date-tree — Remarks of Shaw on the Propagation and Treatment of the Palm — Arab Mode of cultivating the Sandy Tracts in the Neighbourhood of Bengazi — Journey to Carcora — Completion of the Coast-line from that Place to Bengazi — Return to Bengazi, and Departure for Teuchira and Ptolemeta — Description of the Country between Bengazi and these Places — Remains observable in this Track — Correspondence of the Tower called Gusser el Towēl with that of Cafez, mentioned by Edrisi — Probable Site of Adriane — Arrival at Birsis — Remains in its neighbourhood, at Mably (or Mabny), considered as those of Neapolis — Hospitality of the Arabs of Birsis — Remains of Teuchira — Position of the City — Quarries without the Walls covered with Greek Inscriptions — Teuchira a Town of Barca — Walls of the City repaired by Justinian — No Port observable at Teuchira — Mistake of Bruce in confounding Teuchira with Ptolemeta — Good Supply of fresh Water at Teuchira — The excavated Tombs of the ancient City used as Dwelling-houses by the Arabs of the Neighbourhood — Indisposition of our Chaous (or Janissary) — Route from Teuchira to Ptolemeta — Remains at Ptolemeta — Port and Cothon of the ancient City — Other Remains observable there — Ptolemaic Inscriptions — Picturesque Ravines in the Neighbourhood of Ptolemeta — Position of the City — Remains of Bridges observed there — Advantages of its Site — Extreme Drought at Ptolemeta, recorded by Procopius — Reparation of the Aqueducts and Cisterns by the Emperor Justinian — Existing Remains of an extensive Cistern at Ptolemeta, probably among those alluded to by Procopius — State of the Town, its Solitude and Desolation — Luxuriant Vegetation which encumbered its Streets when the Place was first visited by our Party — Change of Scene on returning to it in Summer-time.

THE soil of the Hesperides does not now produce that variety of fruit which we find that it did in the days of its prosperity; but the palm and the fig-tree still flourish there in great abundance, and it is merely from the want of attention, and not from any actual change in the soil itself, that it does not afford the same variety as formerly.

The fruit of the palm-tree forms too essential a part of Arab food to allow of the necessary precautions being neglected for insuring the growth and the ripening of dates; but the fig-trees are for the most part wild, and produce only, a diminutive fruit, which never comes to any perfection. It is a well-known fact in natural history, that "these trees are male and female, and that the fruit will be dry and insipid without a previous communication with the male." This peculiarity was discovered at a very early period, and has been noticed by writers of various ages with much perspicuity and detail. There appears to have been but little variation at any time in the mode of performing these operations; and the manner in which the palm-tree is described, by Pliny, to have been impregnated, is the same with that which prevails in the present day.

A part of the blossom from the male tree is either attached to the fruit of the female; or the powder from the blossoms of the male is shaken over those which the female produces. The first of these methods is practised in Barbary, (one male being sufficient, as Shaw has observed, to impregnate four or five hundred female); and the latter is common in Egypt, where the number of male trees is greater. Both these methods are described by Pliny, (Hist. Nat. lib. xiii.) and the whole account which is there given of the palm-tree and its several varieties is extremely accurate and interesting. The attachment of this tree to a sandy and nitrous soil, and its partiality at the same time for water; its inability to thrive in any other than a dry and hot climate, its peculiar foliage and bark, and the decided distinction of sex which is observable in it, are all mentioned in detail by the Roman naturalist.

The remarks of Arab writers on the distinction of sex in the palm-tree are nearly the same with those of Pliny; and a most extraordinary confirmation of it will be found in a Persian anecdote quoted by Silvestre de Sacy; from which it will clearly appear that an unrequited and secret attachment to a neighbouring date-tree had nearly caused the death of a too-susceptible female palm!

Osmai relates (says the story in question) that an inhabitant of Yemama, a province in Arabia, once made him the following recital. "I was possessor of a garden in which was a palm-tree, which had every year produced me abundance of fruit; but two seasons having passed away, without its affording any, I sent for a person well acquainted with the culture of palms, to discover for me the reason of this failure. "An unhappy attachment" (observed the man, after a moment's inspection) "is the sole cause why this palm-tree produces no fruit!" He then climbed up the trunk, and, looking round on all sides, discovered a male palm at no great distance, which he recognised as the object of my unlucky tree's affection; and advised me to procure some of the powder from its blossoms, and to scatter it over her branches. This I did (said the Arab,) and the consequence was, that my date-tree, whom unrequited love had kept barren, now bore me a most abundant harvest!"

The value of the palm-tree is not generally appreciated in Europe, but it is highly prized in Asia and Africa. The followers of Mahomet (as appears from Kazwini) believe it to be peculiar to those favoured countries where the religion of the Prophet is professed. "Honour the palm-tree," (says this writer, in the words of Mahomet himself,) "for she is your father's aunt;" and this distinction (he tells us) was given to it, because the tree was formed from the remainder of the clay of which Adam was created! It is propagated chiefly (as Shaw has informed us) from young shoots taken from the roots of full-grown trees, which, if well transplanted and taken care of, will yield their fruit in the sixth or seventh year; whereas those that are raised immediately from the kernels will not bear till about their sixteenth. Nothing further is necessary to the culture of the palm-tree, than that it should be well watered once in four or five days, and that a few of the lower boughs should be lopped away whenever they begin to droop or wither. "These" (observes Shaw), "whose stumps, or pollices, in being thus gradually left upon the trunk, serve, like so many rounds of a ladder, to climb up the tree, either to fecundate it, to lop it, or to gather the fruit, are quickly supplied with others which hang down from the crown or top, contributing not only to the regular and uniform growth of this tall, knotless, beautiful tree, but likewise to its perpetual and most delightful verdure. *To be exalted* (Eccles. xxiv. 14.) or *to flourish like the palm-tree*, are as just and proper expressions, suitable to the nature of this plant, as to *spread abroad like the Cedar*."—(Psalm xcii. 11.)

In the immediate neighbourhood of the palm-trees above mentioned (we mean those to the N.E. of Bengazi) are the sand-hills, which form (together with the date-trees) the most remarkable objects on this part of the coast. The occasional mixture of a little manure with the sand, and the decay of vegetable matter, have contributed to produce at the foot of these hills a very excellent soil; portions of which are inclosed within hedges of the prickly-pear and aloe, and near them may be seen a few miserable huts, the abodes of the several proprietors. The chief produce of these little gardens may be stated to be—melons and pumpkins of several kinds, melonzani, or egg-plants, cucumbers, tomatas, red and green peppers, and some few of the plants called bàmia.

The sand itself, with a little labour, is also made to produce very abundantly; so much so, that any one who had seen the place only in the summer time, would scarcely recognise it as the same in the winter season, when covered with luxuriant vegetation. The right of cultivation appears to be general; and a piece of ground may be said to belong to the first person who takes the trouble of inclosing and working it. This, in fact, is no more than just; since the cultivated tracts, in this part of the plain, are merely so many portions rescued from the sandy waste by the industry of the individuals who select them; and must therefore be considered as so many additions made by the original occupiers to the general stock.

The first care of the cultivator is to turn up the sand, and spread layers of faggots underneath: the sand is then replaced, and over it is sometimes spread a mixed stratum of sand and manure.

Upon this the seeds are sown, and care is taken to keep the land irrigated by means of numerous wells of a few feet only in depth. Some of these are built round with rough stones, but the water is always brackish, and occasionally stinking, owing to the quantity of decayed roots, and other vegetable matter, with which they are suffered to be clogged. By the adoption of this short and simple process, the sand is soon rendered so productive, that the Arabs prefer cultivating it, to the trouble of clearing the rich soil beyond it, to the southward, of the broken stones and fragments of building with which it is thickly interspersed.

When the rains had subsided, and the health of Lieutenant Beechey (which had latterly prevented him from travelling) allowed of it, we set out on our journey to Carcora; in order to complete that part of the coast which had been left unfinished between Carcora and Bengazi: two of our party had before made a trip, along the coast, to Ptolemeta, and returned in high spirits with what they had met with in that delightful part of the Pentapolis. On our route to Carcora we had been very much annoyed with a violent and parching sirocco wind, the heat of which would have been sufficiently disagreeable and oppressive, without the extreme annoyance of thick clouds of sand, whirling everywhere in eddies about us, which were driven with such force into our eyes as almost to prevent our making use of them.

Having completed the unfinished part of the coast-line, we returned back to Bengazi, and found everything prepared for our journey to the eastward, through the diligence and activity of Lieutenant Coffin, who had been left at Bengazi for that purpose. During our absence at Carcora, Bey Halil had left the town, and pitched his tents in the fine plain of Merge, a large tract of table-land on the top of the mountains which bound Teuchira and Ptolemeta to the southward. The object of his journey was to collect the tribute from the neighbouring Bedouin tribes, and this is generally a work of much time and trouble, without which the contribution would not be paid at all. We had previously arranged with him that Hadood, Shekh of Barka, should have camels in readiness (on our return from Carcora) to carry our tents and baggage to the westward; but finding they had not arrived, we with difficulty procured others, and set out from Bengazi on the seventeenth of April for Teuchira, Ptolemeta, and Cyrene.

The road from Bengazi to Teuchira and Ptolemeta lies through a very fertile and beautiful country, though a comparatively small portion of it only is cultivated. It may be described as a plain, thickly covered with wood and flowering shrubs, stretching itself from the sea to the foot of the mountains which form the northern limits of the Cyrenaica, and narrowing every mile as you advance towards Ptolemeta, where the mountains run down very close to the sea. We have already stated that the space between this range and Bengazi is about fourteen geographic miles; and the distance between it and the sea, at Ptolemeta, is no more than a mile, or a mile and a half; the whole length of the plain, from Bengazi to Ptolemeta, being fifty-seven geographic miles. The sides of the mountains are also thickly clothed with wood, chiefly pine, of various kinds, and the juniper is found in great quantities among the other shrubs which overspread them.

Ravines, whose sides are equally covered with wood and verdure, cross the road very frequently, in their course from the mountains to the sea; and most of these, as there is nothing like a bridge over any of them, must be nearly impassable in winter. The force with which the water rushes down the ravines in the rainy season is evident from the slightest inspection; the ground being furrowed and torn up in the parts which form the beds of the torrents, and encumbered with trees and stones of various sizes, washed down from the mountains and from the sides of the ravines. Open spaces are occasionally met with in the woods, some of which are of considerable extent; these were probably once cultivated, but are now thickly covered with grasses of various kinds, among which we often observed a great proportion of oats produced spontaneously from the soil.

Several towers of very solid construction are scattered over this plain in various directions; and one of them will be found to correspond very well with that called Cafez, by Edrisi. It is situated at about the same distance (four miles) from the sea; and has likewise a wood to the eastward of it, as he mentions. It may be reckoned at fifteen miles from Bengazi, and not far from it, also to the eastward, are the lakes described by Edrisi in the neighbourhood of Cafez, separated, exactly as he mentions, from the sea by ridges of sand, and running along parallel with the beach. The water of these lakes is stated by Edrisi to be sweet, but it is certainly, in the present day, brackish. The Arab name of one of these (Zeiana, or Aziana) would seem to point out the neighbourhood of Adriana, laid down by Cellarius between Berenice and Arsinoe, or Teuchira; and many ground-plans of buildings, chiefly dwelling-houses, may be observed at the distance of about three-quarters of a mile from the lake, which probably occupy the site of that town.

At sunset, on the second day, we arrived at Birsis, where there are a number of wells, and mutilated fragments of building, of which it would be impossible to make any satisfactory plan, without a great deal of previous excavation. Birsis occupies a very fertile plain, where there is usually an

Arab encampment, and is distant about thirty-one miles from Bengazi, and seven from the city of Teuchira. It is five or six miles from the Cyrenaic range, and about a mile and a half from the sea. A little to the S.W. of Birsis, are other remains of building, which assume a more decided character, and appear to have formed part of a town. Several arched doorways are still remaining, and some of the walls of the houses are standing, to the height of about ten or twelve feet from the present level. The spot on which they stand is now much overgrown with high grass and shrubs of various kinds, and the buildings have been occasionally added-to by the Arabs; so that it requires a good deal of attention to make out their original plans. We were cautioned by the natives, who saw us making our way through the high grass and bushes which encumber the ruins, to beware of the serpents, which they said were very numerous in the place; we, however, saw no more than two, one of a dark colour, about five feet in length, and another of smaller dimensions. The Arab name for this place is Mabny, and Mably (as we heard it pronounced by different persons residing on the spot); and appears to be a corruption of Napoli, or Neapolis, with no other change than might reasonably be expected from the peculiarities of Arab pronunciation.

Neapolis is, however, laid down by Ptolemy between the cities of Teuchira and Ptolemeta; and Mably (or Mabny) is seven or eight miles to the S.W. of the former of these places; so that it will not correspond in position with the city which its name appears to indicate. We may at the same time observe, that in the position assigned by Ptolemy to Neapolis we could perceive no remains which were indicative of a town; that we know of no town, described under another name, as occupying the site of Mably; and that the resemblance of that appellation to Nably, which would be the Arab pronunciation of Neapolis, is too close to be wholly overlooked.

Between Birsis and the sea (from which we have already said it is distant about a mile and a half) are the remains of two towers, occupying the summit of a range of sand-hills on the beach, and which we were unable to visit, in consequence of the marsh which runs along the foot of the range, and separates it from the cultivated land. The country about Birsis and Mably is highly productive, wherever it is cultivated, and agreeably diversified with shrubs and brushwood, among which are a few fig-trees. The plain is here about six miles in breadth (from the sea to the foot of the mountains); and its general appearance, as the Arab tents were seen to rear themselves among the low wood and cultivated lands in which they were pitched, was highly indicative of what one might imagine of patriarchal comfort and tranquillity. We found the Arabs very hospitable and obliging, and one of our party, who had strayed from the rest, and taken shelter at night-fall in one of their tents, was received and entertained with great kindness and liberality; a sheep having been killed expressly for his supper, and the women of the family employed for two hours in preparing it, in the most savoury manner with which they were acquainted. While the mutton was occupying the united attention of the most accomplished cooks of the household, (the mother, one of the wives, and the two eldest daughters of the host) another wife had prepared a large dish of barley-cakes and fried onions, over which was poured some hot melted butter: a great portion of this very speedily disappeared before the repeated attacks of the hungry guest, whose appetite for the savoury meat which was afterwards served up to him was not quite so great as the dish deserved; the skill of the young wife who had cooked the first mess was in consequence highly commended by her spouse, who could no otherwise account for the great portion of meat which was left, than by supposing that the first dish was most to the stranger's taste; never dreaming that a pound of dough, besides butter and onions, could in any way tend to diminish a man's appetite.

Six miles beyond Birsis (in a north-easterly direction) are remains of a much more imposing nature than any which we had hitherto beheld. They are those of an ancient city, completely inclosed within walls of uncommon strength and thickness, which are connected at intervals by quadrangular towers, and entered by two strongly-built gateways, placed opposite to each other on the east and west sides of the city. The town of Teuchira (for it is that to which we allude) is situated close to the sea, which, in this part of the plain, is distant about four miles from the foot of the mountains. A part of the town, as well as of the walls, is built upon a rising ground, and the rest is on a level with the plain; one portion of it (to the westward) has been built round a quarry, and what appears to have been the citadel is also constructed on the edge of another quarry to the eastward, which considerably strengthens its position.

Without the walls on both sides of the town (we mean on the east and west sides) are also very extensive quarries, in which the tombs of the early inhabitants of the place have at various periods been constructed. In these, as well as on the inner part of the city walls, are a great many Greek inscriptions; such of which as our time allowed us to copy, will be found at the end of the chapter, with further details of the buildings; and in the mean time we refer our readers to the plan of the city annexed.

Teuchira, or Tauchira, was a town of Barca, of considerable antiquity: its name was changed under the Ptolemies to Arsinoe, and subsequently (by Mark Antony) to Cleopatris; but its original appellation has survived the others, and it is to this day distinguished by the name of Tauchira, or Tocra, under which it is known to the Arabs.

The walls of Teuchira (we are informed by Procopius) were repaired under the emperor Justinian, and they still remain in a state of perfection which sufficiently proves the solidity of the work. They are built of very massy blocks of stone, conformably with the statement of the historian, many of which have formed parts of much earlier buildings, as the inscriptions found upon them demonstrate.

Very little of the history of Teuchira has come down to us; and we scarcely know more of it, than that it formed one of the cities of the Pentapolis. Although it is situated close to the sea, which washes the northern face of it, Teuchira could never have been a port; as it affords no protection whatever for vessels derived from its natural position, and there are not the slightest traces now visible of anything like a cothon having been constructed there; which, indeed, it would have been folly to have attempted in the exposed situation of the place.

Traces of Christianity are still visible in the remains of a handsome church in this city, which may perhaps be attributed to the piety or the munificence of Justinian, so conspicuously displayed in similar structures throughout his extensive dominions. The account which Bruce has given us of Ptolemeta proves evidently that he confounded it with Teuchira, since he tells us of its *walls*, "which he found *entire*, on which were a prodigious number of Greek inscriptions;" whereas there are no remains of walls at Ptolemeta, (with the exception of a noble gateway by which those which once existed were connected,) that are more than a foot above the ground; and we have already stated, that the walls of Teuchira correspond with Bruce's description. The same writer adds that he found nothing at Arsinoe, or at Barca, and we are somewhat at a loss to know what places he intends to point out as the spots which he considers to have been occupied by the two cities mentioned. We have given the details which we were enabled to collect of Teuchira at the end of the present chapter, and shall therefore abstain from further mention of it here, and proceed with the other parts of our narrative.

We may, however, remark that it abounds in wells of excellent water, which are reserved by the Arabs for their summer consumption, and only resorted to when the more inland supplies are exhausted; at other times Teuchira (we were informed) is uninhabited. Many of the excavated tombs, which we have mentioned above, are occupied as dwelling-houses by the Arabs during their summer visits to this part of the coast; and from the circumstance of their being much cooler at that season than the external atmosphere, are certainly very pleasant abodes.

Here also, as at Carcora, we were very much annoyed with the parching sirocco wind; and our Chaous, from Bengazi, a very stout active fellow, was seized, in consequence, with a violent fever, and was unable to continue his journey. We left him, however, in very good hands, and he rejoined us, on his recovery, at Ptolemeta.

From Teuchira to Ptolemeta is about eighteen miles (geographic), and the road between these places leads along the sea-coast, which gradually approaches the mountains. The soil is excellent, and the country is for the most part well cultivated; the wood being chiefly confined to the sides of the mountains and to those of the ravines which cross the road. In approaching Ptolemeta, the attention is first arrested by a large and very lofty quadrangular tomb, constructed on a basis of solid rock, which has been purposely insulated from the quarry in which it stands, and shaped also into a quadrangular form. This object assumes the appearance of a lofty tower, and forms a very striking feature in the scenery about Ptolemeta, being seen from a considerable distance.

Signor Della Cella has supposed that this noble monument, "veramente" (as he observes) "di regia grandezza," was erected by the seventh of the Ptolemies surnamed Physcon, or Euergetes the Second, purposely as a tomb for himself.

It is probable, however, that the restless and ambitious spirit of this prince looked forward at all times to the sovereignty of Egypt, even after the mediation of the Romans, by which the Cyrenaica was assigned to him as a kingdom. However this may be, it will be seen, from the plan and section of the structure in question, (which we have given in the details of Ptolemeta,) that it was not intended for the tomb of a single person, but as that of a numerous family, in which no one appears to have been particularly distinguished from the rest. There was originally, perhaps, some inscription over the entrance of the tomb by which the name and the honours of the persons it inclosed were set forth; but as this part of the structure has been purposely injured, it is probable that the inscription, if ever there existed one, was at the same time effaced.

At any rate, though we looked very attentively for some appearance of letters, we were unable to distinguish any; and we will merely suggest, with regard to this mausoleum, that it was certainly appropriated to some family of distinction, (it may be to some part of that of the Ptolemies,) since there is none so conspicuous or so handsome in any part of the neighbourhood of Ptolemeta.

The next object which presents itself in approaching the town is the insulated gateway which we have mentioned above, standing now like a triumphal arch overlooking the town, but which was originally connected with the walls. On reaching the summit of the elevated spot upon which this gateway has been erected, the remains of Ptolemeta lie before you, stretched out in various parts of the beautiful plain in which it is built, sloping down from the mountains to the sea. It appears to have occupied about a square mile of ground, and a more agreeable position could not anywhere have been chosen, on this part of the coast of the Cyrenaica, than that which has been fixed upon for the port of Barca.

The harbour has been chiefly formed by art (one side of it only being sheltered by nature); and the remains of the cothon are still very conspicuous, though much encumbered with sand.

An Amphitheatre and two Theatres are still visible at Ptolemeta: the latter are close to the remains of a palace, of which three columns only are now standing; and the former is constructed in a large quarry, in which the seats have been partly excavated, those parts only having been built which could not be formed in the quarry itself. The interior court of the palace above-mentioned is still covered with tessellated pavement, and beneath it are very spacious arched cisterns, or reservoirs, communicating with each other, and receiving air and light from the court-yard above them. The remaining columns of this building, which we imagine to have been a palace, are those which Bruce has described as forming part of the portico belonging to an Ionic temple, and as having been executed "in the first manner" of that order. The details of them, (he adds,) with all the parts that could be preserved, are in the King's collection. The proportions and style of the columns in question do not (we must confess) appear, in our estimation, to partake much of the early character of the Ionic; but were the resemblance in reality much greater than it is, the existence of a Greek inscription which is built into the basement of the columns, bearing the names of Cleopatra and Ptolemy Philometor, (together with another, turned upside down, mentioning that of Arsinoe conjointly with Ptolemy and Berenice,) would prevent our attributing an earlier date to them than the reigns of the sovereigns recorded.

The ravines which form the eastern and western boundaries of Ptolemeta (particularly that to the eastward) are wild and romantic in the extreme; and one might imagine one's-self transported, in winding along them, to the beautiful secluded valleys of Switzerland and Savoy. It is true that in the Cyrenaica nature is on a less extended scale than in the mountainous districts we have mentioned; but it appears in a form no less captivating on that account; and we will venture to say, that if a person who had travelled in those countries should be suddenly dropt into the eastern valley of Ptolemeta, without being told where he was, he would certainly suspect himself to be in one of them. He would never, for a moment, dream of being in Africa—that parched and barren region of desert monotony so horrid in European estimation. For our own parts we shall never forget the delight which we experienced, at every new turn of the valley, as fresh objects of interest presented themselves to our view on either side of this enchanting retreat.

We had already passed through a very interesting country, in our journey from Bengazi to Ptolemeta; and we had long forgotten the dreary swamps and insipidity of the Syrtis, where only *one tree* had been seen to rear itself in a space of more than four hundred miles.

It could not, therefore, be contrast that made the vallies of Ptolemeta appear to us in such captivating forms and colours—it was the simple impression which Nature's favourite spots never fail to create on the imagination—heightened only, perhaps, by the solitude of the scene, and the wild, romantic elegance of its character. There are beauties which may be felt, but cannot be described; and the charm of romantic scenery is one of them.

We will not therefore attempt any other description of the eastern valley of Ptolemeta, than by remarking that it rises gradually from the sea, winding through forests of pine and flowering shrubs, (which thicken as the sides of the mountain on which they grow become higher and more abrupt,) till it loses itself in the precipitous part of the range which bounds it to the southward, and which presents a dark barrier of thickly-planted pines, shooting up into the blue sky above them. The windings of the valley greatly add to its beauty, and the scenery increases in interest at every turn, in tracing it up towards the mountains in which it loses itself. Sometimes the path is impeded by trees, which throw their branches across it, leaving only a narrow passage beneath them; and sometimes, on emerging from this dark and difficult approach, a broad sweep of verdant lawn will suddenly present itself, fenced in, apparently, on all sides, by high walls of various-coloured pines, rising one above the head of the other, in all the grandeur of uniformity. On reaching the opposite end of this verdant amphitheatre, a new scene presents itself, before unsuspected; and the rambler, bewildered with variety, finds himself utterly incapable of deciding which pleases him most, or when he shall feel himself equal to the task of tearing himself away from the spot. We confess that, when first we discovered this valley, the shades of night surprised us before we thought the sun had set, far in its deepest recesses; and we never afterwards visited it without regretting that our occupations would not allow us more leisure to admire it.

Among the trees which clothe the sides of the mountains are many handsome stone sarcophagi of Greek and Roman workmanship, all of which, however, we found had been opened; and among them seats of the same material were occasionally observed to have been placed, as if the spirits of the dead loved to linger about the spot which had so much delighted them when living. We should willingly have devoted a great portion of our time to the same pleasing occupation, and have passed whole days in wandering among the tombs, in making plans and drawings of them, and searching for inscriptions: but fate had not decreed us so agreeable a lounge, and after securing in our portfolios some of the principal objects of the place, we set out without further delay for Cyrene, which we had determined (as our time was now limited) should form the chief object of inquiry. We had, however, arranged that, on our return from Cyrene, the plan of the town and neighbourhood of Ptolemeta (which will be found annexed) should be completed; and that drawings should be made of such of the most conspicuous objects as had not been already secured, all of which was eventually accomplished.

It will be seen, by a reference to the plan of Ptolemeta, that the position of the town was remarkably well chosen. In its front was the sea; and on either side a ravine, along which are still seen traces of fortification, secured its flanks from any sudden attack; while the only passes by which it could be approached from the high ridge of mountains to the southward, were defended (as will appear in the plan) by strong barriers drawn completely across them: the whole town, at the same time, was originally inclosed within a wall which may still be traced to considerable extent, running parallel with the mountains at the back, and extending from these, along the banks of the ravines, to the sea. Two bridges appear (from the existing remains) to have been thrown across each of the ravines; one of which is to this day tolerably perfect, and is faithfully represented, in its actual condition, in the drawing which is given of it (page 362); several forts were also scattered about in various directions, both within and without the walls, contributing at once to the beauty and security of the place. The situation of the town in other respects was also remarkably good. It sloped down gradually from the high ground which forms the foot of the mountains at its back, (and which sheltered it from the southerly winds,) and must consequently have enjoyed the full benefit of the cool northern breezes, so grateful in all hot climates. In fact, there is no place on the coast of Northern Africa, between Ptolemeta and Tripoly, which can at all be compared with the former of these places, for beauty, convenience, and security of position, Lebda alone excepted. We are, however, informed, that the town of Ptolemeta suffered at one time so severely from want of water, that the inhabitants were obliged to relinquish their houses, and disperse themselves about the country in different directions. The reparation of the aqueducts and cisterns of the town, which, it seems, had fallen into decay, restored Ptolemeta to its former flourishing state; and this act is recorded, among many others of a similar nature performed at the command of Justinian, in the eulogy of that emperor by Procopius. As Ptolemeta is unprovided with springs, the care of its reservoirs and aqueducts must have been at all times peculiarly essential; and we find that its buildings of this class are among the most perfect of its existing remains.

It is probable that the cisterns we have mentioned above, as being situated under the tesselated pavement of the edifice which Bruce calls a temple, were among those alluded to by Procopius. They consist of two divisions of arched chambers, running parallel with each other, which are connected by others of shorter dimensions, running in an opposite direction. They communicate mutually, by means of small door-ways, of the form which will be seen in the plan (page 367), and circular apertures were left at intervals in the roof, which received light and air from the court-yard above them, and might have served equally as entrances to the cisterns, or as places from which the water might be drawn up in buckets. They have all of them been coated with an excellent cement, which is still, for the most part, very perfect, and occupy a square of about an hundred feet. We may suppose that these reservoirs were occasionally available as supplies for the general use of the town, since the remains of an aqueduct leading from them through the centre of it are still visible, as will appear in the plan of Ptolemeta. There are also remains of stone conductors leading into these cisterns from the mountains at the back of the town, and as rain usually falls in great quantities during the winter they must have been for the most part well supplied. We searched in vain for some inscription on the walls of these buildings which might throw light on the period of their construction or restoration, but were unable to discover one in any part of them: the arches which form the roofs are well turned and constructed in the usual manner, with a key-stone. We may add, that these cisterns still afford a very copious supply to the Arab tribes of the neighbourhood, although no care is taken to lead the rain into them; and we found the water which they contained on our arrival at Ptolemeta uncommonly cool and delightful.

The greater part of the town, on our first visits to it, was thickly overgrown with wild marigolds and camomile, to a height of four and five feet, and patches of corn were here and there observable growing equally within the city walls. The solitude of the place was at the same time unbroken by animals of any description; if we except a small number of jackals and hyænas, which strayed down after sunset in search of water, and a few owls and bats which started out from the ruins as we disturbed them by our near and unexpected approach. Appeals of this kind are always irresistible; and the contrast which presented itself between the silence and desolation which characterized the city of Ptolemeta when we visited it, and the busy scene which a spectator of its former wealth and magnificence would have witnessed under the Ptolemies and the Cæsars, afforded a striking and, we must say, a melancholy example of the uncertainty of all human greatness.

If the exuberant vegetation we have mentioned appeared to be rather out of its place, it was not less a source of inconvenience than regret, for we had the pleasure of being obliged to wade through it up to our arm-pits in making our way to the different buildings; and it may readily be imagined that this tiresome operation, after the heavy rains which fell occasionally at night, was no treat on a cool cloudy morning. The brushing through a turnip field, or one of mangel-wurzel, which many of our readers have no doubt often tried with a double-barrelled gun upon their shoulders, is nothing to the tramping we have mentioned; for not only our boots and trowsers were quickly wet through with the heavy drops which we brushed from their lodgments, but our shirt-sleeves and jackets, and sometimes even our turbans, were also well soaked on these occasions. A very different scene presented itself on our return from Cyrene, when the summer heat had begun to exert its influence. Not a leaf or a stalk remained of all the impediments we have alluded to, and the prevailing colour of the place, which we had left a bright green, had been succeeded by a dusky brown. The corn had been cut and carried, leaving scarcely any traces of its having been formerly growing; and the ruins were left exposed, in all their naked desolation, glaring on the eye of the spectator. We had now to encounter inconveniences of a very different nature from those which had originally presented themselves; but although they were by no means less disagreeable, we had reason to rejoice in the exchange. No impediment now remained to obstruct our approach to, or to prevent our view of the buildings, and we were able to trace the plans of them with much greater ease and accuracy than we could on the former occasions. Having given a general view of the country and remains between Bengazi and Ptolemeta, we will now retrace our steps, and notice a few of the ruins which present themselves in the route with somewhat more attention to detail.

Of the buildings which occur in passing from Bengazi to Teuchira, the most conspicuous is that which we have already mentioned under its modern name of Gusser el Toweel (the high tower), and which we have supposed to be the same with that called Cafez by Edrisi, and placed by him at the distance of a day's journey from Soluc. It is a quadrangular building of about thirty-six feet by twenty; which is entered by a single door placed in the centre of one of its longest sides. On one side of the building is a narrow chamber, occupying the whole breadth of the interior, and on the opposite side is a low archway, (of not more than six feet in height from the floor, and sunk about four feet below it,) which is now almost filled up with rubbish, and of which, we must confess, we were unable to discover the use. The intervening space is left vacant, forming a single room of something more than seventeen feet in length, and occupying, like the narrow chamber which communicates with it, the whole breadth of the inner part of the building.

A window has been formed in part of the wall for the purpose of giving light to an upper story, which, together with the window itself, appears to have made no part of the original plan; an addition has also been made to the exterior, (marked by shading lines in the ground-plan,) and forming, with what has been already described, a square of something less than fifty feet. There is no appearance of any door in this additional wall, which has been very strongly built, and it completely prevents all access from without to the door of the original building. The object of this has no doubt been security, and the whole structure appears to have been intended as a station for troops and was probably one of the fortresses repaired by Justinian. Its height may be about five-and-twenty feet, (we mean the height of the original building, for the added part does not seem to have been ever raised to half that elevation), and it is still surmounted by a cornice part of which is, however, cut away. There are several other strong towers at no great distance from Gusser el Toweel, nearer to the foot of the mountains, and a communication appears to have been kept up all the way from Bengazi to Ptolemeta. There are also several well-built and spacious arched cisterns, and other structures partly built and partly excavated, in this tract of country; as also many subterranean storehouses for grain; and a month or two might certainly be spent with great advantage in examining the space between the sea and the mountains, from Bengazi to Birsis and Teuchira.

FOOTNOTES:

Vide Scylax, Theophrastus, and others.

Signor Della Cella has remarked (p. 185,) that there are *a few* palm-trees in the neighbourhood of Bengazi, and a tract or two of land sowed with barley ("alcune palme, e qualche tratto seminato col orzo"—) all the rest is (he tells us) neglected and uncultivated. But there are a *great many* palm-trees in the neighbourhood of Bengazi, on both sides of the harbour, and a great proportion of cultivated land.

The following is the process mentioned by Shaw.—"In the months of March or April, when the sheaths that respectively enclose the young clusters of the male flowers and the female fruit begin to open (at which time the latter are formed and the first are mealy), they take a sprig or two of the male cluster, and insert it into the sheath of the female; or else they take a whole cluster of the male tree, and sprinkle the meal, or farina of it over several clusters of the female." (Travels in Barbary, vol. i., p. 259-60).

The same author remarks that the palm-tree arrives at its greatest vigour about thirty years after transplantation, and continues so seventy years afterwards; bearing yearly fifteen or twenty clusters of dates, each of them weighing fifteen or twenty pounds.

"Si parmi les palmiers (says the author of a treatise on agriculture quoted by Kazwini, in the words of Silvestre de Sacy), "Si parmi les palmiers on rapproche les individus mâles des individus femelles, ces derniers portent des fruits en plus grande abondance, parceque le voisinage favorise leurs amours; et si, au contraire, on éloigne l'arbre femelle des mâles, cette distance empêche qui'il ne rapporte aucun fruit. Quand on plante un palmier mâle au milieu des femelles, et que, le vent venant à souffler, les femelles reçoivent l'odeur des fleurs du mâle, cette odeur suffit pour rendre féconds tous les palmiers femelles qui environnent le mâle."

Shaw has observed that "the method of raising the Phœnix (φοινιξ) or palm, and, what may be further observed, that when the old trunk dies, there is never wanting one or other of those offsprings to succeed it, may have given occasion to the fable of the bird of that name dying and another arising from it."

(So Pliny, lib. xiii. c. 4.) Mirumque de ea accepimus cum phœnice ave quæ putatur ex hujus palmæ argumento nomen accepisse, emori ac renasci ex seipsa.

The palm-tree, however, though a beautiful tree, is sometimes, it appears, a very obstinate one; and the means which we are told, on Arab authority, should be used to render it more docile on these occasions would astonish the horticulturists of Europe.

When a palm-tree refuses to bear (says the Arab author of a treatise on agriculture), the owner of it, armed with a hatchet, comes to visit it in company with another person. He then begins by observing aloud to his friend (in order that the date-tree should hear him) "I am going to cut down this worthless tree, since it no longer bears me any fruit."—"Have a care what you do, brother, returns his companion; I should advise you to do no such thing—for I will venture to predict that this very year your tree will be covered with fruit." "No, no, (replies the owner,) I am determined to cut it down, for I am certain it will produce me nothing;" and then approaching the tree, he proceeds to give it two or three strokes with his hatchet.—"Pray now! I entreat you, desist" (says the mediator, holding back the arm of the proprietor)—"Do but observe what a fine tree it is, and have patience for this one season more; should it fail after that to bear you any fruit, you may do with it just what you please." The owner of the tree then allows himself to be persuaded, and retires without proceeding to any further extremities. But the threat, and the few strokes inflicted with the hatchet, have always, it is said, the desired effect; and the terrified palm-tree produces the same year a most abundant supply of fine dates!!! (Extract from Kazwini, Chréstomathie Arabe, tom. iii. p. 319.)

The sandy tract here alluded to is merely formed by deposites from the beach, and extends scarcely half a mile inland; the country beyond it, all the way to the mountains, is a mixture of rock and excellent soil, with no sand whatever, and is for the most part, as we have mentioned, well wooded and covered with vegetation.

A species of wild artichoke is also very commonly found here, which is eaten raw by the Arabs; chiefly however for amusement, as we see raw turnips eaten in other countries.

See the plan of this tower. It is called by the Arabs Gusser-el-toweel—the high tower—and is seen from a considerable distance.

Cafez autem est turris sita in media planitie Bernic, habetque ad latus suum orientale sylvam propinquam mari, et ipsa distat à mari IV. M. P. Non procul etiam à Cafez, ex parte orientali adest lacus cum longitudine maris porrectus, et collis arenæ ab eo divisus, cujus tamen aquæ dulces sunt: occupat hic sua longitudine XIV. Milliaria, latitudine medium fere milliare.—(Geog. Nubiensis, p. 93.)

The M is frequently pronounced by the Arabs instead of N; and the B always for the P, a sound which they have not in their language; the L and the N are also often confounded by them, as we find them to be frequently by the natives of other countries.

The Neapolis here mentioned must not be confounded with that which has been identified with Leptis Magna.

As we repassed the same plain in July, many heaps of corn and barley were collected in various parts of it, and the greater part of the verdure had disappeared. We found the oxen of the place very busily employed in treading out the grain, in the good old-fashioned way practised before the invention of flails; while the Arabs, availing themselves of a little breeze of wind, were occupied in tossing up the grain into the air which had been already trodden out, in order to separate it from the husks, after the manner often alluded to in Scripture. Among other instances of this allusion, we may mention the fragments of Nebuchadnezzar's image, which are compared in Daniel (ii. 25.) to "the chaff of the summer threshing-floor carried away by the wind."

The practice of excavating tombs in the neighbourhood of ancient cities, in the quarries from which the stone was procured for building them, is very general in this part of Africa, and was probably first adopted from its convenience; little more being necessary than to shape the excavated spaces to the size and form required after the stone had been extracted for architectural purposes.

De Aedificiis.

The water is also too deep to admit of one, and becomes so on a sudden within a few feet of the beach.

A further description of the Harbour and Cothon will be found, with other details of Ptolemeta, at the end of the chapter.

See the plan of these in the plate prefixed to page 367. The columns are given in the vignette at the beginning of this chapter.

The inscriptions will be found in the plate prefixed to Chapter 14.

After sowing the corn, the Arabs leave it to enjoy the advantages of the winter rains, and never return to it till it comes to maturity and is ready to be cut and carried away.

CHAPTER XIII.

OBSERVATIONS ON THE CITIES OF TEUCHIRA AND PTOLEMETA.

Actual Condition of the City of Teuchira — Perfect State and great Strength of its Walls — Suggested Period of their Erection — Mode in which they are constructed — Gates of the City — Narrow Passage communicating with them — Probable Advance of the Sea at Teuchira — Line described by the Walls — Estimated Circuit of them according to Signor Della Cella — Greek Inscriptions cut in various parts of them — Suggestions of Signor Della Cella respecting them — Actual Nature of the Inscriptions — Excavated Tombs in the Quarries of Teuchira — Egyptian Names of Months generally adopted by the Inhabitants of the City — General Nature of the Plans of the Tombs — Some of the Bodies appear to have been burnt, and others to have been buried entire — No Difference appears to have obtained at Teuchira between the Modes of Burial adopted by its Greek and Roman Inhabitants — Encumbered State of what are probably the earliest Tombs — Solitary instance of a Painted Tomb at Teuchira — Remains of Christian Churches, and other Buildings within the Walls — Disposition of the Streets — Remains without the Walls — No Statues, or Remains of them, discovered by our Party at Teuchira — Remarks on the Wall of Ptolemeta — Remains of a Naustothmos, or Naval Station, observed there — Other Remains of Building on the Beach near the Station — Further traces of the City-Wall — Dimensions of Ptolemeta — Remains of Theatres found there — Description of the larger one — Ruins described by Bruce as part of an Ionic Temple — Other Remains in the Neighbourhood of these — Remarks on the Style of some of the Buildings of Ptolemeta, as contrasted with those of Egypt and Nubia — Probable Date of its existing Remains.

IT will be seen, by a reference to the plan of the city of Teuchira, that there is little now remaining within the limits of its walls to call for any particular details. The destruction of the town has, in fact, been so complete, that it is scarcely more than a heap of confused ruins; and the various fragments of building which are scattered over its surface encumber the ground-plans so effectually, that more labour and time would be necessary for their removal than the buildings would probably merit. It is evident that Teuchira has been intentionally destroyed; and that the solidity of its walls has alone prevented them from being confounded in the general wreck. The perfect state in which these still continue to remain will, however, compensate for the losses we have sustained within their limits; and we may consider them as affording one of the best examples extant of the military walls of the ancients. Procopius has informed us that the city of Teuchira was very strongly fortified by the Emperor Justinian; and the restoration of the original wall which inclosed it (which we may suppose to have been laid in ruins by the Vandals) was probably the chief point to which the historian alluded. We are not aware of any data by which the precise period of the first erection of these walls may be ascertained; but their solidity would induce us to refer them to an epoch anterior to the time of the Ptolemies; while the regularity with which they have, at the same time, been constructed would prevent us from assigning to them a very early date. It is well known that the most ancient walls which remain to us are as remarkable for the irregularity as they are for the solidity of their structure; and the term *Cyclopean*, which has been generally applied to them, has almost become synonymous with *irregular*.

The existing walls of Teuchira have undoubtedly been constructed at a period when architecture had attained great perfection; the mode of building adopted in them is uniform and regular, well calculated from its nature to save labour and expense, and is such as could only have been successfully employed where the blocks of stone used were large and heavy. Two ranges of stone, longitudinally placed, form the outer and inner surface of the structure; and these are crossed by a single block at regular intervals the length of which is the thickness of the wall: a space is left between the longitudinal ranges, about equivalent to the breadth of the stones which compose them; and this is filled up with what is usually termed rubble, (which here appears to be the refuse of the material employed,) and occasionally with a single stone. Little or no cement has been used in the building (so far at least as we were able to discover); and, indeed, the weight of the several blocks, with the pressure upon them, would seem to render it wholly unnecessary.

Six and twenty quadrangular turrets contribute at the same time to the strength and the defence of the wall; and two gates flanked with buttresses, projecting inwards, by which the entrance is defended, and placed opposite to each other on the east and western walls, are the only approaches to the town. The entrance through these (as is usual in ancient towns) is by means of a narrow passage formed by the buttresses mentioned above; but the gate itself is not placed within the line of the walls, as we find to have been the case with that of Mycenæ, but ranges with them. Nearly in the centre of the southern wall there are two turrets of considerably larger dimensions than the rest, which are at the same time of a more recent construction, and immediately opposite to them is an outer wall of a semicircular form. We naturally searched here for another entrance to the town, but could find no appearance of there ever having been one: yet, except it were for the defence of a gateway, there does not seem to be any sufficient reason why these turrets should be larger than the rest; and if there were no entrance through them to the town there has been none on the south side at all. On the north side of Teuchira (it will appear in the plan) no part of the city wall is remaining, and it is probable that it has been undermined by the sea which appears to have here advanced (as it has on other parts of the coast) beyond its original bounds.

The line described by the walls, although somewhat quadrangular, is by no means a regular figure—a diagonal drawn from the opposite corners, at the north-east and south-western angles, would be a line of about three thousand two hundred English feet; while that which would pass through the north-west and south-eastern angles would be about nine hundred feet shorter. The circuit of the walls has been estimated by Signor Della Cella at about two miles; but we found it, by measurement, to be less than a mile and a half; being comprised in a line of eight thousand six hundred English feet. On the interior of the wall, as we have already stated, there are a good many Greek inscriptions; but we were not fortunate enough to find their contents quite so interesting as Dr. Della Cella has supposed they might have been, when he tells us, that "all the annals of the city might perhaps be found registered on its walls." We examined the whole space, however, very attentively and found only a collection of names, which we should scarcely have thought it worth while to copy had not the Doctor's assertion made it necessary to shew what portion of information the inscriptions actually contained. They will be found, with other inscriptions from the excavated tombs of Teuchira, in page 386; and it will be seen that the names are chiefly Greek, and the character, for the most part, Ptolemaic; but no other dates could be found, on any part of the surface mentioned excepting the few which appear in the plate. The inscriptions alluded to by Signor Della Cella, on a quadrangular building towards the centre of the city, consist also wholly of names and dates; they are encircled by a wreath, and it will be seen by the plate that these names are for the most part Roman. A few names, within a similar enclosure, were also visible on the wall of a turret, one of which (the most legible) we have copied.

The excavated tombs in the neighbourhood of Teuchira contain a vast number of Greek inscriptions; but these also afford only names and dates, of different countries and periods; and the most interesting piece of information that we were enabled to derive from them, was the proof which they afford of the Egyptian names of months having been in general use in this part of the Cyrenaica.

Many of the tombs, and it is probable also most of the earliest, are now buried under a mass of drifted sand; and among these it is not unlikely that dates might be found of very considerable antiquity. From the wreck of materials, also, which encumber the city, some valuable inscriptions might possibly be obtained, but the labour of clearing the ground to search for them would perhaps be too great to be undertaken with propriety, on the mere chance of such discoveries.

Of the tombs at Teuchira into which we were able to penetrate, (we mean such as are not buried in sand,) there are none, that we could find, of any particular interest. They appear to have been at all times very rude, compared with those of Egypt and Cyrene, and the inscriptions upon them are in many instances very rudely cut. Most of them have only one chamber, three sides of which are sometimes occupied by places cut into the wall for the reception of bodies. Some have only two, and others again only one of these places, in which case (we mean the latter) it is usually found opposite to the door. In several of the tombs there are no places discernible for bodies, and rudely-cut columbaria are all that can be perceived in them; in others again we find both, but seldom placed in the same position with regard to each other.

We may infer from these circumstances, that some of the bodies were burnt, the ashes only being deposited in the tomb, and that others were buried entire after being, most probably, embalmed: and here we have a mixture of the Greek and Egyptian modes of burial, as might naturally, indeed, be expected.

Not a trace of the mode in which the bodies had been embalmed, nor indeed of any bodies at all, could we perceive either at Teuchira or Ptolemeta. Not a single fragment, either of any cinerary urn or of vases of any description. The dampness of the climate, in the winter season, would no doubt contribute very materially to the destruction of the bodies when the covers were once removed from the excavated places which contained them; but it is at the same time somewhat remarkable that not a single fragment of linen or bone could be met with (though we searched for them with great attention) by which the mode of burial could be ascertained. The cause of this is most probably the occupation of the tombs by the Arabs who, as we have stated above, make use of them occasionally as places of residence for themselves and their cattle; and would naturally throw out any similar remains when they chanced to be seized with a fit of cleanliness or industry.

The pottery would also very speedily disappear before the repeated attacks of the children; and such urns or vases as were found at all perfect would be employed by the women for culinary purposes, and depôts of various kinds, and would naturally be broken in the course of time however carefully they may have been preserved. The fragments thrown out would soon be buried in sand blown up into the quarries, in heaps, from the sea;

and thus all traces might easily be lost as well of the bodies themselves, as of the vases and urns which contained the ashes. There appears to have been no difference whatever in the mode of burial practised by the Greeks and Romans of Teuchira, since many of the tombs, which are similar within, have on them the names of one and the other nation indiscriminately, and they are often seen mingled together on the same.

It is probable that the early tombs would be interesting, and that they would be found at the same time more perfect than the rest; for the sand has accumulated about them in such heaps as to have blocked up all access to them for ages. Those most buried are the tombs which are nearest the town, and they are also, we should imagine, the oldest; but we had no time to employ in excavating any of them, although we very much wished to do so.

There is one example of a painted tomb at Teuchira, in very bad taste, and this was the only one we could perceive that was so; it is probable, however, that most of them have been originally painted, and that what we see at present are the mere skeletons of the originals.

Of the buildings contained within the walls of the city, the most interesting of those whose plans were distinguishable, appeared to us to be the two Christian churches which will be found, with all the details we could procure of them, in the plate, page 367. In both these it will be seen, that the part devoted to the altar was on the eastern side of the building; but the extreme length of one of them is much greater than usual, and it is not unlikely that the portion at its western extremity, although comprised in the same line of wall, was part of another building.

Near one of these (that to the eastward of the town) we found part of an entablature in the worst taste of the lower empire, which we conjectured to be the remains alluded to by Signor Della Cella, as probably having formed a part of the temple of Bacchus: it is true that they are mentioned by the Doctor as capitals and not as parts of the epistylia; but as the fragment is small, it is possible that such a mistake may have been made; and if this be not what is alluded to in the passage below, we confess that nothing else could be found among the ruins which would at all correspond with the description.

The streets of Teuchira appear to have been built in squares, and to have crossed each other at right angles. One large street seems to have passed completely across the town, from the eastern to the western gateway; and towards the centre of this we found some columns and the arch of a gateway which probably stood across the street. In various parts of the city, to the north-east and south-west of it in particular, there are imposing remains of fallen columns and entablatures, which have no doubt belonged to buildings of more than ordinary importance; but without excavation it would not be possible to give any satisfactory account of them, and we have not ventured, in our plan of the town, to hazard any attempt at restoring them. There are also some interesting remains of buildings at the north-eastern angle of the city, where part of a quarry has been enclosed within the walls for the better defence of the place, to which indeed it effectually contributes; a strong fort has been built at this angle, in an elevated and commanding position, which appears to have been the citadel, or *strong-hold* of the town. Without the walls, to the westward of the town, there are also some interesting remains, the plans of which we attempted to complete without success: we found there a group in alto-relief, apparently of Roman workmanship, of which we have given an outline at page 367. There were probably, in earlier times, many statues in the city of Teuchira; but none of them at present remain, not, at least, that we could discover; and they have, perhaps, not survived the barbarism of the Vandals, or the fanaticism and ignorance of those who have succeeded them.

We now pass to the remains of Ptolemeta; and shall begin by observing, that no traces of the wall, which originally enclosed it would present themselves to the notice of a casual observer in taking a general view of the town. On examination, however, in the neighbourhood of the gateway, with which it seems probable that walls have been connected, we discovered traces of them running straight down to the quarry, in which we have already mentioned the amphitheatre was built and excavated. Here we found that the wall had passed through the quarry; and that a portion of the rock had been left on each side of it, in the line of the wall's direction, connecting the part which ran down from the gateway with that which we discovered on the opposite side of the quarry, extending itself from thence to the sea. The remains of the wall between the quarry and the sea are very conspicuous and decided; they run down quite to the water's edge, and are here about eight feet in thickness, and, in some parts, as much as twelve and thirteen feet in height. Without these (to the westward), almost buried in sand, are the remains of the Naustathmos (or naval station), built for the protection of vessels: they begin from the wall, following the line of the beach towards the mouth of the western ravine, and were themselves protected from the sea by a breakwater of about fourteen feet in thickness. The walls of the υφορμοι (uphormoi) are seven feet in thickness, and the spaces which they inclose, where the vessels were stationed, as much as thirty and forty feet across, in those parts which the sand had not altogether covered. To the westward of the ravine, other traces of wall are visible, extending themselves from that (in a line with the beach) along a road which leads towards the quarries, in which are the insulated tombs already alluded to, represented in plate (p. 355). Further traces of walls are observable running round this harbour towards the point marked A in the plan; and it seems to have been altogether divided from the inland country, as we find to have been usual with the ancients, more particularly in time of war. We had no opportunities of ascertaining whether any other remains of a cothon are to be seen between the points A and B, where the χηλαι (keelai, or cornua), the claws, or horns (as they were called) of the harbour, would be looked for if any such had formerly existed. Remains of a wall running round the small port within the town (on the eastern side of point B), and which we may call the eastern harbour, are still visible; and a strong fort yet remains on either side of it, at the eastern and western extremity of the wall, which appears to have been often the case.

The Pharos, or light-house, if any such existed, was probably erected on the high ground on point B, in the neighbourhood of the fort at its eastern extremity, and columns and other fragments of building, at the back of the western port, point out the places of those structures usually erected by the ancients near their harbours, for the accommodation of the merchants and sailors: here also are the remains of a bridge which was formerly thrown across the ravine, running down to the wall of this port.

We have already said that traces of the city-wall are observable between the quarry which contains the amphitheatre and the gateway; and a portion of it may also be remarked extending from the latter to the mountains at the back of the town; where they are connected with other parts of it running along the foot of the range to the inner bank of the eastern ravine. There again decided remains of the wall may be traced running parallel with the same ravine; and which, passing near the bridge represented in plate (p. 362,) continue towards the sea as far as the remains of the second bridge which we have already mentioned. Beyond this we could perceive no more traces of the wall; although it seems more than probable that it extended on this side to the beach, (as we find it to have done on the opposite side to the westward,) and that it passed along parallel with the sea, till it joined the portions connecting the two forts of the eastern harbour, which we have already observed to be remaining. We could not discover any traces of a gateway in the eastern wall of the city; but it is probable that there was formerly one on this side also, leading to the upper bridge, where some very strong works are still extant, in the form of a curve, as will appear by a reference to the plan.

It is difficult to say how these works were connected with the remains of the wall between them and the mountains; and had our time allowed it, we should have excavated about them for the purpose of discovering the connection.

We may reckon that the walls of Ptolemeta, when entire, inclosed a quadrangle of eighteen thousand English feet in circuit; and the line of wall which may be traced from the existing remains covers a space of at least thirteen thousand. A line drawn through the centre of the city, from north to south, would be about four thousand eight hundred feet in length; and that which should be drawn across it from east to west, about four thousand four hundred. The whole circuit of the city would thus be somewhat less than three English miles and a half; its length, from north to south, something less than a mile, and its breadth from east to west something more than three-quarters.

Such of the plans of the buildings at Ptolemeta as could in their present state be satisfactorily made out, will be found in plate (page 385;) but although the forms of the theatres and amphitheatre prevent their being mistaken for other buildings, it would not be possible without excavation to make out their details with any accuracy. We have given our idea of the larger of the two theatres, from the appearance and the measurements of the existing remains of it, but the smaller one was too much ruined, and too much encumbered, to allow of our hazarding a similar attempt, and we have confined ourselves to its general dimensions, as given in the plan of the town. We may reckon the diameter of the orchestra of the larger theatre at about one hundred and forty-five English feet, and that of the part appropriated to the cunei, at about fifty of the same. The whole diameter of the theatre would thus be two hundred and forty-five feet. It will be observed that the area of the orchestra is very considerably larger than that occupied by the same part of the building in Greek and Roman theatres in general, and that the passages leading into it are wider in proportion to the cunei than usual. It will also be seen, from the absence of any præcinctions, that there were no interior communications in this theatre, by which the spectators dispersed themselves over the body of the house: the only approach to the seats having been by means of passages communicating directly with the orchestra from without, which appear to have been nearly on a level with the orchestra itself; the roofs of them, only, sloping somewhat in the direction of the seats themselves. As these (the seats) were comparatively few, and the spaces between the passages inconsiderable, there was no necessity for staircases, and we accordingly find no appearance of any communications of this nature. As it seems, however, that the lowest range of seats was raised a few feet above the level of the passage and of the orchestra, a short flight of steps would have been necessary, to render the access to them easy; and we thought we observed traces, in two or three of the divisions, of there having been one originally in each. The arched roofs of all the passages have fallen in, and every part of the theatre has suffered materially from the effects of rainy winters, rather than of time.

The depth of the proscenium appears to have been, as we have given it, about twenty-five feet, but we could recover no part of the stage with any tolerable accuracy, so that we have omitted it altogether.

The amphitheatre has been chiefly excavated (as we have already observed) in the quarry in which it stands, and a small portion of it only has been built, where the rock could not be made to serve. Here, as in the theatres, there appear to have been no interior communications; and the approach to the seats was probably from above, as well as from below, by means of the staircases between the several cunei only, no passages being anywhere observable. The whole of this is so ruined, that we shall give no further details of it than we have offered to our readers, merely stating, that its form appeared to have been round, in which particular it differs from amphitheatres in general, which are usually of an oblong figure. The diameter of the circle may be reckoned at about two hundred and fifty English feet, including the cunei and arena.

The remains marked (*a*) are the same which Bruce describes as those of an Ionic temple; there is nothing, however, (that we can perceive) in the disposition of what still exists of their plan, to authorize such a conclusion; and we have considered them as the remains of a palace, or other residence of more than ordinary importance. The three remaining columns appear to have formed part of a colonnade extending itself round the court-yard, which has already been described as situated above an extensive range of cisterns: remains of tessellated pavement are still observable in the court-yard, and the walls which inclose it are very decided; the columns have been raised on a basement of several feet in height, as will be seen in the vignette in which they are represented. Without these, to the northward, are ranges of fallen columns of much larger dimensions than those we have just mentioned; but they are so much encumbered, that we have not ventured to lay them down in the plan: they are of the Corinthian order, and the capitals are well executed. A little beyond these, to the northward and north-eastward, are other remains of columns, which once belonged to a building of some importance, the plan of which cannot be given without excavation; and, indeed, we may observe, with respect to the numerous masses of fallen columns, and other parts of various buildings of more than ordinary consequence at Ptolemeta, that very little satisfactory information can be obtained of their plans, without a good deal of labour in clearing them, from the accumulation of soil, and the fragments of fallen building, with which they are encumbered. There is a structure of very large dimensions at the north-eastern part of the town, the outer walls of which are still standing to a considerable height; but the plan of its interior is not sufficiently apparent to authorize any restoration of it, and we will not even hazard a conjecture of its nature. On its northern face are three large quadrangular tablets of stone, built into the wall, each five feet in length by four in height, on which are cut the Greek inscriptions (marked 1), given in plate (page 385); and to the westward and south-westward of this building are many interesting remains of private dwelling-houses, palaces, baths, &c., which require a great deal of excavation. On a pedestal in one of these, is the inscription (4) in plate (page 385); most of them appear to have been Roman, and the capitals and bases of some of the columns belonging to them are very fanciful and overcharged with ornament. Some of the shafts of small columns in this mass of building are spiral, and formed of coloured marbles; and may probably be attributed to the time of Justinian, when the city revived under his politic munificence. If the taste displayed by the Greeks and Romans of this period had been at all in proportion to the expense which they lavished upon their public and private edifices of almost every description, the result would have been splendid in the extreme; but the costliness of material, and the labour employed in ornament, will not compensate for the absence of this true test of genuine excellence; and we cannot venture to commend the strange mixture of received orders, and the wayward fancy employed in the invention of new ones, which are conspicuous in several parts of Ptolemeta.

It has been observed by Signor Della Cella, that the remains of this city are purely Egyptian; but we must confess that we were unable to discover the slightest resemblance of style in Ptolemeta to that which characterizes the architecture of Egypt. There is nothing at Ptolemeta (that we could perceive) which is not either Greek or Roman; and the profusion of unnecessary ornament, which generally distinguished the later productions of both these nations, is very different from that which is observable in Egyptian remains. The style of Egypt, though highly ornamental, is founded on established principles; and there is nothing incongruous or unmeaning in the most laboured decorations which are peculiar to it: proportion and simplicity are very rarely violated in the buildings either of Egypt or Nubia; and the great variety of ornament which appears in them never disturbs the general effect, or detracts from the imposing grandeur of the masses. Whenever the general form and larger parts of a building are simple and well proportioned, a great deal of ornament may be adopted in the detail, without injury to the effect of the whole; and as this is particularly the case in Egyptian architecture, the mind is strongly impressed with the pleasing character of the general mass, before it has time to notice any other peculiarities.

The same may be observed with respect to Gothic architecture; in which the almost infinite detail which it presents is not found to diminish either the simplicity, the grandeur, or the elegance of the whole. When the attention is turned from the general mass to the subdivisions, every portion, however small, is observed to have a meaning, in both styles of architecture here alluded to; and there is seldom any part of the ornament, either in Egyptian or in Gothic examples, which we wish to have removed from its place. In the capitals and shafts of Egyptian columns, (which are usually composed of different parts of the lotus, the leaves, the stalks, the open flower, or the bud, so combined and arranged as not to interfere with the simple and, generally, graceful outline of the whole,) the detail gives a lightness to the general mass which tends to improve its effect; and the simplicity of the general form exhibits the decoration to advantage: but in the later productions of Greece and Rome, a profusion of unmeaning ornament is employed, which rather gives an air of heaviness to the detail, than any appearance of lightness to the mass. The general forms are not, in fact, sufficiently important of themselves to create a favourable impression; and it will usually be found difficult, if not impossible, to make amends for this fault by decoration. We do not mean to assert that there are no examples of good taste at Ptolemeta; but it appears to us that by far the greater part of the buildings now remaining have been constructed since the place became a Roman colony; and that there are none to which a higher antiquity may be safely assigned (with the exception of some of the tombs) than the period at which the country was occupied by the Ptolemies.

FOOTNOTES:

Many of the stones employed in the restoration of the walls have belonged to more ancient buildings, and parts of handsome cornices, friezes, and capitals are often seen built in with the original structure; among these may be noticed fragments of Ptolemaic inscriptions, which are evidently not in their original places.

We must except a low, narrow door, through one of the turrets at the south-west angle, the mode of constructing which will appear in page 367. It seems to have been intended as a sally-port and one person only can pass through it at a time. From the remains about this angle, there appears to have been an outer wall of very inferior strength, but it seems to have made no part of the original plan.

Nearly opposite to these turrets, without the wall, are the remains of a very strong fort; and this circumstance would perhaps seem to favour the idea of there having been a gate in the place here alluded to, the entrance to which would have been well defended by the fort.

The turrets attached to the walls are also described by the same author as *round*; and it is difficult to imagine what could have occasioned this mistake, since they are all of them quadrangular, as will appear by the plan.

Le mura della città sono talmenti tapezzate di Grechi inscrizioni che forse trovansi qui registrati tutti gli annali di questa città. (Viaggio da Tripoli, &c. p. 199.)

The practice of burying the body entire was, however, very frequently adopted by the Greeks in other places, as we shall hereafter have occasion to mention.

Plans and sections of some of the tombs will be found in page 367, and we think the reader will not be able to trace so much resemblance between the style of Teuchira and that of Cyrene as Signor Della Cella has discovered, when he tells us that "Il fabricato di Tochira, dello stessissimo stile di quello di Cirene, la stessa copia, e struttura di tombi, conferma ciocchè di questa città lasciò scritto Erodoto, *che usava le stesse leggi de' Cirenei.*"—(Page 199.)

Vi si scorgono pure gli avanzi di un tempio che io credo essere stato dedicato a Bacco, a giudicarne da' capitelli, che giaciano affastellati fra le sue rovine, guarniti di foglie di viti con grappoli pendenti.—(P. 199.)

We mean, of course, in their present ruined state, for the original height of the wall cannot now be ascertained.

These divisions, composing the Naustathmos, were termed ορμοι (ormoi), υφορμοι (uphormoi), or ναυλοκοι (naulokoi), as mentioned in the account of the ports and harbours at the end of the Narrative.

See account of ports and harbours, (p. 21).

Ibid.

480 feet less.

480 less.

440 more.

See plate.

CHAPTER XIV.

JOURNEY FROM PTOLEMETA TO MERGE.

Departure from Ptolemeta — Romantic and Picturesque Appearance of the Road — Luxuriant Vegetation which adorned it — Arrive at the Summit of the first Range — Bedouin Tents on the Plain above — Pleasing Manners of their Inhabitants — Character of the Scenery on the Summit of the Lower Range — Beauty of the Route continues — Arrive at the Plain of Merge — Character and Position of the Plain — Our Camel-Drivers refuse to proceed — Artful Conduct of Abou-Bukra — Appeal to Bey Halil — Projected Mission to Derna — Abou-Bukra comes to Terms, and brings his Camels for the Journey — Pools of Fresh Water collected in the Plain of Merge — Use made of them by the Arabs — Prevalence of a Virulent Cutaneous Disease among the Arab Tribes of Merge and its Neighbourhood — Remains of a Town at one extremity of the Plain — Remarks on the District and City of Barka — Testimonies of Strabo, Pliny, Ptolemy, and Scylax, respecting the Port of Barca — Remarks on the Position of the City of that Name — Arab Accounts of Barca — Edrisi, Abulfeda, &c. — Unsatisfactory Nature of the Accounts in Question — Mode of reconciling the Arab Accounts of Barca with those of Scylax — Suggested Position of the Ancient City — Peculiarity of Soil attributed to Barca — Observations on its Produce and Resources — State of Barca under the Arabs — Decay of the Ancient City after the building of Ptolemais on the Site of its Port — The Barcæans remarkable for their Skill in the Management of Horses and Chariots — Their Country formerly celebrated for its excellent Breed of Horses — Degeneracy of the present Breed — Account of Barca by Herodotus — Other Accounts of its Origin — Siege and Plunder of the City by the Persians under Amasis — Subsequent state of the City till the building of Ptolemais.

ON our arrival at Ptolemeta, we had discharged the camels which we hired from the people of Bengazi, and waited the arrival of those which Hadood, Shekh of Barca, was to furnish us with, under whose escort we were to proceed to the eastern limits of the Bashaw's dominions.

At Teuchira we had been joined, as we have already stated, by Abou-Bukra, the son of Hadood, and four days after our arrival at Ptolemeta the camels which we expected were brought from the mountains, and we set out on our journey to Cyrene. We left Ptolemeta on the twenty-seventh of April, and took the road leading through Merge, a large and fertile plain, situated on the top of the range which we have already described as lying to the southward of Ptolemeta. After repassing a part of the road, by which we had formerly travelled, we began to ascend a most romantic valley, a little to the westward of the town of Ptolemeta and leading up from the coast towards Merge. As we wound along the steep and narrow pathway which skirted the bed of the torrent below us, we found the place much more remarkable for its wildness and beauty than it was for the goodness of its roads; and had not our camels been accustomed to the mountains they would probably have given us a good deal of trouble. The sides of the valley were thickly clothed with pines, olive trees, and different kinds of laurel, interspersed with clusters of the most luxuriant honeysuckle, the fragrance of which, as we passed it, literally perfumed the air. Among these we distinguished myrtle, arbutus, and laurestinus, with many other handsome flowering shrubs, a variety of wild roses, both white and red, and quantities of rosemary and juniper. Scenes of this kind even in Europe would be highly appreciated; but to travellers in Africa, it may readily be imagined they could not fail of being more than usually grateful; and every fresh beauty which opened itself to our view was hailed with enthusiastic delight.

The very difficulty of the road added interest to the scene; and the mixture of what (with us) would have been garden shrubs, blooming, more luxuriantly than we ever see them in northern climates, amidst the wild crags of a neglected ravine, gave a finish and an elegance to its rugged forms which produced the most agreeable association of ideas.

But if we begin to indulge ourselves in recollections of this nature, we shall soon lose the thread of our narrative; and restraint is the more necessary on the present occasion, as the scenes which presented themselves one after the other, in our route from Ptolemeta to Merge, were nothing but a continued succession of beauties from the beginning to the end of our journey. In about an hour from the time when we began to ascend, we reached the top of the first hill, and were saluted by a wild-looking, dark-featured Arab, who presented us some honey in the comb which is procured in quantities from the neighbouring mountains. This was the first person we had met with in our passage up the ravine, and there was a wildness in his accent as well as in his appearance which suited admirably with the character of the scene. A little farther on we reached some Arab tents, scattered here and there among the bushes and trees, and such of the Bedouins whose tents we passed nearest to came out, and questioned us on the objects of our journey. We observed in these people the same peculiarities of look and accent which had struck us in our friend of the honeycomb, and they had a bluntness and independence of manner and appearance which afforded us, together with their simplicity, a good deal of pleasure and amusement. They welcomed us in the true patriarchal style, with an offer of shelter and refreshment, and we should have liked nothing better than spending a week or two among them, and rambling about the beautiful country which they occupied.

It often happens, however, that pleasure and duty are disagreeably inconsistent with each other; and the fine Arcadian lounge, that we should willingly here have indulged in, would not have much forwarded the objects of the mission. The view which presented itself from the top of the hill was no less pleasing than those which we had enjoyed so much in ascending it. It had less of wildness than those of the ravine, but quite sufficient to give additional interest to the broad sweep of open country which lay stretched out before us, comprising a rich and varied succession of hills and vallies which lost themselves in the blue horizon.

The open tracts of pasture and cultivated land scattered over this charming scene were most agreeably diversified with clumps and thickets of trees, and with flowering shrubs and flowers, in greater profusion and variety than we had seen in our passage along the ravine. Everything around us was green and smiling; and whether we looked, in our progress, from the hill to the valley, or from the valley to the side of the hill, the view was equally delightful.

After quitting the Arab tents, we entered a most beautiful valley extending itself in a north-easterly and south-westerly direction; and three hours more, over hills and through vales, which it would be useless and almost endless to describe, we arrived at the plain of Merge, a long sweep of flat country of mingled pasture and cultivation, bounded on either side by a range of wooded hills about five miles distant from each other, and stretching from north-east to south-west as far as the eye could reach. The water from the mountains inclosing the plain settles in pools and lakes in different parts of this spacious valley; and affords a constant supply, during the summer months, to the Bedouin tribes who frequent it. Although the ranges of hills which we have described as inclosing it give to Merge the appearance of a valley, it must be recollected that it is situated on the top of a chain of mountains of no inconsiderable elevation; and if we have mentioned it as an extensive plain, it must also be considered as a tract of table-land raised far above the level of the sea. In looking over what we shall presently have occasion to mention respecting the town and the neighbourhood of Barka, it will be necessary to bear this in mind; but before we enter upon the subject we must add to our journal the few incidents which occurred during our stay at Merge.

It was not our intention to have remained a moment in this valley, as we were anxious to get to Cyrene as soon as possible; but on signifying our intentions of proceeding farther, (for the day was not half spent,) the camel-drivers refused to go on, alleging that Abou-Bukra had hired them only to Merge. Abou-Bukra himself was not present at the time, having ridden towards the other end of the valley where the tents of Bey Halil, who had been some days at Merge, were pitched near the tomb of a celebrated Marábut. As we had no means of disproving the compact alleged, and the camel-drivers persisted in their refusal to proceed, we did not think it worth while to take any further trouble in endeavouring to overcome their scruples; we therefore ordered the tents to be pitched and rode on to Bey Halil, fully expecting that he would furnish us with other camels to enable us to continue our journey on the following morning. The Bey received us as usual with the greatest civility, and promised the camels at an early hour the next day, by which time, he added, Shekh Hadood would most probably arrive and take the charge of escorting us to Cyrene. The next day, however, no camels arrived, and we again rode down to the tents of Bey Halil to learn the reason of this unseasonable delay. We found the Bey's tent filled with Bedouin Arab Shekhs, who appeared to be in grand consultation, and Halil had either been, or pretended to have been, persuading them to furnish us with camels for the journey. The result of the conclave was not, however, by any means favourable, for none of the worthy Shekhs present would let us have their camels for less than eighty dollars; a demand so extremely exorbitant that we did not hesitate a moment in declining it, and offered them at the same time thirty, expecting that they would relax, as is usually the case with them, when they found that we persisted in our refusal.

Half the day was, however, spent in sending backwards and forwards and still we could get no camels, Abou-Bukra himself making a thousand professions of his readiness to oblige us on all occasions, but giving us no proofs of it whatever. It required very little penetration to discover that this was evidently a concerted manœuvre; and that Bey Halil was either unable to make any satisfactory arrangement for us, or was himself a party in the plan. Abou Bukra was certainly the principal agent in the affair, and the whole plot was doubtless got up by him. He had mentioned no difficulties of the kind at Ptolemeta, because the camel-drivers of Bengazi would have offered to proceed with us to Cyrene, had he declined supplying us on reasonable terms. The eighty dollars required by all the Bedouin Shekhs was the sum which he wished to extract from us, and the circumstance of the whole assembly being unanimous in the demand was intended to be a proof of its fairness, he himself having made no offer whatever, on the plea of not having camels enough at his disposal. Bey Halil very probably did not wish to interfere in preventing his Arab friend from making what profit he could of us (such an act being considered by Mahometans in general as extremely unbrotherly, and not by any means called for); and with regard to the Arabs, they willingly lend their services to one another on all occasions of a similar nature.

Finding the chances against us on this tack, we determined to try another; there being no end to Arab extortion when you have once given them reason to suppose that you will submit to it. We accordingly arranged that two of our party should set out with all speed for Derna, to request Mahommed Bey would furnish us with camels, which we knew he would immediately do. This manœuvre succeeded, as we expected it would, in bringing about a favourable change; but we had determined, in the event of being obliged to put the threat in execution, to transport a tent and some provisions to Ptolemeta, on the horses, where our time would be employed to advantage till the camels from Derna arrived; and, as the distance from Merge to Ptolemeta was only a few hours, and the road could not be mistaken, this plan would have been easily effected.

Abou-Bukra, however, no sooner perceived that we were in earnest, than he offered to supply us himself with camels at a price of forty dollars; but as thirty was the sum we had ourselves proposed, we declared that we would not make any other alteration in it than by meeting him half way in his demand; and as he had begun to suspect that we kept to our word he made no further difficulty in the matter, and agreed to bring his camels at thirty-five. This he accordingly did, and Shekh Hadood not having yet arrived we quitted Merge the next day, under convoy of Abou-Bukra and our Bengazi Chaous, Rabdi, who had now recovered from his illness, and joined us to resume his office.

During the time of our stay at Merge, we received a present of several sheep from Bey Halil, for which we made a suitable return to the Chaous who brought them, and took the opportunity of sending by him a token of our regard to our old friend Hashi, the Bey's secretary.

We have already said that the water of Merge is collected in pools in different parts of the valley; and we soon found that in exchanging that of the wells and cisterns which we had quitted for it, we had not much improved the quality of our liquor. It was soon discovered that the water we procured from the pools was not quite so clear as it might have been, and we thought we perceived a peculiar taste in it which did not seem to be its natural flavour.

A very little observation convinced us we were right; for the pools were used by the Arabs, not only for drinking, but for washing and bathing also; and we soon found that the last-mentioned ceremonies, though not often resorted to by Arabs in general, were more particularly essential to the comfort of those at Merge, from circumstances which we would willingly conceal; since they will scarcely be considered as perfectly in character with the highly-romantic features of the country which they inhabited.

We are not, at the same time, prepared to assert, that the causes which more peculiarly call for ablution (considered as a matter of comfort) did not actually exist in patriarchal days amidst scenes such as we have described; and if we do not find them hinted at in the allusions to early times which are made in this age of refinement, it is only, perhaps, that too minute a detail would be inconsistent with the ideas which we wish to excite of our forefathers.

In confessing that the Arabs who washed themselves in the pools of Merge were induced to do so more frequently than they would otherwise have done, from the alleviation which this operation afforded to the pain of a well-known cutaneous disease, that it will not be necessary to name, we must state, at the same time, that it is by no means peculiar to them alone; since the greater part of the Arabs from Bengazi to Derna are afflicted with a similar complaint. As they have either no effectual remedy for the disorder, or neglect the precaution of applying it, the consequences must be distressing in the extreme to them; and it is certain, that their appearance is not often remarkably prepossessing, and, perhaps, as we have said, not altogether in character with the beautiful scenery about them. We shall insist, notwithstanding this unlucky objection, that the scenery of the country in the neighbourhood of Merge, is among the most beautiful that we have ever beheld; and that the people who inhabit it are not the less patriarchal in their manners, and customs, and appearance, because they happen to be afflicted with a cutaneous disease the name of which has not usually been associated, in modern times, with ideas of pastoral, or any other enjoyments. At the same time, we confess that we did not feel ourselves called upon to fill our water-skins any more from the pool which we had hitherto used, when we found for what purposes it was occasionally employed; although the Arabs themselves could see no sufficient reason why it should not be drank on that account.

Near the centre of Merge is a ruin now called Marábut Sidi Arhooma, and a few miles to the south-east of it are remains of an inconsiderable town which the Bey informed us had been built by a celebrated Shereef, but of which so little is now remaining that the plans of the buildings could not be satisfactorily ascertained.

The extensive plain (or valley) of Merge, for it is equally one and the other, may be considered as occupying a part of the territory within the ancient limits of Barca; and before we proceed with the details of our journey, it will be proper to turn our attention to the imperfect notices which have come down to us of the celebrated city of that name. The limits assigned to the district of Barca by the Arab historians and geographers comprise not only the whole of the Cyrenaica, but, according to some, the whole tract of country between Mesurata and Alexandria; while its actual limits (as we have stated elsewhere) commence at the bottom of the Syrtis, extending themselves eastward as far as Derna, and, as we were also informed, to the eastern extremity of the Bashaw of Tripoli's dominions. The ancient country of Barca was, however, confined to the western parts of the Cyrenaica, and extended no farther in that direction than to the eastern limits of the Hesperides. The port of Barca, under the Lagidæ, received the name of Ptolemais, and we have the authorities of Strabo and Pliny for considering the last-mentioned city and that of Barca as the same. Ptolemy has, however, distinguished Barca from Ptolemais, and Scylax has described the former of these cities as situated at the distance of one hundred stadia from the sea; so that no doubt can remain of their having been different places. As the distance of Scylax from the port to the city of Barca is given in distance from the sea, we must look for the latter (supposing the one hundred stadia to be correct, which we have no sufficient reason to doubt) in some part of that range of mountains which bounds the country between Bengazi and Ptolemeta to the southward; and it appears extremely probable, that its site should be looked for in some part of the plain of Merge: it may be, in the remains which have already been mentioned in the south-eastern part of the valley. Here, however, a considerable difficulty occurs, if the accounts of the city of Barca, which are given by early Arab writers, are at all to be depended upon as correct; for although these accounts, in many respects, will be found to be extremely unsatisfactory, they all appear to concur in placing the city in the neighbourhood of a mountainous country, but, at the same time, rather in a plain at the foot of it than in any part of the mountains themselves. The distance, however, of Barca from the coast unavoidably places it in some part of the range which we have mentioned; for there is no part of the plain between this range and the sea, (as will clearly appear by the chart,) which is distant anything like one hundred stadia from the coast, with the exception of that to the southward of Bengazi; and to suppose the town of Barca there would be absurd, for it would then be fifty miles distant from its port and only nine or ten from the more convenient harbour of Berenice. Edrisi has given us several distances to and from Barca; as—from Barca to Augela ten stations (or days' journey), equal to two hundred and fifty Roman miles. From Barka to Alexandria—twenty-one stations, or five hundred and fifty M. P. From the promontory of Khanem (Cape Mesurata) to Barka—four hundred and eighty M. P. The intermediate places between Barca and Alexandria, and between Mesurata and Barka, are, at the same time, mentioned in detail; but as few of them correspond with the existing names of places in the same routes we have no means of checking the numbers as they occur, or of reckoning the distance of any known places in its neighbourhood from the city of Barca described. If the distances, also, be taken in the aggregate, they will be found too considerable to fix the site of the city with any sufficient precision. Were the places of Aurar and Alásal clearly decided upon we should have more available data; and particularly if distances had been given by Edrisi between Teuchira and Barca, and between Ptolemeta and the last-mentioned city. The other Arab accounts, which we allude to, of Barca, are as follows:—

In the work of Azizi, as cited by Abulfeda, we are told that "there are *two mountains belonging to Barca*, in which there is a great proportion of excellent soil, numerous springs of fresh water, and many tracts of cultivated land." Provisions are mentioned as being at all times very cheap there, and the inhabitants exported wine, and pitch, extracted from the pine, to Egypt; together with a great many head of cattle of a small breed.

This refers to the *district* or territory of Barca; and the *city* of that name is described by the author just quoted as "situated in *an extensive plain*, the soil of which is of a reddish colour; it has been surrounded" (he adds) "with a wall ever since the time of Motewakkel, that is to say, from the year of the Hegira 240."

Another Arab writer, whose name has not come down to us, informs us, as cited by Silvestre de Sacy (*Chrestomat. Arabe*, Tom. ii., p. 521), that "the city of Barca is situated in a country where the soil and the buildings are red; whence it happens that the clothes of those who reside there partake of the same colour."

It is then stated that, *"at six miles from Barca, is a mountain,"* and without mentioning at all in what direction, the author goes on to say, that provisions were at all times very abundant and very cheap in the country; that the cattle thrived and multiplied in its pastures; and that the greater part of those killed in Egypt were supplied from it. Bricks, honey, and pitch (he adds) were also exported to Egypt, the latter of which was prepared in a place dependant upon Barca called Maka, situated on a high mountain, of difficult access, which it was impossible to ascend on horseback. In the *city of Maka* (he goes on to state) was the tomb of Rowaïfa, one of the companions of Mahomet, (for it seems there were two of that name,) and *this city* was called, in the Greek language, *Pentapolis*, which means (says our author) five cities. The country (he adds) produced a great variety of fruits, and there was a great proportion of it covered with juniper; the people about it were of different Arab tribes, and of those called Lewata. On the road from Barca (he still continues) to Africa proper, is the valley of Masouyin (the pronunciation of which name, says De Sacy, is uncertain) in which are found remains of arches and gardens to the number, it is said, of three hundred and sixty; some of the gardens are cultivated, and the wilderness, or desert tract, from which the honey is procured, is situated in this valley.—(*Chrestomat. Arabe*, Tom. ii. p. 521, 2.)

In the Geographia Nubiensis, Barca is described as a town of moderate dimensions and narrow limits; and as being celebrated for an earth called by its name, which was of great service, when mixed with oil, in cutaneous diseases. It was of a reddish colour, and if thrown into the fire smelt strongly of sulphur, emitting at the same time a very offensive smoke: its taste is described as *execrable*. (*Geog. Nubien.* p. 92.)

There can be no question that these writers had all of them the same place in view: the peculiarities which they attribute to it agree too well to doubt it; but there is nothing in the description of any by which the position of the city of Barca can be fixed (at least we cannot see that there is) with any tolerable degree of accuracy.

The only mode of reconciling the Arab accounts of Barca with the distance which Scylax has given of that city from the sea, is to suppose that the authors of them intended to describe it as situated in some plain within the limits of the range of mountains mentioned above; and, under this idea, the extensive plain of Merge appears to be the most eligible spot we are acquainted with for the position of the town we are speaking of.

The position of Merge with regard to Ptolemeta, which has already been identified with the ancient port of Barca, is extremely favourable to this supposition. Two ravines, one of which is an extremely good road, lead up directly to it from Ptolemeta; and the distance of any town, which might be built upon its plain, from the sea would correspond sufficiently well with that which we have quoted from Scylax. The peculiarities of soil which are attributed by Arab writers to Barca, are at the same time observable in the soil of the plain of Merge, which is of a decided reddish colour, and stains the clothes of those who lie down upon it, as we have occasion to know by experience. Again, one account says, that "six miles from Barca is a mountain;" and the ranges of mountains which inclose the plain (or valley) of Merge are also six miles distant from each other. Honey is also found in the valleys leading to Merge, as it is said to have been in those leading to Barca; and the Arabs are still in the habit of extracting a kind of resin, or turpentine, from the fir, which might be the "kidràn" of the writers we have quoted. These are all of them vague proofs, but, in the absence of better, we are content to receive them in corroboration of the idea that Merge is the plain intended by the writers in question; although, after all, it does not absolutely follow that the town described by them as Barca should be clearly established as the *ancient* town of Barca required.

The peculiarities ascribed to the territory of Barca—its numerous springs, its excellent soil, its large supplies of cattle, its various kinds of fruit trees, are all of them observable in the mountainous districts of the Cyrenaica; and there can be no doubt that these tracts are part of the country alluded to by Arab writers as the territory of Barca. Barca, under the Arabs, was a considerable province, but it suffered materially from the tyranny of Yazouri, and a great part of its inhabitants abandoned their country and established themselves in Egypt and other places. Many of the emigrants settled in Alexandria; but when that city was afterwards laid waste by the plague, in the dreadful manner described by Abd' Allatif, more than twenty thousand persons quitted it for Barca, and the province again assumed a flourishing appearance.

The city known by the Arabs under the name of Barca never appears to have been (in their time) of any importance; but the ancient city so called was (after Cyrene) the most considerable town of the Cyrenaica; and continued to flourish down to the time of the Ptolemies when it appears to have been eclipsed by Ptolemais. Its inhabitants were celebrated, like those of Cyrene, for their skill in the management of horses and chariots; the former of which arts they are said to have received from Neptune, the latter from Minerva; which is stating in other words that at a very early period nothing was known of the origin of this custom in Africa. In the age of Pindar the Cyrenaica was still celebrated for its excellent horses, and we find that it enjoyed the same reputation in the times of the Arab historians. The breed has, however, (from whatever cause,) degenerated considerably from its original character, and the horses of Barca are not now to be compared with those of Arabia and Egypt. The origin of the ancient city of Barca, or Barce, is related by Herodotus (Melp. 160.), and many interesting particulars of it are given in detail by the same writer. He states it to have been founded by the brothers of Arcesilaus, King of Cyrene, (probably about five hundred and fifteen years before the Christian era,) who left him, in consequence of some dissensions, to inhabit another part of the country; where, after some deliberation (says the historian,) they built the city which was then, as it is at present, called Barce.

Others have supposed it to have been of Phœnician or Libyan origin, Barca being a Phœnician name well known on the northern coast of Africa, as we learn from Silius Italicus and other writers.

Servius intimates that its citizens came originally from Carthage, which might suggest the probability that Barca, Dido's brother, who accompanied her into Africa with some of his countrymen, established himself there and gave the name to the city and territory by which they were afterwards distinguished. The city was taken and plundered by the Persians, under Amasis, after a long and difficult siege (related in detail by Herodotus), and many of its inhabitants were sent prisoners to Darius Hystaspes, in whose reign this event took place, and settled by that monarch in a district of Bactria which was after them called Barce. The descendants of Battus were, however, left unmolested in the city; which continued (perhaps) to flourish, as we have already mentioned, till the building of Ptolemais on the site of its ancient port; to which place its inhabitants are said to have retired in order to enrich themselves by commerce.

FOOTNOTES:

It was to the rus in urbe that our destiny called us—to the πολίς Ἑλλενίς παλαιον ονομα και σεμνον—νυν πενης, και κατηφης, και μεγα ερειπιον! as Cyrene is pathetically described by Synesius; and we are sorry to say that the term *rus in urbe* may now be well applied to this once beautiful city with even more correctness than to Ptolemeta; which we have already described as covered with vegetation, and presenting the appearance of a solitary grass-grown tract of country, rather than of a once populous town. Cattle feed everywhere among the ruins of Cyrene, and its whole aspect is infinitely more rural than civic.

One of the reasons alleged for putting so high a price upon the camels was the probability of their eating the silphium which grows in the country we were about to visit, and which has sometimes very fatal effects upon them.

Ειθ' ἡ Βαρκη προτερον, νυν δε Πτολεμαις.—(Strabo, Lib. xvii.) Deinde Ptolemais, antiquo nomine Barce.—(Hist. Nat. Lib. v. c. 5.)

So also Stephanus; Βαρκη, πολις Λιβυης, ἡτις και Πτολεμαις.

Εκ δε λιμενος της Κυρηνης μεχρι λιμενος του κατα Βαρκην σταδια φ▯ , ἡ δε πολις ἡ Βαρκεων απο θαλασσης απεχει σταδια ρ▯ . (Perip. p. 109.)

(لاقطران) el kidrān, (goudron).

The Arab word is ضـــطابلس Bintàblis.

Yazouri was Grand Khadi and governor of Egypt and Barca, in the reign of the Caliph Mostanser-Billah. He was stripped of these posts, and of that of Vizier, which he also held, in the year 450.

This author relates, that he himself was credibly informed, that on *one* single day (a Friday) the Imam at Alexandria had read the funeral service over *seven hundred people!*—and that, in the space of a month, the same property had passed to fourteen persons who inherited it in succession.

POSITION and Plan *of* CYRENE. BY *Captn. F. W. Beechey* R.N.

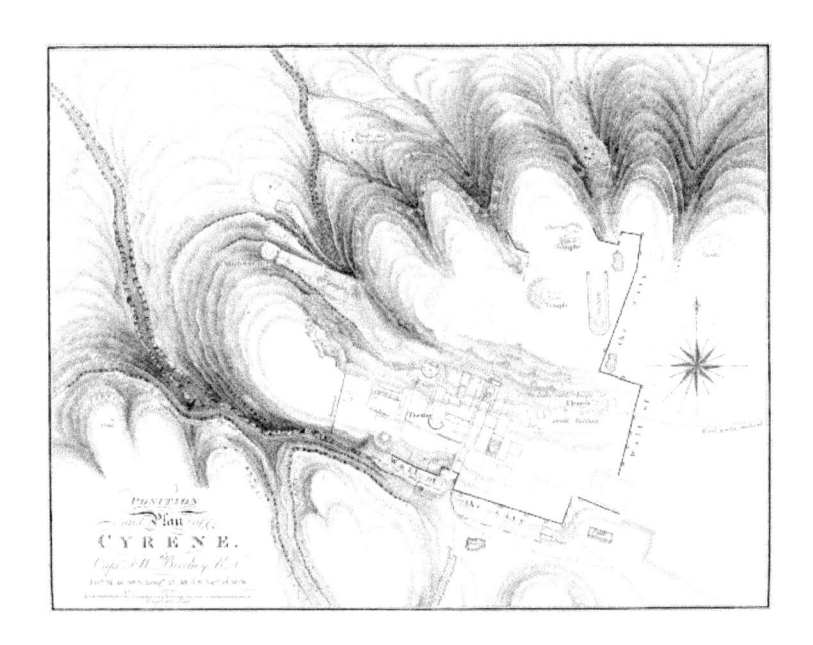

J. & C. Walker Sculp^t.

Published as the act directs, April 1827, by J. Murray, Albemarle S^t. London.

Plan *of the RUINS and ENVIRONS of* CYRENE. BY *Captn*. *F. W. Beechey R.N.*

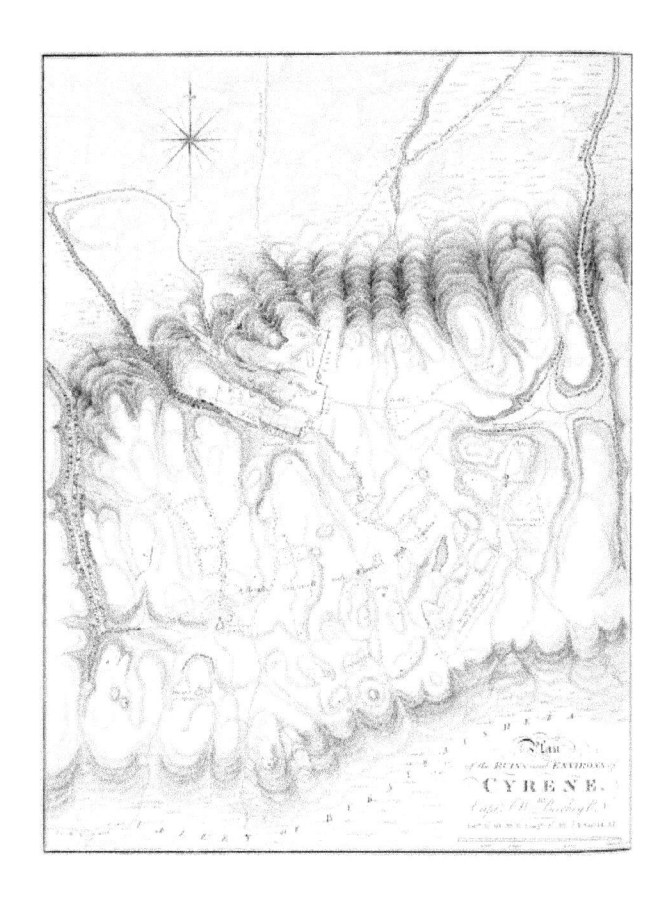

J. & C. Walker Sculp.^t.

Published as the act directs, April 1827, by J. Murray, Albemarle St London.

CHAPTER XV.

JOURNEY FROM MERGE TO CYRENE.

Departure from Merge — Deep Marks of Chariot-wheels on the Stony Road indicative of an ancient Track — Valley of Bogràta — Ancient Wells observed there — Valley of Hareebe — Beauty and Luxuriance of the Country continue — Roses of the Cyrenaica mentioned by Athenæus as celebrated for the excellence of their Perfume — Oil (or Ointment) of Roses made at Cyrene in the time of Berenice (probably the Daughter of Magas) — Difficulty and Danger of some Parts of the Road — Apprehensions of our Arab Conductors — They appear to have been groundless — Arrive at Margàd — Bad State of the Road continues — Quarrel between Abou-Bukra and one of our Servants — Consequences of the Quarrel — Departure of Abou-Bukra — Continue our Route alone and succeed in finding the right Track — Return of Abou-Bukra and his people — Satisfactory Termination of the Disturbance — Oppressive Sirocco Wind — Nature of the Country on approaching Cyrene — First Appearance of a Plant resembling the Daucus, or Wild Carrot — Resemblance of this Plant to the Silphium, as expressed on ancient Coins — Points in which it differs from it — Remarks on the Silphium as mentioned by ancient Writers — Testimony of Herodotus, Arrian, Theophrastus, Pliny, Athenæus — Bill of Fare of the Kings of Persia, stated by Polyænus to have been discovered in the royal Palace by Alexander the Great — Silphium mentioned in this among other articles of Food — Description of the Plant by Theophrastus and Pliny — Celebrity and Scarcity of the Silphium and of the Extract from it — Extraordinary Cause of the first Appearance of the Silphium in the Cyrenaica, as mentioned by Pliny on the authority of Greek Writers — Effects produced by the Plant on the Sheep and Cattle who were allowed to eat it — Similar Effects produced by the Plant observed by the Expedition on Camels — Extraordinary Medicinal Qualities imputed to the Silphium by Pliny — The use of it recommended by the Roman Naturalist as a sovereign remedy for almost everything but the Tooth-ache — Fatal Consequences recorded by Pliny, of applying it in the Case last mentioned — Silphium offered by the People of Cyrene to their first King Battus, as the most valuable Production of their Country — State in which the Plant observed by the Expedition most resembles the Silphium on the Coins of Cyrene — Partition of the Road from Merge to Cyrene — Extensive Traces of Building observed along the ancient, or lower Road — Approach to Cyrene indicated by innumerable Sarcophagi and Tombs — Position of these along the sides of the Roads, as observable at Pompeii and other ancient Towns — Frequent Traces of Chariot-wheels still observable along the Roads, deeply indented in the rocky Soil of the Place — The earlier Tombs distinguished by their simplicity and good taste — The later by a more ornamented and less perfect style — Busts and Statues scattered everywhere about among the Tombs — Difference of Style and Character observable in these — Remains of an Aqueduct — Fountain of Cyrene.

ON the morning of the 29th, we left the plain of Merge and proceeded on our journey to Cyrene. The road, after crossing the plain, leads over a rugged hill in which it has been cut; and we soon found from the deep and continued marks of chariot-wheels that we were following an ancient track. From the hill we descended into a beautiful valley named Bogràta where we found some ancient wells situated upon a rising ground in the centre of it, at which we watered our horses. From hence we proceeded through a hilly country, well clothed with trees of various kinds, and pitched our tents for the night at Hareebe, a delightful valley, studded with olive-trees, and possessing two wells of good water. The next day we passed through other remarkably fine vallies, which we found for the most part cultivated, and through copses and thickets of pine, cedar, laurel, laurestinus, carob, cypress, myrtle, box, arbutus, and various other trees and shrubs, which were flourishing in the greatest luxuriance. Among these the convolvulus and honeysuckle twined themselves; and red and white roses, marigolds, and other flowers, with a great variety of beautiful ferns, were everywhere scattered over the hills and vallies. The forms of the landscape were at the same time remarkably picturesque; and here and there a ruin of some ancient fortress, towering above the wood on the summit of a hill, contributed to give character to the scene.

Our attention was occasionally called away (in climbing up, or descending the steep and rocky sides of some of the hills over which we passed) by the difficulty and danger of the roads; and our horses were continually slipping on the hard glassy surface which they presented; notwithstanding we had used the precaution of taking off one of their shoes and the others were frequently dropping off of themselves, owing to the wearing away of the nails. As we passed some of the woods our guides begged we would keep together lest we should be fired at by some ill-disposed persons from among the bushes; but we soon found this caution to be perfectly unnecessary, and continued to stray away in all directions without experiencing the least molestation.

On the second night we pitched the tents at Margàd where we found a supply of water in an ancient cistern belonging to a fort on the hill close to it. Here were also several Arab tents, with flocks of sheep feeding about them. The Arabs received us very civilly, always offering milk and lèban, although our guides would have made us believe that they were greatly averse to our passing through their country. On quitting Margàd, we pursued our route through a country very similar to that of the preceding day; but along a much worse road, which obliged us to lead our horses nearly one half of the way. We had not gone far before a quarrel took place between Abou-Bukra and one of our servants, and the former, pretending to be seriously affronted, took the opportunity (never neglected by an Arab) of letting us know how necessary he was to us and declared he would stay no longer. He accordingly rode off, and all his people followed him, leaving the camels without any drivers, in expectation no doubt that we should immediately ride after them and entreat them to resume their occupations.

In this, however, we were determined not to gratify them, and took no other notice of their departure than by telling our servants to drive the camels on themselves, which they managed to do very well. The worst part of the story was our ignorance of the road, and we were greatly at a loss, among the many narrow pathways that led through the thickets, to determine on which we ought to take. Unluckily our chaous knew no more of this road than ourselves; but we took the direction which we imagined to be the right one, and contrived to get on with tolerable success.

Abou-Bukra had before been often trying to persuade us that the Arabs of the place were much averse to our passing through their territory, and expatiating on the value of his protection and influence; he probably imagined that we should be greatly alarmed at the idea of being left to ourselves in a hostile country; and he knew, at the same time, that we could not possibly be acquainted with a single step of the road. His disappointment must, therefore, have been very great, when he found that no one rode after him, or took any measures towards effecting a reconciliation. In the mean time we continued to get on very well, and were convinced that if we did so we should soon be rejoined by the deserters; accordingly, before the day was concluded the whole party returned, and of their own accord entered upon their several duties as before, just as if nothing had happened. This was precisely what we had expected, and we made no comments either upon their arrival or departure as if we had been indifferent to both. Abou-Bukra was now all civility, and his people drove the camels much better than ever they had done before! Towards the close of the day we arrived at some Arab tents, and pitched our own close to them for the night, in a valley for which we could obtain no name; but which, whatever might have been its title, was certainly a very delightful one. During the last two days a hot sirocco wind had been blowing, which rendered the travelling extremely oppressive, especially during the heat of the day; on the afternoon of the third day, however, it suddenly changed to the north-west and brought a smart shower of rain, which cooled the air a good deal, and was the first which we had had for some time.

The country from Margád to Grenna, the present Arab name for Cyrene, is of the same hilly nature as that already described; but on approaching Cyrene it becomes more clear of wood, the vallies produce fine crops of barley, and the hills excellent pasturage for cattle.

It may here be proper to mention that, on the day after our departure from Merge, we observed a plant about three feet in height very much resembling the hemlock, or, more properly speaking perhaps, the Daucas or wild carrot. We were told that it was usually fatal to the camels who ate of it, and that its juice if applied to the flesh, would fester any part where there was the slightest excoriation. This plant had much more resemblance to the silphium of ancient times (as it is expressed on the coins of Cyrene) than any which we had hitherto seen; although its stem is much more slender than that which is there represented, and the blossoms (for it has several) more open. In some parts of the route from Merge to Cyrene we lost sight of this plant altogether; while at others we found it in considerable quantities, growing chiefly wherever there was pasturage. Immediately about Cyrene we observed it in great abundance; and soon ceased, from its frequent occurrence, to pay any particular attention to it.

It is extremely probable that the plant here mentioned is the laserpitium or silphium in such repute among the ancients; and it may not here be amiss to collect a few of the remarks which have been made at various periods respecting it.

According to Herodotus the silphium originally extended from the island of Platea to the beginning of the Greater Syrtis, a space including the whole of the mountainous district of the Cyrenaica; and Scylax, after mentioning the islands Aedonia and Platæa, informs us that, beyond these (in passing from east to west) are the regions which produce the silphium. We may also infer from a passage in Arrian, that the silphium extended itself over the whole of the fertile part of the Cyrenaica to the confines of the desert which bounds it; since he tells us that the fertility of this country continued as far as the limits of the silphium itself, and that beyond these boundaries all was desert and sandy. Theophrastus also observes that the silphium was found in the Cyrenaica, and that the greater portion of it was produced from the country of the Hesperides in the parts about the Greater Syrtis. It appears to have sprung up in the grass, or pasture lands, as the plant we have mentioned above also does, and the sheep are reported to have been so fond of it that whenever they smelt it they would run to the place, and after eating the flower, would scratch up the root and devour it with the same avidity. On this account (says Arrian, who has recorded the fact just mentioned) some of the Cyreneans drive their sheep away from the parts in which the silphium is produced; and others surround their land with hedges, through which the sheep are not able to pass when they chance to approach near the plants. Silphium appears to have been found in many parts of Asia, as well as in some parts of Europe; but that of Cyrene was much the most esteemed and constituted a material part of the commerce of that country, as we find from various authorities. In the time of Pliny silphium (or laserpitium) had become so scarce in the market, that a single stalk of it was presented to the Emperor Nero as a present (no doubt) of extraordinary value; and Strabo tells us that the barbarous tribes who frequented the country about the Cyrenaica had nearly exterminated the plant altogether (in an irruption which they made on some hostile occasion) by pulling it designedly up by the roots; from which we may infer that the destruction of the silphium was considered as a material injury to Cyrene. We have already mentioned in our account of the Syrtis (on the authority of the same writer) that the silphium and the liquor which was extracted from it formed material articles of a contraband trade at Charax, where they were exchanged with the Carthaginians for wine. And we have ventured, on the same occasion, to differ in opinion with Dr. Della Cella as to the propriety of adopting the change in Strabo's text proposed by that gentleman (p. 79); as it sufficiently appears, from various authorities, that both the plant and the extract were articles of commerce, and not the extract only, as the Doctor has stated. This is evident from the remarks of ancient writers on the subject; and it is also certain that the liquor (or οπος του σιλφιου, in Latin termed Laser) was obtained from the stem as well as from the root, as Theophrastus, and Pliny (on his authority) have testified.

It is evident also from both these authors that the stem of the silphium was in request as an article of food, and was eaten in several ways. This appears equally in Athenæus; and we find both the extract, and the plant, very decidedly mentioned in the bill of fare of the Persian monarchs, as given by Polyænus (Stratagemata, Lib. iv.) and which was discovered by Alexander the Great, engraved on a brazen column in the royal palace. Here we see two pounds, and upwards, of the extract, or juice of the silphium, termed by Pliny Laser; and a talent weight (about sixty-five pounds) of the plant itself in the list. What the extract of the silphium was like we will not pretend to say; but the stem and the root appear to have been eaten much in the same way that we eat celery, (which indeed it very much resembles,) either stewed or boiled.

The silphium is described by Theophrastus as a plant with a large and thick root; and the stem, he tells us, resembled that of the ferula, and was of about the same thickness. The leaf which, he says, was termed maspetum (μασπετον), resembled that of parsley: the seed was broad and foliaceous:

the stem annual, like that of the ferula. Pliny's account is copied from that of Theophrastus; but he has given us at the same time whatever information he could collect of the silphium and its properties in the age in which he himself lived. He informs us that—the celebrated plant Laserpitium, which the Greeks call silphium, was found in the Cyrenaica; and that the juice, or liquor, extracted from it was termed Laser; a drug so famous for its medicinal qualities that it was sold by the denarius, seven of which, or eight drams, were equal to the English avoirdupois ounce, which was the same with the Roman.

For many years past (he continues) no silphium has been found in the Cyrenaica; the owners of the land having thought it more profitable to turn their sheep and cattle into the pasture lands (where the silphium, as we have before mentioned, is produced) than to preserve the plant as formerly. One only stem of it (it is Pliny who speaks) has been found in my recollection, which was sent to the Emperor Nero. And of late no other laser has been brought to us than that which grows extensively in Persia, Media, and Armenia, and which is very inferior to that of the Cyrenaica, being at the same time adulterated with gum, sagapeum, and pounded beans. We learn from the same author that in the consulships of C. Valerius, and M. Herennius, thirty lbs. of laserpitium was brought into Rome, which seems to have been considered as a very fortunate occurrence; and that Cæsar, when dictator, at the commencement of the civil war, took from the public treasury, with the gold and silver which he carried away from it, an hundred and eleven pounds of the silphium (or laserpitium); which proves how valuable the plant was at Rome, as, indeed, might be reasonably inferred from the circumstance of its being found in the treasury at all.

The first appearance of the silphium in the Cyrenaica is said by Pliny (on the authority of Greek writers) to have been occasioned by a sudden and heavy fall of rain, resembling *pitch*, which completely drenched the ground in the neighbourhood of the Hesperian Gardens and of the eastern confines of the Greater Syrtis. This miraculous shower is said to have occurred seven years before the building of the city of Cyrene; which was erected (says Pliny) in the year of Rome 143. He adds, also, on the authority of Theophrastus, (the author to whom he chiefly alludes in quoting Greek authorities above,) that the silphium extended itself over a space of four thousand stadia, and that its nature was wild and unadapted to cultivation, retiring towards the desert whenever it was too much attended to. We have already observed that great care was taken by the ancients to preserve the silphium from the sheep and cattle, the former of which were remarkably fond of it: when allowed to be eaten, it first acted medicinally upon the animals, and afterwards fattened them exceedingly; giving at the same time an excellent flavour to the flesh. Whenever they were ill, it either speedily restored them, or else destroyed them altogether; but the first of these effects was most usual. It is probable, however, that it only agreed with those animals which were accustomed to it; at least the plant now observable in the Cyrenaica, which answers to the description of the silphium, is very frequently productive of fatal effects to the animals (particularly the camels) who eat of it, not being accustomed to the soil. One of the reasons advanced by the son of Shekh Hadood, Abou-Buckra, for putting a high price upon his camels at Merge (on the occasion already before the reader) was that they were going into the country where the silphium was found, which, he said, was very dangerous for them to eat; and the camels which were sent to us from Bengazi, when we were about to leave Grenna, were kept muzzled during the whole time of their stay in those parts where the plant was known to be produced.

With regard to the effects of the silphium upon bipeds, (we mean those of the human race,) a few extracts from Pliny will fully suffice to convince us that it does not yield in omnipotence even to the famed balm of Gilead; or to that well known specific, and sovereign remedy for all complaints, distinguished by the humble title of Eau de Cologne. Certes, (observes this author, in concluding the remarks which we have quoted below upon the wonderful efficacy of his specific,) "if I should take in hand to particularize of the vertues that laser hath, being mingled with other matter in confections, I should never make an end;" and the reader will probably be somewhat of his opinion, before he has waded through half the wondrous qualities attributed to the omnipotent silphium. We give them in the good old English version of Holland.

We may add that the silphium was offered by the people of Cyrene to their first king, Battus, whom they deified, as the most valuable production of their country; and we have already observed that a representation of the plant is found on the reverse of their coins.

The resemblance of this representation to the plant which we found in the Cyrenaica is most conspicuous when the plant is young; and before the flower has quite opened, or the stem has attained its greatest height.

A little to the north-west of Margàd the road branches off in two directions towards Cyrene. The lower road, or that which is to the northward of the other, is the proper and ancient road; and traces of building are every where discernible in passing along this route, as we were able to ascertain in our return from Cyrene, which will hereafter be described. The southern road, however, is that which Abou-Bukra selected in escorting us from Merge to Grenna; and we afterwards learnt that he had done so in consequence of the feud which he had upon his hands, (already alluded to above,) which rendered it unsafe for him to travel along the road most usually frequented.

We had passed the remains of some strongly built forts in our route from Margàd to Cyrene, and after ascending the high ground to the northward of Wady Boōkasaisheēta we came in sight of the numerous, we might almost say innumerable, tombs which encumber the outskirts of the town. It is well known that the burial-places of the ancients were usually without the walls of their cities; and we find the tombs of Cyrene, (like those of Pompeii and other places,) ranged along the sides of the roads by which the town is approached, and occupying, at the same time, the greater part of the space intervening between one road and another. When we reflect that the inhabitants of this celebrated city have laid their mortal remains on the soil which surrounded it for more than twenty-four centuries, we shall not be surprised at the multitude of tombs which are everywhere scattered over its neighbourhood. They are all of stone, either constructed on the surface, or excavated in the rocky soil of the district; and as most of them have been defaced, or laid in ruins, (for there is not one of them which has not been opened,) the wreck of material with which the soil is encumbered may be more easily imagined than described. The road, when we had descended into the plain of Cyrene, continued to wind through the tombs and sarcophagi, and along the edges of the quarries in which the subterranean tombs have been excavated, for more than a mile and a half; we observed that it was occasionally cut through the rocky soil, and that marks of chariot wheels were still very evident in many parts of its stony surface.

These approaches to the town, for there are several of them, as will be seen by the plan, have the appearance of ruined and deserted streets; the tombs ranged on each side of them supplying the places of houses. The solemnity, we can scarcely say the gloom, of this effect is, however, enlivened by the variety of style which characterises the architecture, as well as by the difference in the plans and sizes of the tombs, and in the degrees of labour and finish bestowed upon them. The earlier tombs may be distinguished by their simplicity and good taste, the later by a more ornamented and a more vitiated style. A similar difference of style may be observed in the busts and statues, which are scattered about among the tombs; some of which have the Greek and some the Roman cast of countenance and costume, portrayed in the several manners peculiar to each nation, according to the age of the performance.

We were at first induced to stop at every object of importance which presented itself in our passage through these regions of the dead; but we soon found that such delays, however agreeable, would make it night before we reached the city itself if we continued to indulge in them as our inclination prompted; and we bade our conductor (the chaous from Bengazi) lead on to that part of it which he himself considered to be most worthy of particular attention. The taste of the African displayed itself on this occasion precisely in the manner which we had expected it would do; and after passing for some little distance along the edge of a ravine where we perceived the remains of an aqueduct, he descended by a gentle slope into a level spot of ground, overspread with remains of building, till we found ourselves at the foot of a perpendicular cliff and heard the grateful sound of running water. Nothing further was necessary to rouse the drooping energies of our horses, fatigued with the day's journey, and parched with thirst from the heat of the weather; they sprang forward instinctively, without the stimulus of whip or spur, and plunging up to their knees in the cool clear stream drank deep of the fountain of Cyrene.

We are by no means indifferent to the beauties of antiquity,—nay we often imagine ourselves to be among their most ardent admirers; but we confess, to our shame, that, on this occasion, we followed the example of the poor beasts who carried us, and, springing from our saddles, took a copious draught of the fountain before we turned to pay our homage to the shrine from which it flowed.

FOOTNOTES:

The flowers of the Cyrenaica are stated by Athenæus to have been famous for the odours which they emitted; and we learn from the same author that a most excellent oil, or ointment of roses, was made at Cyrene in the time of Berenice (the great Berenice, as the author here terms her, who was probably the daughter of Magas). Both Arsinoë and Berenice are said by Athenæus to have been great patronesses of fragrant oils and ointments at Alexandria; and we may believe with probability, that the Rigges and Gatties of Cyrene were equally encouraged by the royal protection. The roses which we saw had however no smell, (probably from want of attention,) although the woodbine and other plants were remarkably fragrant. Athenæus's words are: ηκμασε δε και τα εν Αλεξανδρεια, δια πλουτον, και δια την Αρσινοης και Βερενικης σπουδην, εγινετο δε και εν Κυρηνη ροδινον χρηστοτατον, καθ' ον χρονον εζη Βερενικη ἡ μεγαλη.— (Deipnosoph. Lib. xv. c. 12.)

Και το σιλφιον αρχεται απο τουτου (the harbours of Menelaus and Aziris), παρηκει δε απο Πλατεης νησου μεχρι του στοματος της Συρτεος το Σιλφιον.—(Melp. ρξθ).

Mr. Beloe is of opinion that Herodotus intended in this passage to point out the limits of a place or province called Silphium, so named originally without any reference to the plant; and in his remarks on another passage in the same book—εισι δε και γαλαι εν τω σιλφιω γινομεναι . . . (ρчβ .) he observes—"I cannot help thinking that the herb was named from the place and not the place from the herb." But the space here included by

Herodotus comprehends the whole of the Cyrenaica, and there is no mention on other occasions of this term as substituted either for Pentapolis or Cyrenaica, with which it would, however, be synonymous if the reading proposed were adopted. We will not venture to dispute a point of this nature with a writer of Mr. Beloe's talents and judgment; but there does not (on the whole) appear to be, in our estimation, any reason why το Σιλφιον, in the first passage quoted, should not be translated Silphium, (the plant;) or why the words τω σιλφιω in the one last mentioned should not be supposed to mean exclusively the place, or region, in which silphium is produced.

For a great many curious and valuable remarks on the silphium, in which the origin of the term is also alluded to, see the comments on Theophrastus by Johan. Bodæus at the end of the account of the plant.—(Theoph. περι Φυτων, Fol. Amst. 1644.)

Αλλ᾽ ἡ Κυρηνη γαρ της Λιβυης εν τοις ερημοτεροις πεπολισμενη, ποιωδης τε εστι και μαλθακη, και ευυδρος, και αλσεα και λειμωνες, και καρπων παντοιων και κτηνεων παμφορος, ες τε επι του σιλφιου τας εκφυσεις· υπερ δε το σιλφιον, τα ανω αυτης ερημα και ψαμμωδεα.—(Hist. Ind. cap. xliii.)

Τροπον δε πολην επεχει της Λιβυης. πλειω γαρ φησιν η τετρασχιλια σταδια. τα πλειονα δε γενεσθαι περι την Συρτιν απο των Ευεσπεριδων.—(Theophrast. περι Φυτων. L. iv. c. iii.)

The effects of eating silphium (according to Pliny) were manifested in sheep by their falling asleep, and in goats, by sneezing. Si quando incidit pecus in spem nascentis, hoc deprehenditur signo: ove, cum comederit, dormienti protinus, capra sternuenti.—(Lib. xix. c. iii).

Επι τωδε εν Κυρηνη ως μακροτατω απελαυνουσιν τας ποιμνας των χωριων, ινα και αυτοις το σιλφιον φυεται· οἱ δε και περιφρασσουσι τον χωρον του μηδ᾽ ει πελασιεν αυτα τα προβατα, δυνατα γενεσθαι εισω παρελθειν.—οτι πολλου αξιον (he adds) Κυρηναιοις το σιλφιον. (Exped. Alex. Lib. iii. c. xxix.)

Among others, see Strabo, Lib. xvii. and Pliny, Lib. xix. and xxii.

It appears, however, that the laser, or extract of the silphium, was not difficult to be met with in the reign of Severus, as we learn from Galen (de Temperant. L. iii. c. iii. simpl. Medic. Fac. L. viii. and de Antidot. L. ii. p. 440. Edit. Basil.) The plant, at the present day, is common in the high grounds about Cyrene, but we did not meet with it in the neighbourhood of Berenice and the Hesperian gardens, where it seems to have been formerly most abundant.

This was probably the φοινικιος οινος (or palm wine) of Athenæus, much esteemed by the ancients; or the vinum Byblinum another Carthaginian wine in great repute, and said to be at first taste more grateful than the Lesbian. Τον δ' απο φοινικης ιρας τον βυβλινον αινω (says Archestratus as quoted by Athenæus) . . . εαν γαρ εξαιφνης αυτου γευση, μη προσθεν εσθι θεις, ευωδης μεν σοι δοξει του Λεσβιου ειναι μαλλον.—Deipnosoph. Lib. i. c. 23. Palm wine was drunk at Susa and Babylon by the Kings of Persia, as we find from Polyænus, Stratagem. Lib. iv.

Among others Athenæus (in the words of Eubulus) as quoted in the Deipnosophista—(Lib. 1.) . . . καυλον εκ Καρχηδονος και σιλφιον. Here we see the stalk or stem decidedly mentioned with either the root or the extract of the silphium (more probably the former) as an article of export from Carthage; and procured (we may infer) by the Carthaginian traders from Charax, since they had no silphium in their own country. Again, Antiphanes (the ηδιστος Αντιφανης) as quoted by Athenæus; ος εν τω φιλοθηβαιω φησιν.—Λιβυς τε καυλος εξηργασμενος ακτισι θειαις σιλφιου παραστατει.—(Lib. xiv. c. iv).

Succus duobus modis capiebatur, e radice atque caule.—(Hist. Nat. L. xix).

Οπον δε διττον εχει (says Theophrastus) τον μεν επι του καυλου, τον δε απο της ριζης. διο καλουσι τον μεν καυλιαν, τον δε ριζιαν—(Lib. iv. περι Φυτων).

Post folia amissa (says Pliny) caule ipso et homines vescebantur, decocto, asso, elixoque:—Theophrastus' words are,—μετα δε ταυτα καυλον εσθιεσθαι παντα τροπον αγαθον, εφθον, οπτον.—(Lib. iv.)

Οπου σιλφιου δυο μναι . . . σιλφιου ταλαντον σταθμω.

If the king supped at Babylon, or at Susa, half the quantity of wine supplied for the meal was palm wine, the other half, the juice of the grape. οταν δε η εν Βαβυλωνι, η εν Σουσοις, τον μεν ημισεα εκ των φοινικων οινον παρεχει, τον δε ημισεα αμπελινον.—Polyæni Stratagem. Lib. iv. 32.)

Taking the mina at 1 lb. 1 oz., the talent (which was always sixty minæ) would give sixty-five pounds.

Among a great many other articles, consumed every day at the dinner and supper of the Persian kings, as enumerated in the list we have quoted, we find four hundred sheep, one hundred oxen, thirty horses, three hundred lambs, thirty stags, or gazelles, four hundred fatted geese, three hundred pigeons, and six hundred other birds of various kinds! So much solid food was not, however, cooked without a proportionate seasoning; and we find a talent weight (say sixty-five lbs.) of garlic among the numerous other condiments employed on these occasions.

The Macedonians in the suite of Alexander, while they expressed their astonishment at its profusion, applauded the magnificence of the royal table, and the good taste of the Persian monarchs. But the ardent son of Philip (though by no means a friend to abstinence) was prudent enough to discourage, on this occasion, the commendation of luxuries so superfluous and expensive, and ordered the column to be taken down, observing at the same time that so prodigious a meal was unnecessary; that such excess of indulgence and prodigality could scarcely fail to produce timidity and effeminacy; and that they who had dined or supped so enormously must necessarily afford an easy victory to their opponents.

Το δε σιλφιον εχει ριζαν μεν πολλην και παχειαν, τον δε καυλον ηλίκον ναρθηξ. σχεδον δε και τω παχει παραπλησιον. τον δε φυλλον, ὁ καλουσι μασπετον, ομοιον το σελινω. σπερμα δ' εχει πλατυ, φυλλωδης, οιον τον λεγομενον φυλλον.—(Lib. iv. c. iii.)

Ad pondus argenti denarii pensum.

Most probably the laser or extract, which was the most valuable; though Pliny's word is laserpitium.

The leaves of the plant, steeped in white wine, were, it seems, a most extraordinary specific; and "the root is singular" (it is Pliny who speaks) "for to cleare the windpipes, and to take away all the asperitie and roughness in these parts; and being applied in the form of a liniment it helpeth imposthumat inflamations proceeding from the ranknesse and ebullition of blood. A liniment thereof made with wine and oile is a most familiar and agreeable medecine for the black and blue marks remaining after stripes; but if the same with some adition of wax be reduced into a cerot it helpeth the kings evill. As for the liquor laser (continues our naturalist) issuing from Silphium, in that manner as I have shewed, it is holden for one of the most singular gifts that nature hath bestowed upon the world, and entereth into many excellent confections and compositions. Of itselfe alone, it reduceth those to their natural health who are starven and benumbed with extreme cold. Taken in drinke it allaieth the accidents and grief of the nerves. A great restorative it is with meat, and quickly setteth them on foot who have lien long and been brought low by sicknesse: for laser, if it be applied in due time, is as good as a potentiall cauterie to raise a blister: outwardly applied no man maketh doubt but it is of singular operation and worketh many effects. Taken in drinke it doth extinguish the venome left in the bodie, either by poisoned dart or serpents' sting: and if the wounds be annointed with the same dissolved in water it is the better; but particularly for the pricks of scorpions it would be applied with oile. Being laid too, with rue or honey, or by itselfe alone, (so that the place be annointed over it with some viscous gum to keepe it too, that it run not off,) it is excellent for the carbuncle and the biting of dogs. Being incorporate with sal-nitre and well wrought withall beforehand, and so applied, it taketh away the hard horns and dead corns arising in the feet, which commonly bee called in latin morticini. Tempered with wine, and saffron or pepper, if it be but with mice-dung and vinegre, it is a good incarnative in ulcers; and an excellent drawer to the outward parts for to fill up the skin and make a bodie fat. A good fomentation there is made of it and wine for to bath kibed heels; for which purpose it is boiled in oyle and so applyed."

"In like manner it serveth to soften hard callosities in any place whatsoever: and for the foresaid corns of the feet especially, if they be scraped and scarrified before, it is of great efficacee. Singular it is against unwholesome waters, pestilent tracts, and contagious aires; as in times suspected of infection. Soveraigne it is for the cough, the fall of the uvula, and an old jaundice or overflowing of the gall; for the dropsie also, and horsenesse of the throat; for presently it scowreth the pipes, cleareth the voice againe, and maketh it audible. If it be infused and dissolved in water and vinegre, and so applyed with a spunge, it assuageth the gout. Taken in a broth, or thin supping, it is good for the pleurisie, especially if the patient propose to drinke wine after it. Being covered all over with wax to the quantitie of one cich pease it is given very well in case of contractions and shrinking of sinews, and namely to such as carrie their heads backward perforce, by occasion of some crick or cramp. For the squinance it is good to gargarize therewith. Semblably it is given with leeks and vinegre to those that wheaze in their chest and be short-winded, and have an old cough sticking long by them: likewise with vinegre alone to such as have supped off and drunke quailed milke which is cluttered within their stomacke. Taken in wine it is singular for the faintings about the heart; as also for colliquations and such as are falne away and far gone in a consumption, and for those that be taken with the falling sicknesse: but in honied water it hath a speciall operation respective to the palsie, or resolution of the tongue. With sodden honey and laser together, there is made a liniment very propor to anoint the region of the hucklebone where the sciatica is seated; and the small of the backe to allay the paine of the loins. I would not give counselle (continues our author) as many writers doe prescribe) for to put it in the concavatie or hole of a decayed tooth, and so to stop up the place close with wax, for feare of that which might ensue thereupon: for I have seene the fearfull sequele of that experiment, in a man, who upon the taking of that medicene, threw himself headlong from an high loft and broke his necke; such intolerable pains he sustained of the toothach: and no marvelle; for doe but annoint the mussle, or nose of a bull therewith it will set him on a fire and make him horne mad: and being mingled with wine, if serpents (as they are most greedie of wine) chance to lap or licke thereof, it will cause them to burst. And therefore I would not advise any to be annointed with it and honey of Athens incorporat together; howsoever there bee physicians who set downe such a receit." (Nat. Hist. Book xxii. c. xxiii.)

Nam folia ad expurgandas vulvas pellendosque emortuos partus decoquuntur in vino albo odorato, ut bibatur mensura acetabuli a balineis.—Adde—Laser, e silphio profluens fæminis datur in vivo. Et lanis mollibus admovetur vulvæ ad menses ciendos.—(Hist. Nat. Lib. xxii. c. xxiii.)

Ciceris magnitudine cera circunlitum.

This plant, from its succulent nature, is very difficult to preserve; and we are sorry to say that the specimens which we had collected of it (together with many others of the Cyrenaic plants) got mouldy for want of more attention than we were able to bestow upon them. We understand, however, that Captain Smyth has succeeded in bringing over a specimen of the silphium in good condition, and that the plant is now growing in Devonshire and thriving remarkably well.

It was not, however, unfrequent to bury persons of more than ordinary worth and consideration within the walls; and the most frequented and conspicuous places were in such cases selected for the tombs, or monuments, which the gratitude of citizens reared in the midst of their families. The Lacedæmonians, whose laws and customs were usually in direct opposition to the other states of Greece, allowed the dead to be buried indiscriminately within the walls of their cities, as we are told by Plutarch in his life of Lycurgus.

The fountain of Cyrene was a consecrated stream, and the face of the rock from which it flows was originally adorned with a portico like that of a temple.

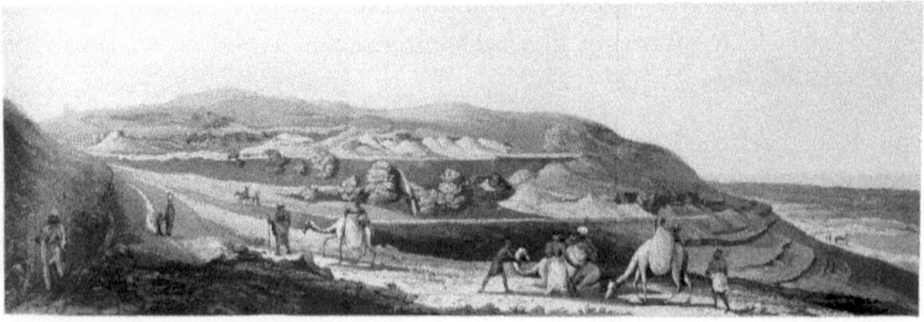

Engraved from a Drawing taken on the spot by H. Beechey. POSITION OF THE AMPHITHEATRE, THE FOUNTAIN OF APOLLO & SOME OTHER REMAINS WITHOUT THE TOWN OF CYRENE.
Published March 1827, by John Murray, London.

Drawn by H. Beechey. Engraved by E. Pinden.

ENTRANCE TO THE FOUNTAIN OF APOLLO. *Published March 1827, by John Murray, London.*

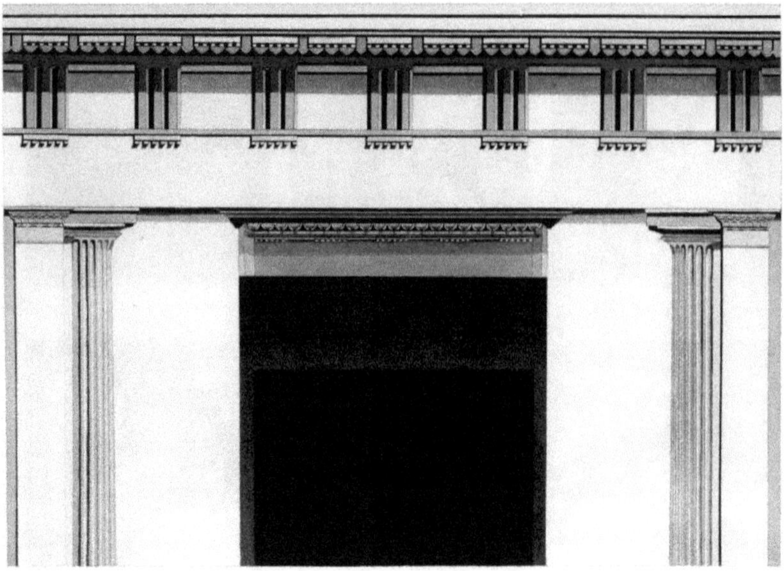

Engraved from a Drawing taken on the spot by H. Beechey.

ELEVATION OF THE INTERNAL FAÇADE OF AN EXCAVATED TOMB AT CYRENE.

SHEWING THE COLOURS AS THEY NOW EXIST.

Published March 1827, by John Murray, London.

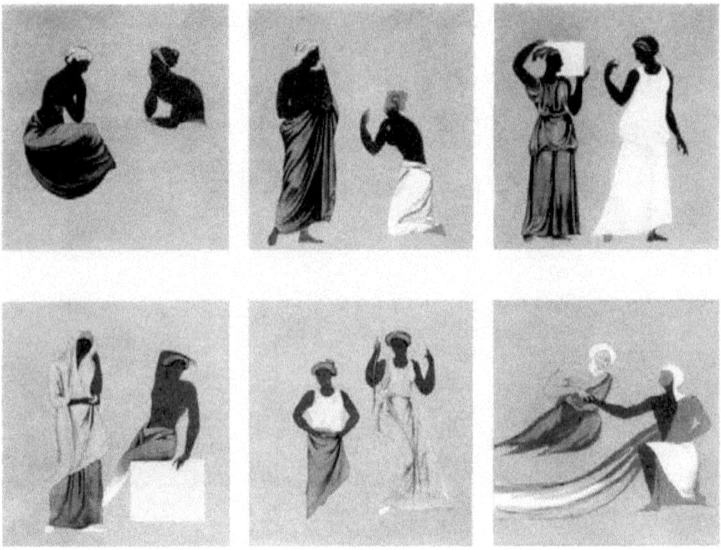

Engraved from a Drawing taken on the spot by Henry Beechey.

SUITE OF ALLEGORICAL FIGURES.

PAINTED ON THE MOTOSSES OF ONE OF THE EXCAVATED TOMBS AT CYRENE.

Published June 1827, by John Murray, London.

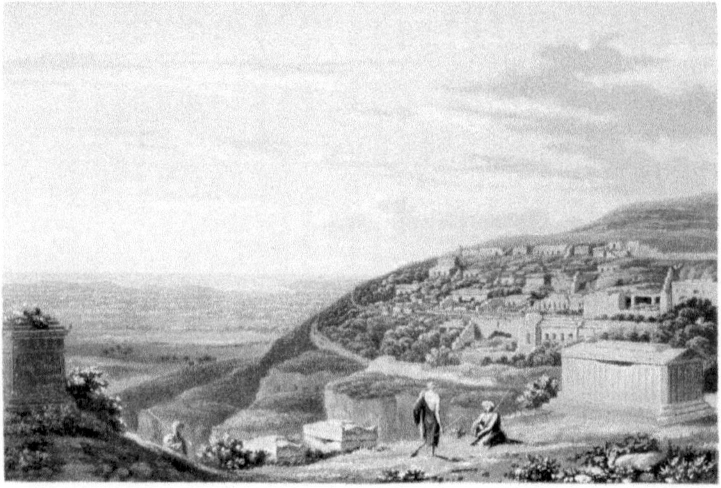

Engraved from a Drawing taken on the spot by H. Beechey.

PARTIAL VIEW OF THE TOMBS ON THE HEIGHTS OF CYRENE.

Published March 1827, by John Murray, London.

CHAPTER XVI.

Description of the Fountain — Excavations which enclose it — Sculptured Tablet discovered at the entrance of one of the Chambers — Early Character of its Style — Beautiful Bas-Relief in white Marble discovered near the Fountain — Indications of Porticoes in front of the excavated Chambers — Greek Inscription cut over one of them — Remains in front of the Fountain — Aqueduct above it — Peripteral Temple, probably of Diana — Female Statue discovered there — Position of Cyrene — Delightful View from the Town — Excavated Galleries and Tombs — Nature and Style of the Tombs — Variety displayed in the disposition of their Interiors — Remains of Painting discovered in them — Suite of what appear to be Allegorical Compositions, painted on the Metopes of one of the Doric Tombs — Practice, at Cyrene, of painting the several Members of Architecture — Remarks connected with this Practice.

IT is not often that an Arab takes an interest in his part when he finds himself called upon to support the character of a Cicerone; but Chaous Rabdi had no sooner quenched his own thirst, and allowed his tired horse to drink as much as he chose, than he was eager to point out to us such of the wonders as were congenial with his taste for antiquities. He entered upon his office by desiring us particularly to remark, that this water was not stagnant like that of the wells which we had seen in other parts of the country; but that it actually *ran*, exactly like a river, and afforded a copious and a constant supply, even in the driest seasons! The exultation with which our sturdy chaous pronounced the latter part of his harangue was fully equal to that which the most ardent of antiquaries might display in pointing out a valuable coin or gem in his collection, which he considered to be the only one of the kind ever found; and we were no doubt considered by our worthy conductor as little less than Goths or Vandals, when, after having given a short assent to the truth of this remark, we turned towards the mountain from which the water issued, and entering an excavated chamber which presented itself, began to examine its connexion with the stream.

We found that a channel had been cut from this apartment far into the bowels of the rock, (at the height of about five feet from the level of the chamber,) along which the water flowed rapidly from the interior, and precipitated itself in a little cascade into a basin, formed to receive it, on a level with the floor of the apartment: from hence it passed out into the open space in front of the mountain. The channel forms a passage of about four feet in height, and is about three feet in breadth; the sides and roof are flat, but the bed of the stream, which occupies the whole width of the passage, is worn into irregular forms by the strong and constant action of the water.

We inquired of the Chaous how far the channel continued to wind into the heart of the rock, and what it eventually led to; but he could only inform us that its length had never been ascertained, and that it was known to be the haunt of demons and fairies, as the Arabs of the place (he said) could testify! It would have been useless to assert our disbelief of this statement, that is, of the latter part of it; and having satisfied ourselves by examining this mysterious passage, as far as the day-light extended, and ascertaining that it continued still farther into the mountain, we determined to take an early opportunity of bringing lights and exploring it to the end, and proceeded to examine the other parts of the excavation. On one side of the cascade are two excavated chambers, or rather one chamber divided into two compartments; and in the farther division is a second basin, sunk below the level of the chamber, which appears to have originally communicated with the stream by means of a small aperture in the rock just above it; but no water at present finds its way through this opening, and the basin would be dry were it not for the rain which washes into it from without during the winter season. It is probable that this reservoir was originally devoted to the service of the priests who had the charge of the sacred stream, in the performance of their religious ceremonies. Nearly opposite to it is what appears to have been the principal entrance; and we found here a tablet, broken in two pieces, which seems to have fallen from over the doorway, and near it the fragment of a fluted, engaged column. On the tablet is sculptured three female figures, joining hands as if performing a sacred dance: the mode of executing the draperies in this bas-relief would seem to point it out as belonging to a very early period; and the difference of style between it and another bas-relief which we found near it, representing a female figure crowning a term, will be obvious on a reference to the plates of the two performances given. The last-mentioned tablet is of white marble, in excellent style, and finished with all the delicacy and taste of the most refined periods: the upper part of it appeared at first sight to be naked, but on a more attentive inspection it was found to be covered with what is evidently intended for a light, transparent, drapery, the few folds of which are very slightly, though very clearly defined, and result with great propriety as well as simplicity from the easy and graceful action of the figure. As the tablet has lain for ages with its face towards the ground, the polish still remains very conspicuously upon its surface; and contributes to give an additional air of finish to this tasteful and interesting performance.

The group we first mentioned is executed in sandstone; and it will be seen that the style of it, although characterised by archaism, is by no means deficient either in sentiment or taste, or distinguished by an ignorance of the rules of art. The faces in both of these tablets have been mutilated, and other parts of the compositions, as will be seen by the plates, are wanting.

In front of the fountain two porticoes appear to have been erected, if we judge from the channels which are cut in the surface of the rock, into which the pediments seem to have been inserted; and on a part of the cliff, at right angles with the face of the rock, is an inscription in Doric Greek recording the name of a priest who built one of the porticoes in question.

It is probable that the separation of a part of the cliff from the rest, in consequence of the foundation having given way, was the cause of the destruction of the portico of Dionysius, (the name which is mentioned in the inscription;) no other indications of which now remain except the marks we have alluded to in the surface of the rock. The front of the fountain is however much encumbered with soil, washed down by the winter rains from above; and parts of the portico may yet be found beneath it should this place be excavated at any future period: the chambers within are also much encumbered with the same material, washed in through the entrance where the tablet was discovered, and it is by no means improbable that interesting remains might be found underneath the soil which is collected there.

There is a good deal of building in front of the mountain (without the limits which we may suppose to have been occupied by the portico of Dionysius,) of which it seems difficult to establish the nature; if it be not in some way connected with the reception of the water, and its distribution over the town of Cyrene. It appears to us that the stream was originally confined, and raised by lateral compression to a height sufficient to allow of its being conducted into different parts of the town, the level of which is considerably above that of the fountain itself; but in what precise manner this object was accomplished we will not here venture to suggest. The remains of an aqueduct are still visible on the brow of the hill, from which the cliff descends perpendicularly to the fountain, leading from thence to the brink of a ravine on the opposite side, down which also flows another stream of excellent water. From the traces of building which we perceived about this ravine we should imagine that the aqueduct had been formerly thrown across it, and the water distributed over the cultivated grounds which lie without the walls of the city; at present the stream which flows down it, as well as that of the fountain already described, finds its way over the country below into the sea, and is no otherwise serviceable than as it affords an occasional draught to the Bedouins who frequent the neighbourhood during the summer, and to the cattle who drink with their masters. The excavated chambers of the fountain of Apollo are occupied at this season by flocks of sheep and goats, and the whole of the level space in front of the mountain is thickly covered at such times with these animals, as well as with numerous herds of cattle, attracted thither by the water which now strays over its surface. When we first arrived at Cyrene these intruders had not made their appearance; and we rambled about, to our great comfort and satisfaction, without meeting a single living creature besides those of our own party in the day time, and a few jackalls and hyænas in the morning and evening, which always ran off on our approach.

After satisfying our thirst, and, in some degree, our curiosity, at the fountain, we descended a few feet to some remains which we perceived on a level piece of ground below it; and found that they were those of a peripteral temple which, from the fragment of an inscription that we discovered among its ruins, mentioning the name of the Goddess, appears to have been dedicated to Diana.

Little more than the ground-plan of this temple is now remaining, and most of the columns are buried beneath the soil; we were able, however, to ascertain that the portico was hexastyle, and the columns about four feet and a half in diameter: those on the south side are so completely buried that no traces of them whatever are visible; but from those which are still in their places on the opposite side we were led to suppose that the number of columns was no more than ten, instead of eleven, which is the usual proportion in peripteral temples according to the rules laid down by Vitruvius. As the number of lateral intercolumniations would not, with this disposition, be double the number of those in the front, the whole length of the temple in question could not be equal to twice its breadth, which we accordingly find to be the case: and it is probable, therefore, that the ædes, or body of the temple, was built before the other parts of it, and that the columns and porticoes were added at a subsequent period, and the number of pillars regulated by the dimensions of what was already constructed. At the same time the width of the intercolumniations does not appear to have been greater than seven feet, which is scarcely more (as compared with the size of the shaft) than the shortest space allowed between columns in Greek and Roman architecture. There are no columns, at either end, between the antæ in this temple; and the walls of the ædes must have been continued from the angle till they reached the jambs of the doorways. If the statue of the deity looked towards the west (as recommended by Vitruvius, chap. v.) it must have been placed in the pronaos, and not in the cella, to have been seen through the doorway from without; for the wall which divides the cella from the pronaos continued too far across the interior to have allowed of any door in the centre of it, opening from one of these to the other, (as will appear by the plan;) and it would be absurd to look for a communication between them in any other part of the wall. Under this disposition, had the statue been in the cella, and its face turned towards the west, it must have looked against the wall in question; and could not have been seen at all from the western front of the temple. From the portions of Doric entablature which we perceived among the ruins of this temple, we may conjecture that it was of that order; but we could no where discover any parts of the capitals belonging to the columns, and the bases, if ever there were any, are buried under the soil which has accumulated about the building. It will be seen by the plate (page 430) that there is a building attached to this temple on the northward which has no connection with its original plan; and there are other remains of building beyond these, and to the westward of them, which will require excavation to determine their plans. We have already mentioned the fragment from which we have ventured to conjecture that the temple was dedicated to Diana; and we may add that a mutilated female figure (of which we have given a drawing, page 427) was also found close to its northern wall. The statue, it will be seen, is in a sitting position; and a part of the chair only was visible when we first discovered it among the heavy fragments of building with which it was encumbered, as well as with the soil which had accumulated about it. We succeeded, however, after some trouble in clearing it, and were rather disappointed at finding so little of it remaining. The girdle which encircles the waist of this figure has been executed with great care and precision; it is represented as closely tied, and the ends of it, which hang down in front, are finished with little tassels strongly relieved from the surface of the drapery; this object, in fact, seems to have been one of primary importance with the sculptor, and may have been intended (if we suppose it to have been the statue of Diana) to point out symbolically the peculiar characteristic of the goddess, her attachment to (or rather her profession of) perpetual celibacy.

It was between the remains of the temple of Diana and the fountain that we discovered the beautiful bas-relief of white marble which we have already mentioned above; and near it we found the torso of a male figure the size of life (also of white marble) executed in the best style of Grecian sculpture.

A little beyond this temple the level tract of ground stretching out from the base of the cliff from which the fountain issues is terminated by a strongly-built wall, the top of which is even with the surface; it has been built for the purpose of keeping up the soil, which would otherwise, from the abrupt descent of the ground, be washed down by the winter rains and the buildings upon it exposed to be undermined. This wall, which is a very conspicuous object from below, must have formed in its perfect state an admirable defence, as it would have effectually precluded the possibility of any approach to the place from the country beneath. Since the waters of the fountain have been left to their natural course the stream pours itself over the top of the wall in a pretty, romantic-looking cascade; the effect of which is heightened by the trees growing up against the barrier, amongst whose branches the water dashes in its passage to the plains below. A few paces beyond the first wall the ground again descends abruptly and is kept up by a similar structure; after which it continues to do so more rapidly, each descent being quickly succeeded by another, till they finish altogether at the foot of the mountain.

The position of Cyrene is, in fact, on the edge of a range of hills of about eight hundred feet in height, descending in galleries, one below another, till they are terminated by the level ground which forms the summit of a second range beneath it. At the foot of the upper range, on which the city was built, is a fine sweep of table-land most beautifully varied with wood, among which are scattered tracts of barley and corn, and meadows which are covered for a great part of the year with verdure. Ravines, whose sides are thickly covered with trees, intersect the country in various directions, and form the channels of the mountain-streams in their passage from the upper range to the sea. The varied tract of table-land of which we are speaking extends itself east and west as far as the eye can reach; and to the northward (after stretching about five miles in that direction) it descends abruptly to the sea. The lower chain, which runs all along the coast of the Cyrenaica, is here, as it is at Ptolemeta and other places, thickly covered with wood, and intersected, like the upper range, with wild and romantic ravines; which assume grander features as they approach the sea. The height of the lower chain may be estimated at a thousand feet, and Cyrene, as situated on the summit of the upper one, is elevated about eighteen hundred feet from the level of the sea, of which it commands an extensive view over the top of the range below it. For a day or two after our first arrival at Cyrene a thick haze had settled over the coast, and we were not aware that the sea was seen so plainly from the town as we afterwards found it to have been. When the mist cleared away the view was truly magnificent; and may be said to be one of those which remain impressed upon the mind, undiminished in interest by a comparison with others, and as strongly depicted there after a lapse of many years as if it were still before the eyes. We shall never forget the first effect of this scene (on approaching the edge of the height on which Cyrene is situated) when the fine sweep of land which lies stretched at the foot of the range burst suddenly upon us in all its varied forms and tints; and imagination painted the depth of the descent from the summit of the distant hills beneath us to the coast, terminated by the long uninterrupted line of blue, which was distinguished rising high in the misty horizon. If we knew in what the powers of description consisted we should be tempted to employ them on this occasion; and would endeavour to convey to the minds of our readers the same impressions of the beautiful position of Cyrene which the view of it suggested to ourselves. But one glance of the eye is, we fear, worth more, in calling up the feelings which are produced by fine scenery, than all that description is capable of effecting; and the impressions which time will never efface from our own minds would never (it is probable) be stamped, by words of ours, on the minds of those in whom we could wish to excite them. Under this conviction we will turn from the view before us, and proceed to describe a very remarkable peculiarity in the northern face of the heights of Cyrene. We have already stated that the side of the mountain descends abruptly, in this direction, to the plain below; not by a single, unbroken descent, but in ledges, or galleries, one above another, which terminate only in the plain itself. The Cyreneans have judiciously taken advantage of this formation, and shaped the ridges alluded to into practicable roads leading along the side of the mountain, which have originally communicated in some instances one with another by means of narrow flights of steps cut in the rock. The roads are to this day very plainly indented with the marks of chariot wheels deeply sunk in their smooth stony surface; and appear to have been the favourite drives of the inhabitants who enjoyed from them the delightful view which we have despaired of being able to place before our readers. The rock, in most instances, rises perpendicularly from one side of these aërial galleries, and is excavated into innumerable tombs, which have been formed with great labour and taste, and the greater number of them have been adorned with architectural façades built against the smooth side of the rock itself, contributing materially to increase the interest, and to add to the beauty of the drives. When the rock would serve for the porticoes in front of the tombs, without any addition of building, it was left in the forms required; and if only a part of it would serve, the remainder was added by the architect. This mode of proceeding added greatly to the strength of the work, and was probably attended, at the same time, with a saving of labour. The outer sides of the roads, where they descended from one range to another, were ornamented with sarcophagi and monumental tombs, and the whole sloping space between the galleries was completely filled up with similar structures. These, as well as the excavated tombs, exhibit very superior taste and execution; and the clusters of dark green furze and slender shrubs with which they are now partly overgrown, give an additional effect, by their contrast of forms and colour, to the multitude of white buildings which spring up from the midst of them. We have endeavoured in the drawing here annexed, to give some idea of this remarkable scene; but although we have copied it with fidelity, and with all the care which our time allowed, the effect of our view falls very far short of that which is produced by the scene itself.

On leaving the fountain and the temple of Diana we descended the side of the hill and took our course along the galleries we have mentioned, passing with some difficulty from one to another, through the thick furze with which the ground is overspread, and entering the most conspicuous of the excavated tombs which we passed in our route along the roads.

They usually consisted of a single chamber; at the end of which, opposite the doorway, was an elegant, highly finished façade, almost always of the Doric order, cut in the smooth surface of the rock itself with great regularity and beauty of execution. It generally represented a portico, and the number of columns by which it was supposed to be supported varied according to the length of the tomb. The spaces between the columns themselves also varied; the porticoes being sometimes monotriglyph, and sometimes ditriglyph, according to the fancy of the architect. Between the columns were the cellæ (if we may call them so) for the reception of the ashes or the bodies of the deceased, cut far into the rock, at right angles with the façade; and the height of these was necessarily regulated by that of the columns from the level of the chamber. As the spaces between the columns were wider, or otherwise, the width of the cellæ varied accordingly, there never being more than one of these recesses between any two of the columns. The cellæ had often separate façades on a smaller scale than the principal one, but always of the same order; and they were occasionally made to represent doorways: the entrance to them appears to have been originally closed with a tablet of stone on which there was probably some inscription recording the names of the persons within. In some instances part of such a tablet was left standing, but we never found one entire in any of the tombs, and very rarely saw fragments of them at all. As most of the chambers are, however, much encumbered with soil washed in by the rains through the doorway of the tomb, it is probable that some of these might be found entire on excavating either the chambers themselves, or the ground immediately about the entrance to them. The cellæ were sometimes sunk to a considerable depth below the levels of the chambers, and contained ranges of bodies or cineral urns placed one above another, each division being separated from that above and beneath it by a slab of stone, resting on a projecting moulding which was raised on two sides of the cella. There are also divisions, in many instances, in the length of the cellæ, some of them containing three and four places for bodies on the same level, but these are always ranged (to use a naval phrase) head and stern of each other; and we never saw an instance in which any two of them were parallel. In fact, the width of the cella, which, we have already stated, was regulated by the space between the columns, would have rendered such an arrangement impossible, since it was of the same breadth in all parts, whatever might be its extent in length and depth. For a more complete idea of these elegant mansions of the dead we refer our readers to the plates containing the ground-plans and elevations of such of them as we had time to secure on paper. It will be seen that the proportions of the several members of the entablature varied considerably in the few instances given; and indeed, we may say that there are scarcely two façades where the measurements exactly correspond.

There were, however, very few instances in which the established laws of proportion, so far as propriety and apparent security are concerned, were in any way materially violated, (at least, we may say, not in our opinion;) and the eye is seldom offended by an appearance either of weakness or clumsiness in the columns, or of heaviness or insignificance in their entablatures. There is at the same time a good deal of variety in the disposition of the interiors, and the workmanship is usually very good, and occasionally, indeed very frequently, admirable. In several of the excavated tombs we discovered remains of painting, representing historical, allegorical, and pastoral subjects, executed in the manner of those of Herculaneum and Pompeii, some of which were by no means inferior, when perfect, to the best compositions which have come down to us of those cities. In one of the chambers, which we shall hereafter describe, we found a suite of what appear to be allegorical subjects, executed with great freedom of pencil and still exhibiting uncommon richness of colour. The composition and design of these groups display at the same time great knowledge of the art, and do credit to the classic taste and good feeling of the painter. It appears extremely probable that all the excavated tombs were originally adorned with paintings in body colour representing either compositions of figures or of animals, or at any rate devices and patterns. We ascertained very clearly that the different members of the architecture have also in many instances been coloured; and these examples may be adduced in further confirmation of what has been inferred from the recent discoveries at Athens—that the Greeks (like the Egyptians) were in the habit of painting their buildings; thus destroying the simplicity and sullying the modest hue of their Parian and Pentelic marbles! We do not allude to the representation of figures or compositions, which might rather, perhaps, be considered ornamental than otherwise; but to the actual disfigurement of the several members of the architecture by covering them with strong and gaudy colours; a practice as revolting to good taste and propriety as that of dressing the Apollo (if we may suppose such profanation) in a gold-laced coat and waistcoat; or the Venus of Praxiteles in stiff stays and petticoats. We are sorry to observe that the practice we allude to does not appear to be the result of any occasional caprice or fancy, but of a generally established system; for the colours of the several parts do not seem to have materially varied in any two instances with which we are acquainted. The same colours are used for the same members of the architecture in so many of the tombs at Cyrene, that we can scarcely doubt that one particular colour was appropriated by general consent or practice to each of the several parts of the buildings. The triglyphs, for instance, with their capitals, were invariably painted blue in all the examples we know of where their colours are still remaining; and the regulæ and mutules, together with their guttæ, were always of the same colour, as was also the fillet which we have described as intervening between the capitals of the triglyphs and the cymatium below the corona. The soffit of the corona was also painted blue, in the parts which were occupied by the mutules; and the space between the latter, together with the scotia, were at the same time painted red: the sides of the mutules, and the upper part of the moulding which we have mentioned as running along the tops of the metopes, together with the tænia, or fillet, below the triglyphs, were equally of a red colour. Patterns were at the same time very frequently painted, chiefly in blue and red, on the cymatia of the entablature and of the plinths of the capitals; and this was equally the case when the patterns were cut as well as when they were put in in outline. The central annulet was usually painted blue and the upper and lower ones red; and when there were only two they were both painted red, which was sometimes the only colour employed when there were three. We could not ascertain what particular colour was used for the abacus and echinus, for we seldom found any traces of colour remaining either upon them or upon the shafts of the columns. In one or two instances, however, the abacus seems to have been red, and in one which we have given in plate (p. 452), it appears to have been something of a lilac colour. The colours of the metopes and architraves must also be left in uncertainty; and, indeed, it may perhaps be inferred from our never finding any positive colour remaining upon them, that the larger parts of the entablature were left plain, and that the smaller, or ornamental, parts only were painted. We are ourselves inclined to think that this was the case, as well with regard to the entablature as to the columns; for we should otherwise have found the parts in question occasionally painted, which we do not recollect to have decidedly seen.

It may here be remarked, with respect to what appears to have been the established colour of the triglyphs at Cyrene, that there is a singular correspondence between this practice of the Cyreneans and that which is attributed by Vitruvius to the artificers of early times when wood was used instead of stone in the construction of their buildings. For the parts which, in the wooden structures alluded to, corresponded to the triglyphs of later periods, are said by this author to have been covered with *blue wax*; and we have already stated that *blue* was the prevailing colour of the triglyphs in buildings of all classes at Cyrene. It would thus appear that the colours, like the forms, of buildings, were adopted in imitation of early custom; and this circumstance will alone sufficiently account for the uniformity, in point of colour, of one building with another; and may be considered as a reason why fancy or caprice were not allowed, in these instances, to have their usual weight among a people who were strenuously attached to the practices and customs of their ancestors. "In imitation of these early inventions, and of works executed in timber," (says Vitruvius, in the words of Mr. Wilkins, his English translator,) "the ancients, in constructing their edifices of stone or marble, adopted the forms which were there observed to exist. It was a general practice among the artificers of former times to lay beams transversely upon the walls; the intervals between them were then closed, and the whole surmounted with coronæ and fastigia of pleasing forms, executed in wood. The projecting parts were afterwards cut away, so that the ends of the beams and the walls were in the same plane; but the sections presenting a rude appearance, tablets, formed like the triglyphs of more modern buildings, and covered with *blue wax*, were affixed to them, by which expedient the ends, which before offended the eye, now produced a pleasing effect. Thus the ancient disposition of the beams supporting the roof is the original to which we may attribute the introduction of triglyphs into Doric buildings." (Wilkins's Vitruvius, vol. i. p. 63, 4.)

Whatever may be the truth of these remarks of Vitruvius respecting the origin of the triglyph, it is singular that there should be so decided a coincidence between the practice which he has mentioned and that of the Cyreneans; we have in consequence been induced to lay the passage just quoted before the reader, and to submit to those who are most competent to decide the question, how far this analogy may be the result of accident, or how far it may be safely considered as obtaining in compliance with ancient custom.

Among the tombs which have been excavated on the northern face of the heights of Cyrene there are several on a much larger scale than the rest; some of these appear to have been public vaults and contain a considerable number of cellæ; others seem to have been appropriated to single families, and in two instances we found large excavated tombs containing each a sarcophagus of white marble ornamented with figures and wreaths of flowers raised in relief on the exteriors. We suspect these to be Roman; but the workmanship of both is excellent and the polish still remains upon them in great perfection.

We have already mentioned a ravine to the westward of Cyrene, on the brink of which stands a portion of the aqueduct of which traces have been described as still remaining above the fountain.

This ravine, which forms the bed of a stream of excellent water, is highly picturesque and romantic; it deepens gradually in its course towards the sea, and is thickly overgrown with clusters of oleander and myrtle which are blooming in the greatest luxuriance amidst the rocks overhanging the stream. On the western side of the ravine we found that galleries had been formed, similar to those already described on the northern face of the rock of Cyrene, and that tombs had equally been excavated there to which the galleries in question conducted. The deep marks of chariot wheels along the galleries prove that these also had formerly been used as roads; and the romantic beauty of their situation, on the very brink of the steep descent to the bed of the torrent below, must have rendered them very delightful ones. There seems to have been originally a parapet wall along the dangerous parts of the road, (we mean those where the descent is very abrupt,) for there are considerable traces of one still extant about three feet from the ground: in some places, however, (where the road is not more than three feet in width, with the high, perpendicular rock on one side, and an abrupt descent to the torrent on the other,) there is no such defence now remaining; and the passage from one part of the gallery to the other is not here quite so safe for nervous people as it might be. The steep sides of the descent are thickly overgrown with the most beautiful flowering shrubs and creepers, and tall trees are growing in the wildest forms and positions above and below the roads. The Duke of Clarence (when the choice of his death was proposed to him) had a fancy to be drowned in a butt of malmsey; and we think, if we found ourselves in a similar dilemma, that we should pitch upon some part of this charming ravine, as the spot from which we could hurl ourselves through myrtles and oleanders into the pure stream which dashes below, with more pleasure than one could leap with from life into death in most other places that we know of. We must, however, confess that in passing along the dangerous parts of the galleries here alluded to, no such fancy ever entered our heads; and we took especial care, notwithstanding the beauty of the descent, to keep closer to the high rock on one side of the road than to the edge of the charming precipice on the other.

There is a good deal of building, of very excellent construction, about the stream which runs along the bottom of the ravine; and the water seems originally to have been inclosed, and covered in, and (we think) also raised to a considerable height above its bed, (as appears to have been the case in the fountain of Apollo,) to be distributed over the country in its neighbourhood. It is difficult to say in what precise manner this end may have been accomplished; and whether or not the water so raised was connected with the aqueduct which has already been mentioned as running down to this ravine from the edge of the cliff above the principal fountain; and which we have also stated appears to have crossed it, and to have been continued on the opposite side. As the supply from both fountains is plentiful and constant it would be well worth the labour and expense of preserving; and the level of both would render them comparatively useless to the town, as well as to the high ground about it, unless some means of raising the water were resorted to. They who had leisure to examine the remains of building connected with these two streams, attentively; and were able, at the same time, to bring to the search a sufficient knowledge of the principles of hydraulics and hydrostatics, would find the inquiry a very interesting one; for our own part we confess that, without enjoying either of these advantages, we were usually tempted to bestow a portion of our time, when passing along the ravine in question, in trying to collect from the existing remains how far they may have been conducive to the object we have attributed to them. At something less than a quarter of a mile from the commencement of this ravine, the stream which flows down it is joined by another, issuing out from the rock on its western side, and a basin has been formed in the rock itself for its reception. In front of this third fountain there are considerable traces of building, which are however so much buried by the accumulation of soil, and encumbered with shrubs and vegetation, that nothing satisfactory can be made out from them. The spot is now (like that in front of the fountain of Apollo) a favourite retreat for the sheep and cattle of the Bedouins who occasionally visit Cyrene; and our appearance often put them to a precipitate flight, and the old women and children, who usually tended them, to a good deal of trouble in collecting them together again. These annoyances (we must say, in justice to the sex) were borne for the most part very good-naturedly; and we usually joined them in pursuit of the family quadrupeds with every disposition to assist them to the utmost. Indeed the Arab women in general, of all ranks and ages, are remarkable for patience and good nature; and we have often seen both these qualities in our fair African friends, put to very severe trials without suffering any apparent diminution. Their greatest failings seem to be vanity and jealousy; and these are surely too natural and too inconsiderable to merit any serious reprehension, more especially in a barbarous nation. Curiosity is at the same time, with them, as it is said to be with the sex in general, a quality in very extensive circulation; and if we could have stopped to answer all the various odd questions which the good ladies of Cyrene proposed to us, we should have employed the whole day in replying to them. By the help of a few little trinkets, however, which we usually carried about with us, we contrived to put an end to the conversation, without any offence, whenever it began to exceed moderate limits; and continued our route under a shower of pious wishes that the blessing of God might attend us.

In passing along the galleries we have mentioned in this ravine, there are a great many excavated tombs, some of which are very beautifully finished, and one of them presents the only example which we remember to have met with at Cyrene of a mixture of two orders of architecture in the same part of a building—the portico in front of this tomb being supported by Ionic columns, surmounted with a Doric entablature. The whole portico is formed out of the rock itself, which has been left in the manner formerly alluded to, and advances a few feet before the wall of the chamber in which the door is excavated. The proportions are bad, and no part of the tomb has anything particular to recommend it to notice beyond the peculiarity we have stated it to possess; but as it is the only instance which we observed of the kind, we have thought it as well to advert to it. The tympanum is here placed immediately over the zophorus, without any cornice intervening, and the mutules are in consequence omitted. Like many other excavated tombs at Cyrene, the one now in question has no cellæ beyond the chamber; and the places for the bodies were sunk in the floor itself and covered with tablets of stone. In such cases we often see that two, or more, bodies have been ranged parallel with each other round the sides of the chamber, in the manner represented in the ground-plans (page 464), a circumstance which never occurs in the cellæ, as we have already stated above.

The galleries which are formed in one side of this ravine lead round the cliff into another valley, somewhat broader, in which are also several excavated tombs. In one of these, which has been furnished with a Doric portico, Mr. Campbell discovered the suite of beautiful little subjects which we have given with all the fidelity we could command in the plate (page 456). They are painted on the zophorus of an interior façade, of which we have given the elevation; and each composition occupies one of the metopes, the pannel of which appears to have been left plain in order to set off the colours of the figures. The outline of these highly finished little groups has been very carefully put in with red: the local colour of the flesh and draperies have then been filled in with body colour, and the lights touched on sharp, with a full and free pencil, which reminded us strongly of the beautiful execution of the paintings at Herculaneum and Pompeii. There is no other attempt at light and shadow in any of them but that of deepening the local colour of the drapery in two or three places, where the folds are intended to be more strongly marked than in others; the flesh being left (so far as can at present be ascertained) with no variation of the local colour produced either by light or shade. The colours employed are simply red, blue, and yellow; but whatever may be their nature they still are brilliant in the extreme, and appear to have stood remarkably well. There seem to have been two reds used in these pictures, (for so we may call the several groups in question,) one a transparent colour resembling madder lake, the other like that colour with a mixture of vermilion or of some other bright, opaque red. These colours appear so rich and brilliant, when sprinkled with water, that one would imagine they had been passed over gold leaf, or some similar substance, as we observe to have been the case in pictures of Giotto and Cimabue, as well as in the earlier works of the Venetian and other schools. We are not, however, of opinion that this practice was adopted in the paintings now before us, although the brilliancy of their colours would suggest the employment of some such expedient. The yellow appears equally to have been of two kinds; an orange colour was first used to fill in the outline, and the lights were touched on with a brighter yellow over it; the whole together presenting that golden, sunny hue, so delightful to the eye both in nature and art. The same process seems to have been adopted with respect to the blues; but the lights, in this instance, appear rather to have been made by a mixture of white with the local colour than by a second blue of a lighter shade.

It may be inferred from the copies which we have made of these designs, (which, although they are as good as we could make them, naturally fall very short of the perfection of the originals,) that the drawing of the figures is in excellent style, and the actions at once expressive, easy, and graceful; what we have most failed in is the expression of the countenances, which, though produced merely by a single outline, we were wholly unable to copy at all to our satisfaction. The characters and features are what are usually called Grecian, and remind us strongly, in the originals, of those of the figures represented on some of the most highly finished Greek (or in other words, Etruscan) vases. The draperies are well arranged, and executed with great taste and freedom; they appear, like the other parts of the compositions, to have been painted at once, without any alteration, and with the greatest facility imaginable. It will be observed that the turban has in several instances been adopted; and the shape of some of these is more oriental than any which we remember to have seen in Greek designs. It is singular also that all the figures appear to have been black, with the exception of that of the old man in the last group, which has certainly been red; yet there is nothing either Moorish or Ethiopian in the characters represented; which, from the outlines, we should suppose to be Grecian. We have no solution to offer for this apparent inconsistency; and will not venture to suggest what may have been the subjects of the several pieces. They appear to represent some connected story; yet the same persons are not certainly introduced in all, if indeed in any two of the compositions. In the first group two females, both of them young, appear engaged in some interesting conversation. The second may perhaps represent the same persons, but it is difficult to say whether the rod in the hand of the standing figure is raised for the purpose of chastisement, or whether it is intended to represent the performance of some magic ceremony. The finger which is raised towards the lips of this figure seems rather to be indicative of imposing silence than of conveying admonition; and the arm and hand of the person kneeling appear to be more expressive of veneration or submission, than of either alarm or supplication. There is a curious appearance on the head of this figure which somewhat resembles in form the twisted lock of the Egyptian Horus, but its colour is decidedly red, while that of the other parts of the head are uncertain. The lower part of this figure has been so much rubbed as to be nearly unintelligible, and the face has disappeared altogether. A similar accident has happened to one of the preceding figures, the lower part of which is not now distinguishable. In the third group we see a female figure with a helmet closely fitted to the shape of the head, bearing on her shoulder an ark, or canistrum; a second female, attired in white, is represented walking, and looking back towards the other, whom she is beckoning to advance. The folds of the white drapery have nearly disappeared, and little more is left of it than the outline. The helmet of the first-mentioned figure of this group is painted red, and the back part of it, with a portion of the arm, is rubbed out. The fourth design represents a young man asleep, and a matron apparently watching over him, who appears, from her countenance and action, as well as from the garment which is thrown over her head, to be labouring under some affliction. In the fifth we observe a female figure sitting, and apparently employed in spinning; by her side is a youth of ten or twelve years old, with a turban of a different form from those with which some of the other figures are furnished: this appears to be merely a family-party, and the careless and schoolboy-like action of the youth whose thumbs are stuck into the folds of his garment, is well expressive of youthful unconcern. The last group represents an old man in a reclining position, who appears to be welcoming or taking leave of his son, who is kneeling by the side of his couch: the complexion of the old man is decidedly red, but that of the youth is very uncertain, as this picture has suffered more than any of the rest. The head and trunk of the old man, so far as they remain, are designed in the best style of Grecian art, and, indeed, we may say of the groups in general that they exhibit a perfect knowledge of the figure, as well as great taste in the mode of displaying it; and we cannot but regret that the rude hands of barbarians, rather than those of time, have deprived us of any part of these beautiful compositions. Enough however remains to make them very interesting; and we present them to the public as examples of Grecian painting at Cyrene, with the impression that they will not be thought unworthy relics of the genius and talent of the colony.

The colours employed in the architecture of this tomb (so far as they at present remain) are faithfully given in the elevation of the interior façade, (page 452), and appear to have been confined to the entablature, and to the capitals and plinths of the columns and pilasters.

There is only one cella, in this instance, for the reception of the dead, and it appears to have been allotted to a single body only; but as the interior is much incumbered with soil washed in through the door-way from without, we could not say decidedly that there is no place for a second body beneath the upper one, without some previous excavation.

The cella is not placed opposite to the entrance of the tomb, as is usual in other examples, but on the right hand side of it in entering; and this arrangement has been made in conformity with the position of the rock in which it is excavated, and not from any caprice on the part of the architect. The date of this tomb would appear, from its architectural details, to be posterior to the time of the Ptolemies; but no degeneracy of style is observable in the paintings, which would not disgrace the best periods of Grecian art. We must at the same time recollect, that the architecture employed in the decoration of excavated tombs is not to be judged by so severe a standard as that which is applicable to the exteriors of *buildings*; the details in the first case are purely ornamental, and may be placed in the same scale with those of interiors, in which the fancy of the architect is always left more at liberty than it can be allowed to be in external decoration: and what would therefore be bad taste in one of these instances is not necessarily such in the other. Neither does it appear to have been the practice of the ancients to give an air of gloom or sadness to the abodes which they allotted to the service of the dead, and on which they have bestowed, at all periods, so much labour and expense. We find historic, allegorical, and pastoral subjects represented on such occasions in the gayest colours; as if it had been their wish to disarm death of its terrors, and to moderate the intensity of affliction by diverting the mind from the loss of the deceased to the honours which are paid to their memory. The shades of the departed were also supposed to take delight in the attention bestowed upon their mortal remains; and to wander with complacency over the gay and costly chambers which piety and affection had consecrated to their use. A departure from the established practice of the ancients in the exterior decorations of their temples and public buildings, ought not then perhaps to be received, in the instances mentioned, as a mark of vitiated taste, or of the recent date of the fabric in which such anomaly may be observed: and in applying this remark to the excavated tombs at Cyrene (scarcely any two of which are alike in their proportions) we have the more reason to regret the almost total absence of inscriptions, by which the dates of the several fabrics might be clearly ascertained. It is probable that many of these might be found on tablets, once let into, or placed over, some part of each tomb; and now buried beneath the soil and the wrecks of the exterior façades, which incumber the chambers and the approaches to them. In many instances busts have been placed over the pediments of the outer porticoes, and we often found fragments of statues in the chambers and cellæ within. So many of the tombs are however filled up to a considerable height above the level of their pavement with an accumulation of soil from without, that it is scarcely possible to say what they contain; while the entrances are usually incumbered with the fragments of the fallen porticoes which once formed the ornaments of the exteriors. On the day of our arrival at Cyrene we perceived the marble bust of a female figure, from which the head had been recently broken, lying in front of one of the excavated tombs; and on inquiring of some straggling Arabs, who had preceded us, what was become of the remainder, they at first pleaded ignorance on the point altogether; but on our proving to them, from the whiteness of the fractured parts, that we were certain the head must have been very lately broken off, they asked us what we would give them if they should find it. A bargain was now made that if the head were at all perfect, so as to be worth our taking it away, they should have a Spanish dollar for bringing it; but if we left it in their possession they were only to have the head for their pains. The words were no sooner uttered than one of the fellows scrambled into a tomb close at hand, and brought out with him the relic in question; which was, however, so much defaced by the process which had been employed in severing it from the body, as to be wholly unworthy of removal, and it was left by the side of the trunk with the full and free consent of both parties. We are sorry to say that the practice of breaking heads from the figures has been very general at Cyrene; and has been occasioned in many instances by the inability of the Arabs to carry off a whole statue to Bengazi or Tripoly (where they might have a chance of disposing of it to advantage) and their eagerness to secure the profits which might result to them from the transport and sale of a part of it. We took care to make it generally understood, after this discovery, that we would never purchase anything that had been recently mutilated; and that we should certainly complain to Bey Mahommed at Derna whenever we heard that any injury of the kind had been committed on his Highness's property.

If the excavated tombs of Cyrene have been pointed out as objects of no trivial interest, those, also, which have been *built* in every part of its neighbourhood are no less entitled to our attention and admiration. Several months might be employed in making drawings and plans of the most conspicuous of these elegant structures; and the few examples which our short stay allowed us to secure them (as given in the plate, page 464) will give but an imperfect idea of the variety observable in their forms and details. Many of these are built in imitation of temples, although there are scarcely two of them exactly alike; and their effect on the high ground on which they mostly stand, as seen from different parts of the city and suburbs, is more beautiful than we can pretend to describe. A judicious observer might select from these monuments, as well as from the excavated tombs above mentioned, examples of Grecian and Roman architecture through a long succession of interesting periods; and the progress of the art might thus be traced satisfactorily, from its early state among the first inhabitants of Cyrene, to its degeneracy and final decay under Roman colonists in the decline of the empire.

The larger tombs were usually divided in the centre by a wall along the whole length of the building (which is the case in one of those represented in the plate, p. 464), and several bodies were disposed one over the other in each of the compartments thus obtained. Every place containing a body was covered with a slab of marble or stone, in the manner of those described in the excavated tombs; and there were sometimes two of these places abreast of each other, and the same number at their head or feet, according to the size of the tomb. Innumerable busts and statues originally adorned the constructed tombs (as we have already observed to be the case in those which have been excavated in the mountain), and many of these are still seen half buried beneath heaps of rubbish and soil, at the foot of the buildings they once surmounted. Those entirely above ground we usually found broken in several pieces, or mutilated so as to be much disfigured; but we have not the least doubt that there are many of them still existing in a perfect state, within a few feet, and often a few inches, of the surface, which might easily be obtained by excavation.

Two Arabs of the place, who had one day observed us looking at some of the statues here alluded to, came the next morning to our tent, and gave us to understand that they knew of one, in a perfect condition, which they could point out to us for an adequate reward. We made the only bargain with them which it would have been safe to conclude, among so many mutilated pieces, lying round us in all directions, which was simply, that if it proved to be worth taking away we would give them a certain number of dollars for the information which they had afforded us. On our accompanying them to the place where the figure lay, they soon cleared the earth from a female statue, in very good style, and tolerable preservation, excepting that the surface of the face and upper part of the body had entirely lost its polish and become extremely rough. As the statue was of larger dimensions than life, and consequently very heavy, it would not, under these circumstances, have been worth our while to remove it from the place where it was; and we accordingly gave the Arabs a *bakhshees* for their trouble, and told them that we did not think it good enough to remove; but that if we should ultimately take it away we would give them the reward before specified. With this arrangement, however, (though a perfectly just one,) they proved to be so little satisfied, that on the following morning in passing by the place, we found that the statue had been placed upright, and pelted with stones for their own or their children's amusement. The lips were knocked off, and the face and body otherwise mutilated; though not to the degree which we expected when we first observed the figure placed up as a mark for every idle passenger to amuse himself with throwing at. We were not a little concerned to see the mischief which we ourselves (however innocently) had in fact been the cause of, and gave out that we intended to write to Mahommed Bey that he might discover and punish the delinquents! adding, that if any similar outrage should be practised in future, the severest retaliation might be expected.

After this we were careful, when we discovered a good statue, to bury it an inch or two in the soil which surrounded it, effacing at the same time all traces of our work; and never indulged ourselves in looking at any object of importance when we thought ourselves observed by the Arabs. For such is the inconsistency of Arab character, that the very same statue which they would walk over continually without ever honouring it with more than a glance en passant, would in all probability be broken in pieces the moment it became an object of particular notice. The style of architecture in which the monumental tombs have been constructed varies according to the dates of the building, and apparently, also, to the consequence of the persons interred in them; the order employed is almost always Doric, particularly in the earlier examples. It seems probable that the custom of burying the entire body obtained very generally in Cyrene and other cities of the Pentapolis; and this is one of the few instances in which we perceive any analogy between the customs of the Cyreneans and those of the Egyptians. It is certain, however, that the practice of burning the bodies, and of preserving the ashes in urns, prevailed also among the inhabitants of the Cyrenaica as it did in other Grecian states. At the present day there are no remains either of bodies or of cinereal urns in any of the tombs with which we are acquainted, one of them only excepted: in which a leg and foot, which appeared to have been rather dried than embalmed, was found in a very perfect state. There are places formed in the wall, at the extremity of one of the cellæ in an excavated tomb, for the reception, apparently, of cinereal urns, as will be seen in the elevation we have given of it; but this is the only example of the kind we have met with, and we are left to determine, in other cases, from the dimensions of the cellæ, whether they contained bodies or ashes. The reason of this is that (from whatever cause) all the tombs, whether excavated or constructed, have been opened and rifled of their contents; and we never saw a single instance in which this had not been the case. In the constructed tombs, when the cover was too heavy to remove without a great deal of labour, a hole was always found knocked in the side of the sarcophagus; and the tablets or slabs of stone or marble which closed the cellæ and the places for the bodies, in those which were excavated, were in no instance found in their places entire by any individual of our party. The tombs of persons of distinction, at Cyrene, appear to have been erected in conspicuous positions without any regard to order or arrangement; at the will, perhaps, of the deceased themselves, or of those at whose expense they were interred: but the sarcophagi of those of inferior consideration were ranged in line, whenever the ground would allow of it, so as to take up as little space as possible, and to present an appearance of regularity; the sizes of the latter very seldom varied materially, and their forms were usually alike. The arrangement of the sarcophagi was not always the same; but they were almost invariably placed at right angles, in the manner represented (page 464) in the ground-plan and elevation which we have given of them. The sarcophagus itself was generally composed of a single block of stone, hollowed out roughly for the reception of the body; and its cover consisted of another single stone shaped into the form represented in the plate, without any great attention to finish, but always with considerable regularity.

This form of sarcophagus was common among the ancients in other parts of the world, and continued in very general use to a late period of the Roman empire. In the plain below the city (to the northward) there is a considerable number of handsome tombs, both excavated and constructed (those of the latter sort naturally preponderating); and among these there must be many (we are sorry to say) which we never had an opportunity of examining: our route over this tract of country having chiefly been confined to the road from Cyrene to Apollonia (now Marsa Susa) its port; situated at the foot of the range of high land the summit of which forms the plain in question: and as the ground in this part is thickly wooded, and crossed by ravines in different directions, the buildings which might still exist upon it would not be seen by passengers unless they lay immediately in their track. There are also many to the southward of the town which we had no leisure to examine; our researches among the tombs having for the most part been limited to the more immediate neighbourhood of the city, where there is still a very ample field for inquiry, without trespassing on the ground we have just mentioned.

The summit of the mountain on which Cyrene is built has been cleared of the wood which no doubt once incumbered it, and we easily found a convenient place for our tents, which were pitched, on our arrival near the centre of the town. The whole of this tract, as far as the eye could reach, was thickly covered with the most luxuriant vegetation, to the height of four and five feet; and as the place had not been visited since the rainy season, we found none of the grass trodden down, and were obliged to commence the operation of levelling it before we could make ourselves comfortable in our abodes.

The heavy dews which fell immediately after the sun was down made our passage through this obstruction rather inconvenient from five or six in the evening till nearly mid-day, and there was no part of Cyrene which we could pass to between those hours without being completely wet through. In a few days, however, we had formed several footpaths to the principal points of attraction, and many of these led over fallen columns and statues which wholly escaped notice till our feet struck against them. Indeed so much was the whole town encumbered with vegetable matter that very few objects were presented to the eye when first we arrived at the place: and we almost despaired of finding any matter of interest unconnected with the fountain and the tombs. Every wetting that we got, however, added to our satisfaction, by augmenting the list of the remains; and we soon perceived that we had established ourselves in the neighbourhood of two theatres and of several other objects well worth attention. The road to the fountain was (it may be imagined) one of the first which was made; and the passage of our servants and horses along it, as they went to fetch water for the consumption of the party, soon rendered it the most practicable of any. It led also to the galleries which we have already mentioned along the northern face of the mountain; and became very shortly such a favourite path to every individual of our number, that each of us, in first coming out of the tent, turned as naturally into it as if there were no other. About midway between our tents and the fountain, the track which had been made through the high grass about us passed close along the scene of one of the theatres, the largest of the two just alluded to; but before we proceed to the description of this building, and of others which engrossed our attention at Cyrene, we shall turn from the subject and lay before our readers the contents of the following chapter.

FOOTNOTES:

ΛΙΓΔΙΟΝΥΣΙΟΣΣΩΤΑ ΙΕΡΕΙΤΕΥΩΝΤΑΝΚΡΑΝΑΝ ΕΓΞΣΚΕΥΑΣΕ

In speaking of the fountain to which the Libyans conducted the founders of Cyrene, Herodotus says, αγαγοντες δε σφεας επι κρηνην λεγομενην ειναι Απολλωνος, ειπαν—"Ανδρες Ελληνες, ενταυτα υμιν επιτηδεον οικεειν· ενταυτα γαρ ὁ ουρανος τετρηται."—(Melp. ϱνη▯).

And as the stream here alluded to is the principal fountain of the place we may suppose it with probability to have been that of Apollo.

There are, however, many exceptions to this rule, which does not appear to have been by any means generally adopted by the Greeks. The number of columns on the flanks of temples seem to have been usually (at the same time) *more* than double the number in front, and seldom *less* by more than one, the proportion given by Vitruvius.

The pycnostyle is the least intercolumniation allowed by Vitruvius, and is one diameter and a half of the column at the bottom of the shaft; but neither this proportion, nor that of the systyle, which is equal to two diameters of the column, are recommended by him for general adoption: since "the matrons (he adds) who go to their supplications, mutually supporting each other, cannot pass through the intercolumniations (those of the pycnostyle and systyle dimensions are intended) unless they separate and walk in ranks. The view of the entrance, and of the statues themselves, is also obstructed when the columns are placed so little apart; and the ambulatory, whose width is governed by the interval between the columns, is inconvenient from its being so narrow."—Wilkins's Vitruvius, vol. i. p. 11, 12.

"The temples of the gods ought to be so placed that the statue, which has its station in the cella, should, if there be nothing to interfere with such a disposition, face the west; in order that those who come to make oblations and offer sacrifices may face the east, when their view is directed towards the statue: and those who come to impose upon themselves the performance of vows, may have the temple and the east immediately before them. Thus the statues they regard will appear as if rising from the east and looking down upon the suppliants."—(Wilkins's Vitruvius, vol. i. p. 79.)

The most ancient position of temples appears to have been east and west, with the entrance, or frontispiece, towards the west; and the statue of the deity looking towards the same point; so that they who worshipped should have their faces turned towards the rising sun. The contrary aspect was, however, adopted at an early period, and appears to have been universal in later ages whenever local causes did not interfere with such an arrangement.

The closely-drawn girdle of the ladies of antiquity, like the snood of the Scottish maidens, was symbolical of an unmarried state; and to loosen it was part of the nuptial ceremony.

The height of the upper range from the level of the sea, as obtained by Captain Smyth from a sea base, was 1575 feet.—The dip of the visible sea horizon, repeatedly measured by us with a theodolite from the summit, was 42' 00", which, adding $\frac{1}{14}$ for terrestrial refraction, gives 2003 feet for the height—the mean of these, which we have adopted, is 1805 feet.

We may add, that the circumstance of being obliged to reduce our drawing (which is a large one) to the size of a quarto plate, has, at the same time, operated to its disadvantage, as might naturally indeed have been expected.

It must be recollected that these façades were merely representations of porticoes, and that the columns did not project farther from the surface than half their own diameter.

All the excavated tombs were not provided with antechambers, and the cellæ in such cases commenced from the surface of the external façade.

The metopes are often far from being square, and the mutules are placed at different distances from the triglyphs according to the fancy of the architect. The capital of the triglyphs is very rarely continued, in the same line, across the metopes; but is almost always deeper in the last-mentioned division, forming a moulding in the space between the triglyphs, which gives an air of finish to this part of the entablature. Above the capital of the triglyphs, between it and the cymatium below the corona, there is usually a band or fillet, of the same depth, for the most part, with the capital, and on the same plane with it; and the capital itself sometimes projects a little beyond the femora of the triglyph, and sometimes is on the same level with it. The cymatium below the corona is for the most part much deeper than the usual proportion of that member; which appears to have been done in order to show the ornament upon it, which would not otherwise, from the projection of the corona and the depth of the mutules, be conspicuous. The proportion of the corona itself also varies, and the scotia beneath it is sometimes introduced, and sometimes omitted altogether. Much difference exists in the depth of the cyma, as well as in that of its fastigium; and the lions' heads, which are often sculptured upon it, are sometimes introduced and sometimes omitted. Whenever these are placed, as they usually are, over the axes of the columns, an ornament representing the end of a tile is often found to accompany them, placed on the fastigium, exactly over the centre of the metopes. There is also a difference in the depth of the regulæ and mutules, as well as in the thickness and depth of the guttæ, the form of the latter being sometimes conical and sometimes cylindrical, and on some occasions almost square. The upper part of the two outer channels of the triglyphs are sometimes cut parallel with the line of the capital; but more frequently inclined a little downwards, so as to meet the bottom of the moulding above the metopes, which we have already stated is not often in a line with that of the capitals of the triglyphs. The depth of the tænia, also, and that of the epistylium (or architrave) varies in different instances; as well as the proportions of the columns themselves, and those of their abaci, or plinths: the latter are generally surmounted with an elegantly proportioned cymatium, which is itself almost always crowned with a fillet. We may add that the curve of the echinus also varies, but is usually of a light and elegant proportion; and the annulets sometimes follow the line of the curve, and sometimes range with that of the hypotrachelium: the number of these occasionally two, but more frequently three; and the upper and lower ones (in the last-mentioned instance) are frequently cut square, while the central one forms an angle, the apex of which projects beyond the two others. This, however, only occurs when the annulets range with the shafts of the columns, for when they range with the line of the echinus they are generally cut like the teeth of a saw, as the central one is in the instance just mentioned. We observed that for the most part when annulets were adopted there were no channels, or grooves, hollowed in the hypotrachelium, and this equally obtained whether the annulets followed the line of the echinus or that of the shaft. There was commonly a fillet dividing the channels, or fluting of the shaft, the proportion of which was not always the same, and we rarely saw any fluting where these were not adopted, and very seldom any columns where the shafts were left plain. The difficulty of preserving the edges of the fluting with nicety, and of keeping them from being chipped and broken, appears to have been the reason for adopting the fillet; for as the proportions of the façades, particularly those of the interior ones, were necessarily on a small scale, the edges of the fluting, where no fillet was used, must have been nearly as sharp as the edge of a sword, and consequently very liable to accident. We may add that the width of the fillet accommodated itself to the entasis of the shaft, and was continued round the upper part of the channels, so as to form the crown of the hypotrachelium, when no annulets were made use of; for in that case the channels finished in these, forming an elegant curve from the line of the column to the lowest of the annulets, which sometimes projected considerably from the upper part of the shaft. With regard to the disposition of the triglyphs with respect to the columns, we usually found them placed over the axes of the latter, with sometimes one, and sometimes two intervening, as we have already mentioned above; with the exception, however, of those at the extremities of the zophorus, which were sometimes placed in the angle, and sometimes a little removed from it, being in the latter case placed over the joint centre of the half column and pilaster which usually terminated the façade at both extremities. We must remark, with respect to the introduction of the pilaster conjointly with the columns at the angles, that the shafts and the capitals were not wholly relieved from the surface, although they were more so than half their diameter. It must be recollected at the same time that the whole façade was generally formed in the rock itself, and had consequently no weight to support, and no internal arrangements to which it was necessary that it should be accommodated. The placing of the triglyphs was therefore purely optional, and might be adapted to the taste or the fancy of the architect, who was thus enabled to follow his own ideas of proportion and arrangement, without reference to any standard but the eye.

In the tomb of Theron at Agrigentum we have a similar instance of a Doric entablature supported by Ionic columns.

An operation which is at present necessary, in order to make them bear out.

Each of these customs (as practised by the Greeks) had well-founded claims to great antiquity; for interment appears to have been in use in the time of Cecrops, and burning must at any rate be allowed to have been practised by the Grecians, as far back as the Trojan war, if we rely upon the testimony of Homer. The custom of burning was perhaps the most peculiar to the Greeks, of the two modes in question; for Lucian, in enumerating the various methods resorted to by different nations in the disposal of their dead, expressly assigns burning to the Greeks, and interment to the Persians—διελομενοι κατα εθνη τας ταφας, ὁ μεν Ἕλλην εκαυσεν, ὁ δε Περσης εθαψεν . . . (περι πενθους, § 21.) Some, however, considered the former as an inhuman custom, and philosophers were divided in their opinions on the subject: each sect esteeming that method the most reasonable by which bodies would, according to their tenets, be soonest reduced to their first principles.—See Potter's Archæologia, vol. ii. p. 207-8, &c.

Plan of DERNA, BY *Captn. F. W. Beechey R.N.*

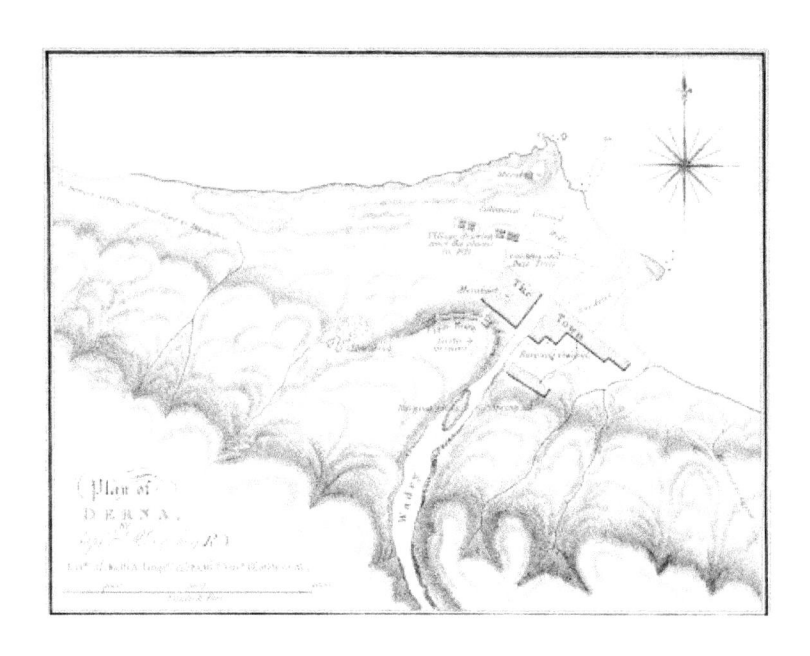

Plan of MERSA ZAFFRĀN, BY *Captn. F. W. Beechey* R.N.

J. & C. Walker　　　　　　　　Published as the act directs, April 1827, by J. Murray,
Sculp.̇　　　　　　　　　　　　　　　　　　　　　　Albemarle S.̇ London.

Plan *of the* PORT *and* RUINS *of* APOLLONIA, *now called* MERSA SUZA: BY *Capt*.ⁿ *F. W. Beechey* R.N.

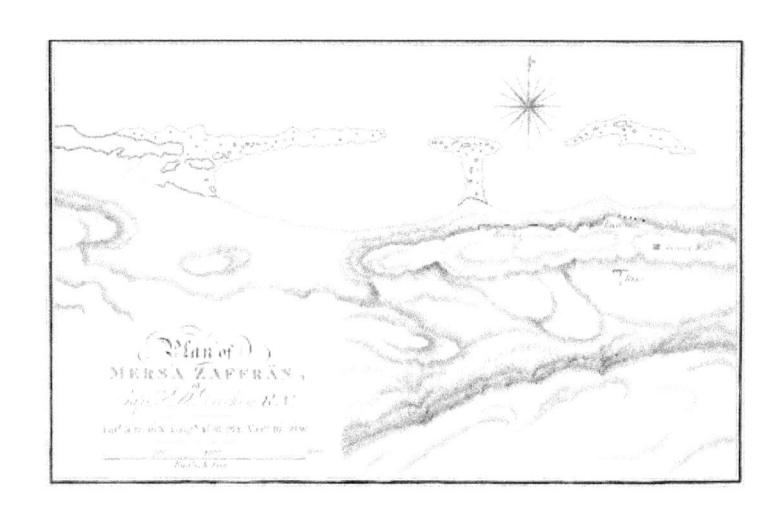

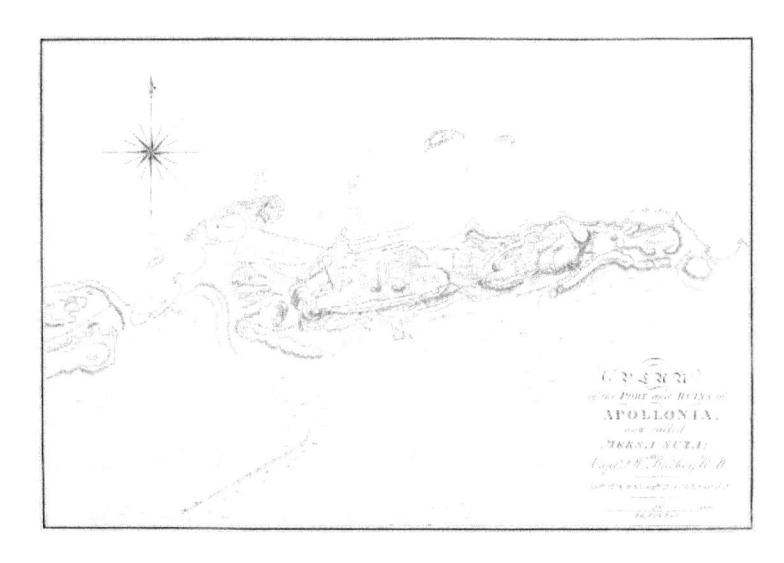

- 357 -

J. & C. Walker   Published as the act directs, April 1827, by J. Murray,
Sculp‸.   Albemarle S‸. London.

(Large-size)

Engraved from a Drawing taken on the spot by H. Beechey.

SINGULAR POSITION OF TWO INHABITED CAVES IN THE NEIGHBOURHOOD OF APOLLONIA.

Published March 1827, by John Murray, London.

CHAPTER XVII.

Arrival of Captain Smyth at Derna — Our Party set out from Cyrene to meet him — Remains of Ancient Forts, and Sarcophagi observed on the Journey — Marks of Chariot-wheels in the Stony Track indicative of an ancient Road — Barren Appearance of the Mountains which rise at the back of Derna — Perilous Descent from their Summit to the Plain below — Exhausted condition of our Horses in accomplishing it — Arrive at Derna, where we found the Adventure, and wait upon Captain Smyth — Description of the town of Derna — Ravages occasioned by the Plague there — Prompt Measures of Mahommed Bey in subduing it — Some Account of Mahommed Bey — Civility and attention received by our Party from Signor Regignani the British Agent at Derna — Take leave of Mr. Tindall, who sails on board the Adventure — Departure from Derna on our road to Apollonia — Gradual increase of Vegetation observed on the Route — Thickly-wooded Ravines and dangerous Passes on this Road — Beautiful Stream at Elthroon — Arrive at El Hilal — Capacious Harbour at that place — Ancient Remains observed there — Arab Encampment at El Hilal — Dishonest Conduct of our Chaous — Arrive at Apollonia — No Water to be found there — Begin to dig a Well in order to procure some, our stock being wholly exhausted — Bad Success of this attempt — Continue our Journey to Cyrene — Miss the Path over the Mountain, and lose our way among the thickets and underwood — Inconvenience of this mistake to all Parties — Find the right track, and at length reach the Fountain of Apollo — Rencontre of our Servants with some female Inhabitants of the Mountain — Singular position of the Caves which they lived in — Gain intelligence at Cyrene of a Spring in the neighbourhood of Apollonia — Set out again for that place — Description of the Road — Architectural Remains, and beautiful appearance of the Country through which it passes — Meet with an Hyæna in the dusk of the evening — The forest much infested by these animals and Jackalls — Peculiarities of both — Arrive at Apollonia, and find the Spring described to us — Other Caves in the Mountain — Unwillingness of their Inhabitants to admit us — Description of the City of Apollonia.

WE had been about three weeks at Cyrene, busily employed in walking over the ground, and in making plans and drawings of the remains of antiquity which it presented, when news was brought to us from the Vice-Consul at Derna that H. M. S. the Adventure had arrived there. As we particularly wished to communicate with Captain Smyth, we left Mr. Campbell in charge of the tents and set out on our journey to the eastward. We continued to descend for the first hour, taking the route of Safsaf, where there are extensive remains of building, and soon came to a stony, uninteresting country, partially cultivated, and much overrun with brushwood; at noon we had reached a place called Tereet where we perceived the remains of ancient forts and those of some tombs and sarcophagi. We found ourselves here in the neighbourhood of an Arab encampment, and continuing our route over a country that appeared to have been cleared for the purposes of building, arrived by two o'clock at Lamlada, another ancient station, occupied, like that already mentioned, by Arabs. The nature of the ground continued very much the same with that which we had already passed over, except that it was more hilly; and by five we had arrived at Goobba, where we found many remains of building and a welcome supply of fresh water from a spring. We observed that the tombs here had architectural fronts similar to those which we have spoken of at Cyrene. As the evening was fast closing in, we did not stop to give these much attention, but proceeded on to Beit Thiarma where we pitched our tent late at night. At this place there is a spring of fresh water, built round, and upon a hill close to it the remains of an ancient fort. We had reason to conjecture from the frequent remains of building which we had met with in our journey to this place, as well as from the occasional marks of chariot-wheels impressed in the rocky soil we had passed over, that the road which we had taken was the same with that formerly used in travelling from Cyrene to Darnis now Derna.

The next morning we continued our course east-south-east, and began to ascend by a very bad, stony pathway, which took us four hours to surmount, winding all the time through olive and fir trees thickly planted in every direction. About noon we reached the brow of the range which separated us from the town of Derna, and here began the most difficult part of our journey, the descent into the plain below. The face of the mountain is devoid of vegetation, occasionally polished like glass; and its inclination approaches in many places far too closely to the perpendicular to render it safe as a road. Indeed it is in so many parts scarcely practicable, that we could not help wondering, when we arrived at its foot, how we had contrived in any way to descend it without breaking our own and our horses' necks in the attempt.

There was neither road nor pathway to be found, and we were obliged to scramble down in the best way we could, sometimes stumbling over rugged and encumbered parts of the mountain, and slipping along at others over a hard, polished surface, which was still more difficult to pass than they were. When we arrived at a descent more than usually perpendicular, we had the greatest difficulty, after sliding down ourselves, to make our poor horses follow us; and it was truly distressing, as well as provoking, to see these fine animals reduced to a condition in which they did not appear to have the power of exerting the slightest portion of their natural energy. Their eyes appeared starting from their heads, and their nostrils were distended to the utmost extent; a mass of white foam was collected round their mouths, mixed with blood which the sharp Mamaluke bit had drawn forth in our endeavours to keep them from falling down the cliff, and the perspiration which terror and fatigue (without mentioning the heat of the sun) had drawn forth, literally ran down in streams from their bodies. They became at length so helpless and so completely overcome, that we doubted whether we should ever get them down the cliff at all, and indeed our own fatigue and continued anxiety would not have rendered us very effective conductors if the descent had lasted much longer. Yet our horses had been accustomed to roads of every description, or rather to countries with no roads at all, and had often laboured through deep and heavy sands, and over rugged and mountainous passes, in the course of their journey from Tripoly. They had also an advantage in having only three shoes, which prevented them from slipping about so much as they would otherwise have done; and in short they went through this arduous part of their journey much better than most horses would have done, and much better perhaps than we had any reason to expect from the nature of the pass which they descended. It will scarcely be necessary to add that on reaching the bottom of the precipice (for so we must call it) we stopped to recruit the exhausted strength of all parties before we set out for the town: our horses had had several very heavy falls, but fortunately experienced no material injury; and after leading them on till they were sufficiently recovered, we were able to mount them again and continue our route along the sea-side to Derna, where we arrived in the evening and found the Adventure at anchor in the roadstead. We lost no time in waiting upon Captain Smyth, who informed us that he had succeeded in completing the coast line between Derna and Alexandria.

The town of Derna is situated at the mouth of a large ravine, and is built on a low point of land running out from the foot of a range of barren mountains distant about a mile from the coast. It is supposed to be built on the site of the ancient Darnis, but there are scarcely any remains of building at the present day which have claims to particular notice. It is amply provided with water (the first requisite for a town in hot climates), and well situated at the entrance of a large ravine, or fiumara, along which a part of it is built.

The houses are much better than those at Bengazi and are surrounded by gardens producing abundance of grapes, melons, figs, bananas, oranges, greengages, and other fruit; they have also the advantage of being well sheltered by thick groves of date-trees, which give a very pleasing appearance to the town, and contribute materially to the comfort of the inhabitants by forming a perpetual shade. A delightful stream of water gushes out from the rock above the town, passing through several streets in its course, and irrigating the gardens, and even the corn-fields in its neighbourhood. In short the actual resources of Derna give it a very decided advantage (in point of comfort) over every other town in the Bashaw's dominions. A very pleasant wine (we were told) is made from the grapes of this place, all of which is consumed by the natives themselves, in spite of the prophet's injunctions.

The ravine at the mouth of which the town is situated is of considerable depth and extent, winding up far into the mountains; some of the gardens are formed upon its sides, and about them a few trees occasionally appear, where the soil has been able to lodge. In the rainy season a considerable body of water rushes down from the mountains to the sea, and is sometimes so deep and so rapid as to become wholly impassable: at such times it separates one half the town from the other and occasions a consequent inconvenience. In the summer, however, it is dry, and the market is held upon its shining bed.

It may readily be imagined that natives of Africa complain little of any inconvenience which fresh water may chance to occasion them; and we doubt even whether the inhabitants of Derna would not rather run the risk of losing a part of their town every winter, than be deprived of the pleasure of seeing and admiring so large a portion of this valuable fluid, and of enjoying the consciousness that, at least once a year, they have more of it than they know what to do with.

The water which flows from the spring we have mentioned above was conveyed through the streets (as the people informed us) by one of their former Beys, a native of Egypt, who is said to have expended a considerable sum of money in beautifying and improving the place, and to have erected a large and handsome mosque which stands in the centre of the town.

The streets of Derna are for the most part narrow and irregular, and not without that quantity of rubbish and dirt which may be supposed indispensable to Arab towns and tastes; but the luxuriance of its gardens and groves are however quite sufficient to balance these objections; and the abundance of grapes which overhang the walls and houses, the terraces, covered walks, and every part of the town, give it a highly pleasing and picturesque appearance.

On the eastern bank of the ravine is the principal burying-ground of the place, distinguished in particular by a lofty and handsome tomb raised on four arches, under which the body is placed, with its usual simple covering of snow-white cement, and the stone carved turban at its head. The town is undefended both by sea and land, and may at any time be destroyed by no greater force than could be brought to bear against it by a brig of war. Upon a hill at the back of it are the remains of a castle built some years ago by the Americans; but the guns are now thrown down, and the castle itself is little more than a mere heap of ruins. As this is a conspicuous object in sailing along the coast, the observations for latitude and longitude were reduced to it. Some large building-stones and fragments of columns bedded in the walls of the Arab houses are all that we could perceive of ancient remains in Derna. Above the town there are a few tombs extant, but in a very mutilated state, excavated in the side of the mountain. What is called the port affords some protection for small vessels with the wind from north-west to south-east; but even these cannot remain with a northerly or north-east wind: during the fine weather, however, some few anchor in it and load with corn, wool, and manteca, the produce of the inland country.

The plague has made dreadful ravages at Derna, as is evident by the number of deserted houses on its outskirts. The year previous to our arrival it was brought (we were told) from Alexandria, and the mortality which it occasioned was very considerable: the prompt measures of the Bey, however, subdued it, who ordered the clothes of all persons attacked with it to be burnt, their houses to be properly ventilated, and the streets to be cleared of everything that was likely to communicate the infection. These exertions were probably assisted by the general healthiness of the place, and the constant change of atmosphere produced by the passage of water through the town: the only remedy we heard of for the disease was the favourite application of a hot iron to the tumours, which we understood to have been peculiarly successful in many cases.

Derna is the residence of Bey Mahommed, eldest son to the Bashaw of Tripoly, who commands the whole district extending from the frontiers of Egypt (the eastern part of Bomba) to Sidi Aráfi, one short day west from Grenna. Mahommed Bey is well known for his active and turbulent spirit, and for his rebellion against the Bashaw's authority, which once obliged him to seek refuge in Egypt. His bold and enterprising measures succeeded in quelling the marauding tribes of Arabs who infested the country and levied contributions on the peaceful inhabitants of the towns; but his courage and conduct were sullied by cruelties which we do not feel inclined to justify from their necessity, however well we might probably succeed in attempting to do so before an Arab or Turkish tribunal. Indeed so many acts of cruelty and extravagance are related of this prince, that we should scarcely know how to reconcile them with the noble qualities which many allow him to possess, if we did not know from experience that such inconsistencies are common in barbarous countries; and that it is possible for the same man to be cruel and forgiving, avaricious to extortion, and liberal to profusion, generous and mean, open and intriguing, sincere and deceitful, temperate and dissipated, in short anything but cowardly and brave.

We resided while at Derna in the house of the British agent (Signor Regignani) appointed by the Consul at Tripoly, from whom letters had been forwarded, which arrived before us, with orders for our proper accommodation. The Bashaw had also written to his son, Bey Mahommed, to afford us his assistance and protection, and although the Bey was absent, collecting the tribute, during the time of our stay at Derna we had no reason to complain of any want of attention to the applications which we occasionally made to him. From Signor Regignani we invariably received the greatest attention and kindness, and although his influence in Derna was certainly very limited, and he himself often exposed to unavoidable insult, drawn upon him in a great measure by his religious persuasion, yet there was nothing which he had it in his power to command, that he did not very freely afford us.

At Derna we took leave of one of our companions (Mr. Tindall, a young officer attached to the Adventure), who had accompanied the Expedition from Tripoly.

The field of our operations, on arriving at Cyrene, was limited to a comparatively small tract of country, and we were enabled in consequence to dispense with this gentlemen's services, which we knew would be useful on board. We were sorry to part with Mr. Tindall, who had materially assisted us in our operations, and whose frank and spirited character, and joyous disposition, had so often enlivened the frugal board of our little party. We took our leave at the same time of Captain Smyth and the officers of the Adventure, from whom we had received many friendly attentions, which we often look back upon with pleasure. Our arrangements completed, the Adventure sailed from Derna, and as soon as we had finished plans and drawings of the town, we set out on our return to the tents.

We left Derna on the second of June, and pursued our course along the beach towards Apollonia, with the intention of returning to Cyrene by that route. After travelling along a stony flat running out from the base of the mountain, we reached El Hyera, where there is a well of fresh water within a few feet of the sea, and the remains of a fort upon a small eminence a little above it: at night we stopped at Bujebàra, close to the cape of the same name, with which Derna forms a large bay; and which has three rocky islets lying off it. The mountains, which extend in a range along the coast, at a distance of from a mile to a mile and a half, are continually broken by deep ravines which cross the beach in their passage to the sea, and make the road in some places nearly impassable.

It was curious to observe the gradual increase of vegetation in passing from Derna to Apollonia by this route: the mountains at the former place, as we have already mentioned, are perfectly destitute of any; in advancing, a little underwood is here and there seen, and a few bushes sparingly dotted about the plain; these increase by degrees, as the country becomes bolder, and gradually spread themselves over the sides of the hills, ascending higher and higher every mile, till, in approaching El Hyera, one continued wood reaches down from the top of the mountains to the sea. On the third, we pursued our journey along the coast by a very indifferent road, and at two miles' distance from Bujebàra the range comes down close to the sea and terminates in perpendicular cliffs, along the edge of which we were obliged to pass to the great risk of our horses and camels. At the foot of these, which is washed by the sea, we noticed a small rocky point with a quarry upon it, extending itself in a semicircular form so as to afford some protection for boats which might also be hauled upon the sandy beach within it. Eight miles to the westward of Bujebàra we came to a deep ravine, through which ran the largest body of water which we had seen in Africa; it is called Wady Elthroon. The sides of this ravine, which proceeded from an immense fissure between the mountains, were thickly clothed with pine, cypress and olive-trees, and the river, which ran with some rapidity, was studded with small islands covered with oleanders, which we found in full bloom as we passed. Along the brink of the stream was spread a beautiful turf, which opened in little plots, broader or narrower, according to the nature of the ground, on which we threw ourselves down to take a few minutes rest and enjoy a long draught of the clear cool water and a short dream of Arcadian felicity. In truth, the spot was delightful—we scarcely recollect to have seen a more pleasing one anywhere—and to meet with such a scene in an African climate was to render the view doubly grateful.

Ascending the opposite side of the ravine, we entered a country fertile in corn and which seemed to be very well peopled; here we found some ruins very much decayed and mutilated, apparently those of an ancient town of small dimensions, which, as its situation will be found to correspond, we will venture to suggest as the Erythron of Ptolemy; and indeed the similarity of the names would naturally lead to this conclusion.

On leaving Elthroon the road took a westerly direction, at the foot of the range, through a country well cultivated in some parts and in others overrun with pine-trees. At every mile we were interrupted by a provoking ravine, which we hardly knew whether most to admire for its beauty, or to exclaim against for the serious impediments which it presented. Night brought us to El Hilàl, a mountain so called. The point of El Hilàl extends to the north-east and forms a bay of about a mile in depth, in which even large ships might find shelter with the wind from north to south-east by east. It is in this spot that Cellarius has placed a naval station and town, and there are certainly remains at the present day about it indicative of an ancient site, while the harbour itself would be sufficiently qualified for a naval station to correspond with that part of the description. Two ancient forts are seen in ruins on the cliff and we noticed an ancient tomb which is excavated in the rock, close to the ravine, retaining still a very handsome façade. Three miles to the eastward of the forts at El Hilàl are some others, also in ruins, and the remains of strong walls in the neighbourhood of stone-quarries, all of which would seem to point out the spot as an ancient station. This place has also the peculiarity of being the only part of the coast which can be seen from Cyrene, from which it is distant about fourteen miles. In Ptolemy's chart we find a naustathmos (or naval station) placed on the western side of this promontory; but we saw nothing that would answer to the position in that direction. Ras El Hilàl, with Bujebàra on the south-east, forms an extensive bay; and another with Cape Rasát on the north-west near the centre of which is situated (now called Marsa Suza) the Port of Cyrene, Apollonia. From El Hilàl commence two ranges of mountains extending themselves to the westward, one along the coast, from it to Ptolemeta, forming the southern boundary of the plain on which Apollonia is built; the other rising in a range above these, diverging towards Merge and abreast of Cape Ras Sem. At El Hilàl we found an Arab encampment and obtained from it a goat and some corn for our horses. The Bedouins were civil and obliging, and brought us out a very acceptable present of kuskusoo, for which we made a suitable return. They would, however, have had but little reason to be satisfied with the conduct of strangers whom they had treated with courtesy, if we had not very fortunately made a discovery on leaving them which our Chaous had not probably anticipated. We had made it a practice in the course of our journey to pay the Arabs for whatever we had of them; and although this practice is considered by Turks not only as superfluous but very plebeian, we found it more consistent with our ideas of propriety, and at the same time more politic than if we had adopted a line of conduct more dignified and less honest.

Our Chaous had received from us a sufficient sum of money to make a liberal return to the Bedouins of El Hilàl for the corn and the goat which they had supplied us with; but instead of complying with our orders on this head he thought it more adviseable to keep the piasters in his purse than to distribute them as he had been directed: and we should accordingly have left behind us a much worse character for liberality than we deserved, if this discovery had not been made before we took our departure. Chaous Massoud looked rather foolish when the charge was brought home to him, too well substantiated to admit of denial, and we afterwards found that his honesty in other matters was not greater than on the occasion here alluded to. On our arrival at Grenna we sent him back to Derna and procured another Chaous from Bey Mahommed. Massoud was an Egyptian, and took every occasion to show his superiority, in point of civilization, over the Arabs and Moors of the west. He was particularly proud of his singing; and as his lungs were nearly equal to his conceit, was never tired of displaying his fancied abilities to the utmost extent of his voice, not dreaming for a moment that any of his auditors could possibly be less amused with his efforts than himself. With this view, he always kept close to our side, adapting the pace of his horse to ours, and quavering without intermission. His voice was good, and had he been able to moderate it, and to use it only on proper occasions, would rather have cheered than annoyed us on the road; for his songs had some subject, and were infinitely preferable to the tiresome monotony and endless repetition of two or three unmeaning words which had been so unmercifully dinned into our ears ever since we left Tripoly. The songs of the Arabs are however not always without a subject, as the examples which we have of their poetry in England will testify; but we are obliged to confess that the greatest attempts at invention which we ourselves noticed in a journey of seven or eight hundred miles were nothing more than short allusions to what was going forward at the time, or to something which was in anticipation. For instance, in ascending a hill, the song of our Arab companions would be—"Now we are going up the hill—now we are going up the hill." And in descending—"Now we are going down—now we are going down." Each sentence being repeated all the time the action alluded to was going forward, without the slightest variation of any kind. In approaching a town, the song would consist of something about the time we were likely to arrive there, or what good things were to be had at the place—eating being usually the summum bonum. On our return to Bengazi in June the whole burthen of our camel-driver's song for three days was the reward which he expected to have for driving his camels so fast.

It was late in the evening when we arrived at Apollonia, without having met with a single human being; our road led chiefly over a stony country intersected by deep ravines, which our horses had the greatest difficulty in crossing.

We were told at El Hilàl, that we should find Arab tents and plenty of water at Apollonia, but neither of these had we the good fortune to meet with, after a long and very diligent search.

We accordingly began to dig a well in the sand, but the water which drained into it was too salt to drink, and our labour was wholly thrown away. The day had been hot, and the exertions which were necessary in getting our horses safely across the deep and numerous ravines which obstructed our passage from El Hilàl to Apollonia, had tolerably exhausted the strength of our party before we arrived at our journey's end; but the circumstances in which we were placed had the effect of renewing it for a time, and it was midnight before we discontinued our search for Arab tents, and our efforts to procure a supply of water. As no hopes of finding either appeared to be left us, we gave over the search, and retired to our tents; the water-skins were carefully drained, and afforded us something less than a pint, which was divided amongst the party, consisting of eight, and we laid ourselves down to sleep away the inconvenience which we had not been able to remedy. At daylight on the fifth we rose to make our way to Cyrene, which we knew could not, at all events, be more than half a day's journey to the southward; but ill fortune still pursued us, for neither our Chaous, nor the camel-driver, had any knowledge whatever of the road. As we knew, from our actual position, that we could not well be mistaken in the direction of Cyrene, we set out upon the chance of finding some track which might eventually lead to the point required; and after following several paths, one after the other, all of which only led us into the wood and left us, a great part of the day was consumed without effect. It was too late to think of returning to El Hilàl, for it would not have been safe to cross after dusk the many deep ravines which interposed in that route, and we determined to make our way over the mountains which lay between us and Cyrene, since we could not find a pass leading through them. We knew that on reaching the summit of the range we should have a view of the place we were bound to, which could not, in a straight line, be far from us; but our project was soon discovered to be more easily projected than executed: for the sides of the mountain were thickly covered with wood, among which we were obliged to scramble as we might, and after dragging our horses for several hours through these impediments, and over the rough stony ground and slippery parts of the rock, we found, on reaching the top of one hill, that another was before us, as difficult to pass as the one we had just surmounted; and that a thickly-wooded valley must be crossed before we could attain even the foot of it. By this time the camels which had pursued a different track were discovered on the opposite side of a ravine, and we flattered ourselves that they had succeeded in finding the right path; it was impossible however for us to join them without retracing our steps, and we knew that we should never have been able to get our horses down the hill, which had cost them so many leaps and heavy falls to ascend; nothing therefore was left but to push on as well as we could, and after four hours' labour, such as we never experienced, and have certainly no wish to encounter again, we reached the top of the range and stopped a few minutes to refresh our horses, who were covered with foam, and trembling so much with terror and fatigue that a halt had become unavoidable. They had been, like ourselves, for nearly two days without water, and the heat of the weather, joined to the exertions which were necessary, had rendered thirst doubly annoying. On arriving at the summit of the range our view was still impeded by wood, and though we climbed several trees, to look out for an object which might guide us on the way which still remained for us to take, we could not succeed in overtopping the forest which lay between us and Cyrene. Our course was therefore still doubtful, and in a short interval which we devoted to rest, it was proposed that some of us should push on in advance, leaving the horses in charge of the others, and endeavour to find some opening: this was accordingly done, till our voices could scarcely be heard by each other, but still without any success. Beyond this distance it would not have been prudent to go, as we should scarcely have found one another again, had we ventured to ramble out of hearing. As it was, we experienced some difficulty in re-assembling our little party, consisting of four, and began once more to lead our horses forward who were very unwilling to move. After some further search, we came suddenly on a path which crossed us at right angles in our course; and as it was broad and evidently led through the wood, we determined at all events to follow it. It continued to be practicable and commodious, to our great relief and satisfaction; and we forgot, for a time, all our troubles, in the prospect of a speedy release from the embarrassment which our trip over the hill had brought upon us.

This path was very fortunately the right one, and led direct from Cyrene to Apollonia; but as it came into the plain at some distance from the point at which we began to ascend, and was wholly concealed by the wood which covered the sides of the mountain, it escaped our observation altogether, till we crossed it at the top of the range. After following it for some time we came to an open space, and were gratified with a view of Cyrene, which in the course of a few hours more we reached, and found ourselves once again by the side of the fountain which appeared to us, after our long abstinence, more attractive and beautiful than ever.

We found on inquiry that our camels and baggage had not arrived, a circumstance which rather surprised us, as we expected from the view which we had had upon the road that they would have been in advance of us. Two men were immediately despatched in search of them, carrying a skin of water which we knew from our own experience would be acceptable, and after sun-set we had the pleasure of seeing them arrive without any material loss or accident. It appeared that the road up the mountain which they had been observed to take terminated abruptly at the foot of a precipice, a circumstance which greatly surprised them, for the track which they followed was undoubtedly trodden, and, as it seemed to them, very recently. No outlet, however, was on any side visible, and as they stood pondering on the object of a road which led only to the base of a high perpendicular cliff and was closely hemmed in by thickets and brushwood, they thought they heard a mill at work, the sound of which seemed to come from above. As they looked up with astonishment towards the side of the mountain, from which the noise apparently came, they clearly heard a soft female voice issue from it, and soon perceived two very pretty young Arab girls looking out of a square hole on the side of the precipice, at the height of about an hundred and fifty feet above their heads—the place being not only inaccessible from below but equally so from above, and indeed on all sides of it, owing to the smoothness and perpendicular surface of the cliff in which it was formed.

When their surprise was a little abated our servants requested some water, but were told that there was none in the house; the girls inquiring at the same time where our people were going, and if they belonged to the English at Grenna. They replied in the affirmative, and said they had lost their way. One of the females then asked how many the party consisted of, and were answered, fifteen, though there were only two; the remainder, it was added, were close at hand in the wood. This embellishment was intended as a defensive measure to conceal the actual weakness of the company, for the elevated position of their fair auditors had not made the most favourable impression upon our servants; who suspected that persons living so far out of reach, must have stronger reasons for moving so far from their fellow-creatures, than was consistent with honesty and peaceable intentions. Accordingly when the girls had explained that the road which they were seeking led over the plain below, (where their fathers, they said, were cutting corn,) our wanderers turned to retrace their steps and descend the mountain-path as fast as possible; not a little anxious with regard to the reception they might experience on their route from neighbours of a more formidable description than the elevated little personages who had addressed them. As they began to descend one of the girls again called to them, and letting down a long rope made of twisted skins with knots in it two feet apart, desired them to make their water-skin fast to the end of it, with which, as the skin was empty, they willingly complied, choosing rather to run the risk of losing it altogether than to forego a possible chance of getting it replenished. The skin was quickly hauled up, and disappeared through the hole, leaving its owners in anxious suspense, not so much on account of the hide itself as of its anticipated contents. They had however no reason to repent of their confidence, for the skin very shortly made its appearance again and proved to be nearly full of water, to the delight of our thirsty attendants; who after expressing their gratitude for the supply, continued their journey with renewed strength and spirits, and arrived at Cyrene in the evening, as we have already mentioned above.

We found Mr. Campbell in quiet possession of the tents. He had had a good deal of trouble with our escort Boo Buckra, who had caught a fever, and nearly lost his life in consequence of repeatedly cramming himself with bazeen immediately after he had been physicked and bled.

On arriving at Cyrene we began to make inquiries respecting the water which we had been told we should find at Apollonia, and discovered that a spring in reality existed, at a short distance only from the place, but situated in the depth of a ravine, so as not to be easily perceived. We had observed the remains of an aqueduct, leading in the direction of this very ravine, and had an idea of exploring the wady in search of the spring which originally supplied it. But finding no stream crossing the plain or issuing from the ravine (or wady) in question, we concluded that it existed no longer; and as we had little time to spend in curiosity determined upon pushing on as fast as possible to Cyrene, where we knew that our resources were certain. Having made this discovery, which secured our supply of water, we determined to return without delay to Apollonia, and remain there till the fast of Rhamadàn should be concluded, during which time no Mussulman is allowed to eat or drink while the sun is above the horizon, and consequently the excavations would go on but slowly which we had already begun at Cyrene. Apollonia remained to be explored and laid down in our map, as no opportunity had been hitherto enjoyed of bestowing more than a slight inspection upon it.

While we were making the necessary arrangements for our departure, Shekh Aàdam, a man of some influence in the place, waited upon us with an order from Bey Mahommed enjoining him to render us every assistance in his power. We thought him accordingly a very proper person to accompany us in our visit to Apollonia, as his knowledge of the country would probably be of service in our researches, while his influence at the same time might prevent interruption. We had not indeed met with a single individual either at or in the neighbourhood of the place, excepting the two fair tenants of the cliff who dwelt among the haunts of the eagle; but as Arab tribes have in general no fixed habitation, but move as the season or circumstances direct, we could not tell how long we might remain unmolested in our rambles among its antiquities. Shekh Aàdam was in consequence attached to our party; and we again left Cyrene, on the 7th of June, with the intention of proceeding direct to Apollonia.

The road which leads to that place from the fountain winds along the foot of the upper range on which Cyrene is situated, and then taking a north-easterly direction, through a tolerably level and very fertile country, passes through the ruins of an ancient village, where a number of sarcophagi are still visible, ranged on either side of the path. Here the road turns more to the northward, and leading through a wood, over some stony hills, continues along a ridge between two deep ravines to the brow of the mountains which overlook Apollonia, down which it then winds in a zigzag direction, till it reaches the plain on the sea-coast below at no great distance from the port.

The whole of this road has been anciently paved, excepting the parts which have been cut through the rock, where deep marks of chariot-wheels are still observable. It has also had tombs on both sides of it, extending the greater part of the way, and has been defended by forts, the remains of which are visible near the edge of the lower range of hills. The country through which it passes is highly interesting and beautiful; near Cyrene it has been cleared from the wood which originally covered it, and appropriated to the cultivation of grain: this part is fertile in the extreme, and is succeeded by beautifully undulating ground overspread with flowering shrubs, which thicken as they approach the top of the lower range, where they are lost in dark forests of pine extending themselves down to the beach. The intermediate space between the corn-land and the forest has probably been laid out in villas and country residences, for we observed many ground-plans of buildings scattered over it which are not those of tombs or military works. As this part is wooded, the remains are not visible till they are very closely approached, so that there are probably many which have never been visited and certainly many which we never examined ourselves; not indeed owing to want of inclination, but to the circumstance of our not having more time at our disposal than was necessary for objects of more immediate importance.

On our return to Apollonia, by the road which we have just described, we noticed several excavated chambers in similar positions to those which our servants had mentioned: they were cut in a ravine to the westward of our path, many hundred feet above the level of the torrent, in places apparently inaccessible. We found, on inquiry, that whole families resided in them, ascending and descending by means of ropes; and indeed we ourselves could see persons in some of them who appeared to be reconnoitring our movements. It was late in the evening before we reached the plain upon which Apollonia is situated, and so dark in the thicker parts of the wood which reaches from the top to the bottom of the hills that we could scarcely distinguish our way. As we were leading our horses down a very steep part of the road we came suddenly upon a large hyæna, which we should not have seen if he had not been perched upon a mass of rock somewhat higher than our heads, lying close by the side of the path. The foremost of our party had drawn a horse-pistol and was in the act of presenting it to this unwelcome visitor, when he opened a howl which so startled our horses that we had the greatest difficulty in holding them, and turning himself round, walked slowly up the side of the hill, evidently in no way disconcerted at our appearance. As we did not wish to fire if it could have been avoided, we made no attempt to molest him in his retreat; for the report of our fire-arms would have alarmed the whole forest, which we understood to be much infested by hyænas and jackalls. As it was, the dismal howl which our shaggy friend uttered was echoed immediately by the shrill cries of numberless jackalls, none of which, however, were we able to see, and the plain was reached without interruption. We had been so much accustomed to the cry of the jackall, an animal very common in northern Africa, that it would not of itself have engrossed our attention for a moment; but although we had very frequently been disturbed by hyænas, we never found that familiarity with their howl or their presence could render their near approach an unimportant occurrence; and the hand would instinctively find its way to the pistol before we were aware of the action, whenever either of these interruptions obtruded themselves closely upon us either by night or by day. It must, however, be confessed that the cry of the jackall has something in it rather appalling, when heard for the first time at night; and as they usually come in packs, the first shriek which is uttered is always the signal for a general chorus. We hardly know a sound which partakes less of harmony than that which is at present in question; and indeed the sudden burst of the answering long-protracted scream, succeeding immediately to the opening note, is scarcely less impressive than the roll of the thunder-clap immediately after a flash of lightning. The effect of this music is very much increased when the first note is heard in the distance, (a circumstance which often occurs,) and the answering yell bursts out from several points at once, within a few yards, or feet, of the place where the auditors are sleeping. The jackall can never be a formidable animal to anything but sheep and poultry, unless, perhaps, when the number assailing is very great; but it is usually so little molested by the Arabs, whose dogs protect their live-stock from harm, that we have frequently gone close up within a few yards of one, before he would turn to walk away. The same indifference in retreating is also peculiar to the hyæna, who not only walks away very slowly when advanced upon, but appears at the same time to have a limping motion, as if he were lame of one leg. The hyæna most commonly seen in the north of Africa is that which is striped in the back, black and grey; its paws are scarcely more formidable than those of a large dog, but its teeth and neck are very strong, and there is no animal fiercer when wounded or closely attacked.

We arrived at Apollonia late in the evening, and set out early the next morning, to find the spring which was said to exist in a neighbouring ravine. We followed the course of the aqueduct mentioned above, which appeared to us to finish at the mouth of the wady; but our companion, Shekh Aàdam, pointed out to us a spot where it was continued over the hill and along the side of the precipice: this was probably done to avoid the rush of water which thunders down the vallies after rain, and brings with it large stones, trunks of trees, and other matters, sweeping everything before them in their course. As the aqueduct was constructed of stone, and covered over apparently with the same materials, besides being coated in the inside (or water-course) with cement, there does not seem to be any objection to its having been carried out of the level. We proceeded up the ravine nearly a mile and a half, and then came to a stream of water issuing out of the rock at some distance above, which descended in little cascades and was lost in the bed of the wady. The sides of this ravine are nearly perpendicular, and about five hundred feet in height: near the top we observed two caves, situated as those were which have already been described; and had some conversation with the people who appeared at the entrance of them. We made them understand that we should like to ascend and pay them a visit in their aërial abodes, but as they seemed to be unwilling to admit us, we did not press the subject any further. The lower parts of the ravine are thickly covered with pine, olive, and carob trees, and the whole has a very wild and picturesque appearance.

The town of Apollonia, now called Suza Hammàm, from the number of wild pigeons that frequent it, is situated at the bottom of an open bay, formed between Ras El Hilal and the cape known by the name of Ras Sem. It stands close to the sea, upon a small eminence, or long narrow slip of elevated ground; and is situated at the extremity of a fertile plain, which extends itself from the foot of a ridge of mountains, distant a mile and a half from the sea coast, and running in an east and westerly direction. The length of the city may be reckoned at nearly three thousand English feet, and its greatest breadth at scarcely more than five hundred. It has been completely surrounded by a very strong wall, with quadrangular turrets on three of its sides, and circular ones of much larger dimensions on the remaining side (that to the westward). As the wall has been carried along the brow of the hill, more attention has been paid to its strength than to its symmetry, but the turrets are for the most tolerably equidistant, being about eighty yards apart. The two circular turrets at the north-western angle of the wall have been built with even greater attention to solidity than other parts of this well-defended town; for they have been exposed for ages past to the wash of the sea without suffering any material injury. On the northern and north-eastern sides, however, the sea has made considerable inroads, and very few traces of the wall are there remaining, some parts being wholly without any. The east end of Apollonia appears to have been fortified as a citadel, for which its elevated position above the rest of the town appears to have been admirably adapted. The cliff on which it stands rises perpendicularly from the lower part of the city, and could only be approached by a narrow pass and by a gate in the outer wall. The walls themselves are here doubled and still rise, though not entire, to a height of thirty and forty feet. The quarries which have been excavated about this and other parts of the walls, serving the purpose of an excellent fosse, contribute also very materially, as will be observed in the plan, to the strength of the city of Apollonia. The entrances to the town are all of them narrow (the widest of the gates being no more than five feet across); and their positions, in the angles formed by the wall with the turrets, are remarkably well chosen for the purposes of security and defence. There appear to have been seven gates on the south side of the city, including that belonging to the citadel, and one, near the centre, on the western side, which are all that we were able to discover any traces of: indeed this number of gates, for the size of the city, will be considered unusually large; and were it not for the intervention of the quarries between the city walls and the plain, would have tended to weaken the position. Opposite the largest of the gates on the south side of the town is a spacious semicircular excavation, the sides of which rise perpendicularly to a considerable height, and which appears to have formed an approach to the gate here alluded to. Close to this is a remarkably strong fort, built with sloping sides, like those at Ptolemeta, and others already described in the Syrtis. Here also pass the remains of the aqueduct which formerly supplied the town from a spring of most delightful water, situated at the extremity of the ravine which we have mentioned above, and distant nearly four miles from the town. The sea has encroached very considerably at Apollonia; and it is difficult to say, in what the shelter of the harbour consisted: the line of coast is too strait to afford any protection; and it seems probable, that the small island to the northward of the town, and a reef of rocks a little to the south-westward of this, constituted the only shelter which it afforded. We had imagined, that a communication might formerly have existed between the island and the reef of rocks here alluded to; but it soon appeared that the water was much too deep between these, to allow of any such idea being reasonably entertained. The same cause would also have operated very effectually in preventing the construction of an artificial communication between the points which we have just mentioned; for the heavy sea which rolls into the port in windy weather would soon have swept away anything less than the Breakwater at Plymouth. Had such a communication ever existed, the harbour would have been a most excellent one; but as we cannot suppose that it ever did, from the reasons which we have stated above, we may conclude, perhaps, that vessels usually laid under the lee of the island, and that when this was impracticable, they were drawn up on the beach. We may believe at the same time, that what art could effect in the flourishing periods of Cyrene was done for the improvement and the security of its port, as we find it to have been with regard to the defence of the town. Extensive remains of building, apparently the foundations of a quay, are still visible, stretching out from the beach into the sea, at the depth of a few feet under water. Some quarries, which have been formed in the rock to the north-eastward of the town, are also now under water; and the insulated tomb, which forms so striking an object in the view we have given of Apollonia, is always surrounded by the sea when the wind sets in strong from the northward. Other tombs on the beach are likewise filled on these occasions; as well as some large cisterns to the north-eastward of the town, through which the water roars with a noise like thunder, and dashes up through the apertures formed in them above. The cisterns here alluded to were probably appropriated to the use of the vessels in the harbour, which might have been watered from them very conveniently; and they might at all times have been kept filled with excellent water by means of the aqueduct mentioned above. We have already noticed the encroachments of the sea upon the land, which we ourselves have had occasion to observe in several parts of the coast from Tripoly to Bengazi, as well as those mentioned by other writers on the coasts of Tunis and Algiers. The present state of Apollonia affords another decided instance of the advance of the sea to the southward; and portions of the elevated ground on which the front of the town has been built are continually falling in from this cause. The scene of the principal theatre situated without the wall, to the eastward of the town, has been wholly swept away by the waves, although the quarry in front of it must have greatly contributed to break the force of the sea in this quarter. It will be seen by the plan of the town of Apollonia, that a part of this theatre is built against the wall of the citadel, and the other part against the high ground behind the subsellia. The seats appear in consequence to have been approached from above, we mean, from the ground on a level with the uppermost range; and as the greater number of the ranges are still very perfect, the effect of the whole building is that of a stupendous flight of steps leading down from the elevated ground against which they lean to the beach on a level with the orchestra. It is this effect, we presume, which induced Signor Della Cella to notice the seats of the theatre as a "magnificent staircase;" and it must be confessed that a more noble flight of steps will not often be seen than the one which is in question. This building, like those of a similar nature at Cyrene and Ptolemeta, has no interior communications; and the body of the people appear to have entered from above, as we have already observed. It is probable, however, that some approach to the orchestra (where the seats allotted to persons of rank were usually placed) was contrived from the lower ground upon a level with it; but the whole of that part has been so completely washed away, that we had no means of ascertaining what arrangements had been made there. The road to the theatre appears to have been through the quarries to the south-eastward of the town; and the gates by which the audience approached it were probably the two which lie to the eastward of the aqueduct, and that which was appropriated to the citadel.

Within the walls, to the southward of the town, there appears to have been a small building of a circular form, sunk below the level of the soil about it, in which there are traces of several ranges of seats, which might have belonged to a small theatre of some description, perhaps to an Odeum; but the whole is so much buried with soil, in which grass (when we saw it) was growing, that it would be impossible to obtain any details of it, without a good deal of previous excavation. It will be seen by a reference to the plate, p. 500, in which those details are given, that the ground-plans of some of the buildings of Apollonia may be made out with tolerable certainty. The Christian churches, in particular, are very decided; as well as the remains of a noble building of a similar form at the western extremity of the city. The handsome marble columns, which now encumber the structures which they once contributed so materially to adorn, afford evident proofs that no expense had been spared in the erection of these magnificent buildings; for the material of which their shafts are composed is not found in this part of the coast of Africa, and must have been transported at great labour and cost from the quarries of distant places. On the centre of the shaft of some of these columns we found the figure of a large cross engraved; they have all been originally formed of single pieces, some of which still remain entire, and would be no unappropriate or inconsiderable ornaments to churches of modern construction. The discovery of these splendid monuments of Christianity in a country now labouring under ignorance and superstition, afforded pleasing memorials of early piety, and recalled the active times of Cyprian and Anastasius, of the philosophic Synesius, (himself a Cyrenean) and other distinguished actors in those memorable scenes which northern Africa (from Carthage to Alexandria) once presented to an admiring world. But the grass is now growing over the altar-stone, and the munificence which gave birth to the structures here alluded to is visible only in their ruins.

FOOTNOTES:

This observation is not applicable to the latter part of the ground we travelled over, which could not certainly have ever formed part of a road either ancient or modern; and it was wholly owing to the ignorance of our Chaous, who persisted that we were in the right track, that we were induced to attempt it.

Signor Regignani was of the Jewish persuasion, and it is well known that in Mahometan countries the Jews are a persecuted race.

The mill used for grinding corn by the Arabs is nothing more than a small flat stone on which another is turned by the hand, and this is usually placed in the lap of the women, who are the only millers and bakers in Arab families.

Apollonia, formerly the port of Cyrene.

These are the caves which we have given in the drawing, p. 493.

The port of Apollonia is mentioned by Scylax, in conjunction with that of Naustathmos, as having been secure against all weathers; and his description of the little rocky islands and projecting points in this neighbourhood is, even at the present day, very correct.

We are sorry to say that this view, with some others, which we could have wished to introduce, have been unavoidably omitted.

Sulla spiaggia v'hanno maestosi ruderi di caseggiati, con avanzi di *magnifica scalinata* presso al mare. (p. 155.)

These remarks will be better understood by a reference to the plan of Apollonia annexed.

We had proposed to give these plans in a separate plate, upon a larger scale, but a subsequent arrangement has prevented us from doing so, and we refer to them accordingly as they are found in the plan of the city.

Probably from the shores of the Red Sea, where there is a great variety of coloured marble.

The bishopric of Ptolemais was transferred to Apollonia (then called Sosuza), as that of Cyrene had been formerly to Ptolemais. The present Arab name of the port is Marsa Susa, which is evidently a corruption of the Christian appellation of this ancient harbour of the Cyrenaica.

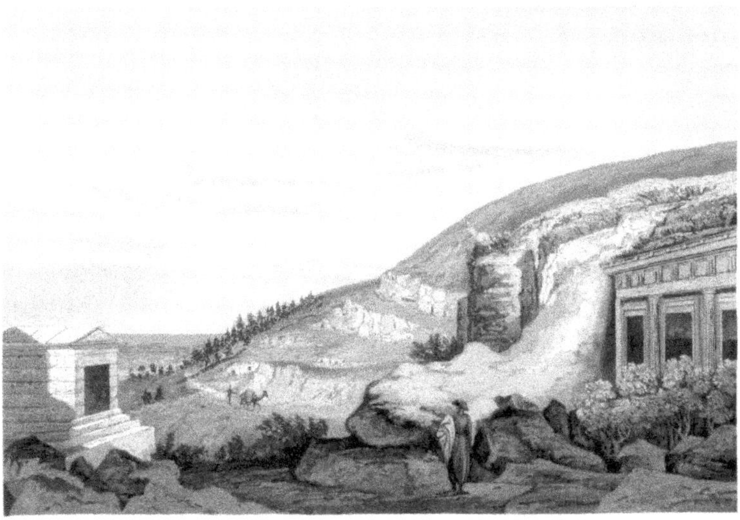

Engraved from a Drawing taken on the spot by Henry Beechey.

ARCHITECTURAL FRONT OF THE DORIC EXCAVATED TOMBS AT CYRENE.

Published June 1827, by John Murray, London.

CHAPTER XVIII.

Observations on the Position of Ras Sem — Remarks of Bruce connected with this place — Difficulty of reconciling the several positions assigned to it — Extravagant Stories related of its Petrifactions, supposed to be those of Human Beings — Fallacy of these Statements as recorded by Shaw — Report of Petrified Remains at Ghirza made to Captain Smyth by Mukni (Bey, or Sultan, of Fezzan) during the progress of his Excavations at Lebda — Journey of Captain Smyth in search of the objects described to him — Description of the actual Remains at Ghirza — Monumental Obelisk discovered there, and Tombs, combining a mixture of the Egyptian and Grecian styles of Architecture — Indifferent Taste and Execution of these Remains — Veneration in which they are held by Mahometans of all classes, who suppose them to be Petrified Human Beings of their own persuasion — Geographic Position of Ghirza determined by Captain Smyth — Further Observations on the Remains at Apollonia — Return of our party to Cyrene — Account of that City continued.

IN concluding our account of that part of the coast which lies between the promontory called Ras Sem and Derna, we may observe that the name of the first-mentioned place, however it may have originated, is not at the present day known to the Arabs, at least not to any of whom we inquired for it. Bruce and Dr. Shaw have described it as situated in the interior; the former at five long days, the latter at six days' journey to the *southward* of Bengazi. The term Ras, which in Arabic signifies a head, is the usual Arab term for a promontory, and it is in this sense that we find it adopted in modern charts to distinguish the headland above mentioned. But the place which is alluded to by Shaw and Bruce is not, as we have stated, on any part of the coast, but lying at a distance of several days from it, that is to say, south of Bengazi; and Bruce translates the name which has been given to it differently, calling it the Fountain and not the Head of Poison, as Ras Sem is commonly interpreted; probably from the indifferent quality of the water which he found there in a very disagreeable spring impregnated with alum. We are not prepared to reconcile the different positions assigned to the fountain or the promontory in question; but have chiefly adverted to it on account of the fictions which have been circulated with respect to its alleged petrifactions. It appears, as reported by a Tripoline Ambassador resident in London about an hundred years ago, on the authority of a friend of his, a person of *great veracity*, and of a thousand other people besides—all, no doubt, of equal respectability—that "a large town was to be seen at Ras Sem, of a circular figure, which had several streets, shops, and a magnificent castle belonging to it." "Olive and palm trees were found there, among others, turned into a bluish or cinder coloured stone, and men were conspicuous in different attitudes, some of them exercising their trades and occupations, others holding stuffs, bread, &c., in their hands. Women at the same time were observed giving suck to their children, or busy at the kneading trough or other occupations. A man was to be seen on entering the castle lying upon a magnificent bed of stone, and guards were still visible standing at the doors armed with their pikes and spears. Animals of different sorts (nay, the very dogs, cats and mice) were observed by some persons converted into stone, and all of the same bluish colour." Here we have evidently the description of an ancient city, with its buildings and statues, converted by the fertile imagination of the Arabs, and other ignorant spectators of its remains, into the fancied semblances mentioned. It is probable that one of the cities of the Pentapolis, Cyrene perhaps, as having most statues, was the petrified city in question; and we may venture to say that there is scarcely an individual who has travelled in Mahometan countries who has not been induced to take journies of inquiry on the authority of similar fictions. Happy are they who find the least resemblance between the description which they have heard and the reality!—for it often occurs that amplification and hyperbole have less to do in such accounts than pure invention. Shaw was encouraged, as he himself informs us, to undertake a very tedious and dangerous journey to Hamam Meskouteen in Numidia upon the authority of Arab reports; he had been assured, with the most solemn asseverations, that a number of tents had been seen there, with cattle of different kinds, converted into stone. On arriving, however, at the place, he had the mortification of finding that all the accounts which he had heard were idle and fictitious, without the least foundation, unless in the wild and extravagant brains of his informers. "Neither (he continues) will the reports concerning the petrified bodies at Ras Sem deserve any greater regard or credibility, as will appear from the following relation."

A similar disappointment was experienced by Captain Smyth, who was induced, from the report of the Sultan of Fezzan, an eye-witness of the scene he described, to undertake a journey to Ghirza; and as he has obligingly favoured us with the details of it, we submit them to the inspection of the reader in the form in which they were extracted from his private journal.

"During the time I was excavating amongst the ruins of Leptis Magna, the Arab Sheiks who visited my tent frequently remarked that I should have a better chance of finding good sculpture in the interior, and made many vague observations on the subject, to which I paid little attention at the time. On my return to Tripoli however, Mukni, sultan of Fezzan, had just returned from a marauding expedition into the interior; and in a conference I held with him, he assured me that within the last month he had passed through an ancient city, now called Ghirrza, abounding in spacious buildings, and ornamented with such a profusion of statues as to have all the appearance of an inhabited place. This account, supported by several collateral circumstances, impressed me with the idea of its being the celebrated Ras Sem, so confusedly quoted by Shaw and Bruce, and consequently inspired me with a strong desire to repair thither."

"Accordingly Colonel Warrington and I waited on the Bashaw, requesting permission to undertake the journey, with which he immediately complied. Only, as his eldest son, the Bey of Bengazi, was in rebellion against him, and might by seizing the Consul-general and myself demand terms which his Highness would find it difficult to accede to, he wished us to proceed with a small force to the mountains, and there be reinforced according to the actual state of the country. His Highness also signified his desire that Seedy Amouri, his son-in-law, and Seedy Mahomet his nephew, should accompany us. He moreover furnished us with his Teskerah (an authority for being gratuitously subsisted by the Arabs), though we never used it but to insure a supply, and always made a present in return, proportionate to the value of the articles provided, being of opinion that availing ourselves otherwise of this document would be detrimental to future travellers."

"On the 28th of February 1817, we left Tripoli before sunrise, accompanied by the two Seedies, an escort of twenty-six Moorish cavalry, and several camels. Proceeding by the fertile grounds of Sahal, we rode southward in the direction of the hills; but before quitting the plain, our companions saluted us and each other by firing their guns whilst riding at full speed, in imitation of desultory attack and defence, which, allowing for the difference of weapon, shewed a striking resemblance to their Numidian ancestors. As we advanced up the hills we found the country beyond the tower of Grara, neglected; the clothing and equipments of the inhabitants were also more rude and scanty than in the plains."

"On the 2nd of March we passed an old tower called Gusser-Kzab, in the plain of Frussa, where, about three years before, a considerable treasure had been discovered in gold and silver coins, of which however I was unable to procure a single specimen, they having been all taken to the coast of Tripoli, where they were most probably melted, and their date and story lost for ever. Proceeding from Frussa over a sterile and fatiguing district, we arrived about noon on the 3rd at the Wadie of Benioleet, where, having been expected, the principal people came out to welcome us, and some met us even as far off as the valley of Mezmouth. This, though only a distance of four or five miles, is a very laborious and dreary ride, over a rocky tract, exhibiting a remarkably volcanic appearance, from a black substance resembling porous lava, lying upon a bed of tertiary limestone, and forming, perhaps, a part of the Harutsch of Horneman. The melancholy aspect of these hills renders the first view of the Wadie of Benioleet, with its houses, fields, and palm trees, extremely picturesque, and the additional bustle occasioned by our arrival gave great animation to the whole scene."

"Benioleet consists of several straggling mud villages on the sides of a fertile ravine, several miles in length, and bounded by rocks of difficult access. The centre is laid out in gardens, planted with date and olive trees, and producing also corn, vegetables, and pulse. This valley is subject to inundation during the winter rains, but in summer requires to be watered with great labour by means of wells of extraordinary depth. It is inhabited by the Orfilla tribe, which amounts to about two thousand souls, subsisting chiefly by agriculture and the rearing of cattle, aided only in a trifling degree by a manufacture of nitre; they are accounted hardy, brave, and industrious, but at the same time dishonest and cruel. A large and ill-proportioned building called the castle, near one of the pleasantest spots in the ravine, was prepared for our reception, and a plentiful supply of victuals and forage provided. Though commanded at almost every point, this is the principal fortress; it contains several apartments, good stabling, and a large court-yard, but the water must be drawn from a very deep well at the distance of a musketshot. The walls are badly perforated for musketry, and flanked with round bastions, too weak to bear artillery."

"Having found several people here who had recently arrived from the place I was bound to, I repeated my inquiries respecting the sculpture, and again received positive assurances that I should see figures of men, women, children, camels, horses, ostriches, &c., in perfect preservation; and the belief of their being petrifactions was so prevalent, that doubts were expressed whether I should be able to remove any one of those whom it had pleased Providence thus to punish for their sins."

"On the 6th, after our party had been joined by three mountain chiefs, Mahmoud, Abdallah, and Hadgi Alli, with twenty-five Janissaries, and fifteen camels laden with water, barley, tents, &c., we proceeded over a hilly and bare country to the southward. On the 7th we arrived at a well of bad water called Kanaphiz, in an open space nearly surrounded by the Lodz hills. We found a small Kaffle there from Fezzan, and purchased of the Moors a quantity of exquisite Sockna dates, and some dried locusts. We were exceedingly tormented here by the numerous ticks that swarmed over the whole plain, and teazed alike both ourselves and our horses. On the 8th having passed the range of Souarat, we advanced through a pretty valley called Taaza, neglected, but evidently capable of improvement, from the luxuriant myrtle, lotus, juniper, cypress, and other plants, flourishing spontaneously. I also observed many trees called Talha, from which a gum exudes resembling that brought from the forests on the north-west of the Zaara; and probably it is the same tree, for it is of stunted growth, with small brownish leaves, though its character is rather that of a rhamnus than a mimosa."

"In the evening we arrived at a brackish well of great depth called Zemzem, from having been blessed by a holy Marabut, and thence is derived the name of the whole Wadie, which running towards the north-east reaches the Syrtis below Turghar. Intending to pitch our tents here, we had first to burn away the stubble to destroy a species of venomous spider, from the bites of which we had two or three narrow escapes, saving ourselves only by killing them suddenly on the spot with a smart blow, the moment we saw them upon us. Ghirrza, the scene of the extraordinary story so extensively propagated, being only within three or four miles of this place, occasioned me a restless night: so that early on the morning of the 9th I eagerly sat off over the hills, and after a short ride the ruins of Ghirrza abruptly met my sight."

"I instantly perceived the error of some writers, in ascribing cold springs and moving sands to this spot, for the site is mountainous and bare, presenting only dreary masses of lime and sandstone, intersected with the ramifications of the great wadie of Zemzem. And although I had not allowed my imagination to rise at all in proportion to the exhilarating accounts I had heard, I could not but be sorely disappointed on seeing some ill-constructed houses of comparatively modern date, on the break of a rocky hill, and a few tombs at a small distance beyond the ravine. On approaching the latter I found them of a mixed style, and in very indifferent taste, ornamented with ill-proportioned columns and clumsy capitals. The regular architectural divisions of frieze and cornice being neglected, nearly the whole depth of the entablatures was loaded with absurd representations of warriors, huntsmen, camels, horses, and other animals in low relief, or rather scratched on the freestone of which they are constructed. The pedestals are mostly without a dye, and the sides bore a vile imitation of arabesque decoration. The human figures and animals are miserably executed, and are generally small, though they vary in size from about three feet and a half to a foot in height, even on the same tombs, which adds to their ridiculous effect; whilst some palpable and obtruding indecencies render them disgusting."

"Across a fine but neglected valley, to the south-eastward, in which were numerous herds of wild antelopes, and a few ostriches, is a monumental obelisk of heavy proportions, and near it are four tombs of similar style and ornament with the first set. These are remarkable however as more strongly combining a mixture of Egyptian and Greek architecture, and are placed so as to give a singular interest to the scene. There are but three inscriptions, and those are comparatively insignificant, nor can other particulars be learned, the whole of them having been opened, in search probably of treasure, but as no person permanently resides near the spot, I was deprived of any local information. A wandering Bedoween, who had been some time in the Wadie, brought me a fine medal, in large brass, of the elder Faustina, which he had found in the immediate vicinity."

"The tombs appear to have remained uninjured by the action of either the sun or the atmosphere, excepting only a deep fallow tint they have imbibed;—the sculpture therefore, as we must call it, remains nearly perfect. As these edifices are near the Fezzan road, people from the interior have occasionally tarried to examine them, and being the only specimens of the art they ever saw, yet representing familiar objects, they have described them on their arrival at the coast in glowing colours. It is this nucleus, which rendered more plausible, perhaps, by the story of Nardoun, soon swelled into a petrified city, and at length attracted the curiosity not only of Europe, but obtained universal belief in Africa. It has been deemed a species of pilgrimage to resort thither, as the caravan passes, and inscribe a blessing for the supposed unfortunate petrified Moslems, and with these the pedestals are actually covered. Thus, notwithstanding the diminutive size and despicable execution of these bas-reliefs, the Turks who accompanied me eyed them with admiration and respect, pointing out to my notice that the horses had actually four legs, and other similar trifles. Never, in fact, has a palpable instance occurred to me, so strongly indicative of the degradation of mind inflicted by the Mahometan tenets on its votaries; nor could I but regret to find men, in many respects estimable, so benighted, and so glaringly deficient in the discernment bestowed by education."

"Ghirrza is situated near some barren hills called Garatilia, and from its want of water, and sterile, comfortless appearance, could only have been a military post in communication with Thabunte, and the stations along the shores of the greater Syrtis. The wadie, indeed, may have been formerly well cultivated, being even now covered with spontaneous vegetation and flourishing talha, cypress, lotus, and other trees. I observed no traces of roads or aqueducts, during my short stay, but I was too much occupied with my operations for determining the geographical position of the place, to extend my researches to any distance."

"On the 11th I wished to proceed to Towergha, and Mesurata, and thence to Lebida, but we had so many men and camels belonging to Benioleet, that it became necessary to return to that place. On our arrival there, we found the inhabitants eager to learn our opinion of the petrifications of Ghirrza, and they were evidently chagrined when they found we had brought some specimens away with us, thereby dissolving the favourite axiom respecting the futility of attempting to remove them."

Such was the result of Captain Smyth's journey to the petrified city at Ghirza; by which, notwithstanding it fell short of his expectations, more was obtained than those travellers are generally fortunate enough to meet with who have an opportunity of comparing the objects described with the florid description of them by Turks and Arabs. With regard to the Ras Sem of Shaw and Bruce, it is difficult to say what place is intended in the accounts which these writers have given of it; for we have already observed that no part of the Cyrenaica is known at the present day by that name to the Arabs of the district, at least not that we were able to ascertain; and we are inclined to believe that one of the cities of the pentapolis is in reality the place originally alluded to in the extravagant reports of the natives, and of others who may have visited the country in question. The distance of five and six days *south* of Bengazi would not certainly correspond with the position of any one of these cities; but it appears to us more probable that a place of some importance would be selected, in preference to one of inferior consideration, as the theme of a tale so marvellous; and there can be no remains in the position alluded to which may at all be compared with those of the Pentapolis.

We shall now resume the thread of our narrative, and proceed to finish our account of Apollonia.

It will be observed, in referring to the plan of that city, that the greater part of the wall is remaining; and we have never seen so good an example of ancient fortification (the wall of Teuchira excepted) as that which it still affords. It has been strengthened by quadrangular turrets, at intervals of about eighty yards, and the gates have in general been placed in the angles formed by the wall with the towers, a position which rendered them less accessible when besieged than if they had been otherwise situated. All the turrets, however, are not square; for one at the south-west corner is circular, as are also two of much larger dimensions on the north-western side of the city, which are about eighty feet in diameter, and have been built uncommonly solid to resist the wash of the sea. At the opposite corner of the town there is nothing remaining but the foundations of one of the towers and a part of the wall extending westward from it along the beach: these were, however, sufficient to determine the limits of the town in that direction. It will be observed that this wall is only apparent as far as (m), beyond which is a large space where everything is buried in sand, and a conjecture arose whether it might not have continued along the cliff leading to the tower (n); but traces of it were again discovered near point (o), with two turrets and other evident remains to the westward of it, which determined its continuation along the beach to (p). We afterwards found that the cliff just alluded to formed a boundary to that portion of the town which appears, from its great strength, contracted limits, and elevated position, to have been the citadel. There are but two approaches to this fortress; one from the town at (r), and another by a very narrow gate at (s) from without. The whole of the south-eastern corner is high, and extremely difficult of access, on account of the quarries which surround it forming a trench of considerable dimensions.

The town appears to have been purposely destroyed, and the wreck of building with which it is incumbered renders the examination of the ground-plans very difficult and tedious, indeed for the most part impossible. Of the five principal buildings laid down in the plan of the city we contrived to obtain, with a good deal of trouble, some comparatively satisfactory measurements, (a) and (b) were unquestionably Christian churches; and must have been erected at great expense, from the costliness of the material employed for their columns (a species of marble somewhat resembling Tripoline).

The building marked (d) has been one of no ordinary importance, and seems to bear more resemblance to a Basilica than to any other public edifice. It will be observed that the semicircular part of this structure has a different aspect from those of the churches, both of which are at the eastern extremities where the altars appear to have been placed. The columns of the basilica (if so we may call it) are also composed of handsome coloured marble—we mean the shafts of the columns, for the capitals are of white marble. The remaining two, (c) and (e), appear to have been dwelling-houses of a superior description, (e) has had immediate communication with the turret close to which it is placed on the southern side of the town; and a long colonnade running parallel with the sea has been erected close to the other dwelling-house leading along the edge of the cliff towards the eastern church. On the south side of the town, without the walls, there is another large building (h), which seems to have been a fort and to have contained quarters for soldiers. A road, inclosed by large stones placed upright, has been purposely carried close along the eastern side of this structure, and turning short round it through an archway has led to the semicircular excavation opposite to the gate (l), one of the principal entrances to the city. We will not pretend to fix with any certainty the date of the buildings we have here alluded to; but we should consider them to be decidedly Roman, and the employment of Corinthian capitals and shafts of coloured marble would seem to favour this opinion. It is not improbable that the churches may have been erected in the time of Justinian, although we do not recollect that they are mentioned by Procopius in his account of the works of that emperor.

In the quarries which inclose the walls, serving, as we have already stated, the purpose of trenches, there are a good many excavated tombs; but they are all so much decayed that it was not worth while making plans of them, and those farther from the city are in no better state; some are filled with sand washed in by the sea, which has encroached considerably upon the land at Apollonia, and surrounds occasionally some very conspicuous tombs which form striking objects to the westward of the town.

On the two islands which are opposite the town there are some excavations and remains of building; but as we had no boat with us, and none is to be found in the neighbourhood, Apollonia, not being used in modern times as a port, we were unable to ascertain their precise nature. The islands are very small, but the town receives great protection from them in northerly gales, although the shelter which they afford is not sufficient, we should imagine, for vessels, even if there should be water enough inside them.

By the 20th June we had completed our plan of Apollonia, which, from the incumbered state of the ruins, was no easy task to accomplish, and we think that little more could be satisfactorily made out without removing the heavy blocks of stone which are everywhere scattered over the town: but this labour would probably be greater than the object appears to demand, since the ground-plans which remain are not of any great antiquity, and, with the exception of the churches, and perhaps the other buildings which we have given, do not seem to call for much more attention than we were able to bestow upon them. We must confess we should have liked to remain there a little longer to have excavated about the larger theatre, where statues would probably be found; we say the larger theatre, because a circular space within the town appears, as we have mentioned, to contain one of smaller dimensions, which must be cleared from the soil and vegetable matter with which it is covered before anything can be determined with certainty respecting it. If a theatre has stood here it must have been a very small one, of a circular form, and, unless appropriated to musical performances, appears, to be unfit for any other. Without the town, to the westward and southward, excavation would probably be interesting; and indeed there is hardly a spot in the habitable parts of the Pentapolis where objects of interest would not in all probability be found. In the space between Apollonia and Derna there are remains of several ancient villages and stations, where we could have very much wished to excavate; and in that between Apollonia and Cyrene there appears to be a great deal of matter for inquiry. The embarkation of heavy objects would be difficult at Apollonia on account of the little depth of water near the beach; it might, however, be managed, and would at any rate be preferable to the transport by land-carriage to Bengazi or Derna, which indeed may be said to be wholly impracticable on account of the frequent deep ravines and dangerous mountain-passes which intervene.

During the time, about a fortnight, of our absence from Cyrene, the changes which had taken place in the appearance of the country about it were very remarkable. We found the hills on our return covered with Arabs, their camels, flocks, and herds; the scarcity of water in the interior at this season having driven the Bedouins to the mountains, and particularly to Cyrene, where the springs afford at all times an abundant supply. The corn was all cut, and the high grass and luxuriant vegetation, which we had found it so difficult to wade through on former occasions, had been eaten down to the roots by the cattle: the whole face of the country was parched by the sun, and had assumed a deep brown and yellow tint instead of the rich green which it had worn on our first arrival; a hot wind was blowing, which had all the character of a sirocco, though coming from a north-west quarter, and the thermometer stood constantly at 97° in the shade, a degree of heat we had not before experienced at Cyrene.

The scorching quality of the north-westerly gale may probably be attributed to the heat of the ground in the hollows about the place, for we did not experience any great degree of heat at Apollonia (we mean, not from the wind, for the sun was very powerful) where the same breeze came to us immediately from the sea. The excessive dryness of the atmosphere of Cyrene at this time may be readily conjectured from the indication of a very good hygrometer which we had with us, which showed 55 during the period in question, an extreme which we had never before seen it mark.

We found afterwards that at Malta, on the same days, they had experienced a strong sirocco wind, and had had the thermometer at 95°. It may be remarked generally of the heat of northern Africa that it has not often that oppressive quality so much complained of in other hot latitudes; and it does not appear to be at all unhealthy, as we often find it to be in damp climates. The sun, however, is uncommonly powerful, and it is necessary for those not accustomed to its influence to keep the head well covered if they would avoid a coup-de-soleil. The force of habit will at the same time enable Europeans to encounter much more heat than they would venture to subject themselves to on first arriving from more temperate regions: we found that we could walk about the whole of the day (which we were obliged to do in making our plans) without feeling more than what may be termed inconvenience; and the greatest annoyance was the reflection from the ground on our eyes and lips, which the masses of white stone among which we had to scramble, in examining and taking measurements of the ruins, made stronger than is felt in cultivated places: these become so hot from ten or eleven o'clock till sunset that the atmosphere about them is like that of an oven; the heat which is reflected from them absolutely scorches, and the eyes of persons long exposed to its influence would probably suffer materially. For the rest, the heat may be borne without prejudice (especially through the folds of an ample turban) unless a greater freedom of diet be indulged in than is prudent in any hot climate. We saw very few serpents in the Pentapolis, and very few scorpions, even among the ruins, where they are generally fond of hiding themselves; but the grass land, at Cyrene in particular, is much infested by a dark-coloured centiped, almost black, with red feelers and legs; we usually found half a dozen of them in taking up the mats in our tents, and had great difficulty in killing them. Any part which chanced to be separated from the rest of the body would continue to run about as if nothing had happened, and were the reptile even divided into twenty pieces each part would travel about, as if in search of the others, without any of them seeming to be the worse. The only mode by which we could kill them at once was by crushing the head, which effectually destroyed life in every other part instantaneously.

On arriving at Cyrene we immediately resumed our examination of the antiquities of the place, and were able to make out the ground plans much better than on former occasions; in consequence of finding the grass eaten up by the cattle and sheep of the Bedouins, whom the scarcity of water, as we have already mentioned, had driven to the heights where the fountains are situated.

At the conclusion of the sixteenth chapter we have noticed two theatres, near which our tents were pitched, and shall proceed to give some description of them. We found them both so much incumbered with the soil which had accumulated about them, in which the grass springs up to a considerable height, that, had it not been for the semicircular shape of the green masses which presented themselves to our view, we should not have suspected them to have been theatres. The columns which once ornamented the back of the scene in the largest of these buildings had been thrown (for they could scarcely have fallen) from the basement on which they formerly stood, and crossed our track in various places along the whole length of the range: among them were several statues, which appeared to have been portraits, executed with great freedom and taste, and beyond were the Corinthian capitals of the columns which had rolled, in their fall, to some distance from the shafts. These, as well as the bases, were composed of a fine white marble, the polish of which was in many cases very perfect; and the shafts (of coloured marble) were formed of single pieces, which added considerably to the effect produced by the costliness of the material. From these circumstances, as well as from the resemblance of the draperies in which the statues were wrapt to the toga, it seems probable that this theatre was Roman; but the execution of the capitals and bases have none of that degeneracy of style which characterizes the works of the lower empire; and we should be disposed to attribute them to the time of Augustus or of Hadrian, when Roman art was undoubtedly entitled to our respect, and (we may also say), in various instances, to our admiration. The whole depth of the theatre, including the seats, the orchestra and the stage, appears to have been about one hundred and fifty English feet, and the length of the scene about the same. The porticoes at the back of the seats are two hundred and fifty feet in length, and the space between these and the colonnade at the back of the scene is of equal extent. The whole building would thus appear to have been included in a square of two hundred and fifty feet, not including the depth of the portico behind the subsellia, which is at present rather uncertain. The theatre has been built, like many of the Greek theatres, against the side of a hill, which forms the support of the subsellia; and the highest range of seats appears to have been upon a level with the platform from which it was approached at the back. On this level also are the porticoes behind the seats; which would seem to prove, if other evidence were wanting, that the cunei were not approached by internal passages, of which there are no indications, but from the platform just mentioned (on a level with the highest range of seats) from which the spectators descended to the lower ranges. There appears to have been a row of columns, inclosing the uppermost range of seats; and as we found several statues in the orchestra, close under the subsellia, it may perhaps be supposed that the upper part of the theatre was decorated with these ornaments, the place of which was probably between the columns of the peristyle in question, since the statues appear to have fallen from some place above the level of the seats; and we know of no situation more appropriate for them than along the colonnade we have mentioned.

This theatre is placed by the side of the road leading down to the fountain, and must have been a beautiful object when perfect; the richness of the materials of which the columns were formed, adding greatly to the effect of the building, if not in point of taste, at least in point of costliness and splendour. The style and execution of the remaining parts of this structure have not however been neglected; and we often stopped to admire the beauty of the Corinthian capitals, which were carved with great sharpness and freedom, and exhibited considerable taste of design. The position of this building will be seen in the ground plan of the city (p. 520); it is the most northern, and the largest of the two. The plan of the other theatre differs materially from that of the one which we have just described, and its proportions are also very different. The depth of the orchestra is much less in proportion to its width, and the space allotted to the seats is at the same time greater for the size of the building. Instead of being approached from above, as that which we have first mentioned appears to have been, there are five passages (or vomitoria), by which the spectators entered, and two communicating with some place beneath the front of the stage which are so much blocked up with rubbish, occasioned chiefly by the fall of the roof, that we could not explore them to the end. These passages descend very abruptly towards the centre, and appear to communicate with the same point, or with each other; they have been arched with blocks of stone, ranged longitudinally, and are of very good construction. We were able to go down thirty-two feet in one of them, after some little trouble in clearing the entrance; but the impediments which then presented themselves were too serious for our time and resources. A casual observer would not have been aware that there were any passages in this theatre by which the spectators entered, so much was the whole building covered with soil and vegetation; and it was only on close examination, that some appearance of the arched roofs which covered them was discernable; and we determined upon excavating in the same line below.

It soon appeared, that passages really existed; and we succeeded in clearing one of them sufficiently to determine the fact beyond dispute. We found that the roofs descended with the seats, some of which they probably supported, but the floors appear to have been level; or, at least, the inclination is so slight (if there be any) as not to be ascertained by the eye. In the course of this excavation we found that some of the rows of seats were hollow; and were in hopes of discovering a further confirmation of the circumstance mentioned by Vitruvius, that the Greeks were in the habit of appropriating hollow spaces beneath the seats of their theatres to the reception of brazen vases, by means of which the sound was considerably improved. We were led to imagine the possibility of this, from the fact of the spaces to which we allude having been carefully formed, and not left merely for the purpose of saving material, or adding to the lightness of the building. We found nothing, however, which could be said to verify the conjecture; and a few fragments of pottery, which were picked up in some of these apertures, were all that presented themselves, in confirmation of the practice alluded to, during the progress of our excavation.

We must observe, with respect to the passages which we have supposed to have been used as entrances to the theatre, that they were all of them on the same level, and had no other communication than with a præcinction, a few feet above the orchestra; how many cannot well be ascertained, as we could not, in the present state of the building, determine the position of the lowest range of seats, and the height of it from the level of the orchestra. The sides of the passages were cased with stone and marble, and decorated with architectural ornament; but we could not ascertain the elevation of the front presented to the stage, no portion of which is standing: perhaps, among the ruins which encumber the orchestra some details of this might be found; but the little time which we had to excavate did not allow us to search for them long, and some fragments of Doric columns were all that we dug out, except blocks of stone and marble. The passages were perfectly strait, and communicated direct with the lower ranges of seats, from which the spectators must have ascended to the upper ones; but we could not perceive any remains of staircases, which were not perhaps necessary, considering the moderate size of the building. No portion of the stage, except the lower part of a wall, is now remaining, which indeed seems rather to have formed a part of the proscenium, as it appears to be somewhat in advance of the stage itself. The width of the orchestra where it joins the proscenium is not more than sixty feet, and its depth about eighty. The depth of the whole space occupied by the seats is not more than forty feet. There are extensive remains of building which appear to have been attached to this theatre, on its eastern side: they seem to have inclosed public walks, and have been surrounded by porticoes, and strong walls of considerable height, in one of which a gate still remaining has been formed communicating directly with one of the principal roads. In the neighbourhood of the theatre we have last mentioned, there are still many statues above ground, in excellent style. One of these, from the representation of the Ammon's head, and the eagles which ornament the armour, is probably a statue of some one of the Ptolemies; and near it is a female statue, one of the Cleopatras, Berenices, or Arsinoës, perhaps, of the family.

We wished to have introduced a drawing which we made of the figure first mentioned, the ornamental parts of which are beautifully executed; but our limits will not allow of it. The head and limbs are wanting, but the trunk, clothed in armour, is a beautiful example of taste and execution. It is of white marble, much larger than life, as is also the female statue near it, of corresponding dimensions.

There are several other statues above ground in this part of the city, in the best style of Grecian art; and many good examples of Roman sculpture, or it may be Roman portraits, executed by Greek artists, which we should rather conclude from the excellence of the workmanship employed in them, and from the fact of Cyrene having been a colony of Greeks, even when under the dominion of Rome.

Every part of the city, and indeed of the suburbs, must have formerly abounded in statues; and we are confident that excavation judiciously employed, in many parts even indiscriminately, would produce at the present time many admirable examples of sculpture.

We will now proceed to give some account of the amphitheatre, of which considerable remains are still extant without the walls to the westward of the town, and which must have been in its perfect state a very conspicuous object from the sea. It has been constructed on the verge of a precipice, commanding a most extensive and beautiful view, and receiving in all its purity the freshness of the northern breeze, so grateful in an African climate. Part of it is built against the side of a hill which formed the support of the ranges of seats fronting the precipice; and that portion of it which bordered upon the verge of the descent rose abruptly from the edge, like a stupendous wall, overlooking the country below. The foundations of this part of the amphitheatre were, it may be imagined, remarkably strong, and they still remain to a great extent very perfect; but all the seats which they supported have been tumbled at once from their places, and lie in masses of ruin beneath. This appears to have been occasioned by a part of the substructure having given way; and as we imagine the whole side to have fallen at once, the crash must have been a tremendous one. On the opposite side, (that which rests against the hill,) nearly forty rows of seats are still remaining, one above the other; and as each of these are fifteen inches in height, the edge of the precipice appears from the upper seats to be close at the foot of the ranges, although the whole of the arena intervenes, and it often made us giddy to look down from them. As the lower ranges of seats are not in their places, it is difficult to ascertain the diameter of the arena, but it seems to have been more than a hundred feet across; and to have been, like that which we have mentioned at Ptolemeta, of a perfectly circular form. There is no appearance of any præcinctions, owing probably to the absence of interior communications, which are not to be found in this building; and it seems to have been chiefly approached from the top, which is equal in height with the level summit of the hill, against which the seats are on this side built. The most natural approach would certainly have been that which leads from the fountain of Apollo, along the edge of the descent which we have mentioned: this will be evident from the plan of the city; but strong walls, which are undoubtedly of ancient construction, cross the road here so completely as to preclude the possibility of any approach from the city to the amphitheatre in this direction. If the walls which we allude to had not been standing at the present day many feet above the level of the road, we should have concluded that they must originally have contained gates which led to the arena; but there is no appearance whatever of such communication, even supposing that the gates were approached by flights of steps, which would not have been an unreasonable conjecture.

The only road which remains (under the difficulties stated) must at the same time have been a circuitous one; and as it communicated merely with the level summit of the hill, against which the seats rested, any approach to the arena, or other lower parts of the amphitheatre, must have been by descents, right and left to them, from the terrace (or platform) which surrounds the upper range of seats, or by the staircases leading from it to the lower ranges, of which decided vestiges are still remaining. The arena seems to have been about a hundred English feet in diameter, and the seats to have occupied a space of about eighty feet in depth; if we reckon the level space (or platform) inclosing the amphitheatre at twenty, the whole building will have stood upon three hundred feet of ground. It could not be ascertained whether any subterranean chambers existed communicating with the arena, as this part is incumbered with the ruins of the fallen seats, and we had neither time nor means to excavate in search of them; we should rather conclude that there were not; for on the north side, where no seats are remaining, (all this portion of the building having fallen down the cliff,) the substructure is very apparent, and no arrangement appears to have been made for vaults. There are remains of a Doric colonnade along the edge of the cliff, forming the north side of one of the spaces walled in to the eastward of the amphitheatre, the capitals of which are beautifully formed, exhibiting all the sharpness and taste peculiar to the early manner of executing the order. Both these inclosures appear to have been appropriated to the amphitheatre,—perhaps as public walks for the use of the audience; but it is difficult to say how they were approached, either from the east or from the west; and the two other sides are inaccessible, in consequence of the abrupt descent of the cliff to the northward, and the rise of the mountain to the southward of the inclosures. We have already said that there is no appearance of any gates, by which the amphitheatre could have been accessible from the eastward, through the walled spaces here alluded to; but we think there must have been a communication originally, although there are at present no traces of any. There is a small building close to the eastern wall of the inclosures, apparently of very early construction: it is a simple quadrangle, without any interior divisions; and the remains of several columns, all of which are not apparently in their original places, are still visible on the north side of the structure, but none are observable on the other sides. This building has also no gate, and it is evident from the appearance of the walls, all of which are standing, that there have never been any formed in it; we will not pretend to say for what purpose it may have been erected.

In returning from the amphitheatre to the city, the road skirts the edge of the cliff, which descends everywhere abruptly, and the soil is kept up by strong walls along the brink of the descent, without which it would be washed down by the winter rains, and the buildings in time undermined. It is over a part of this wall that the fountain of Apollo (which in ancient times was copiously distributed over the city and fertile lands of Cyrene) now precipitates itself, as it probably did in its natural state, into the plain, and finds its way to the sea. Near the end of this wall begin the ranges of tombs which skirt the northern face of the mountain below the city, descending in galleries one above another, till they reach the level of the plain at its foot. The summit is occupied by part of the city; and the edge of the descent was here, as in front of the fountain, skirted by a wall running along the whole line of the cliff, till it joined that which enclosed Cyrene to the westward. From this portion of the mountain descend five large ravines, once thickly wooded with pine and other trees, which have been cleared for the use of the town, and to disencumber the ground appropriated to the tombs. Some of the ravines are, however, still partially wooded, in many places very thickly, and springs of excellent water are found in various parts of them.

The north side of the town, from its present appearance, does not seem to have been ever much inhabited, and very few remains of dwelling-houses are observable there. The buildings which still exist are however of an interesting character, and excavation would be particularly desirable in this part. Two eminences which rise conspicuously above the general level of the summit are occupied by the ruins of spacious temples, and close to the western wall of the city is all that remains of the stadium. The largest of the temples (we mean the ædes, without the columns) is a hundred and sixty-nine English feet in length, and its breadth sixty-one feet. It is of the Doric order, in its early style; and the capitals, which with the columns are lying on the ground, still exhibit marks of excellent taste and execution, though very much defaced by time; they measure nine feet across, and the capital and abacus are of one piece. The form of this building is peripteral; but the columns on the sides appear to have been twelve in number, which is one more than is allowed to temples of that class by Vitruvius, supposing the edifice to be hexastyle; for in peripteral temples the number of intercolumniations on the flanks should, according to this author, be only double those of the front. That there were twelve columns, however, appeared evident on the first inspection, from the existing number of capitals lying on one of the sides of the temple; and on adding two spaces, and the diameters of two columns to the length of the ædes (or body of the temple), which is, as we have stated from actual measurement, a hundred and sixty-nine English feet, and comparing this measurement with that of twelve columns and eleven spaces, the first number given was two hundred and five, and the latter two hundred and four, which result was quite near enough to be conclusive of the fact. In this calculation we have taken the diameter of the columns, as they measured within an inch or two, at six feet; and supposed the intercolumniation to be systyle, that is two diameters of the columns. The same calculation applies equally to the breadth of the temple, which would seem to prove that the intercolumniation assumed was correct,—six columns and five spaces giving ninety-six,—and the breadth of the ædes, with two spaces, and the diameters of two columns added, ninety-seven; bringing the results within one of each other, as in the instance just given with regard to the length. Traces are still remaining of a pronaos and posticus; but one of the walls of the pronaos (the only one remaining) has a very decided return of two feet (at its central extremity) in the direction of the cella. The depth of the posticus is at the same time much greater than that of the pronaos, and rather more than half as much as that of the cella: this distribution is, however, consistent with the character of the climate; for the rain falls very heavily, and almost incessantly, during the winter season at Cyrene; and the unusual space given to the posticus would be found very serviceable to the inhabitants, particularly as the temple was somewhat removed from what may be called the inhabited part of the town. The same reasoning would apply equally in summer time, for the heat of Cyrene is at that period very great. An additional motive for increasing the posticus so much beyond its usual dimensions would be found in the width of the ambulatory (which is regulated by that of the intercolumniations), for the systyle species is too contracted to afford much shelter on any occasion; and we may probably assume, from the calculations above stated, that the temple in question was in fact of that species, although the intercolumniation could not otherwise be ascertained, on account of the encumbered and ruined state of the building, which we had no opportunity of excavating.

We should mention that the walls of the ædes have decided returns of six feet both in front and rear of the temple, towards the two columns which range in a line with them; they are about four feet and a half in thickness, and one of the stones of which they were composed measured fifteen feet in length.

The smaller temple, like that which we have just described, was built upon a rising ground, and had the additional elevation of a very solid basement or substructure, considerably raised above the level of the summit of the hill, part of which (about four-and-twenty feet) has been left as a kind of terrace round the building. The disposition of the columns is by no means evident in this temple, and the number is very uncertain; but the ambulatory must have been a good deal below the pavement of the ædes, since there is no space allowed for it upon the basement we have mentioned; and it must consequently have been upon the terrace beneath it, which appears to have been left for that purpose. The columns must therefore have been unconnected with the roof, and have merely supported the covering of the ambulatory. Indeed, it seems likely that the portico was altogether detached from the ædes, and judging from the remains of a wall, which appears to be part of the original plan, and the position of a column without it, we may perhaps suppose that it was situated on the edge of the terrace above-mentioned; and that the whole space of four-and-twenty feet between this wall and that of the ædes, was a space between the portico and the body of the temple, which does not appear to have been covered in. In this disposition we imagine the wall just alluded to to have formed the back of the portico, and the column, still remaining, to have been one of the range which supported its roof in front. Immediately below this column the ground descends, and traces may be observed of steps leading up to it.

In the ædes there seem to have been only a pronaos and cella; and in the latter is a detached mass of building, raised above the level of the other parts of it, for which we are wholly at a loss to account, there being no analogy between its disposition and that of any part of a cella in its usual arrangements.

The length of the ædes is a hundred and eleven feet, and its breadth fifty feet; the outer walls are four feet in thickness, and that of the pronaos somewhat more than three. The capitals of some fluted columns which are now lying at the foot of the hill on which the temple stands, are of no established order of architecture, and may perhaps be said to be a mixture of Greek and Egyptian; a coalition which we should certainly expect to meet with at Cyrene, but of which we recollect to have seen only a few instances. Close to this building, on its northern side, is the quarry from which the stone employed in its construction was probably taken, forming a deep trench at the foot of the hill. The aspect of both temples is nearly east, as is usual, we believe, in buildings of such a description.

To the eastward of the larger temple, and close to the city walls, are the remains of the stadium, part of which is excavated in the rocky soil on which it stands, and those parts only built which the rock could not supply. Its length is somewhat more than seven hundred feet, and its breadth about two hundred and fifty. The course is now so much buried, and overgrown with long grass and other vegetation, that the mode in which it was disposed could not be ascertained with any certainty; neither is it easy to decide clearly how much space was allotted to the seats, which do not occupy at present more than five-and-thirty feet on either side. The whole is, in fact, (like the temples,) in a very ruinous state, and nearly all the constructed part has disappeared. There are two masses of building to the north-westward of the stadium, which appear to have had some connection with it, but we will not venture to state any decided opinion with respect to their precise use. One of them is a solid quadrangular mass, now about five feet in height, which appears to have been intended as a station merely, from which the horses and chariots of those contending for the prize might be inspected as they entered or came out of the stadium, for it is not sufficiently elevated to command a view of the course. It is fifty-eight feet in length by eighteen in breadth, without any appearance of having been more than a kind of raised platform, unvaried by architectural ornament; and we have only suggested the use for it mentioned because we cannot in fact assign any other to it. The second may, perhaps, have been a small temple, or some building in which the contending parties, and those who had the management or superintendence of the games, might assemble to make arrangements respecting the course, or to settle any differences which might arise with regard to the race. Its form is similar to that of a temple, without external columns; but there is some appearance of there having been a colonnade attached to it, supported by the walls of the building. It is raised upon a small eminence, about an hundred feet to the westward of the terrace, near the entrance of the stadium. Westward of the circular part of the hippodrome, and to the south-east of the largest of the temples which have been described, is a walled space of ground of considerable extent, which may have been appropriated to the gymnasium; but there is so little at present remaining within its limits, that we will not venture an opinion respecting it. We could very much have wished to excavate in parts of this inclosure, as well as about the temple themselves, but our time and means would not allow of it: the stadium would probably afford little of interest, for the stones which were employed in its construction appear to have been carried away in later times to serve in other buildings; and, indeed, little more could be expected from excavating the temples, than fragments of architecture too much decayed by time to render them particularly useful in furnishing details, or of statues which enthusiasm and bigotry have probably defaced, if they should even have been spared by the hand of time.

The city walls approach closely to the southern extremity of the stadium, and are in this part very decided. They begin from the verge of a deep ravine, as will appear by the plan, and continue in an unbroken line to the spacious reservoirs (at the south-eastern angle of the city) which are mentioned in the publication of Dr. Della Cella. Here we lose traces of them, but they again make their appearance on the south side of the buildings just alluded to, and extend to the brink of the large ravine with which the aqueduct communicated. Beyond this (the aqueduct), a wall was unnecessary, for the mountain descends perpendicularly to the bed of the ravine, and renders all approach to the town in this direction impossible; and as the wall of the aqueduct has not been built with arches, but carried along the mountain in a solid mass, it would have been fully sufficient for the purpose of defence, and was probably built solid with this intention.

Square towers were attached to the city wall in various parts, not apparently at regular intervals, but approaching each other more closely where the ground was low, and consequently more favourable to the attack of an enemy. Several parts of the wall have been excavated in the rocky soil on which they stood, and building only employed where the rock was not sufficiently high to render it unnecessary. It should be stated, that the masses of rock here alluded to were not of the nature of a cliff, but detached masses rising in irregular forms as well from within as without the walls. It is evident, as will appear by the plan of the city, that the line of wall was continued round the large reservoirs above mentioned, so as to inclose them completely within its limits, a precaution which might naturally be expected in a climate where water is so valuable. If the winter rains should fail, which we should scarcely think possible at Cyrene, these cisterns might have been filled from the aqueduct which communicated with the principal fountain, for although it only extended across the high ground to the westward of the town, there are traces of conduits, or water-courses, in every part of the city, leading towards the place on which it has been built.

We ought not to omit on this occasion a few remarks which are necessary on the subject of the reservoirs here alluded to, as they may serve to explain an error into which Signor Della Cella appears to have fallen, with respect to the inscriptions which he found in them. He has informed us, that these inscriptions were in a language altogether unknown to us, each stone of the interior wall bearing a separate letter, so that the inscriptions continued, in parallels with the ranges of stone, along the whole length of the buildings in question. The partial absence of light, and the immediate presence of water in these spacious and gloomy subterranean inclosures, appear to have conspired, with the inconvenient position which it was necessary for the Doctor to take, in preventing him from copying more than a few of them. These, however, he tells us, may probably be serviceable in contributing towards the elements of languages now wrapt in obscurity; languages which are the only means at present afforded us of checking the various statements which have come down to us upon the authority of Greek historians, and other writers in that language, who it is well known (Signor Della Cella observes) were so much attached to every thing peculiar to themselves, that they could not avoid pointing out a Grecian origin for whatever bore the traces of civilization. We give the passage here alluded to in the Doctor's own words, and proceed to mention, that the letters which compose his inscriptions have no other meaning than that which is usually conveyed by what are called quarry marks, and do not form any sentence or any single word. Many of them are Greek letters, which are occasionally reversed, and placed in various positions, so that the same letter might at first sight be taken for several others distinct from itself; sometimes two or more Greek letters appear together on the same stone, (occasionally united in a kind of cipher,) and their forms are often made out so rudely, from the dispatch used in cutting and often scratching them on the blocks of stone, as not to bear a very close resemblance to the usual ones. Some of them are not letters of any kind, but simply marks or characters invented for the occasion, as will be observed by the instances which are given of them below. We fear, too, that even if the characters in question had really been inscriptions of the greatest importance, they must have been for ages lost to the world, and were certainly never intended to meet the public eye by those who had them placed where they are; for the whole interior of the cisterns, or reservoirs, upon the stones of which they are inscribed, have been coated with a thick and very hard cement, which still remains perfect in a great many places. We may add that these cisterns, which are three in number, one at right angles with the two others, are partly built, and partly excavated in the rock, as Signor Della Cella very truly observes. The roofs are arched with stone and beautifully turned; indeed, the whole construction of these vaulted chambers, in which large and very regularly-shaped stones have been employed, is excellent in the highest degree. Externally, the roofs are built up on the sides, and form at the top long platforms, or terraces, each of more than a hundred and fifty feet in length, along which we have often walked with pleasure admiring the beauty of their structure.

The south-eastern part of the city appears to be that which was most thickly inhabited, and the number of small buildings crowded closely together are, in their present state, likely to exercise the patience of those who may endeavour to make out their plans. We gave up the task as a hopeless undertaking after a few days' attentive examination of these remains; and it seems probable, that if we had even succeeded in giving all the details which can now be procured of them, little interesting matter would have resulted from the collection. Those in the centre of the town (in the neighbourhood of the theatres) are of much more importance; and the remains in the space between the theatres and the aqueduct have very considerable interest. We do not think, however, that satisfactory plans could be given of either without a great deal of excavation, and we should certainly hesitate in giving names to any which we have not already described from the details which we were able to procure of them. In the large inclosed space attached to the smaller theatre, where there are still traces of colonnades extending three hundred feet, is a semicircular building situated at the western extremity of one of the porticoes (or colonnades) here alluded to, which resembles in its form the tribunal of a basilica. It is possible that this might have been the forum, as the porticoes would have afforded very ample convenience in any weather for the transaction of business; and its position, close to the principal road leading through the centre of the town with which it communicates by a gateway, would at the same time have been equally favourable. Its situation, however, with regard to the theatre, to which it is decidedly attached, has rather led us to imagine, that this place contained the covered walks, or porticoes, for the convenience, or shelter in rainy weather, of the audience; as which we have mentioned it above. The central space, where there are no traces of building, with the exception of a kind of raised platform opposite the gateway, were most probably in that case laid out as a garden; and the whole together would have somewhat resembled in plan the garden and covered walks of the Palais Royal at Paris. A very strong wall, on the south side of which is the gateway, extends at the present day round three sides of the place; and the southern wall appears to have been continued about four hundred feet farther in the same line (turning then to the north in a line parallel with the eastern wall), and to have inclosed the small theatre within its limits. We have already mentioned the statues which we found in this space, at the back of the theatre now alluded to; and suggested that one of them in all probability was a resemblance of one of the Ptolemies; the head of the statue is wanting, and we fear it has been knocked off at some period by the Arabs of the place, for the chance of disposing of it at Tripoly or Bengazi; a fate which has befallen many a beautiful example of Grecian art, now lying in the city and the neighbourhood of Cyrene. It is possible, however, that it might be found in the course of excavation, although we did not ourselves succeed in discovering it in the parts where we dug for it about the statue. We remember to have been very anxious upon the occasion, and fancied that we should know a head of any of the Lagides, meet with it wherever we might. It was from the decorations carved upon the armour, as we have stated in another place, that we imagined this statue to be the portrait of a Ptolemy; and it is well known that the eagle and the head of Jupiter Ammon are usually borne on the coins of that family. If it had been possible, we should have brought home what remains of this statue (which is merely the trunk), as well as several other very excellent examples of Grecian sculpture in its neighbourhood; and we are convinced, that excavation judiciously employed in the central and eastern parts of Cyrene, would bring to light many beautiful specimens of art, now covered only with the soil and vegetation which have been allowed to accumulate for ages about them. There have been several public buildings of importance immediately without the walls inclosing the theatre, of which plans might perhaps be satisfactorily made, if excavation were employed for the purpose; and it is very probable that inscriptions might at the same time be found, which would help to throw light upon the nature of the buildings, and to ascertain the period at which they were erected. There must be a considerable number of those buried in different parts of the city; for we never saw an ancient town in which fewer inscriptions are to be seen than that of Cyrene; especially for a town in which literature and the fine arts were cultivated with so much success. The few which we copied are scarcely worth inserting, and we shall only give (in addition to that over the fountain) another in Doric Greek, which is given by Signor Della Cella, in the reading of which we also differ in some respects from his copy. It was found upon a stone bearing the form of a pedestal, immediately without the wall above mentioned; and the Doctor has suggested that the remains of a female statue, seated in a chair, which is lying in the road not far from it, was the representation of Claudia Arete, the matron, in commemoration of whose benevolence and virtue the inscription in question was erected by the Cyreneans. We give it below, but are not of opinion that the statue alluded to by Dr. Della Cella ever occupied a place upon the pedestal inscribed. Near this female statue is another of a young man (also without the head) which we never remember to have seen equalled in Greek sculpture, for the taste and execution of the drapery.

There are some extensive remains of building, with a very handsome colonnade, on the high ground between the small theatre and the aqueduct, which appear to be those of a palace or other residence of more than ordinary importance. From the northern colonnade the ground descends abruptly, and the soil is kept up by a wall which forms the back part of the chambers built at the foot of it. These consist of a single range of quadrangular apartments, which appear to have been from twenty-five to thirty in number; their length (at right angles with the wall already mentioned) is about forty feet, and their average breadth (for they differ in some instances) about twenty. It is not at present evident, whether these communicated with the building above them or not; but one of them has had a wall built across it, opposite to that which forms the back of the chambers, in which there is no door, so that there could not have been any access to it from the lower ground. There is at the same time no appearance of any staircase leading down to them from above; and if there had, it would have been necessary to have built a separate one for each, for they have no communication one with another. We do not, therefore, imagine that all of them have been closed, but that they had access to the ground in front of them, and none to the colonnades and chambers above. That which is built across is placed at one angle of the range, and is eight feet wider the average breadth, taking it at twenty feet. If a groom or a coachman were to give an opinion with respect to the use of the chambers in question, with reference to the structure above, they would certainly decide, without the least hesitation, that this uniform, long range of building, was the stabling of the palace, and could only have been appropriated to the horses and chariots of the noble Cyrenean who inhabited it. As we have never seen the stables of any ancient residence, whether Grecian or Roman, we will not venture to assign such a use to these chambers; but it is well known that the Cyreneans were particularly celebrated for their skilful management of horses and chariots, and we must confess, without being either coachmen or grooms, that such an appropriation did more than once occur to us.

There are remains of apartments adjoining each other to the westward of the handsome colonnades which we have mentioned, the plans of which we would not hazard without excavation; nor could we without it complete that of the porticoes, the columns of which are nearly four feet in diameter.

The whole building appears to have extended about three hundred feet in a southerly direction, and to have occupied more than four hundred in length from east to west. There are remains of much larger columns, near the road, at the southern extremity of this large mass of building; and we feel confident that matter of considerable interest is still to be found beneath the rich soil which covers it, in their immediate vicinity and neighbourhood. Corn is now growing over a great part of the ground in question; and an old Arab, who was employed in cutting it down, when we measured the remains of building just described, was greatly astonished at the trouble we gave ourselves in walking over and examining them in a very hot day; when he could scarcely himself make his mind up to cut down his wheat, which was certainly a matter (he said) of much more importance. He had his gun ready charged by his side, and moved it along with him as he changed his position in reaping; a ceremony at which we should have been a little surprised, if we had not before seen frequent instances of similar precaution in the Arabs of the Syrtis and Cyrenaica. In fact, the Bedouin, like the Albanian or the Corsican, never stirs out without his gun, if he has one; for it rarely happens that any individual has not some feud upon his hands, and it is necessary to be provided with the means of defence, in a country where every man is the legal avenger of his own or his family's wrongs. We use the term Bedouin, because, although our swarthy friend was cutting wheat, he was at the same time a wandering Arab; and only visited the place periodically, chiefly during the summer season. For three parts of the year Cyrene is untenanted, except by jackalls and hyænas, and the Bedouins pitch their tents chiefly on the low ground to the southward of the range on which the city is built. Were it not for its elevated position, Cyrene would probably, on account of its luxuriant pasturage, and the abundant supply of fresh water which it possesses, be at all times a favourite haunt of the wandering tribes of the Cyrenaica: but the Arab, for an active man, is one of the most lazy of any race of people with which we are acquainted, and will rather forego a very decided advantage than give himself much trouble in acquiring or maintaining it; he would in consequence easily persuade himself that the advantages which Cyrene must be acknowledged to possess, would be more than counterbalanced by the trouble of ascending and descending its hills, and of driving his flocks and his camels to water in places which would be thought inconvenient.

We are not aware that it will be of any service to dwell further upon the nature and condition of the buildings of Cyrene; as much as we were able to collect (with the time and means which we had at our disposal) has already been given of the objects most worthy of notice; and to say more would only be to offer conjecture, on subjects which do not afford sufficient data to authorise particular description.

In fact, the whole of the existing remains of this ancient and once beautiful city are at present little more than a mass of ruin; and the tombs afford the most perfect examples of Grecian art now remaining in Cyrene. To give plans of half these would be impossible, unless whole years of labour were devoted to the task; but we really believe, that any zealous antiquary, any person with tolerable feeling for the arts, would with pleasure devote every day to such employment should he find himself stationed for years in their neighbourhood.

We never, ourselves, passed our time more agreeably, than in collecting the details which we have been able to procure of them; and shall never forget the sensations of delight—we will not use a less impressive term—which we experienced on our first introduction to these beautiful examples of Grecian art.

The position of the tombs, as well as that of the city, has been already described, and too much can scarcely be said in its praise; we wish that our limits would allow us to give more of the architectural details of the former than can be collected from the general view of them; but we shall probably avail ourselves of some other opportunity of submitting a few examples to public inspection, and can only at present refer for some idea of them to the view which we have just alluded to. To have lived in the flourishing times of Cyrene would indeed have been a source of no trivial enjoyment; and we are ashamed to say how often we have envied those who beheld its numerous buildings in a state of perfection, and occupied, in their former cultivated state, the beautiful spots on which they stand.

We must not, however, take our leave of the city, without adverting once more to the excavated channel that has been formed for the water of the principal fountain, to which we have formerly alluded. We had been so much occupied in walking over the ruins, and collecting the details of Cyrene and Apollonia, that it was only the day before we set out on our return to Bengazi, that we were able to explore this passage to the end. It is formed entirely in the rock from which the stream issues, and runs, in an irregular course, for nearly a quarter of a mile into the bowels of the mountain: the sides and roof of the passage are flat, where time and the action of the current (which is very strong) have not worn them away; but the bottom is encumbered with stones, bedded fast in a quantity of clay which has accumulated about it and against the sides. The general height of this subterranean channel is scarcely five feet, an elevation which we found rather inconvenient, for it obliged us to stoop a good deal in advancing; and as it would not have been possible to examine the place properly, or indeed to have preserved our light, without keeping the head and body in an upright position, we usually found the water making higher encroaches than its chilling cold rendered agreeable.

In some places, however, where there appear to have been originally flaws or fissures in the rock, the roof was irregular, and there was room enough to stand upright, an occurrence of which we very gladly availed ourselves, to the great relief of our knees. We found the average width from three to four feet, although in the places just mentioned it was occasionally as much as six feet; and were it not for the clay which has been collected against the sides, we should often have suffered from their roughness. From the irregularity of the course of the passage we were obliged to take bearings very often; and at each time we stopped for this purpose we took down the distance measured with our chain between the point we stopped at and the last; so that after much trouble we succeeded in obtaining a tolerably correct plan of the whole. The length and course of the channel will be seen in the plan of Cyrene, where it is marked with a dotted line beginning from the cliff, at the foot of which the fountain now discharges itself, and runs across the level ground on which the amphitheatre, and little temple (as we have named it) of Diana are situated. Within forty feet of the end of the channel (that is to say, about thirteen hundred feet from its beginning at the foot of the cliff), it becomes so low, that a man cannot advance farther without creeping upon his hands and knees, and then finishes in a small aperture scarcely a foot in diameter, beyond which of course it is impossible to penetrate. We were not a little surprised at the length of this singular excavation, which seemed, as we advanced, as if it never would finish; and as we could not accelerate our mode of operation without sacrificing the plan of the passage, we had to remain for several hours in the water before we had completed our task. We must say, however, that with all the inconvenience of the stooping position which we were obliged to assume, and the extreme cold of the water, we found the undertaking a very agreeable one, for the interest naturally increased with the length of the passage, and we were more than rewarded for our trouble and temporary annoyance before we reached the end of the passage. In fact we observed after continuing our route for some time, that the clay, which we have already mentioned had been washed down in considerable quantities by the current, was occasionally plastered against the sides of the passage, and smoothed very carefully with the palm of the hand: in this we thought we perceived that something like letters had been scratched, which we should scarcely have thought it worth while to examine, had we not been a little curious to know what Europeans had visited the place before us; we knew of none besides Signor Della Cella, who does not appear from his own account to have penetrated more than a few steps beyond the entrance—probably to the first turning, as far as which the light from without would guide him. Our first conclusion was, that some of our own party had taken this method of writing their names on the wall,—a practice which John Bull seldom neglects in any part of the world which he visits; or that some intrepid Arab had allowed his curiosity to prevail over his fear of evil spirits, and penetrated thus far into the subterranean channel: it never, in effect, for a moment occurred to us, that the characters (whatever they were,), which might be traced on so perishable a surface, were of more than very recent formation. Our surprise may in consequence be readily imagined when we found, on a closer examination, that the walls of the place were covered with Greek inscriptions; some of which, from their dates, must have remained on the wet clay for more than fifteen hundred years, whatever might have been the periods at which others had been written: the preservation of these may certainly be accounted for, by the dampness of the place, and its extreme seclusion, which would conspire to prevent the clay from cracking and dropping off, and from being rubbed off by intruders; but we were not prepared to meet with inscriptions engraved on so yielding a substance, and certainly not to find that, having once been written, they should have remained on it down to the present day, as perfect as when they were left there by those whose visit they were intended to commemorate. They consist, of course, chiefly in a collection of names; many of which are Roman, and the earliest of the most conspicuous dates which we remarked and copied, (for it would take whole days to read and copy them all) were those of the reign of Dioclesian. We could collect no other fact from those which we read, than that a priest appears to have officiated at the fountain, after Cyrene became a Roman colony, whose name and calling (in the form επι ιερεος, &c.) are usually written after the name of the visiter. They are in general very rudely scratched, with a point of any kind (a sword or knife, perhaps, or the stone of a ring,) and often with the point of the fingers. We observed a few Arabic inscriptions among the rest, but were so much occupied in reading over the Greek ones, in order to gain some intelligence respecting the fountain, which might serve to throw light upon the period at which the channel was excavated, or other questions of interest, that we neglected to copy them. There is an appearance in one of the Greek inscriptions of allusion to the name of Apollo, the deity to whom we suppose this fountain to have been sacred; but the letters are not sufficiently clear to establish the fact decidedly, although we do not see what other sense could be given to the words in question, with so much probability of being that which the writer intended; and it is plain, that as the sentence now stands it is incomplete. We could not succeed in finding any Greek dates of antiquity, although the Greek names are very numerous; but a person accustomed to the many negligent modes of writing the character, with plenty of time and light at his disposal, might probably succeed in finding Greek inscriptions of more interest than we were able to discover in the mass of writing here alluded to; a great portion of which, as might naturally be expected, consists of rude scrawls and hasty scratches—mere apologies in fact for letters almost of any kind. That the fountain continued to be an object of curiosity, and probably of religious veneration, after the cession of the country to the Romans, may, however, be inferred from what we have stated; and a minimum may at least be established with respect to the date of the excavated channel, if we cannot ascertain the precise time of its formation, or whether it was cut at one or at several periods.

We have already mentioned that several hours had elapsed, from the time of our entering the channel to that of our re-appearance at its mouth; and we really believe that the Arabs of the place, who had collected themselves round the fountain to see us come out, were extremely disappointed to find that no accident had befallen any one of the party; in spite of the demons so confidently believed to haunt its dark and mysterious recesses. For our own parts, we could not help laughing very heartily at the ridiculous appearance which each of us exhibited on first coming into the light, covered as we were from head to foot with the brown clay accumulated in the channel of the fountain, which had adhered too closely to be washed away by the stream, although its current, as we have mentioned, was extremely rapid.

As the next day was that which had been fixed for our departure, we employed the remainder of the afternoon in making preparations for the journey, and set out early on the following morning for Bengazi. Captain Beechey and Lieutenant Coffin had already preceded us, with the intention of running over to Malta, in order to procure a small vessel for the embarkation of the statues, which we had decided upon removing to Apollonia, where the vessel would have taken them on board. On their arrival, however, at Bengazi, they found a packet of letters from England; and among them, was a despatch from the Foreign Office, which made it necessary that we should alter our plan, and give up any further operations. As the season was far advanced, during which any vessels are found in the harbour of Bengazi, a passage was secured in the last which remained, and camels were despatched to Cyrene to bring away our baggage and tents.

The interval was employed in completing the plans of the buildings and tombs at Cyrene; and that of the excavated channel of the fountain was the last upon which we employed ourselves. We had determined, on first discovering this passage, to explore it as far as it might be found practicable, and the first leisure moment was accordingly devoted to it on the day which preceded our departure.

FOOTNOTES:

See Shaw's Travels in Barbary vol. ii. p. 286.

"About forty years ago, when M. Le Maire was French consul at Tripoly, he made great inquiries, by order of the French court, into the truth of this report; and amongst other very curious accounts relating to the same place, he told me a remarkable circumstance to the great discredit and even confutation of all that had been so positively advanced with regard to the petrified bodies of men, children, and other animals. Some of the Janizaries who, in collecting the tribute, travel over every year one part or other of this district of Ras Sem, promised him that, as an adult person would be too heavy and burdensome, they would undertake, for a certain number of dollars, to bring him from thence the body of a little child. After a great many pretended difficulties, delays, and disappointments, they produced at length a little Cupid, which they had found, as he learnt afterwards, among the ruins of Leptis; and to conceal the deceit, they broke off the quiver and some other of the distinguishing characteristics of that deity."

"M. Le Maire's inquiries (he continues), which we find were supported by the promise and performance of great rewards, have brought nothing further to light. He could never learn, after sending a number of persons expressly, and at a great expense, to make discoveries, that any traces of walls or buildings, animals, or utensils, were ever to be seen within the verge of these pretended petrifactions. The same account he heard from a Sicilian renegado, who attended him as Janissary while in Egypt, and assured him that he had been several times at Ras Sem; and also from another Sicilian renegado, whom the Bashaw of Tripoly had appointed Bey or Viceroy of the province of Derna, where Ras Sem was immediately under his jurisdiction."

The position of Ghirrza, and of several of the most conspicuous objects on the road to that place from Tripoly, are as follows:—

	Latitudes.	Longitudes.
	° ′ ″	° ′ ″
Ghirrza Ruins	31 07 16	14 40 50
Benhoulat Square Tower	31 28 10	14 18 15
Benioleet Castle	31 45 38	14 12 10
Wady Denator-huts	31 52 10	14 03 50
Wou-lad-ben-Merian Pass	32 21 40	13 34 22
Wahryan Mountain-summit	32 07 50	13 02 10

The passage of Vitruvius in question, is as follows, as we have extracted it from Wilkins's translation:—

"From the foregoing investigations,"—those of Aristoxenus on the doctrine of harmony, "brazen vases have been made upon mathematical calculations, proportioned to the magnitude of the theatre. They are so constructed, that upon being struck, they form amongst themselves concords of the fourth, fifth, regularly in succession, on to the double octave. They are then arranged amongst the seats of the theatre according to a certain musical proportion, in cells made for their reception. They ought not to be placed in contact with the wall, but have a vacant space above and around them. They should be inverted, and the edge next the stage raised by means of wedges, six inches in height at the least: apertures ought to be made in the seats of the lower row, opposite to the cells, two feet in width, and one in height."

"If the theatre be not very spacious," continues our author, "thirteen arched cells will be sufficient, in which as many vases are to be placed in the order which he proceeds to point out, by observing which, the voice," he says, "which diverges every where from the stage, as from a centre, striking each of these hollow vases, will acquire an increase of clearness and strength, and at the same time produce corresponding tones in concord with its own sounds." "It may, perhaps, be said," continues Vitruvius, "that many theatres are built every year at Rome, in which no attention has been paid to these points: the objection, however, is not applicable; because it is not considered that all public theatres constructed with wood have many surfaces, which act as sounding-boards. The truth of which will be manifest, if we observe those who sing to the harp; who, whenever they wish to sing in a higher tone, turn themselves to the leaves of the scene; from which they receive the assistance of corresponding sounds. But when theatres are not sonorous, in consequence of their being built with solid materials, such as stone or marble, whether wrought or unhewn, it then becomes necessary to have recourse to the expedient just explained. Many skilful architects, who have built theatres in small towns, have, in order to lessen the expense, adopted vases of pottery instead of brass, of the same pitch; and, by arranging them according to these principles have produced the most useful effects."

We may remark on this subject, that it has hitherto been doubted, by persons well qualified to judge of architectural details, whether the practice alluded to by Vitruvius in the foregoing passage, was ever really adopted by the ancients for the purpose which he mentions. Mr. Wilkins has noticed a passage in Pliny, which alludes to a mode of building peculiar to the walls of theatres; in the construction of which, hollow vessels of earthenware were immured, and whenever it was required to prolong the vibrations, or to increase the powers of the voice, the orchestra was strewn with sand or saw-dust, by which means, the voice being directed to the body of the house, the sounds were carried along the walls so long as there was no impediment to obstruct their course; whereas, in the walls of other edifices, the interior space between the two faces of the wall was filled in with rubble. "In describing this mode of building," continues Mr. Wilkins, "Pliny might have had our author in view; whose mention of vases received a degree of confirmation from the fact, that earthern vessels were sometimes inserted in the masonry of ancient buildings. An instance in which this practice has been adopted, occurs in the Circus of Caracalla. Vases are there found regularly distributed in the stone work above the crown of the arches, which were constructed for the purpose of giving a proper degree of elevation to the seats of the spectators. The object of their introduction seems to be the diminution of weight. Vitruvius confesses (Mr. Wilkins adds) that there was no theatre at Rome which had vases for such a purpose; although he states them to have been in use in the provinces of Italy, and in most of the cities of Greece. It is certain, however, that in the various theatres which have fallen within our observation, no provision has been made for the reception of vases, in the situation which Vitruvius assigns to them."

Since the publication of Mr. Wilkins's Vitruvius, the researches of Mr. William Bankes have fortunately enabled him to throw light upon the subject in question; for in Syria this gentleman discovered a theatre which was constructed in the manner alluded to by Vitruvius, and in which some of the vases were actually found in the situations which he has assigned to them.

We had flattered ourselves on first perceiving the hollow spaces, which were left under the seats of the theatre which we are describing at Cyrene, that we had ourselves discovered a second confirmation of this practice; but no brazen vases appeared in the spaces in question; and the few remains of pottery which we found in some of them, will not even justify us in asserting that they contained originally vases of earthenware.

"Ho trovato che internamente ciascuna di queste pietre era scolpita di una lettera d' un alfabeto a me ignoto; cosi la serie di queste lettere veniva a formare una linea, e queste linee si ripetevano per ogni serie di pietre. Tentai de copiarle, ed entrai con questo progetto nell' aquidotto; ma tra la poca luce che vi trapeleva da soli luoghi ov' era rotto, e l'acqua che spesso a lunghi tratti vi ristagnava, e l'incomoda positura che doveva prendere per ben riconoscerle, dovette ristarmi dall' intrapresa. Benche questi caratteri, del pari che altre iscrizioni segnate sopra queste rovine, appartengano a lingue perdute affatto; tuttavolta io non ho mai avvisato essere inutil cosa il registrarli, quando mi è occorso di trovarne. Oltrechè questi caratteri possono per avventura fornire qualche nuovo elemento agli alfabeti tuttora oscuri di coteste lingue, conservano ancora solenni documenti de' popoli a diversa lingua che in queste contrade mano a mano vennero a stabilirsi. Sono questi i soli documenti che ci ritengano, dall' abbandonarci interamente all' autorità de' Greci scrittori, i quali si sa che mossi da soverchia tenerezza per le cose loro, non sapevan temperarsi dal vedere Greche origine ovunque vedean traccie d'incivilmento, e non videro diffatti che Greci, e discendenti dalla colonia di Tera, nella Cirenaica."—(*Viaggio da Tripoli*, &c. p. 136.)

We take these characters from the last page of Signor Della Cella's book, where they are inserted without any remarks, and presume that they must be those alluded to; since all the other inscriptions which he has introduced in different parts of his work are accounted for, and are either in Greek or Latin. It will be evident, we think, to all who are accustomed to see Greek and Roman quarry marks, that the characters in question are no other, and could never have been found on any single stone.

ΚΛΑΥΔΙΑΝΑΡΑΤΑΝΦΙΛΙΣΚΩ
ΘΥΓΑΤΕΡΑΦΥΣΕΙΔΕΕΥΦΑΝΟΣ
ΜΑΤΕΡΑ ΚΛ·ΟΛΥΜΠΙΑΔΟΣ
ΑΙΩΝΙΩΓΥΜΝΑΣΙΑΡΧΙΔΟΣ
ΑΡΕΤΑΣ ΕΝΕΚΑ ΚΥΡΑΝΑΙΟΙ

ΑΣΖ ΜΥΤΛ
ΕΥΝΟΙΑΣ

The pasturage of Cyrene and Barca was always, as it is at present, abundant; and both cities were remarkable for their excellent breed of horses, and their more than ordinary skill in driving. Pindar gives the epithet Εὔιππος (renowned for horses) to Cyrene; and the Barceans, we are told (see the ἐθνικὰ of Stephanus), derived their art of rearing them from Neptune, and their dexterity in the management of chariots from Minerva. οἵ τας ἱπποτροφίας παρα Ποσειδωνος, ἡνιοχειν δε παρα Αθηνᾶς ημαθον.

Scavato ad arte è lo sbocco di questa fonte, e questo incavo ben oltre si prolunga attraverso la montagna, ove io *per qualche tratto* volli penetrare, a malgrado le minaccie delle mie guide, che credono quella cavità ordinaria stanza di spiriti malevoli.

The Arabs of the present day whom we met with at Cyrene, would on no account be persuaded to enter the passage in question, which they believe (as Dr. Della Cella truly observes) to be the abode of evil spirits.

We imagine the words to have been, επι ιερεος του μεγιστου Απολλωνος, but the ος is wanting after Απολλων, and the μ in μεγιστου; in which latter word also the ε and γ look more like an α and a τ. The rest of the inscription is clear; and were we only to give it as a fragment, επι ιερεος του...ιστου Απολλων.., there would, probably, be no doubt raised with respect to the manner of reading it.

CHAPTER XIX.

Historical Sketch of Cyrene — Its Foundation by a Lacedemonian Colony — Dynasty of the Battiades, or Family of Battus — Cession of the Country to Ptolemy Lagus — And afterwards to the Romans by Apion, the last of the Ptolemies who possessed it — Cyrene becomes a Roman Province, and is united in one Government with Crete — Illustrious Persons who were natives of Cyrene — Tenets of the Sect of Philosophers termed Cyrenaic — Decay of the City, and its final Desertion in Christian times after the Transfer of the Bishopric to Ptolemeta — Return of the Expedition to Bengazi, and its subsequent Departure for Malta.

WE learn from Herodotus, that Battus, a native of Thera, in compliance with the injunctions of the Oracle at Delphi, first landed with a party of his countrymen in Platæa; an island lying close to the northern coast of Africa, and supposed to be that which is at present called Bomba. Here he built a city; and after a lapse of two years proceeded again to Delphi, in order to consult the Pythia (or priestess) with respect to his future proceedings.

The new establishment appearing to be insufficient for the fulfilment of the deity's instructions, Battus removed his colony to Aziris, a part of the continent opposite to Platæa, and described by the historian as a most delightful spot. In this new abode they remained for six years; and on the seventh, (by the advice of the Libyan tribes in their neighbourhood, who promised to conduct them to a much better place,) removed to the high ground then called Irasa, on which they built the city of Cyrene, about the third year, according to Eusebius, of the thirty-seventh Olympiad. We find little more worth relating of Battus, except, perhaps, that he lost the impediment in his speech, for which he had originally consulted the oracle, in the following extraordinary manner. As he wandered abroad one day unattended, a lion sprung very unexpectedly upon him; and the cry of surprise and dismay which he uttered so terrified the monarch of the woods, that he fled with the utmost precipitation. At the same moment Battus discovered that he had lost the infirmity under which he had laboured; for the sudden exertion of voice just alluded to had taken it effectually away. After a reign of forty years, Battus was succeeded by his son Arcesilaus, of whom little further is known, than that he reigned for sixteen years. During these two reigns, no accession appears to have been made to the numbers of the original colony; under Battus the third, however, who was distinguished by the appellation of Ευδαιμων, (the prosperous,) another migration took place from Greece; and the lands already occupied not being sufficient for the accommodation of the new colonists, an inroad was made upon the territory of the Libyan inhabitants, and one of their chiefs, whom Herodotus calls Adicran, was deprived of a considerable part of his dominions.

The Libyans applied for support to the Egyptians; and Apries, who at that time reigned over Egypt, (and is supposed to be the Pharaoh Hophra of Scripture,) despatched a large army to their assistance. The Cyreneans, aware of the approach of their invaders, drew up their forces at Irasa, near the fountain called by Herodotus Theste; and the Egyptians were routed with a loss so considerable, that few of them escaped to bear the tale of their defeat. In the reign of Arcesilaus the third, who succeeded the last-mentioned Battus, dissensions appear to have taken place among the colonists, and the brothers of the king abjured his authority, and left Cyrene with their followers. After some consultation among themselves with respect to their future proceedings, they are said by Herodotus to have founded the city of Barca, and established themselves in that part of the country.

Not content with this measure, the founders of Barca endeavoured to gain over the Libyan tribes to their party, and to stir up dissensions between them and the Cyreneans, in which they partially succeeded; Arcesilaus, in consequence, made war upon both, and the Libyans, either fearing to meet him in the field, or wishing to draw the Cyreneans from their heights to attack them with more advantage in the plains, retreated to the eastward, and joined the native tribes which occupied the country between Cyrene and Egypt. Here they were imprudently followed by the king, and an engagement took place, in which the Cyreneans were defeated, and seven thousand of their heavy-armed troops were left dead upon the field of battle. The consequences of this defeat were fatal to Arcesilaus; for soon after his return to Cyrene he was strangled by his brother Learchus, when disabled by weakness resulting from indisposition; the murderer, however, did not long survive him, for he was himself put to death by means of a stratagem, concerted, we are told, by Eryxo, the wife of Arcesilaus, who revenged in this manner the loss of her husband. To Arcesilaus succeeded another Battus, who is said by Herodotus to have been lame; and in his reign ambassadors were sent to Mantinea (according to the advice of the Oracle), to entreat the mediation of the Arcadians, in the disputes which had already been the cause of so much bloodshed. Demonax was in consequence selected by the Mantineans, a person highly respected for his probity; who, on arriving at Cyrene, divided the Greeks into three separate classes, according to the countries from which they originally came, and gave them a new form of government, which continued in force during Battus' reign. The son of this Battus, however, Arcesilaus, refused to acknowledge the new constitution, by which many privileges of the former kings of Cyrene had been transferred to the body of the people. Insurrections of the populace took place in consequence, and Arcesilaus was obliged to take refuge in Samos, while his mother, Pheretime, went over to Cyprus, in order to implore the assistance of Euelthon, who reigned at that time in the island. The suppliant queen was received with great courtesy, and Euelthon made her several valuable presents; but Pheretime, while expressing her thanks for these attentions, suggested that an army, which might accompany her to Cyrene, and avenge the wrongs which her family and herself had sustained from the people of the city, would be a much more desirable gift. Euelthon, however, adhered to the line of conduct by which he had hitherto been regulated, which was that of a strict neutrality; and sent the queen a distaff and spindle of gold, assuring her that he was acting with much more consideration towards a female, in making her a similar offering, than if he had presented her with an army. Arcesilaus, in this interval, had collected an army in Samos; and went to Delphi to consult the Oracle on the probable consequence of his return to Cyrene. The answer was, as usual, mysterious; and predicted his death if certain events should take place which he was enjoined to avoid; at the same time he was advised to return to his dominions, and adopt conciliatory measures.

On recovering his possessions, Arcesilaus neglected the prudent advice of the Pythia, and commenced a vigorous persecution of those whose revolt had occasioned his flight from Cyrene. Some of them contrived to escape his resentment; but a party of the fugitives who had taken refuge in a tower, were burnt there by order of the king, who caused his people to set fire to the building. In this act, one of the injunctions had been neglected, on observing which the life of Arcesilaus depended; and he was afterwards assassinated in the market-place at Barca, together with Alazir, the king of the place, whose daughter he had taken for his wife. The queen Pheretime had established her son's authority in Cyrene; but on hearing of his death, she fled immediately to Egypt, and persuaded Aryandes, who at that time commanded there as viceroy of Darius Hystaspis, to march an army against the Barceans. Before proceeding to extremities, Aryandes despatched a messenger to the people of Barca, desiring to be informed, if they really had been guilty of the death of Arcesilaus. On their acknowledging the act, he set his army in motion, and gave the command of it to Amasis, while a fleet at the same time was entrusted to Badres, and both proceeded to take vengeance of the assassins. After a long and ineffectual siege, Barca was entered by treachery: and Amasis, who had passed his word to spare the lives of the Barceans, gave them over to the vengeance of Pheretime; by whom all who were concerned in the murder of her son were put to death in the most inhuman manner. The city was plundered by the Persian army, and the lives and property of those persons only were respected, who had been averse to the murder of Arcesilaus.

Their object accomplished, the Persians returned to Egypt, leaving Barca, by desire of Pheretime, in possession of those who had been spared for their adherence to the family of Battus. The cruelties of Pheretime were visited upon her as those of Herod were afterwards punished; for we are told that she was eaten alive by worms, and died in the greatest torments.

The account which has descended to us of Cyrene and Barca, (with that of the various tribes of Northern Africa,) from the pen of the father of history, concludes with the death of Pheretime; which is believed by Herodotus to have been a judgment of the gods for the cruelties of which she had been guilty.

From this time the Cyreneans as well as the Libyans, with whom they appear to have been intermixed, are little alluded to in history till the conquest of the Persian empire. We are informed by Aristotle that, in his time, Cyrene was a republic; and we may perhaps suppose that, on the extinction of the family of Battus, that form of government took place which had been recommended by Demonax; although the Cyreneans may possibly have been tributary to, or under the protection of, Persia. At the period when the dispute concerning the limits of the countries took place between the people of Cyrene and Carthage, we may presume, from the account transmitted of it by Sallust, that democracy was the established form of government at Cyrene; and Strabo has informed us, that the Cyreneans continued to be governed by their own laws, till the reduction of Egypt by the Macedonians. After the death of Alexander, Cyrene became the prey of contending adventurers, and was at length delivered into the hands of Ptolemy by Ophellas; although that general is supposed to have obtained for himself the sovereignty of at least a part of the country. Magas, the brother of Ptolemy Lagus, reigned in Cyrene for fifty years; and it continued to be a part of the empire of the Ptolemies, some of whom resided there at different periods, till it was made over by his father to Apion, an illegitimate son of Ptolemy Physcon, who left it in his will to the Romans. The senate accepted the bequest, but allowed the several cities to be governed by their own laws; and the country was in consequence a prey to civil discord, and exposed to the tyranny and violence of many rival pretenders to supremacy. Lucullus in some measure restored tranquillity, when he visited it during the first Mithridatic war; but the evil was never finally removed till the whole of the Cyrenaica was reduced to the form of a Roman province. This event happened about twenty years after the death of Apion, and seventy-six before the birth of Christ: we find the country afterwards, in the time of Strabo, united with Crete in one government.

The most flourishing period of Cyrene was probably that of the Ptolemaic dynasty, and of the two or three centuries which preceded it; an epoch when Grecian art was in the highest perfection, and literature in great estimation.

At the time when the city, on account of an insurrection, was destroyed by the Roman people (who afterwards, however, rebuilt it,) it is probable that the temples were spared; for the architectural remains of those which we have described are decidedly Greek of an early style; and the same may be observed with respect to many of the tombs, although in these we may find examples of architecture in the style of many different periods.

Philosophy and literature were diligently cultivated at Cyrene; which gave birth to Aristippus, the founder of the sect distinguished by the name of Cyrenaic, and to many other celebrated men; among whom we may reckon Callimachus and Eratosthenes, Aristippus the younger, Anniceris, Carneades, &c.

The philosophy of Aristippus appears to have inculcated, that the soul has two particular motions, or sensations,—those of pain and pleasure; that all pleasures are alike; and that virtue is only to be esteemed inasmuch as it conduces to our gratification. Carneades denied that any thing could be perceived or understood in the world, and was the first philosopher who introduced an universal suspension of assent: he pretended to discover an uncertainty in the most self-evident notions; and vigorously opposed the doctrine of the stoics in his attempt to confute Chrysippus. When Carneades was sent as ambassador to Rome, with Diogenes the stoic, and Critolaus the peripatetic, he pronounced a very learned dissertation upon justice, which strongly convinced all his auditors of its value and importance in society: in another speech, however, the philosopher confuted all the arguments which he had established in his first discourse; and gave no existence at all to the virtue which he had just before strongly recommended. The Roman youth were so captivated with the eloquence and the reasoning powers of Carneades, that they are said, on this occasion, to have forgotten their usual amusements and thought of nothing else but philosophy. The effect produced upon the public mind was at all events so strong, that Cato the censor gave immediate audience to the Athenian ambassadors in the Senate; and dismissed them in haste, expressing his apprehension that they would corrupt the opinions of the Roman people.

Cyrene appears to have not long survived the introduction of Christianity into Northern Africa; for we find it described as—a mass of ruin—by Synesius, who lived in the time of Theodosius the younger. It is probable, that when the bishopric was transferred to Ptolemais, this once beautiful city no longer existed; and it is certain that the remains of Christian churches at Mersa Suza and Ptolemeta, (the Apollonia and Ptolemais of antiquity,) are superior in every respect to those which are found at Cyrene, and apparently of much more recent construction.

In returning from Cyrene to Bengazi, we proceeded by a different route from that which we had taken in approaching it; and passed through a country rich in vegetation, and producing abundance of grain; in which we observed frequent traces of building, particularly on the elevated spots of ground.

At Jenain, about two hours distance from Cyrene, we found two wells of excellent water, apparently of ancient construction; and observed remains of building on a rising ground adjoining, and some tombs excavated in the rock. An hour more, travelling along the brow of the ridge, brought us to Marábut Sidi Arāfi, the division between the territories of Derna and Bengazi. Here also we found several wells, and partial remains of building, which continued all the way along the road to Bĭrāsa, where their number considerably increased. This has evidently been an ancient site; and we have no doubt that the whole of the country, through which we this day travelled, was once very thickly inhabited. Traces of ancient pavement are continually met with on the road, which is occasionally flanked by ancient tombs, similar in construction to some of those at Cyrene, and every pass of importance has been fortified with towers of considerable strength.

At Wady Jeráhib the table land ceases, and a steep and somewhat perilous descent begins into the valley (or wady) here mentioned, down which we with difficulty conducted our horses. A strong fort on the right commands, or rather, formerly commanded the entrance on this side to the wady, and overlooks the country to a considerable extent. The sides of this ravine are quite perpendicular; and in some places more than five hundred feet high; they are filled with excavated caves, like those which we have described at Apollonia, and are entered by ropes in a similar manner, which are always very carefully drawn up after them by the inhabitants.

The road which leads along Wady Jeráhib winds for two hours through woods of pine-trees, some of which were two feet in diameter (the largest size we had hitherto seen in the country), and appear to be well adapted for spars. In the centre of the valley their naked trunks were lying (amongst heaps of stones, and other matter collected about them) in considerable numbers when we passed along it; and the bark of most of those trees which are standing has been worn away for several feet upwards. We may infer from these appearances, that in the rainy season the body of water which rushes along Wady Jeráhib must be very great; and to avoid the inconvenience to which travellers would in consequence have been exposed, we find the ancient road raised several feet above the actual level of the wady in other parts, and occasionally paved, and cut through the rock. At its western extremity, Wady Jeráhib opens out into a very spacious and beautiful, we may say without exaggeration, a magnificent valley: at the entrance of which are the remains of a very large fort, now called by the Arabs Belíggidem; the walls of this are still upwards of forty feet in height. Other valleys are seen from the fort, stretching out far into the blue horizon; and we looked on all sides over the tops of thick forests of pine, which covered the sides and the summit of the wadies, as far as the eye could reach. Belíggidem may be called a very good day's journey from Cyrene, which would more frequently, indeed, be extended to a day and a half. The road from hence winds through a succession of wadies, and we found it to be very indifferent; till, after ascending a difficult hill, it brought us once more to Margàd,—a spot at which we had stopped for the night on our journey from Merge to Cyrene. From this place, our former conductor, Boo-Bukra, had turned off abruptly to the southward, in order to avoid passing through Bĕlĕnege (a part of the road which we had taken in returning), where he understood that the relations of two men whom he had killed were lying in wait for him. The party in advance had learnt this from an Arab at Bĕlĕnege; and it enabled us to account for the circuitous and difficult route along which Boo-Bukra had conducted us on our former journey. We had observed, that in addition to his musket and pistols, the usual arms of an Arab, he always carried a short carbine slung over his shoulder, which he never took off on any occasion; but were not at all aware of the difficulty of his situation, till we heard of the fact just mentioned. The change of route made a difference of two days to us, as nearly as we can recollect; but we do not regret the circumstance, since it enabled us to see a part of the country which we should not otherwise have had an opportunity of visiting. From Margàd we proceeded to Bogràta by the road which we had formerly taken, and from thence to Merge, where we found Bey Halil, for he had not been able to collect all his tribute. From Merge we descended to Ptolemeta, and joined Captain Beechey, who had arrived there the day before from Teuchira, having left Mr. Coffin at Bengazi, to make the necessary arrangements for our embarkation. We had arranged this meeting in order to complete the plans of both these places, which had been left somewhat unfinished in our eagerness to visit Cyrene. Three days were spent at Ptolemeta, and we then continued our journey to Teuchira, where we had no occasion to remain more than a single day, after which we proceeded to Bengazi.

On the 25th of July we had completed all our arrangements, and embarked the same afternoon for Malta.

We cannot close our account of the proceedings of the Expedition without expressing in a public manner our warmest thanks to the officers who accompanied us on our journey: the privations and hardships to which they were exposed might have reasonably drawn forth an occasional murmur; but these have always been patiently and cheerfully borne; and we have cause to be grateful, on many occasions, for services which have materially contributed to forward the objects, and facilitate the advance of the Expedition. To Lieutenant Coffin, in particular, who attached himself as a volunteer to our party, we feel ourselves under considerable obligations; and we should not do justice to the assiduity and regularity with which he kept the camel-track, mentioned above, if we did not state that it has enabled us to lay down the route with much greater precision than we could otherwise have attained to.

END OF THE NARRATIVE.

FOOTNOTES:

The whole of the table-land in the neighbourhood of Cyrene, as well as that upon which the city was built, may probably have been called Irasa, and the fountain of Theste may reasonably be imagined to have been that which we have formerly mentioned at Gobba, where remains of antiquity still exist. We are led to this conclusion, from the nature of the ground in the neighbourhood of the fountain in question; for it is there that the table-land ceases altogether, and the Cyrenaic range descends so abruptly as to be in most places inaccessible. We have mentioned the difficulty which we ourselves experienced in leading our horses down one of the passes near Derna, considered, of course, to be a practicable one; and can readily imagine the disadvantage which an army would labour under in having so formidable a barrier to surmount, as any of the passes alluded to would present; in front of an enemy whose lines were drawn up on the summit of the range, and on the edge of the ascent by which they were advancing.

This position in fact is one, of all others, which would naturally be selected as a line of defence against forces advancing from Derna and Egypt; and the Greeks would hardly have neglected to avail themselves of it, supposing them to be at all acquainted with the country, which can hardly be doubted at the period in question, after so long a residence on the mountain.

This army is said by Herodotus to have penetrated farther to the westward; and the historian believes (what is extremely probable) that the Persians had views on other parts of Libya, besides that possessed by the people of Barca; and that the army of Amasis was intended to reconnoitre the country, if not to reduce it to subjection.

Many pointed observations are recorded of Aristippus the elder, who appears to have possessed a very lively wit. He asked a certain person, who reproached him for having given a sumptuous entertainment—whether he would not have been equally hospitable if it would only have cost him three oboli? When the other replied in the affirmative, Aristippus observed, "It is you then, I find, who are fond of money, and not I of pleasure." Dionysius once sent him three beautiful women, from which the philosopher was desired to select whichever pleased him most; but Aristippus retained them all three; observing that "Paris had greatly suffered by preferring one goddess to another." When some one inquired what Aristippus would expect for the education of his son, he answered five hundred drachmas. "I can buy a slave," replied the other, "for that money." "Do so," said Aristippus, "and then you will have two."

The name of Bĭrāsa will naturally suggest a resemblance between it and Irāsa, the country which is mentioned by Herodotus as that to which the Greeks were conducted by the natives of Libya. We do not mean to infer, that the place first mentioned has any other connexion with the territory upon which Cyrene was erected, than that which we are going to suggest; but if the affinity of the Arabic and Hebrew, or Chaldee, to the old Phœnician, or Samaritan language, (an early dialect of the Hebrew,) be really so great as is generally allowed, the two words in question may bear the same meaning without any forced application. The word *rās* in Arabic, and in Hebrew, signifies a head; and the term is constantly applied by the Arabs to high and mountainous ground, whether inland or on the coast: land on the summit of a mountain may therefore be said to be—*bi-rās*—upon the head, or high ground; and *bi-rās-a* would signify, in Arabic, as it does in the case of the territory in question—a tract of land on the upper part of a range of hills—and might be applied without any impropriety to a similar tract of land of whatever extent. It is not, perhaps, improbable that *rās* had the same meaning among the Libyan tribes, (whom we may suppose to have spoken some dialect of the old Phœnician,) as it bears in Arabic and Hebrew; and that the particle *bi* or *be*, was at the same time used by the Libyans, in the sense which belongs to it in those languages. Irāsa might then be supposed to mean a tract of table land; for the loss of the letter *b* is of little importance, considering that the word comes through a Greek medium; and as the Greeks in the case alluded to were conducted from the low ground to the high, such an application is far from improbable. It is not, however, necessary for this application to insist upon the omission of the *b*; for the *i* in Irāsa might well be a contraction of the article *el* or *il*, signifying *the*, and *I-rāsa* be pronounced for *el-rāsa*, which is consistent with the usual pronunciation of Arabic and other Oriental languages. The whole would then be taken for a part; and the country which the Greeks were recommended to inhabit, would be termed—the summit of the mountain—and in the Libyan dialect (let us suppose) Ir'rāsa, or Er'-rāsa.

We have not been able to publish on this occasion (as we believe we have already stated) more than a limited number of plates; so that several to which we have referred have been unavoidably omitted. Some of the drawings, however, will appear in another publication, with others made in Egypt and Nubia; and in that we shall hope to find means of introducing the greater part of what has been omitted.

The accuracy to which this method of computing distance may be brought, with proper attention, will be seen on referring to the Table, p. xliv. in the Appendix.